Churches and Charity in
the Immigrant City

Churches and Charity in the Immigrant City

Religion, Immigration, and Civic Engagement in Miami

EDITED BY

ALEX STEPICK

TERRY REY

SARAH J. MAHLER

RUTGERS UNIVERSITY PRESS

NEW BRUNSWICK, NEW JERSEY, AND LONDON

LIBRARY OF CONGRESS CATALOGING-IN-PUBLICATION DATA

Churches and charity in the immigrant city : religion, immigration, and civic engagement in Miami / edited by Alex Stepick, Terry Rey, Sarah J. Mahler.
     p. cm.
     Includes bibliographical references and index.
     ISBN 978-0-8135-4459-5 (hardcover : alk. paper)
     ISBN 978-0-8135-4460-1 (pbk. : alk. paper)
     1. Church work with immigrants—Florida—Miami. 2. Church work with
immigrants—Catholic Church. 3. Immigrants—Services for—Florida—Miami.
4. Immigrants—Florida—Miami—Political activity. 5. African American
churches—Florida—Miami. 6. Church work with African Americans—Florida—
Miami. 7. African Americans—Services for—Florida—Miami. 8. African
Americans—Florida—Miami—Political activity. 9. Political participation—
Florida—Miami. I. Stepick, Alex. II. Rey, Terry. III. Mahler, Sarah J., 1959–
BV639.I4C58 2009
261.8089'00973—dc22   2008016732

A British Cataloging-in-Publication record for this book is available
from the British Library.

Visit our Web site: http://rutgerspress.rutgers.edu

Manufactured in the United States of America

CONTENTS

v

ACKNOWLEDGMENTS

This research was part of the Pew Charitable Trusts and its Gateway Cities Initiative. We gratefully acknowledge the Trusts' support and particularly that of Kimon Sargeant, our program officer at the Pew Charitable Trusts. The Sponsored Research office at Florida International University, then directed by Tom Breslin, provided critical financial support in the form of stipends for the graduate research assistants, some of whom not only produced masters' theses, but also became authors of chapters in this volume. Numerous church leaders, organizations, and congregants helped us tremendously. We would like to single out Bishops Augustín Román and Thomas Wenski for the extensive time they spent with us. Rick and Yvonne Sawyer of the Family and Children Faith Coalition in Miami were also exceptionally helpful. We appreciate the generous help and hospitality we received from the congregations at Emmanuel Apostolic Church and Christ the King Catholic Church in Perrine. We owe a special debt of gratitude to Ricky Sant, the leader of Trinidad Catholic Community at Christ the King, and its diligent and pious members. Greg Bowe gave us access to the Florida International University freshmen who constitute the sample for our survey research reported in chapter 11.

We would like to express our profound thanks to the congregants and leaders of the specific churches and communities where we worked: the Catholic churches, St. Agatha, Our Lady of Divine Providence, San Juan Bosco, Notre Dame d'Haiti, Christ the King, and St. Ann Mission; the Protestant churches, Sierra Norwood Baptist, the Episcopal Church of the Ascension, Emmanuel Apostolic, Monument of Faith, First Born Christian Center, Unity Light of the World, Sweet Home Missionary Baptist, the Refugees' Seventh-Day Adventist, and the Disciples Nazarene; the West Perrine Christian Association, the advocates for Virginia Key, and the Richmond Heights Tree Planting Project. All were unfailingly welcoming and generous toward us.

In the early stages of this project numerous colleagues and students at Florida International University provided important assistance. Emmanuel Eugene helped us in the Haitian community. Karla Mendieta assisted in various Hispanic communities. Ikam Acosta worked on the religious aspects of the Elian Gonzalez case. Carol Hoffman-Guzman provided feedback on our research design. Sung Shik Kim helped with Seventh-Day Adventist congregations. Also numerous students helped with the mapping, including Audrey Gelin, Felicia Ingram, Ninette Rodriguez, Nathalie Franco, and an undergraduate class of Terry Rey. We express our gratitude not only to all of these people, but also to the hundreds of religious and lay leaders with whom we spoke.

The map in chapter 1 was produced by Marcos Feldman. Jennifer Wolfe worked on earlier versions of the map.

Through this all Carol Dutton Stepick was project coordinator. She guided all the field research, including the massive mapping task described in the methodology, plus she took care of the innumerable bureaucratic tasks required to make a large project succeed. She also did a very thorough, careful editing of the manuscript, which undoubtedly helped make it much more readable. Without her, this project never would have moved forward.

Fred Kniss and Paul Numrich kindly provided a pre-publication copy of their book *Sacred Assemblies and Civic Engagement: How Religion Matters for America's Newest Immigrants* that significantly helped us with our theoretical framework. Fred Kniss was also especially helpful in addressing issues concerning the photos during the final stages of manuscript preparation. Two anonymous external reviewers provided important feedback that helped focus and organize the manuscript. The book is undoubtedly better because of them. Adi Hovav has provided invaluable assistance as our editor at Rutgers University Press and Connie Rey's skills and brave spirit were a blessing to this project.

Through support from the Pew Charitable Trusts, Jerry Berndt came to Miami and photographed in many of the congregations in which we worked. His photographs provide an insight that we could not provide otherwise.

Churches and Charity in
the Immigrant City

1

Religion, Immigration, and Civic Engagement

ALEX STEPICK, TERRY REY, AND SARAH J. MAHLER

On a typical Sunday in Miami, a Haitian pastor from Port-au-Prince lays hands on the afflicted in a storefront Pentecostal church in Little Haiti, while a few miles west a Catholic priest from Nicaragua says Mass in Spanish to his diverse Latino flock. A few blocks further west, a group of elderly Cuban Catholics plans a fund-raising event for the Diocese of Guantánamo-Baracoa in eastern Cuba. Meanwhile, in Miami's southern suburbs, another Catholic church is receiving the bishop of Trinidad, and further south still, Mexican fieldworkers busily prepare for the feast of their patron saint, Our Lady of Guadalupe. Nearby, tucked away in a large church on a side street, African American Protestants, most of Bahamian descent, respond enthusiastically to their pastor's sermon on the importance of preserving God's land, the good earth that the Lord bequeathed to them.

Miami's diverse religious landscape stretches not only across Miami-Dade County, but throughout the Caribbean and Latin America. Indeed, many of these religious activities may appear to be more foreign than "American," not of the United States. Are they? Do they focus exclusively or even primarily on immigrants' home countries and perhaps isolate the immigrants from U.S. society? Do they impede rather than assist in immigrant integration into Miami and the United States? Are the immigrant churches somehow fundamentally different from American houses of worship?

Based upon ethnographies of immigrant and African American congregations in Miami, complemented by a survey of local youth, this book addresses these questions. Each ethnographic chapter provides in-depth detail of the congregation's activities, both those that are focused inwardly and those that reach out to the broader civil society. The survey provides a broader examination of the relationship between religion and civic engagement among Miami youth. This first chapter reviews previous work on immigrant religion and civic engagement and provides the theoretical framework for the subsequent ethnographic chapters and the discussion of the survey results.

With more than 35 million foreign-born people, the United States at the turn of the twenty-first century is home to more immigrants than ever in its history. The vast majority of these immigrants are racial or ethnic minorities in their new country; i.e., Latinos, Asians, and Blacks. They contribute to the nation's increasing cultural diversity and to the concomitant decline in the majority status of non-Hispanic Whites. Indeed, in many larger cities, particularly those receiving immigrants, native minorities and immigrants are now a majority of the population, a trend that appears destined to become national. Many, if not most, of these immigrants, and many of the native minorities that they encounter while settling in the United States, are highly religious, making religion an essential issue toward understanding the multifaceted and far-reaching influence that recent immigrants are having and will have on American social life.

Driven by the abiding faith of both its native born and its immigrant populations, the United States itself is an extraordinarily religious country, with over 90 percent of its people professing belief in God.[1] In spite of a seemingly apparent trend of secularization in modern Western society, which is assailed by many right-wing Christians, and despite infamous sociological predictions that religion was on the decline in human life (Greeley 2001), there is strong evidence that faith continues to play a key role in American society. For example, a greater fraction of U.S. adults believed in life after death in the 1990s than in the 1970s (Greeley and Hout 1999). Nearly two-thirds of Americans identified with a particular church in the early 1990s,[2] and between 30 and 40 percent of Americans attend church services during any given week. So, whereas formal church affiliations may be in statistical remission in the United States, *religious belief* clearly is not. As we detail below, it is safe to add that immigrants will contribute to a strengthening of this trend.

Church and Civic Engagement

Against this backdrop, it should not be surprising that religion influences the broader civic agenda even at the highest level of American politics. President George W. Bush, who professes to strong evangelical Christian beliefs himself, advocated and implemented policies, generally referred to as the Faith-Based Initiative, to more deeply involve religious institutions in civic society (Milbank 2001; Pipes and Ebaugh 2002; Farris, Nathan, and Wright 2004). More generally, contemporary American politics are thoroughly infused with religion, including religious interpretations in the debates on abortion, homosexuality, the "war on terror," school vouchers, and prayer in schools. While the separation of church and state has been a central tenet of U.S. society since its very inception, many religious organizations are deeply concerned with social and political issues and, inspired by this concern, pursue civic agendas that stretch far beyond the pastoral realm. Many American churches actively promote civic engagement through soup kitchens, Habitat for Humanity, and myriad other charitable works. African American churches, in particular, have been a focal point of leadership development and civic organization. The civil rights movement, for example, was largely church based, and its key leaders were mostly religious clerics. Meanwhile, at the end of the twentieth century, the Christian Right catapulted issues like abortion and prayer in schools to the forefront of American political debate. Indeed, humanitarianism has always been one of the central ethical concerns of Judaism, Christianity, and Islam, embodied forcefully in the Golden Rule, around which each of these major religions centers its social ethics.

It is thus wholly unsurprising that faith communities are at the vanguard of charitable initiatives in the United States, as reflected in a Hartford Theological Seminary survey that found "more than 200,000 congregations supporting thrift shops and more than 120,000 congregations helping to tutor children and youth"; they "are making major contributions to the welfare of their communities through a combination of social and spiritual ministries" (Dudley and Roozen 2001).

At the same time, some religious groups more strongly emphasize direct engagement with civil society beyond their immediate membership. Some congregations and their associated denominations create nonprofit organizations or directly engage in community politics (Ebaugh and Chafetz 2000b; Guest 2003; McRoberts 2003; Wuthnow 2004; Mooney 2007). Others focus on individual salvation with either no connections outside their church or only connections with outsiders in their efforts to evangelize.

At the level of individuals, in general, the more people attend church the more likely they are to engage in civic activities, both inside and outside the church (Smidt 1999, 187; Brooks and Lewis 2001). Wuthnow (1999) found that those who attend church are twice as likely to volunteer as those who do not attend.[3] Similarly, Park and Smith (2000) determined that among Protestants, those who frequently participate in church activities are more likely to volunteer in both their churches and their communities. More specifically, Wilson and Musick (1997) found that church attendance exerts a consistent positive influence on formal volunteering; that is, in activities such as working with a local food bank or with Habitat for Humanity. However, church attendance does not appear to affect rates of informal volunteering, such as helping a neighbor or a family member.

While regular church attendees are more likely to volunteer, denominational affiliation appears to help determine the kinds of activities in which they engage, although precisely how remains unsettled. Brooks and Lewis (2001) maintain that

Catholics place a heavy rhetorical emphasis on volunteering but actually volunteer less for religious organizations, although they still may volunteer for secular organizations. The research on Protestants appears to be contradictory. Wilson and Janoski (1995) found that conservative Protestants are more likely to volunteer for activities within their church as opposed to secular volunteer activities, while Uslaner (2002) claimed that those with more fundamentalist values were more likely to participate in secular causes (also see Regnerus, Smith, and Sikkink 1998). Among White evangelical Protestants, meanwhile, Wuthnow (1999) found no relationship between church attendance and participation in larger outreach efforts. American evangelicals are often believed to be more concerned with their own church communities than with wider societal participation (Wilson and Janoski 1995; Bellah 1996; Wuthnow 1999), especially as compared to Catholic or mainline Protestant congregations (Chaves and Tsitsos 2001).

Research appears similarly contradictory for African Americans. Brooks and Lewis (2001) found African Americans less likely than Whites to volunteer or donate money to nonreligious causes, while Greenberg cites a number of sources that support a "strong link between church attendance and voter turnout, politics in church and political knowledge, and among African Americans, church involvement and collective action" (2000, 380–381). Smith, Fabricatore, and Peyrot (1999) found that among African American Catholics in Baltimore, attending Mass demonstrated a strong association with hours volunteered. Moreover, African Americans were more likely than Whites to devote one to five hours of volunteering a month to their parishes.

The data for Latinos is sparse but appears to be more consistent. According to the 1989–90 Latino National Political Survey and the 1990 American National Election Studies, church is often the primary, if not only, civic association to which Latinos belong (Jones-Correa and Leal 2001). Unfortunately, we do not know if the church prompts them to volunteer or not.

How do immigrants and immigrant congregations fit into this dynamic? Are they as likely as established residents in the United States to incorporate civic engagement into their religion, or are their religious practices more focused on individual spiritual concerns or, perhaps, their home countries? Although numerous scholars have addressed the social and economic adaptation of immigrants and some studies have focused on immigrant religion, the relationship between immigrant religion and "civic life" in the United States has largely been missed by academic radar. This book emerged from the first systematic effort to examine immigrant religion and civic engagement as part of the Pew Charitable Trusts Gateway Cities research initiative, which funded research in Houston, Los Angeles, New York, San Francisco, and Washington, D.C., along with this one in Miami. Although each project was planned and implemented independently, they were all designed to "document how religion contributes to or impedes the civic incorporation of new immigrants" (Sargeant 1998).

Religion and Immigration

There is no doubt that immigration, religion, and civic engagement are themes of rising importance in the United States. Immigration has been on the increase ever since the mid-1960s. The current wave is generally referred to as the "new immigration" in contrast to the "old immigration" that peaked one hundred years ago and was severely curtailed by restrictive immigration laws in the 1920s. While the proportion of immigrants was higher during the last great wave of immigrants at the beginning of the twentieth century, the United States presently has more total immigrants than at any point in its history. Immigrants today, much like one hundred years ago, still tend to concentrate in a few gateway cities (e.g., Miami, New York, and Los Angeles), but they are increasingly spreading out to smaller cities and rural areas. Immigrant gateway cities such as Miami thus portend the impact of this demographic change that will happen, and is happening throughout the United States on a smaller scale so far.

Immigration has assuredly affected the U.S. religious landscape. Most visible are the seeming differences between immigrant and traditional U.S. religions. Not only are signs, texts, and messages in different languages, but non-Western religions from non-Judeo-Christian traditions such as Islam, Buddhism, Hinduism, and others have emerged.[4] Perhaps because these religions are so visibly different, and certainly in the case of Muslims because of 9/11 (September 11, 2001), they receive public attention disproportionate to their numbers. Yet immigrants in the United States, approximately two-thirds of them, in fact, are primarily Christian, while 15 percent claim no religious affiliation (Jasso et al. 2003).[5] Given these percentages, the impact of immigrants on the U.S. religious landscape will be primarily among Christians.

Studies of recent immigrants and religion have only recently begun to emerge. Yet there is no doubt that religion is central to immigrants' personal and communal identity and their social orientation in a new land.[6] Recent immigrants are more likely to attend religious services regularly than either the native-born or earlier-arriving immigrants (Foley and Hoge 2007, 65).[7] Nationwide surveys of Presbyterians reveal that Koreans attend church much more frequently than native-born Americans (Kim and Kim 2001, 82). About 70 percent of first-generation Koreans in Los Angeles reported affiliation with Korean ethnic churches in the United States (Hurh and Kim 1984, 130). There was also an extraordinarily high level of religious participation among Korean American Christians, with 83 percent of those who were church affiliated attending church once a week or more (see also Min 1992, 1371). Bankston and Zhou (2000) have likewise observed similarly high church attendance among Vietnamese Catholics in New Orleans. And Stepick (1998) has documented the extremely high church attendance rates among Haitians in South Florida, while Richman (2005) indicates that for most Haitian immigrants in South Florida the church is central to life in America, perhaps even more so than it was in the homeland.

While certainly not all immigrants are religious, many are.[8] Some even claim that the immigrant experience itself is "theologizing" (Smith 1978; see also Ebaugh and Chafetz 2000b; Hirschman 2004; Kniss and Numrich 2007), that the process of uprooting and transplanting oneself can be traumatic and religion often provides familiar reassurances and meaning (Herberg 1960). Foley and Hoge (2007, 65) assert that immigrants become more religious the longer they are in the U.S. Cadge and Ecklund (2006) argue specifically that migrants who are less integrated into American society are more likely than others to regularly attend religious services.

Why is faith so central to immigrants' lives? Most studies of immigrant faith practices and religion demonstrate its role in reinforcing and perpetuating ties to the homeland culture as a mechanism for both easing the psychological distress occasioned by immigration and providing a community of co-ethnics who can assist each other in adjusting to life in the United States while retaining ties to those they left behind (Chou 1991; Legge 1997; Min 2002). Dolan, for example, found that nineteenth-century letters of immigrants reflected an "understanding of the afterlife as a place of reunion" that mirrored immigrants' separation from their loved ones in the homeland (1992, 153). Socially, religion thus tied immigrants to each other and, symbolically, to the homeland (e.g., DeMarinis and Grzymala-Moszczynska 1995) and helped provide a meaningful social identity that reinforced the immigrant ethnic and national home country identities (Tiryakian 1991; Al-Ahmary 2000).

An entire genre of immigration literature has emerged that focuses on immigrants' ability to live significant portions of their lives across national borders.[9] This includes religion (Levitt 2003, 2007). Broad scholarly consensus proposes that homeland identity reconstruction and reinforcement is a central function of immigrant religion (see Stepick 2005). Tweed (1997) argues that the Miami shrine to Cuba's patron saint, la Virgen de la Caridad del Cobre (Our Lady of Charity), serves to unify an otherwise fractious Cuban exile community. Indeed, the annual festival in her honor fills the Miami Arena with around fifteen thousand believers (Mahler 2002). Similarly, other scholars maintain that for immigrants in the United States religion's most important function is its establishment and maintenance of ties to the homeland, over and above immediate and local spiritual and social concerns (Gans 1994; Remennick 1998). Even in congregations with members from varied ethnic backgrounds, cultural diversity does not mute congregants' respective expressions of homeland identity. Hanging the various flags of congregants' home nations in local churches is common, as is, in Catholic parishes, the displaying of saints who are popular in immigrants' homelands.[10] As seen in the following chapters treating Catholic congregations, the celebration of the feast days of the patron saints of immigrants' homeland nations is a highlight of Catholic life in the

Archdiocese of Miami (Tweed 1997; Rey 2004). Often these celebrations emphasize home country culture, such as food and secular music, as much or even more than religious themes.[11]

During the old immigration, the U.S. Catholic Church self-consciously created ethnic parishes that made it easier for immigrants to continue practicing their faith. That is no longer the policy, but the effect often remains in both Catholic and Protestant denominations. As Lin and Jamal (2001) and Lin (1996) indicate, for contemporary immigrants religion continues to forge cultural identity and social purpose (also see Bankston 1997). Congregations that immigrants attend often are (or soon become) perceived locally as serving a particular ethnic group, often in languages that exclude native-born Americans.[12] Mainly for social and cultural reasons, though often also for less obvious theological ones, such congregations naturally draw people of similar ethnic composition to those already seated in their pews.

Immigrant concentrations are also commonly the sites of social capital formation utilized in the adaptation to the host society. Immigrant congregants may exchange food, loans, and help with finding housing, rides, job referrals, childcare, and other services (Ebaugh and Chafetz 2000b; Richman 2005).[13] Through church, Korean immigrants, for example, develop and reinforce social ties that they self-consciously use for business purposes (Hurh and Kim 1990; Kwon, Ebaugh, and Hagan 1997; Yoo 1998; Chai 2000; Min 2000; Kim and Kim 2001; Suh 2001). This is likely to engage immigrants at least somewhat in the broader society, although not necessarily for civic activities.

Immigrant Religion and Civic Engagement

At first glance, immigrant churches generally do not appear to be civically engaged. All immigrant churches described in the literature emphasize ties to those within the congregation and to the immigrants' homeland. Accordingly, the churches appear disinclined to promote civic or political engagement in the host society. Yet other literature indicates that immigrant religion is closely linked to civic engagement. One of the most important works on assimilation for earlier immigrants, Herberg's *Protestant—Catholic—Jew: An Essay in American Religious Sociology* (1960), argued that religion formed part of the core identity of both immigrants and established residents; i.e., native-born Americans. As such, religion was central to national American identity and to the nation's very social structure. Similarly, Hirschman claims that, historically, "immigrants become Americans by joining a church and participating in its religious and community life" (2004, 1209). Moreover, in the wake of September 11, 2001, for example, Muslims in the United States, most of them immigrants, quickly organized to protect themselves by disavowing terrorist acts (Leonard 2003). Mooney (2007) also notes that some religious groups have a stronger orientation than others toward direct engagement with civil society by founding nonprofit organizations or directly engaging community politics (see also Ebaugh and Chafetz 2000b; Guest 2003; McRoberts 2003; Wuthnow 2004). What accounts for such variation?

In linking immigrant religion and civic engagement, we emphasize four factors: denomination, generation, leadership, and the context of reception, i.e., immigrants' treatment by American institutions and society.

Denomination

The literature by scholars of religion, borrowing from the broader literatures on religion and civic engagement, tends to emphasize the importance of denominational differences. Putnam et al. (1993, 107), for example, argued in his early study in Italy that the Catholic church discouraged civic engagement. Putnam and others (Putnam 2000; Uslaner 2002; Uslaner and Conley 2003) have argued that fundamentalists discourage believers from broader social interaction and from building a bridging social capital with those who are "sinners." Fundamentalists are likely to believe that those who do not share their beliefs, those who have not been "saved," want to deny them their fundamental rights, particularly their public expressions of faith. As a result, they prefer to interact primarily with people like them, with those with whom they have bonding social capital (Hoge et al. 1998; Greenberg 2000). In analyzing fifty pan-ethnic Asian American congregations in northern California, for instance, Jeung (2005) demonstrates how evangelical congregations are more inwardly focused, emphasizing family and professional status. Mainline Protestants, on the other hand, are more likely to be involved in efforts that reach the broader community (Putnam 2000; Wuthnow 2002; Jeung 2005). Kniss and Numrich (2007) also emphasize denomination.[14] They find, for example, that highly sectarian groups, such as fundamentalist Protestants and the Hare Krishna sect of Hinduism, are largely internally oriented rather than civically oriented. Fundamentalist Protestants tend to treat politics as a matter of individual choice and even intentionally distance themselves from political action. In contrast, mainstream groups such as Methodists and Catholics are more externally oriented to broader public concerns and may view political action as a logical consequence of the group's collective identity (Kniss and Numrich 2007, 180–181).

Immigrant Generation

Among immigrants, numerous researchers have pointed out the importance of generational differences, how first-generation immigrants are more oriented to the home country, while the second generation, i.e., those born in the United States of immigrant parents, is likely to be more Americanized (see, for example, Portes and Rumbaut 2006). In the context of religion, this often provokes tension, specifically over the appropriate language for religious services and particular moral codes, usually concerning respect for authority and gender roles (Chai 1998; Lawson 1999; Schrauf 1999; Alumkal 2000; Ebaugh and Chafetz 2000a; Mathur 2001; Vertovec 2001). First-generation immigrants obviously are more fluent in their native language, while the second generation is often bilingual but commonly more comfortable in English. The more-Americanized second generation also has usually absorbed some of America's individualistic culture that includes questioning authority. American popular culture also gives females more freedom to express their sexuality in ways that the more traditional first generation finds objectionable and "immoral." These differences frequently give rise to inter-generational conflicts within immigrant churches and occasionally lead to the second generation abandoning the congregations of their parents (Chai 2000; Stepick and Dutton Stepick 2002; Stepick 2005; Portes and Rumbaut 2006).

Warner (1997) argues that immigrant congregations are likely to take a path parallel to what has been called segmented assimilation, in which immigrant youth assimilate into a U.S. native minority group, such as Latinos, Asians, or African Americans (Portes and Zhou 1993; Portes 1996; Zhou 1997; Portes and Rumbaut 2001). Warner asserts that immigrant congregations will evolve first into single-language (e.g., Spanish) but multinational congregations (e.g., Spanish-speakers from different countries of origin) before further developing a hybrid or *mesitizaje* identity that combines elements of different traditions. Min and Kim (2005) note that immigrant Korean churches have been successful at passing on to the second generation their religiosity, church affiliation, and attendance, but not their Korean culture. In examining Korean American Evangelicals at college, Kim (2006) finds that the one particular aspect of Korean culture that the second generation rejects is the strict hierarchy of their parents' churches. And Ecklund (2005a, 2005b) concludes that first-generation Korean congregations tend to emphasize their Korean culture, while second-generation Koreans are more likely to express concern for the broader local community and value diversity, although those values are attenuated by negative stereotypes of poor and U.S. minorities, particularly African Americans.

Leadership

Leadership also directs a congregation's civic engagement. Foley and Hoge (2007, 48) argue that some religious communities have an organizational style that promotes civic linkages outside the worship community. These civic-leader worship communities may involve congregation members only peripherally or they may provide opportunities for at least some congregants to participate in civic affairs. Kniss and Numrich (2007, 184) argue that this is especially prominent in directing a congregation's civic engagement in the more structured organizations. Catholicism, for example, often has paid professional staff assisted by lay volunteers, frequently directed by priests (see also Mooney 2005;

Palacios 2007). Islam, in contrast to Catholicism, is decentralized. The direction of a mosque, whether it promotes civic involvement in the broader world, is fundamentally determined by its leadership (see, for example, Klausen 2006). Some Christian leaders, such as Jerry Falwell, negatively stereotype Moslems and thus promote an adversarial civic engagement similar to that of fundamentalist Moslems (Kaya 2007). In contrast, Dempsey (2006) found a Hindu temple in New York in which its guru invited the full participation of visitors regardless of not only caste, but also ethnicity, gender, and even religion.

To understand the role of leadership in congregations, we draw upon Max Weber and on criticisms of Weber articulated by Pierre Bourdieu and Peter Worsley. In seeking to understand the legitimation of human authority, Weber adopted the Greek term used in the New Testament, *karism* (gifts of the Spirit),[15] to refer to an inherent quality that makes certain people natural and effective leaders: "The term 'charisma' will be applied to a certain quality of an individual personality by virtue of which he is considered extraordinary and treated as endowed with supernatural, superhuman, or at least specifically exceptional powers or qualities. These are such as not to be accessible to the ordinary person, but are regarded as of divine origin or as exemplary, and on the basis of them the individual concerned is treated as a leader" ([1925] 1969, 241).

Weber articulates three typologies of religious leaders: the prophet (a natural leader), the priest (an appointed leader), and the magician (an entrepreneurial diviner), all of which obviously may and often do overlap. Weber asserts that the prophet, "the purely individual bearer of charisma, who by virtue of his mission proclaims a religious doctrine or divine commandment," is the most effective and the most influential of the three ([1922] 1963, 46). Concerned primarily with "religion as a source of the dynamics of social change" (Parsons 1963, xxx), Weber employs the related notions of *charisma* and *prophet* to theorize "the effect of religious views upon the conduct of life" ([1922] 1963, 9). It is the prophet, thus naturally endowed with charisma, who most abundantly produces such an effect. The most important effect of prophecy is the establishment of a foundational worldview that shapes a faith community's identity and sense of purpose. As Weber explains, "prophetic revelation involves for both the prophet himself and for his followers . . . a unified view of the world derived from a consciously integrated and meaningful attitude toward life. To the prophet, both the life of man and the world, both social and cosmic events, have a certain systematic and coherent meaning. . . . Now, the structure of this meaning may take varied forms and it may weld together into a unity motives that are logically heterogeneous" ([1922] 1963, 58–59).

In this passage Weber forcefully implies that charisma, or effective religious leadership, produces its greatest impact in creating and upholding congregants' worldview. When leaders employ a theology that is both consonant with their congregants' worldview and promotes civic engagement beyond the church doors, then charisma may be transformed into effective civic social capital. To illustrate, a faith community may be led by a highly charismatic cleric whose theology, nonetheless, de-emphasizes civic engagement and hence the cleric's charisma results in more insular spiritual activities, such as faith healing and pilgrimage. On the other hand, where charisma focuses on the social implications of morality, the energy generated by prophecy can result in enthusiastic and wide-ranging social service programs. In most cases that we have studied and which are detailed in subsequent chapters, the impetus for civic engagement flows downward from clerical leadership to the laity, and Weber is apt for understanding these cases where leaders seem to be naturally endowed and have an inherent social vision.

However, leadership may be not necessarily "top-down." Leadership may also emerge from a dialectical relationship between the religious leader and his or her congregation. For these types of cases, Weber is inadequate. We must address not only how congregants respond to charismatic leaders, but also when and how leaders may react to their congregants. We need to understand the agency of congregants as well as the "charismatic" agency of church leaders. Worsley recognizes this, arguing that "Weber's own treatment of the charismatic leader is a bad precedent," since in exclusively emphasizing the personality of the leader it "stops short of examination of the situation out of which leadership emerges, and of the social support for the prophet, when this is exactly one of the most crucial features demanding explanation" (1968, xxxvii). Bourdieu likewise asserts that "Max Weber never produces anything other than a psycho-sociological theory of charisma, a theory that regards it as the lived relation of a public to the charismatic personality" (1987, 129). Bourdieu is critical of such a definition of "charisma as a property attaching to the nature of a single individual" (1987, 131) because it ignores the structures of the religious field and the relationships between these structures and the religious *habitus* ("the matrix of perception") of the laity, which, for Bourdieu, must be the primary object of analysis for the sociology of religion. "Weber consistently fails to establish a distinction between (1) direct interactions and (2) the objective structure of the relations that become established between religious agencies" (Bourdieu 1987, 126). For Bourdieu, "The latter is crucial . . . [since] it controls the form that interactions may take" (1987, 131). While sharing Weber's insistence that the final measure of true prophecy is its capacity to produce effective religious and/or social change, Bourdieu goes on to argue that "prophecy can play such a role only because it has as its own generative and unifying principle, a habitus objectively attuned to that of its addressees" (1987, 131). For immigrants, their habitus presumably must adjust to their new environment. The context of reception, particularly how immigrants are treated by American institutions and society, is likely to have a significant impact on their habitus and consequent civic engagement.

The Context of Reception: Immigrants' Treatment
by American Institutions and Society

Immigrant religious congregations, in spite of often acting as sites of temporary refuge, are not hermetically sealed. Regardless of their spiritual orientation, they of necessity interact with and react to the broader society. Much of the broader literature on immigrant integration similarly emphasizes that how the broader society accepts or rejects immigrants affects how immigrants respond, how easily they integrate, or whether they engage in reactive ethnicity that emphasizes their differences from those discriminating against them (Portes and Zhou 1993; Alba and Nee 2003; Stepick et al. 2003; Portes and Rumbaut 2006).

Context of reception is a concept derived from the broader field of immigration studies. It refers to how the host or receiving society treats immigrants and refugees upon arrival (see Portes 1981; Portes and DeWind 2004; Portes and Rumbaut 2006). This involves government policy toward these groups (favored, disfavored, or treated the same as most others) as well as the overall economic and social climate that the newcomers encounter. Can immigrants readily obtain a legal immigration status? Is the economy growing so newcomers can find work? How nativistic or accepting are the established residents toward the newcomers?

Utilizing a series of measures, the context of reception provides a type of index that factors into the immigrants' likelihood of success. Thus, success does not hinge entirely on the immigrants' own human capital or other characteristics. Immigrants' individual characteristics, such as their level of education and training, are necessary to understanding immigrant incorporation, but they are not sufficient. It also matters fundamentally how the host society receives or welcomes immigrants. Immigrants whom the host society treats well are likely to do better than those whom the host society discriminates against, regardless of the immigrants' background. The concept of context of reception and the associated mode of incorporation have been used primarily to explain immigrants' individual economic success, usually defined in terms of labor market experiences (employment rates, income, occupation), but recently it has also been applied to education outcomes, particularly for the children of immigrants (Portes and Rumbaut 2005).

Context of reception has not been extensively applied theoretically to analyses of religion and civic engagement among immigrants. We believe, however, that it can further our understanding of differences in civic social capital (CSC) among immigrants. This perspective argues that the process of interaction and reaction is more important than such things as what language one may speak or the denomination to which one belongs. Foley and Hoge (2007, 228–229) recount how the rejection of the Irish in the 1800s provoked a reliance upon their Catholic heritage and institutions to become part of America by maintaining their ethnic distinctiveness.[16] Marquardt (2005) discusses a Catholic mission in Georgia with primarily undocumented immigrants from Mexico. The mission priest was charismatic and committed to motivating the congregants to civic engagement. Congregants did participate, but they encountered difficulties in achieving their goals because of their immigration status and because the local community did not provide formal means for incorporating their concerns. Stevens (2004) argues that the new context of reception forces immigrants to choose between their old habitus and a new one. Ghanaian Pentecostals in Chicago must choose between changing their religious culture in order to more comfortably fit into their new context or maintaining their religious culture and the tension that exists between it and their new context. More generally, the context of reception approach leads us to expect that the nature of conflict or accommodation on the part of the local community and the immigrants' response will affect whether immigrants and their churches swing toward engagement with or isolation from U.S. society.

Civic Social Capital

Religious congregations clearly can be a source of social support, solace, and identity formation, in addition to meeting the spiritual needs of their members. Immigrant congregations also generate and embody social capital; i.e., social relationships that have material consequences (see Bourdieu 1983; Coleman 1988b; Portes 1998). These social capital relationships focus primarily on the immigrants' lives in their new homeland, on adapting to their new environment. As a result, they complement the functions of immigrant religious organizations to provide social and symbolic links to their homeland. Similarly, they relate to the central concern of this volume, civic social capital and religion.

The phrase "civic social capital" (CSC) is our own creation. It builds upon and extends the notion of social capital. As summarized by Alejandro Portes (Portes 1998; Portes 2000; Portes and Landolt 2000; Portes and Mooney 2002), the concept of social capital was developed independently by the French sociologist Pierre Bourdieu (1983) and the American sociologist James Coleman (1988a, 1988b). The phrase "social capital" is an extension of economists' notions of financial and human capital. The original and still primary use of social and the other forms of capital has been to explain individual economic achievement. Access to financial capital obviously affects individual economic achievement. Formal education, training, and job experience, all of which constitute human capital, are also likely to affect individuals' economic achievement. Bourdieu's and Coleman's conceptions of social capital extended these ideas by theorizing the cliché, "it's not what you know, but who you know." While Bourdieu and Coleman defined the concept somewhat differently, both converged on the fact that benefits accrue to individuals or families by virtue of their ties with others. These social networks often serve as the basis for economic advancement or as a social safety net tapped in times of need.[17]

Through the 1990s the concept became extremely popular in the social sciences (for a review, see Portes 1998).[18] Most authors used the concept similarly to the original conceptions of Coleman and Bourdieu. The political scientist Robert Putnam, however, employed the same phrase but theorized it fundamentally differently (Putnam 1993, 1995, 1996, 2000). His formulation emphasized the social capital of communities, not individuals; and he was more concerned with the general civic life of a community than with economic achievement. Thus, while Coleman and Bourdieu conceptualized social capital as individuals' investments into social networks for their own individual and primarily economic benefit, Putnam conceived of social capital as a community-level phenomenon. He conceived of social capital as the density of social ties within communities. According to Putnam's conception, communities where individuals have denser (or more overlapping) social networks have more social capital. He examines, for example, membership in PTAs, neighborhood crime watch organizations, churches, and unions. His analysis focuses on benefits accruing not to individuals but to communities, such as reduced crime rates, lower official corruption, and better governance. As Portes (2000) points out, in Bourdieu's and Coleman's original formulations the sources of social capital were clearly associated with a person's networks, while effects were linked to an array of individual material and informational benefits. These individual benefits were clearly separate and distinct from the social networks that produced them. Putnam's formulation of collective social capital or civic-ness, however, lacks this distinct separation.

We share Putnam's interest in civic relations, but we seek to develop a concept that avoids the communalistic pitfalls of his application of the term "social capital." In this vein we employ the term "civic social capital" (CSC) largely to shift focus away from social capital's emphasis on economic benefits to individuals and toward activities that are also civic. We are interested in social ties that extend beyond one's immediate family and friends. More particularly, we will focus on how religious organizations enable or deter social relationships with the broader civic society. Social ties may produce economic benefits for individuals, as conceived in the original formulation of social capital, but they may also expand an individual's definition and sense of community, that is, the civic society of which one is a part. Our concern in this book is the role religious organizations have in developing their members' CSC. In other words, we are concerned with how social relationships based in the church (or other religious organizations) affect individuals' relationships to the broader civic world.

Definitions of "civic" vary widely from a narrow focus on electoral politics, such as voting, to a much broader examination of social ties beyond one's family (Flanagan and Sherrod 1998; Flanagan and Faaison 2001; Hyman 2002). We define "civic" broadly to mean addressing people's needs in a continuum from very close to home to the broader Miami community to outside Miami, including, but not limited to, transnational ties to homelands. This includes, for example, congregants developing relationships not only with other congregants whom they did not previously know, but also with individuals outside their religious organization, which could be youth in other religious youth organizations, co-ethnics who share a concern with the politics of their homeland, and/or other people who share environmental concerns in Miami and use the church as a mechanism for mobilizing social action. We are interested in "citizenship" in broad, fundamental terms, not solely what passport one holds, if one is a legal or undocumented immigrant, or if one is registered to vote and casts a ballot. Following Kniss and Numrich (2007), we are concerned with how religious organizations themselves and immigrant individuals within congregations encourage or discourage acting as members of a variety of broader publics.

We adopt the distinction between *bonding* and *bridging* social capital (Gittell and Vidal 1998; Woolcock 1998; Putnam 2000; Beyerlein and Hipp 2005). Bonding social capital emerges from networks where people share perceived identity relations. It reflects social ties among people defined as socially homogeneous or similar in race, ethnicity, gender, class, and/or religion. People with bonding social capital take it for granted that others in the network are fundamentally similar to themselves and can be trusted (Szreter 2002). Bonding social capital provides emotional support and the solidarity produced by religion that Emile Durkheim associated with group rituals (1915, cited in Wuthnow 2002). With its emphasis on ties to people who are similar, bonding social capital is thus not very civic. It does not reach very far into the broader social world. As such, we do not use the phrase civic social capital for cases that reflect solely bonding relationships.

Bridging social capital, in contrast, ties together people who are socially different.[19] People engage in bridging relationships because they presumably believe that together they can achieve something not possible through using only bonding social capital (Szreter 2002). Ties that bond are generally thought to be stronger, while those that bridge are weaker. Because bridging ties link to people who are different, they are, however, more likely to provide access to different resources.[20] While much of the social capital research addresses economic consequences, our concern is with bridging social ties that link immigrants to the broader civic society. It is argued that bridging is likely to promote a sense of civic responsibility, overcome divisiveness and insularity, and encourage not only tolerance but cooperation that may be useful for addressing large-scale social problems such as crime, poverty, and the ill effects of family disruption and inadequate health care (Skocpol and Fiorina 1999; Wuthnow 2002). Bridging social capital is also believed to be a means of strengthening the larger society (Frank and Yasumoto 1998; Paxton 1999; Wuthnow 2002).[21] Thus, bridging social capital relationships constitute examples of civic social capital.

Another type of CSC is linking social capital (Szreter 2002), also called status-bridging social capital (Wuthnow 2002). Linking social capital refers to social ties established between people who are not only different, but also unequal in power and access to resources (Szreter 2002). Linking social capital spans vertical arrangements of power, influence, wealth, and prestige. Those with less power acquire influence and other resources through linking social capital (Wuthnow 2002). Linking social capital thus is an obvious case of CSC, and it is the particular type most directly tied to the formal sphere of politics, of elected and appointed officials who have control over resources. Linking CSC can emerge also in the broader civic sphere, between private individuals and groups in which one has resources that the other does not have.

Following Portes's (2000) critique of Putnam, we conceptualize CSC as an individual attribute that arises from one's social relations. We do not conceive of social organizations, such as a congregation or other religious organizations, as having more or less CSC. Rather, social organizations are a potential site for the promotion and creation of CSC. In the chapters that follow we specifically view CSC as emerging from the social relations within congregations and embodied in individuals. In this sense, our conception of CSC is similar to Coleman's and Bourdieu's ontological view of social capital. We specifically conceive of congregations as sites that either do or do not encourage, promote, or produce CSC. CSC is a subset of bridging social capital. CSC consists of that bridging social capital that specifically links individuals, in our case members of a specific congregation, to the broader civic society in which they are embedded. Since this is an ethnographic study and the first attempt to analyze CSC, we employ a broad definition of civic society not limited to relatively narrow concerns of political scientists of voting or participation in electoral politics. It is self-consciously exploratory to see the range of relationships and to analyze those that reach beyond the congregation.

Our central question is, around what, if any, civic activities do immigrant religious congregations in Miami (and, by extension, elsewhere) coalesce? If a particular religious body does not engage in any civic activities, why does it not? If a religious body does foster civic engagement, how does it engender and deploy CSC? Do immigrant religious organizations primarily engender CSC toward their homelands? Under what conditions do immigrant congregations promote CSC related to Miami and the United States? When religious bodies engage in civic activities, do they or do they not cross classic sociological lines that have for generations divided Miami into competing sectors (e.g., ethnic, racial, class, gender, income, and neighborhood dividing lines)? Why or why not? What do congregations seek to accomplish by engaging in CSC? And what can we learn from this about broader issues of the future of multi-cultural, multi-class, multi-ethnic/racial cities? In other words, how can focusing on *religious* organizations (as opposed to, or perhaps in addition to, community, racial, ethnic, nationality, etc. groups) advance our understanding of how immigrants and their "native" neighbors negotiate their identities, social status, legitimacy, and power in complex social arenas?

In sum, our central theoretical concept is civic social capital or CSC, which we will employ to examine how congregations do or do not promote bridging social links to the community beyond family and church. Based on the ethnographic and quantitative studies of the authors in this volume, we argue that in religious institutions CSC emerges from denomination, leadership, immigrant generation, and the context of reception.

Miami as a Gateway Immigrant City

Miami is the quintessential new immigrant city. With more than 50 percent of its population having been born in other countries and more than 80 percent having foreign-born parents, it is proportionately the most immigrant city of any major metropolitan area in the United States. Less than half the population speaks English in their homes. Non-Hispanic Whites number fewer than Blacks, not only in the central city but also in the entire Miami-Dade County, which has approximately 2.5 million residents, making it the eighth-most-populous county in the United States. Immigrants, overwhelmingly from the Caribbean, account for all of the Black population growth since 1980.[22]

The 1959 Cuban Revolution that initiated immigration into Miami also occasioned a dramatic, rapid transformation in the city's culture, economics, and politics. Miami is home to the most economically successful Latino population in the United States, Cubans. Economically, Miami has been described as the capital of the Caribbean and even all of Latin America. Local politics are dominated by foreign-born immigrants and their offspring. For the first time in American history, a group of first-generation immigrants has assumed control of local political institutions and risen to the top of the local socioeconomic hierarchy.

The role of religion in Miami is largely unknown simply because very few scholars have seriously or systematically examined it.[23] What little we do know suggests that religious institutions indeed play a significant role. They are at the forefront of efforts to improve interethnic relations. Religious organizations have also played a central, although largely undocumented, role in the integration of immigrants into Miami.

The reception accorded Cubans is a prime example of how context of reception affects both immigrant economic integration and religion. Because they were fleeing a left-wing revolution at the height of the Cold War, Cubans were much more warmly received by the U.S. government than other groups who arrived around the same time. The Cuban Refugee Act provided near instantaneous legal status and bountiful federal assistance to the refugees, administered in many cases through Catholic relief organizations.

In the early years of the Cuban exodus, the Catholic Church was integral to the resettlement of thousands of refugees. Indeed, some have informally argued that the Cuban exodus "created" the Catholic Church in Miami. Before the arrival of Miami's Cubans, Protestantism dominated Miami (Tweed 1995) and the Catholic Church had a small, insignificant role in South Florida's religious community. The Miami diocese was established only one year before the beginnings of the Cuban diaspora, which rapidly transformed the diocese. When Fidel Castro declared Cuba to be atheist in 1961, a disproportionate number of devout Christians, the vast majority of whom were Catholic, fled during the first wave of the exodus.

In a downtown Catholic school, the diocese established the Centro Hispano Católico, which was the first and for a while the only social agency with a bilingual staff when Cuban refugees began to arrive (Badillo 2006). The head of the Miami diocese, Bishop Coleman Carroll, led the effort to establish the federal Cuban Refugee Program, which provided unprecedented and unmatched support to Cuban refugees, a program that per capita has offered Cubans more assistance than any other immigrant or minority group has ever received in the United States (Pedraza-Bailey 1985; Stepick 1992; Stepick and Dutton Stepick 2001).

Much of the Catholic infrastructure fled the "godless communism" of the Cuban revolution and re-established itself in Miami. In September 1961, more than one hundred Cuban priests and over eighty nuns resettled in Miami. The Miami Diocese made major efforts to incorporate these Cuban religious leaders, offering them training in English and assigning them to parish priests to offer services to their newly arrived fellow exiles. The elite Belén Jesuit School that Fidel Castro had attended moved entirely to Miami and was staffed almost exclusively by the same Catholic priests who had staffed it in Cuba.

Soon after the Cuban revolution, Monsignor Bryan Walsh, a local Catholic priest from Ireland, organized the transportation and resettlement of unaccompanied minors from Cuba through a program informally known as Pedro Pan (or Peter Pan) (Triay 1998; Conde 1999). San Juan Bosco Church, described at length in chapter 6 by Isabel del Pino-Allen, became a virtual Cuban national parish. The diocese also constructed a shrine to Cuba's patron saint, Our Lady of Charity, that became the focal point of what Tweed has labeled as Cuba's diasporic nationalism (Tweed 1997).With the arrival of Cuban refugees, Miami became predominantly Catholic and had a Catholic church strongly identified with exiled Cubans and their struggle against Fidel Castro. Just ten years after the Miami diocese was created in 1958, its status was upgraded to archdiocese, reflecting the rapid increase in Catholics and the infrastructure that accompanied the influx of Cuban refugees. U.S. government assistance in conjunction with Catholic services was critical in aiding Cuban exiles to quickly and securely reestablish themselves in Miami and turn their attention to anti-Castro politics.

While continuing to help resettle legal immigrants and provide social services to others, the Catholic Church and numerous Protestant denominations have also led the struggle for Haitian refugees to receive equal treatment. African American churches were among the first to speak in defense of Haitian refugees (Stepick 1982; Stepick 1998). Religious leaders were also at the forefront of the fight for Nicaraguans to obtain permanent legal status (Portes and Stepick 1993; Rodriguez 2000). Numerous churches and religious organizations have also created special programs to integrate immigrants in many established Protestant churches; the Catholic Archdiocese runs programs designed to incorporate immigrants; and independent, primarily small fundamentalist Protestant churches have emerged within immigrant communities. Some of these congregations have been transplanted from immigrants' home countries, while the less structured and less visible traditions of Vodou and Santería (or its less syncretic sibling Lukumi)[24] have also transcended borders. Afro-Caribbean religions have had an important and visible impact on Miami culture. Their vitality is evident to the non-practitioner in the many *botanicas* that sell Santería and Vodou ritual paraphernalia and healing herbs. In many neighborhoods no one is surprised by the remnants of offerings left at crossroads or waterways. After a five-year struggle against city authorities, a leading Lukumi congregation in a Miami area municipality, Hialeah, won a victory in 1993 in the U.S. Supreme Court that ruled in favor of animal sacrifice for religious purposes (Supreme Court of the United States 1993). The victory, however, did not eliminate the tension between the estimated one hundred thousand practitioners of Santería or related traditions in Miami and the broader community. Mainstream churches usually condemn Afro-Caribbean religions even though elements of Santería and Vodou affect, in myriad ways, the worldview and daily lives of most Caribbean immigrants.

All of these dimensions of immigration into Miami make it a strategic research site for examining the role of religion and religious organizations in civic life. Nowhere else is the impact of immigration more visible or profound. Nowhere else has an overwhelmingly mainstream Protestant religious community, with a significant Jewish presence, been so altered by the rapid rise of the Catholic Church, by evangelical Christians who were missionized by Americans before immigrating to Miami, and by a substantial infusion of Afro-Caribbean religious traditions. Moreover, Miami contains contrasts between immigrants who are White and Black, rich and poor, politically powerful and disempowered, those highly connected to religious institutions and those disconnected from churches, Christian and Afro-Caribbean. Because of this diversity on critical social dimensions, Miami is an ideal location for examining the interface of religion and immigrants' incorporation into the civic structures and functions of the United States.

The focus of this volume is congregations. From June 2000 to March 2004, we did ethnographic fieldwork and conducted interviews with church leaders and congregants in twenty congregations in Miami-Dade County. Prior to the ethnographic research we embarked on an effort to map and survey all the religious institutions in Miami's predominantly immigrant and native minority areas. We included all of the non-Christian congregations, such as mosques and Hindu temples, but also the religious paraphernalia stores, particularly the botanicas that serve Afro-Caribbean religious needs since these religions generally do not have permanent public places of worship.

The task proved immense as not only are the churches and other religious buildings many, but there is no systematic listing of religious organizations. Various mainstream Protestant denominations and the Catholic Archdiocese do have directories of their churches, but there are no lists for the far larger number of independent Protestant churches. We did find a few Internet-based directories, but checking them proved them to be very incomplete. The only way to accomplish the task reliably and validly was to drive down every street. We set about the task with the help of numerous students, including one of Terry Rey's undergraduate religion classes. Under the guidance of the project director, Carol Dutton Stepick, each student was assigned a particular area and instructed to cover every block. When a religious institution was found, the researcher noted its name and address and attempted at the time or in a follow-up phone call or visit to make contact with the congregation's leader to administer a short survey that asked denomination, primary ethnicities of the congregation, languages of religious services, and the missions and social services provided. We covered most of Miami-Dade County, concentrating primarily in those areas of immigrant and native minorities. We found over twenty-seven hundred and administered our short survey to nearly one thousand.

Once we had the results of the mapping, we selected congregations theoretically. We first wanted to represent the primary immigrant groups in the area: Cubans, Nicaraguans, Haitians, and West Indians, along with Mexicans, who are numerically not as large as the others locally but important because they are the fastest growing group in South Florida and largest immigrant group overall in the United States. We then sought to achieve some denominational variation within the limitations of our resources. Because Catholicism is the largest denomination in Miami-Dade County, we made Catholic congregations a primary focus. We selected San Juan Bosco, which was initially the center of Cuban worship in Miami but later became predominantly a Nicaraguan parish. We also examined two Catholic parishes in the suburbs. St. Agatha serves primarily older Cubans, and Our Lady of Divine Providence has primarily Nicaraguan congregants. Mexicans are residentially concentrated in the southern, more rural part of Miami-Dade County, and there we worked in Saint Ann's Catholic Mission. Haitians are also predominantly Catholic, and we studied the most important Catholic Church for Miami Haitians and perhaps for all diasporic Haitians, Notre Dame d'Haiti, which has a long history of being civically engaged.

While Catholics remain predominant among Miami's immigrants, Protestantism is undeniably important and growing. We wanted some representation of both mainstream Protestants and the independent churches, which are often small storefront operations. Accordingly, we included two Hispanic[25] Protestant congregations. Both are in Hialeah, which is the second-largest municipality in Miami-Dade County and which is 90 percent Hispanic, including over 60 percent who are Cuban. We studied a Seventh-Day Adventist congregation that consisted primarily of a congregation of Seventh-Day Adventists who had migrated from Cuba along with other Caribbean Hispanics. We also studied a Nazarene church that had begun as a White Anglo church, but as immigrants increasingly settled in Hialeah it became overwhelmingly Hispanic.

For West Indians, we studied one Episcopalian, one Catholic, and various Protestant congregations, including one mainline Baptist church and four Pentecostal congregations which were in small storefront locations. The Episcopal and Catholic churches each had ethnically mixed congregations, although West Indians were the largest groups in each. Specifically, the Baptist and Pentecostal churches were predominantly Jamaican.

We also wanted to overcome a common limitation of immigration studies that analyze only immigrants without putting them in context or comparing them to the broader U.S. population. To do this, we incorporated African Americans specifically because they have a long and well-documented history of melding religion and civic engagement, although no studies specifically of African American churches in Miami have previously been done. For African Americans we had two foci. We studied Perrine, a historically Black neighborhood in the southern part of Miami-Dade County. There we focused on the West Perrine Christian Association and Sweet Home Missionary Baptist Church. We also studied two environmental initiatives in the county. Both were important to African American communities and led by African Americans, almost all of whom had deep roots in their churches.

All of these congregations are Christian. Miami-Dade County does have many synagogues, along with a few mosques and Buddhist and Hindu temples, but they were not included. Moreover, we did not include any practitioners of African New World religions such as Cuban Santería or Haitian Vodou. All of these would have added to the study, but we chose to not include them because Miami's immigrants are overwhelmingly Christian. Miami's immigrants are also predominantly Catholic, and this volume accordingly has more material on Catholics, although of different national backgrounds, than any other single denomination.

Each ethnographer spent at least two years studying the congregations discussed in each chapter. Some of the ethnographies focus on just one congregation. Others examine more than one. Sarah J. Mahler analyzes the two Hispanic Protestant congregations in Hialeah. Teruyuki Tsuji and Christine Ho considered the most congregations of anyone in the study, doing fieldwork in all seven of the West Indian congregations. All of the ethnographers attended not only religious services but other church-related activities. We also interviewed church leaders, church employees, and congregants. In all the congregations where Spanish was the dominant language, the ethnographers were either native Spanish speakers or had previously conducted ethnographic research in Spanish. In the Haitian case, both ethnographers, Alex Stepick and Terry Rey, have conducted extensive research concerning Haitians and speak both Haitian Creole and French. Following Human Subjects Protection protocol, we offered confidentiality to all participants. Almost all of the church leaders declined. In those cases where church leaders or congregants requested confidentiality we use pseudonyms.

The project also had a transnational component. Sarah Mahler worked in Nicaragua. Both Sarah Mahler and Katrin Hansing traveled to Cuba, where Mahler worked primarily with Protestants and Hansing worked with Catholics. Hansing had conducted fieldwork in Cuba before, but for this project she traveled to Guantánamo, which has a relationship with St. Agatha Catholic Church in Miami, on which she reports in chapter 5. Terry Rey worked in Haiti, where he had done previous research. The transnational research is not the subject of this volume, but it did inform the congregational studies.

We coordinated this work by having monthly team meetings of all the researchers, in which we would report our findings and through which our theoretical framework was developed and refined. Two of the editors of this volume are anthropologists while the third is from religious studies. We had two postdoctoral fellows who are also anthropologists, while the graduate students were from either Comparative Sociology or Latin American and Caribbean Studies at Florida International University. While these backgrounds were complementary, we had to overcome disciplinary boundaries and our ignorance of other disciplines. We shared reading lists and had extensive discussions of how to conceptualize the research. The theoretical framework and, particularly, the concept of civic social capital emerged from these interdisciplinary discussions.

Ethnographies generally provide rich detail that reveals not only nuance but also the processes by which social relationships unfold. They provide much greater depth and insight than obtained from survey research. On the other hand, they are almost always unrepresentative of the broader population. Our set of congregational ethnographic studies does not allow us to generalize to the broader set of immigrant congregations in Miami, let alone the United States. To address this limitation, we conducted a survey of freshmen college students at Florida International University, the local state university, where the editors were all based at the time of the study. Although the sample was not selected from the overall county and is obviously younger than the broader population, it turns out to be generally representative in terms of ethnicity and immigrant versus non-immigrant. Thus, it provides a basis for putting the congregational studies into context.

Map 1.1 and table 1.1 indicate where we conducted fieldwork. The map of Miami-Dade County reflects ethnic concentrations of non-Hispanic Whites, Hispanics, and Blacks. The map demonstrates the extreme segregation within the county with nearly all areas having 50 percent or more of one of these three groups. Cross-hatching also indicates the particular residential concentrations of Nicaraguans, Haitians and West Indians. We did not cross-hatch Cuban areas since it would have included nearly all the map that is not either Black or non-Hispanic White. The places we gathered data are keyed by numbers in map 1.1 and are referred to in table 1.1. These indicate all the congregations plus the coalitions with which we worked and the location of Florida International University's two campuses, where we administered the survey reported in chapter 11. Table 1.1 has the names of the churches, their denomination, the primary ethnicity of congregants, and indicates where on the map each is located.

The following chapters examine the intersection of religion and civic engagement among Miami's primary immigrant and native minority groups. In part 1, we examine congregations that exhibit linking civic social capital, which in all of our congregations is motivated by charismatic religious leaders. Sarah J. Mahler's chapter, "So Close and Yet So Far Away," contrasts the development and deployment of CSC in two Hispanic, primarily Cuban, Protestant congregations. Both congregations cultivate CSC through their sermons and actions, but one extends it into the community beyond the walls of the church, while the other focuses almost exclusively internally. In "Refugee Catholicism in Little Haiti," Terry Rey and Alex Stepick emphasize the role of leadership in the promotion and creation of CSC. The founder of Miami's Notre Dame d'Haiti Catholic Church, Thomas Wenski, actively encouraged parishioners to civically engage, particularly in the political struggles in their homeland, and generally in local initiatives supportive of Haitian immigrant rights. His immediate successor, however, emphasized spiritual concerns to the exclusion of civic social issues, causing a perceivable demise in the church's legendary social and political activism. But, he retired soon thereafter, and his own successor returned the parish to the civic social focus of its founder. Su Oltman Fink's "Politics and Prayer in West Perrine" documents the explicit and forceful creation and promotion of CSC among various African American churches in a community that was once a rural agricultural area of Miami-Dade County but has since become part of metropolitan Miami with the attendant social problems of drugs and crime. Prominent pastors mounted a campaign that drew local and even national attention.

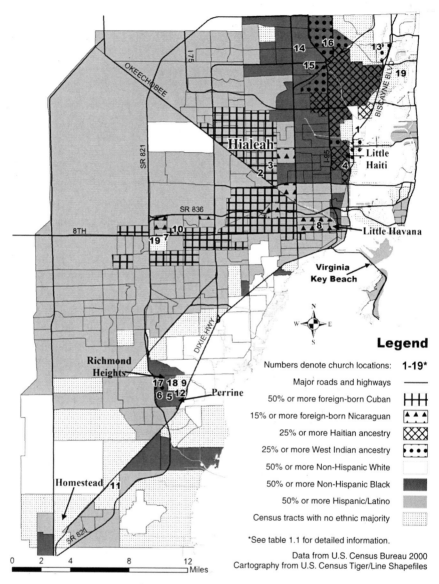

Legend

Numbers denote church locations: **1-19***

Major roads and highways ——

50% or more foreign-born Cuban

15% or more foreign-born Nicaraguan

25% or more Haitian ancestry

25% or more West Indian ancestry

50% or more Non-Hispanic White

50% or more Non-Hispanic Black

50% or more Hispanic/Latino

Census tracts with no ethnic majority

*See table 1.1 for detailed information.

Data from U.S. Census Bureau 2000
Cartography from U.S. Census Tiger/Line Shapefiles

MAP 1.1. Our Congregations and Miami's Ethnic Neighborhoods.

Map by Marcos Feldman.

TABLE 1.1

Key to Congregations

Location	Churches	Denomination	Ethnic majority
1	Miami Catholic Archdiocese	Catholic	Historically important to Cuban refugees
2	Refugees Seventh-Day Adventist	Seventh-Day Adventist	Cuban dominant with other Hispanics
3	Disciples' Nazarene	Nazarene	Mixed Hispanic
4	Notre Dame d'Haiti	Catholic	Haitian
5	Sweet Home Missionary	Baptist	African American
6	West Perrine Christian Association	Various Protestant congregations	African American
7	St. Agatha	Catholic	Cuban
8	San Juan Bosco	Catholic	Cuban leaders with Nicaraguan congregants
9	Mainstream Protestant churches	Various Protestant denominations	African American
10	Our Lady of Divine Providence	Catholic	Nicaraguan
11	St. Ann Mission	Catholic	Mexican
12	Emmanuel Apostolic	Pentecostal	West Indian
13	Monument of Faith	Pentecostal	West Indian
14	First Born Christian Center	Pentecostal	West Indian
15	Unity Light of the World	Pentecostal	West Indian
16	Sierra Norwood	Baptist	West Indian, primarily Jamaican
17	Christ the King	Catholic	West Indian, primarily Trinidadian
18	Church of the Ascencion	Episcopalian	West Indian
19	1,334-person survey	Mix of Christian denominations and other faiths	Mixed ethnicity college freshmen

In part 2, we focus on congregations that produce bridging civic social capital, manifested in service and volunteerism. Katrin Hansing in *"Unidos en la Fe"* (United in Faith) describes the extensive transnational ties between Cuban Catholics in Miami and those in Cuba. She demonstrates the rapidly growing ties that remain informal, unofficial, and often even secretive because of the continuing tense political relations between the United States and Cuba. These ties, as manifest particularly through a relationship between one Miami Catholic church, St. Agatha, and the Cuban diocese of Guantánamo-Baracoa, reflect both Miami Cuban nostalgia and an important means for rapprochement and reconciliation between Cubans on the island and in the United States. Isabel del Pino-Allen, in *"La Catedral del Exilio"* (The Cathedral of Exile), considers another manifestation of nostalgia in her examination of the parish of St. John Bosco, a Catholic church in the heart of Little Havana. St. John Bosco's leaders are Miami Cubans who, more than forty years after the Castro Revolution, maintain the expectation to return to Cuba once *el tirano* (the tyrant) is gone. The church's Religious-Civic-Patriotic School still studies the geography of Cuba as it was before the 1959 revolution. The neighborhood surrounding the church, however, has changed considerably; and many of those who attend the school are Central Americans, especially Nicaraguans, and not Cubans. Despite this ethnic succession, the parish continues to focus on Cuba and anti-communism. The newer arrivals are welcomed into a web of CSC that supports them, but socializes them by reproducing *cubanía*, a specifically Cuban identity. In her contribution, "Black Churches and the Environment in Miami," Eileen M. Smith-Cavros examines the impressive involvement in African American churches in Miami's environmental movement. Across different denominations various African American churches demonstrated environmental connections and priorities to protect threatened natural ecosystems. These concerns not only develop CSC within congregations, but also connect these congregations to the predominantly White environmental movement.

Part 3 examines congregations that focus on bonding social capital primarily through an emphasis on religious and spiritual activities and a de-emphasis on service, volunteering, or other forms of civic engagement. In "Youth and Charity in a Sweetwater Parish," Aidil Oscariz focuses on a parish that experienced ethnic succession. In the early 1980s the congregation of Our Lady of Divine Providence Catholic Church was predominantly Cuban. Less than a decade later, the majority of members was Nicaraguan. The parish priest at the beginning of our study was a Cuban who led the parish in welcoming first the Mariel Cuban refugees in the early 1980s and then Nicaraguans in the mid- and late-1980s. Unfortunately, the priest was also linked to the notorious Catholic sex abuse scandals and he was defrocked in 1999. The scandal divided parishioners, and Oscariz details how the parish's youth group confronts obstacles in constructing CSC. Noemí Báez, María de los Angeles Rey, and Terry Rey, in "Faith in the Fields," focus on the devotion of Mexican Catholics, primarily agricultural and plant nursery workers and day laborers, in the rural south of Miami-Dade County. The celebration of the feast of Mexico's patron saint, the Virgin of Guadalupe, provides a focal point for Mexican immigrants, a spiritual home in an area surrounded by a primarily African American community that mainly ignores the Mexican presence. The Cuban-born priest of St. Ann's Catholic Mission goes out of his way to emphasize the parallels between Miami's Cuban refugees and his Mexican congregation. Yet the civic activities of the church are exclusively focused on the Mexican immigrant community. Because the Mexican immigrant adults work long hours, a core of their youth have assumed a significant role in promoting and realizing this congregation's civic social capital. The West Indian Pentecostal, Catholic, and Episcopal congregations examined by Teruyuki Tsuji, Christine Ho, and Alex Stepick in "The Struggle for Civic Social Capital in West Indian Churches" illustrate an almost exclusive focus on spiritual and social issues. Only one Baptist church with primarily West Indian congregants promotes the development of CSC. All of the West Indian churches, however, have a strong emphasis on rituals that reinforce bonds, primarily religious bonds but also occasionally ethnic ones.

"Religious Practice and Civic Social Capital among Miami Youth" shifts to the relationship between religion and civic engagement among young adults, mostly first-or second-generation immigrants, in Miami. The unique contribution of this chapter is the direct comparison of immigrant and non-immigrant youth, based on a sample survey of over thirteen hundred college freshmen at the local state university, Florida International University. Yves Labissiere, Ann Reeder Goraczko, and Alex Stepick analyze extensive survey data to demonstrate that this population in South Florida is assuredly religious in its belief and practice, quite comparable in this regard to its "local native" cohort. The college-aged youth in this study engage in significant service, political and social activities, with religious commitment being the single most important factor in predicting their combined civic social activities. Some commentators expect immigrants to be less civically engaged (Huntington 2004). The South Florida immigrant youth, however, are as equally engaged as natives. Personal immigration history did not influence either religious practice or civic engagement. Immigrants are different from the native born only in being slightly more religious and using their cultural skills to help other immigrants bridge cultures. In short, being an immigrant may not make as big a difference as those who study immigrants and their religion imply. Yet religion does make an important difference in the broader social engagement of everyone, immigrant and non-immigrant alike.

The final chapter integrates the findings of the empirical chapters to construct theoretical generalizations concerning the relationships between religion, immigration, and civic engagement. We construct a typology of CSC, particularly focusing on the linking CSC of formal politics, the bridging CSC of service and volunteerism, and the bonding social capital of cultural events and religious activities. All of the congregations we studied embody bonding, particularly through religious and spiritual activities. Not all the congregations, however, demonstrate bridging or linking CSC. Service and volunteering activities embody bridging CSC, and to emerge there must be a match between, in Bourdieu's terms, the *habitus* of the religious leaders and their congregants. Religious leaders may promote bridging through service and volunteering, but CSC will not emerge unless the congregants share the bridging goals to be achieved through service and volunteering. Linking CSC was the most uncommon type that we found. To emerge, it requires charismatic religious leaders who can articulate and themselves embody the moral value and mechanisms to link religious congregations to those in the broader society who have power.

NOTES

1. See *http://www.thearda.com.* See also http://extranet.gallup-international.com/uploads/internet/Religiosity%20around%20the%20world%20VoP%2005%20press%20release.pdf.

2. Figures from actual church roll data today suggest that in the United States 59 percent of adults are members of some religious congregation. This is a notable decline since the 1960s, though any remotely parallel decline in *religious belief* is nowhere suggested in the literature.

3. It should be noted, however, that attending church more frequently did not mean one volunteered more. For all denominations together, the significant difference was between those who do and those who do not attend church.

4. There are native-born Americans who practice non-Judeo-Christian religions, too, notably, traditional Native American religions and the African American Muslim community.

5. Estimates of religious diversity within the United States vary according to the source of the data. Jasso et al. (2003) compare immigrants, using the New Immigrant Survey, to the general U.S. population, using the General Social Survey (GSS), and find that 17 percent of immigrants versus 4 percent of the U.S.-born population are non-Judeo-Christians. T. W. Smith (2002), on the other hand, uses the American Religious Identity Survey and finds that only 2.4 percent of the U.S. population is non-Judeo-Christian. Smith does not distinguish between immigrants and the native born.

6. See Stepick (2005) for a recent review of the relevant literature. Until the 1990s, religion received relatively little attention for the current wave of immigrants, both in Miami and the rest of the United States. The primary sourcebooks, such as *The Handbook of International Migration* (Hirschman, DeWind, and Kasinitz 1999) and the first two editions of *Immigrant America* (Portes and Rumbaut 1996/2006), ignored it entirely. Previous studies have focused overwhelmingly on the social and economic impacts of immigration, and only since the mid-1990s have immigration scholars focused on religion among the new wave of immigrants.

7. Foley and Hoge (2007) closely analyze both the New Immigrant Survey (Jasso et al. 2000) and the General Social Survey (GSS). They find that 17 percent of recent immigrants report no religious preference compared to less than 10 percent of the

native-born population. Although Foley and Hoge do not discuss why, we hypothesize that this is a result of immigrants from the Peoples Republic of China, which is both officially atheist and strongly discourages the practice of religion. Foley and Hoge go on to point out that of those immigrants who do express a religious preference, they are more likely to attend church regularly than are the native born.

8. Many immigrants, particularly Chinese, come from areas where religion is either officially discouraged, as in socialist regimes, or not widely observed. Hirschman (2004) summarizes the experiences of Italian immigrants one hundred years ago who were nominally Catholic but seldom attended church. Many contemporary Latin American immigrants are similar.

9. For general literature on transnationalism see Glick-Schiller, Basch, and Blanc-Szanton 1992; Basch, Glick-Schiller, and Blanc-Szanton 1994; Massey, Goldring, and Durand 1994; Mahler 1995, 1998, 1999; Guarnizo and Smith 1998; Laguerre 1998; Guarnizo 2001; and Morawska 2001.

10. The Gesu Catholic Church, in the heart of downtown Miami, in fact, features a statue or painting of the patron saint of each predominately Catholic country in Latin America.

11. Religion in the host country may emphasize an identity that was less important in the home country. Gibb (1998), for example, argues that through immigration to Canada, Ethiopian Harari diminished their ethnic Harari identity but developed an increased collective Muslim identity. Leonard (2000) and Kurien (2001) address how religious differences (Hindus versus Moslems) among South Asian immigrants produce conflict over the definition of Asian ethnic and national identities.

12. Schrauf (1999), in fact, argues that religious practice is one of the few factors that preserves native language among immigrants and their offspring.

13. Religion is more than economics, however. Richman (2005) indicates how Haitian Protestants use the church as their primary social group. Moreover, she explains how Haitians can use Protestantism to escape transnational social obligations that are tied to the traditional religion of Vodou. Protestantism's impact on an individual's direct relationship to God relieves one of Vodou's imperatives to share, give to one's capacity, and engage in reciprocal relationships. Haitian converts to Protestantism are relieved of the burden of sponsoring religious events in the home country and of Vodou's explicit moral imperative to share one's material resources. Richman's arguments are similar to earlier research that addressed why Latin American peasants were converting to Protestantism (Annis 1987; Garrard-Burnett and Stoll 1993; Junker-Kenny and Tomka 1999; Falla 2001; Stewart-Gambino 2001).

14. Because they seek to incorporate non-Christian religions into their analysis, Kniss and Numrich typologize denominations differently from the standard Catholic, mainline Protestant, Evangelical Protestant, Jewish, Muslim, and other. They create three dimensions: sectarianism, moral authority, and moral projects. Sectarianism describes how distinct a particular congregation is from others, how much tension it has with the larger society. Moral authority captures whether the basis of authority is an individual's experience and reason versus being perceived to be in a collective tradition embodied in a shared text or religious hierarchy. Their third dimension, moral projects, captures whether a congregation's morally based activities are either individualistic (i.e., concerned with reforming and empowering individual believers) or more collectivist and directed at broader community-building, social justice, or structural issues (Kniss and Numrich 2007, 9–10).

15. The term *karism* is employed, for instance, in 1 Corinthians 12: 4–11: "Now there are these diversities of gifts [*karisms*] but the same Spirit. . . . For to one is given by the

Spirit, the word of wisdom; to another the word of knowledge by the same Spirit. . . . To another diverse kinds of tongues; to another the interpretation of tongues."

16. For their analysis, Foley and Hoge (2007) draw upon Moore (1986), who also emphasizes the importance of leadership, particularly that of the Irish American archbishop John Hughes.

17. Bourdieu (2003) recognized that the various forms of capital can be, as he stated, "transubstantiated"; that is, they can be transformed from one kind to another. Portes states, "Social capital of any significance can seldom be acquired, for example, without the investment of some material resources and the possession of some cultural knowledge, enabling the individual to establish relations with others" (2000, 2). Bourdieu, however, confused the issue somewhat in his construction of the concept of cultural capital. For Bourdieu, cultural capital was similar to the anthropologists' broad conception of culture as knowledge and understandings, with Bourdieu adding the criterion of knowledge that was potentially economically useful. It thus included both formal knowledge obtained through education and the informal knowledge of such things as manners and presentation of self. Bourdieu's formulation makes sense to anthropologists, but it confuses others because the concept of human capital already includes formal education. Moreover, Coleman (1988a, 1988b) recognized the importance of informal cultural knowledge but did not distinguish it from his general concept of social capital. In reviewing the literature, Portes (1998) indicates that social capital became defined as (1) a source of social control, (2) a source of family-mediated benefits, and (3) a source of resources mediated by non-family networks. The latter usage, exemplified by personal connections that facilitate access to jobs, market tips, or loans, comes closest to Bourdieu's original definition of the concept. By contrast, family-mediated benefits approach his analysis of "cultural capital" since what families do, above all, is to facilitate children's access to education and transmit a set of values and outlooks, variously classified as low- to high-brow culture.

18. A search on Cambridge Scientific Abstracts among social science sources found 2,091 peer-reviewed articles and another 42 books that used "social capital" in the title between 1990 and 2007. If expanded to the abstracts, there were over 4,000 peer-reviewed articles and 139 books.

19. Narayan (1999) uses the term "cross-cutting ties" instead of "bridging social capital."

20. Wuthnow (2002) and Beyerlein and Hipp (2005) note the relationship between bridging social capital and Granovetter's (1973) conception of weak ties, which are weaker but potentially offer more resources.

21. Wuthnow (2002, 670) points out that although he did not use these terms, Alexis de Tocqueville wrote about both kinds of social relationships and described their role in promoting democracy.

22. Miami can have multiple referents, including the City of Miami, Miami-Dade County, and the Miami metropolitan area. The City of Miami, which has about 375,000 residents, is the largest municipality of the thirty-five municipalities in Miami-Dade County. The second largest municipality is Hialeah with about 225,000 residents. Unincorporated Miami-Dade County has more than 1 million people, considerably more than the largest municipality in the county and just slightly less than all the municipalities combined. The metropolitan area is formally defined by the U.S. Census as Miami–Fort Lauderdale–Miami Beach, Florida Metro Area, and includes Miami-Dade, Broward, and Palm Beach counties and has a total population of about 5.4 million. Some people also informally refer to the contiguous urban area within Miami-Dade County as Miami. In this book, unless we otherwise specify, when we use Miami, we mean Miami-Dade County.

23. As discussed in this chapter, Tweed (1997) has examined the creation of a Cuban Catholic shrine in Miami, but he offers very little on the social or political aspects of immigration. Conde (1999) focuses on the experiences of displaced Cuban children in the Pedro Pan project, rather than on the role of the Catholic Church. De la Torre's analysis (2003) does focus on the nexus between Cuban exiles' religion and politics.

24. The term Santería, which literally means "way of the saints," is rejected by many practitioners of Afro-Cuban religion in Miami, who take umbrage with the Catholic nature of the term. Lucumí (or Lukumi), or *la regal de ocha* (the Orisha Rite), is the name of their religion, a worldview more truly African.

25. We vacillated over using Latino or Hispanic for Miami's immigrants from the Caribbean and Latin America. Latino is generally accepted among academics and political activists. In Miami, however, Hispanic has become the predominant term, including among those from Latin America and the Caribbean.

REFERENCES

Al-Ahmary, A. A. 2000. *Ethnic Self-Identity and the Role of Islam: A Study of the Yemeni Community in the South End of Dearborn and Detroit, Michigan.* Knoxville: University of Tennessee.

Alba, R. D., and V. Nee. 2003. *Remaking the American Mainstream: Assimilation and Contemporary Immigration.* Cambridge, MA: Harvard University Press.

Alumkal, A. W. 2000. *Ethnicity, Assimilation, and Racial Formation in Asian American Evangelical Churches: A Case Study of a Chinese American and Korean American Congregation.* Princeton, NJ: Princeton University.

Annis, S. 1987. *God and Production in a Guatemalan Town.* Austin: University of Texas Press.

Badillo, D. A. 2006. *Latinos and the New Immigrant Church.* Baltimore, MD: The Johns Hopkins University Press.

Bankston, C. L., III. 1997. Bayou Lotus: Theravada Buddhism in Southwestern Louisiana. *Sociological Spectrum* 17(4): 453–472.

Bankston, C. L., III, and M. Zhou. 2000. De Facto Congregationalism and Socioeconomic Mobility in Laotian and Vietnamese Immigrant Communities: A Study of Religious Institutions and Economic Change. *Review of Religious Research* 41(4, June): 453–470.

Basch, L., N. Glick-Schiller, and C. Blanc-Szanton. 1994. *Nations Unbound: Transnational Projects, Postcolonial Predicaments, and Deterritorialized Nation-States.* Amsterdam: Gordon and Breach Science Publishers.

Bellah, R. N., ed. 1996. *Habits of the Heart: Individualism and Commitment in American Life.* Berkeley: University of California Press.

Beyerlein, K., and M. Chaves. 2003. The Political Activities of Religious Congregations in the United States. *Journal for the Scientific Study of Religion* 42(2): 229–246.

Beyerlein, K., and J. R. Hipp. 2005. Social Capital, Too Much of a Good Thing? American Religious Traditions and Community Crime. *Social Forces* 84(2): 995–1013.

Bourdieu, P. 1983. The Forms of Capital. In *Handbook of Theory and Research for the Sociology of Education*, ed. J. G. Richardson, 241–258. New York: Greenwood Press.

———. 1987. Legitimation and Structured Interest in Weber's Sociology of Religion. In *Max Weber, Rationality, and Modernity*, ed. S. Whimster and S. Lash, 119–136. London: Allen and Unwin.

———. 2003. La Fabrique De L'habitus Economique. *Actes de la recherche en sciences sociales* 150: 79–90.

Brooks, A. C., and G. B. Lewis. 2001. Giving, Volunteering, and Mistrusting Government. *Journal of Policy Analysis and Management* 20(4): 765–769.

Cadge, W., and E. H. Ecklund. 2006. Religious Service Attendance among Immigrants: Evidence from the New Immigrant Survey-Pilot. *American Behavioral Scientist* 49(11): 1574–1595.

Chai, K.J.W. 1998. Competing for the Second Generation: English-Language Ministry at a Korean Protestant Church. In *Gatherings in Diaspora: Religious Communities and the New Immigration*, ed. R. S. Warner and J. Wittner, 295–331. Philadelphia, PA: Temple University Press.

———. 2000. Protestant-Catholic-Buddhist: Korean Americans and Religious Adaptation in Greater Boston. PhD diss., Harvard University.

Chaves, M., and W. Tsitsos. 2001. Congregations and Social Services: What They Do, How They Do It, and with Whom. *Nonprofit and Voluntary Sector Quarterly* 30(4): 660–683.

Chou, S.-D. C. 1991. Religion and Chinese Life in the United States. *Etudes Migrations* 28(103): 455–464.

Coleman, J. S. 1988a. The Creation and Destruction of Social Capital: Implications for the Law. *Journal of Law, Ethnic, and Public Policy* 3: 375–404.

———. 1988b. Social Capital in the Creation of Human Capital. *American Sociological Review* 94: S95–121.

Conde, Y. 1999. *Operation Pedro Pan: The Untold Exodus of* 14,048 Cuban Children. New York: Routledge.

De La Torre, M. A. 2003. *La Lucha for Cuba: Religion and Politics on the Streets of Miami.* Berkeley: University of California Press.

DeMarinis, V., and H. Grzymala-Moszczynska. 1995. The Nature and Role of Religion and Religious Experience in Psychological Cross-Cultural Adjustment: Ongoing Research in the Clinical Psychology of Religion. *Social Compass* 42(1): 121–135.

Dempsey, C. G. 2006. *The Goddess Lives in Upstate New York: Breaking Convention and Making Home at a North American Hindu Temple.* Oxford: Oxford University Press.

Dolan, J. 1992. *The American Catholic Experience: A History from Colonial Times to the Present.* Notre Dame and London: University of Notre Dame Press.

Dudley, C. S., and D. A. Roozen. 2001. Faith Communities Today: A Report on Religion in the United States Today. *Cooperative Congregational Studies Project.* Hartford, CT: Hartford Seminary. March.

Ebaugh, H. R., and J. S. Chafetz. 2000a. Dilemmas of Language in Immigrant Congregations: The Tie That Binds or the Tower of Babel? *Review of Religious Research* 41(4, June): 432–452.

———, eds. 2000b. *Religion and the New Immigrants: Continuities and Adaptations in Immigrant Congregations.* Walnut Creek, CA: AltaMira Press.

Ecklund, E. H. 2005a. The "Good" American: Religion and Civic Life for Korean Americans. *Dissertation Abstracts International, A: The Humanities and Social Sciences* 65(10): 4006-A.

———. 2005b. Models of Civic Responsibility: Korean Americans in Congregations with Different Ethnic Compositions. *Journal for the Scientific Study of Religion* 44(1): 15–28.

Falla, R. 2001. *Quiché Rebelde: Religious Conversion, Politics, and Ethnic Identity in Guatemala.* Austin: University of Texas Press.

Farris, A., R. P. Nathan, and D. J. Wright. 2004. *The Expanding Administrative Presidency: George W. Bush and the Faith-Based Initiative.* Albany, NY: Roundtable on Religion and Social Welfare Policy.

Flanagan, C., and N. Faaison. 2001. Youth Civic Development: Implications of Research for Social Policy and Programs. *Social Policy Report* 15(1): 3–15.

Flanagan, C., and L. Sherrod. 1998. Political Development: Youth Growing up in a Global Community. *Journal of Social Issues* 54(3): 447–456.

Foley, M. W., and D. R. Hoge. 2007. *Religion and the New Immigrants: How Faith Communities Form Our Newest Citizens.* Oxford and New York: Oxford University Press.

Frank, K. A., and J. Y. Yasumoto. 1998. Linking Action to Social Structure within a System: Social Capital within and between Subgroups. *American Journal of Sociology* 104(3): 642–686.

Gans, H. J. 1994. Symbolic Ethnicity and Symbolic Religiosity: Towards a Comparison of Ethnic and Religious Acculturation. *Ethnic and Racial Studies* 17(4): 577–592.

Garrard-Burnett, V., and D. Stoll, eds. 1993. *Rethinking Protestantism in Latin America.* Philadelphia, PA: Temple University Press.

Gibb, C. 1998. Religious Identification in Transnational Contexts: Being and Becoming Muslim in Ethiopia and Canada. *Diaspora* 7(2): 247–269.

Gittell, R., and A. Vidal. 1998. *Community Organization: Building Social Capital as a Development Strategy.* London: Sage Publications.

Glick-Schiller, N., L. Basch, and C. Blanc-Szanton. 1992. Towards a Transnational Perspective on Migration: Race Class, Ethnicity, and Nationalism Reconsidered. *Annals of the New York Academy of Sciences* 645.

Granovetter, M. 1973. The Strength of Weak Ties. *American Journal of Sociology* 78(6): 1360–1380.

Greeley, A. 2001. The Future of Religion in America. *Society* 38(3 [251]): 32–37.

Greeley, A., and M. Hout. 1999. Americans' Increasing Belief in Life after Death: Religious Competition and Acculturation. *American Sociological Review* 64(6, December): 813–835.

Greenberg, A. 2000. The Church and the Revitalization of Politics and Community. *Political Science Quarterly* 115(3): 377–394.

Guarnizo, L. E. 2001. On the Political Participation of Transnational Migrants. In *E Pluribus Unum? Immigrants, Civic Life, and Political Incorporation*, ed. G. Gerstle and J. Mollenkopf, 213–263. New York: Russell Sage Foundation.

Guarnizo, L. E., and M. P. Smith. 1998. The Locations of Transnationalism. In *Transnationalism from Below*, ed. M. P. Smith and L. E. Guarnizo, 1–32. New Brunswick: Transaction Publishers.

Guest, K. J. 2003. *God in Chinatown: Religion and Survival in New York's Evolving Immigrant Community.* New York: New York University Press.

Herberg, W. 1960. *Protestant—Catholic—Jew: An Essay in American Religious Sociology.* Garden City, NY: Anchor Books.

Hirschman, C. 2004. The Role of Religion in the Origins and Adaptation of Immigrant Groups in the United States. *International Migration Review* 38(3): 1206–1233.

Hirschman, C., J. DeWind, and P. Kasinitz, eds. 1999. *The Handbook of International Migration: The American Experience.* New York: Russsell Sage Foundation.

Hoge, D., C. Zech, P. McNamara, and M. J. Donahue. 1998. The Value of Volunteers as Resources for Congregations. *Journal for the Scientific Study of Religion* 37: 470–480.

Huntington, S. P. 2004. The Hispanic Challenge. *Foreign Policy* 141(March/April): 30–45.

Hurh, W. M., and K. C. Kim. 1984. *Korean Immigrants in America: A Structural Analysis of Ethnic Confinement and Adhesive Adaptation.* Rutherford, NJ: Associated University Presses.

———. 1990. Religious Participation of Korean Immigrants in the United States. *Journal for the Scientific Study of Religion* 29(March): 9–34.

Hyman, J. B. 2002. Exploring Social Capital and Civic Engagement to Create a Framework for Community Building. *Applied Developmental Science* 6(4): 196–202.

Jasso, G., D. S. Massey, M. R. Rosenzweig, and J. P. Smith. 2000. Family, Schooling, Religiosity, and Mobility among New Legal Immigrants to the United States: Evidence from the New Immigrant Survey Pilot. In *Immigration Today: Pastoral and Research Challenges*, ed. L. F. Tomasi and M. G. Powers, 52–81. New York: Center for Migration Studies.

———. 2003. Exploring the Religious Preferences of Recent Immigrants to the United States: Evidence from the New Immigrant Survey Pilot. In *Religion and Immigration: Christian, Jewish, and Muslim Experiences in the United States*, ed. Y. Y. Haddad, J. I. Smith, and J. L. Esposito, 217–253. Lanham, MD: AltaMira Press.

Jeung, R. 2005. *Faithful Generations: Race and New Asian American Churches.* New Brunswick, NJ: Rutgers University Press.

Jones-Correa, M., and D. L. Leal. 2001. Political Participation: Does Religion Matter? *Political Research Quarterly* 54(4): 751–770.

Junker-Kenny, M., and M. Tomka, eds. 1999. *Faith in a Society of Instant Gratification.* Maryknoll, NY: Orbis Books.

Kaya, I. 2007. Religion as a Site of Boundary Construction: Islam and the Integration of Turkish Americans in the United States. *Alternatives: Turkish Journal of International Relations* 6(1&2): 139–155.

Kim, K. C., and S. Kim. 2001. Ethnic Role of Korean Immigrant Churches in the United States. In *Korean Americans and Their Religions: Pilgrims and Missionaries from a Different Shore*, ed. H.-Y. Kwon and K. C. Kim, 71–95. University Park: Pennsylvania State University Press.

Kim, R. Y. 2006. *God's New Whiz Kids? Korean American Evangelicals on Campus.* New York: New York University Press.

Klausen, J. 2006. *Counterterrorism and the Integration of Islam in Europe.* Philadelphia, PA: Foreign Policy Research Institute.

Kniss, F., and P. D. Numrich. 2007. *Sacred Assemblies and Civic Engagement.* New Brunswick, NJ: Rutgers University Press.

Kurien, P. 2001. Religion, Ethnicity, and Politics: Hindu and Muslim Indian Immigrants in the United States. *Ethnic and Racial Studies* 24(March 2): 263–293.

Kwon, V. H., H. R. Ebaugh, and J. Hagan. 1997. The Structure and Functions of Cell Group Ministry in a Korean Christian Church. *Journal for the Scientific Study of Religion* 36(2): 247–256.

Laguerre, M. S. 1998. *Diasporic Citizenship: Haitian Americans in Transnational America.* New York: St. Martin's Press.

Lawson, R. 1999. When Immigrants Take Over: The Impact of Immigrant Growth on American Seventh-Day Adventism's Trajectory from Sect to Denomination. *Journal for the Scientific Study of Religion* 38(1): 83–102.

Legge, J. S., Jr. 1997. The Religious Erosion-Assimilation Hypothesis: The Case of U.S. Jewish Immigrants. *Social Science Quarterly* 78(2): 472–486.

Leonard, K. I. 2000. State, Culture, and Religion: Political Action and Representation among South Asians in North America. *Diaspora* 9(1): 21–38.

———. 2003. American Muslim Politics. *Ethnicities* 3(2): 147–181.

Levitt, P. 2003. "You Know, Abraham Was Really the First Immigrant": Religion and Transnational Migration. *International Migration Review* 37(3): 847–873.

———. 2007. *God Needs No Passport: Immigrants and the Changing American Religious Landscape.* New York and London: New Press.

Lin, A. C., and A. Jamal. 2001. *Muslim, Arab, and American: The Adaptation of Arab Immigrants to American Society.* Seattle, WA: Social Science Research Council Working Group on Religion and Immigration.

Lin, I. 1996. Journey to the Far West: Chinese Buddhism in America. *Amerasia Journal* 22(1): 107–132.

Mahler, S. J. 1995. *The Dysfunctions of Transnationalism.* New York: Russell Sage Foundation.

——. 1998. Theoretical and Empirical Contributions toward a Research Agenda for Transnationalism. In *Transnationalism from Below,* ed. L. E. Guarnizo and M. P. Smith, 64–100. New Brunswick: Transaction Publishers.

——. 1999. Engendering Transnational Migration: A Case Study of Salvadorans. *American Behavioral Scientist* 42(2): 690–719.

——. 2002. *Mapping Transnational Religious Ties for Analysis: Preliminary Lessons from a Comparison of Cuban and Nicaraguan Research.* Paper presented at the Second Biennial Allen Morris Conference on the History of Florida and the Atlantic World, Immigration, Migration, and Diaspora, Florida State University, Tallahassee, Florida.

Marquardt, M. F. 2005. Structural and Cultural Hybrids: Religious Congregational Life and Public Participation among Mexicans in the New South. In *Immigrant Faiths: Transforming Religious Life in America,* ed. K. I. Leonard, A. Stepick, M. A. Vasquez, and J. Holdaway, 189–218. Lanham, MD: AltaMira.

Massey, D. S., L. Goldring, and J. Durand. 1994. Continuities in Transnational Migration: An Analysis of Nineteen Mexican Communities. *American Journal of Sociology* 99(6): 1492–1533.

Mathur, S. 2001. *Acculturation among Indian Immigrants: A Study of Ethnic Identification and Mate-Selection.* Syracuse, NY: Syracuse University.

McRoberts, O. M. 2003. *Streets of Glory: Church and Community in a Black Urban Neighborhood.* Chicago: University of Chicago Press.

Milbank, D. 2001. Bush Unveils Faith-Based Initiative. *Washington Post,* January 30, A01.

Min, P. G. 1992. The Structure and Social Functions of Korean Immigrant Churches in the United States. *International Migration Review* 26: 1370–1394.

——. 2000. Immigrants' Religion and Ethnicity: A Comparison of Korean Christian and Indian Hindu Immigrants. *Bulletin of the Royal Institute for Inter-Faith Studies* 2(1, spring): 121–140.

——. 2002. Religion and Ethnicity: A Comparison of Indian Hindu and Korean Protestant Immigrants in New York. Paper presented at the Social Science Research Council Fellows' Conference on Immigration Religion and Civic Life, University of Texas at Arlington.

Min, P. G., and D. Y. Kim. 2005. Intergenerational Transmission of Religion and Culture: Korean Protestants in the U.S. *Sociology of Religion* 66(3): 263–282.

Mooney, M. 2005. Upward Climb or Downward Slide? Religion and Mediating Social Capital in the Haitian Immigrant Communities of Miami, Montreal, and Paris. *Dissertation Abstracts International, A: The Humanities and Social Sciences* 65(11): 4361-A.

——. 2007. The Catholic Church's Institutional Responses to Immigration: From Supranational to Local Engagement. In *Religion and Social Justice for Immigrants,* ed. P. Hondagneu-Sotelo, 157–171. New Brunswick, NJ: Rutgers University Press.

Moore, R. L. 1986. *Religious Outsiders and the Making of Americans.* New York: Oxford University Press.

Morawska, E. 2001. Immigrants, Transnationalism, and Ethnicization: A Comparison of This Wave and Last. In *E Pluribus Unum? Immigrants, Civic Life, and Political Incorporation,* ed. G. Gerstle and J. Mollenkopf, 175–212. New York: Russell Sage Foundation.

Narayan, D. 1999. *Bonds and Bridges: Social Capital and Poverty.* Washington, DC: World Bank.

O'Brien, D. 2004. *Animal Sacrifice and Religious Freedom: Church of Lukumi Babalu Aye v. City of Miami.* Lawrence: University Press of Kansas.

Palacios, J. M. 2007. Bringing Mexican Immigrants into American Faith-Based Social Justice and Civic Cultures. In *Religion and Social Justice for Immigrants,* ed. P. Hondagneu-Sotelo, 74–90. New Brunswick, NJ: Rutgers University Press.

Park, J. Z., and C. Smith. 2000. "To Whom Much Has Been Given": Religious Capital and Community Voluntarism among Churchgoing Protestants. *Journal for the Scientific Study of Religion* 39(3): 272–286.

Parsons, T. 1963. Introduction to *The Sociology of Religion*, by M. Weber, xix–lxvi. Boston: Beacon.

Paxton, P. 1999. Is Social Capital Declining in the United States? A Multiple Indicator Assessment. *American Journal of Sociology* 105(1): 88–127.

Pedraza-Bailey, S. 1985. *Political and Economic Migrants in America: Cubans and Mexicans.* Austin: University of Texas Press.

Pipes, P. F., and H. R. Ebaugh. 2002. Faith-Based Coalitions, Social Services, and Government Funding. *Sociology of Religion* 63(1): 49–68.

Portes, A. 1981. Modes of Structural Incorporation and Present Theories of Labor Immigration. In *Global Trends in Migration: Theory and Research of International Population Movements*, ed. M. M. Kritz, C. B. Keeley, and S. M. Tomasi, 279–297. New York: Center for Migration Studies.

———. 1996. *The New Second Generation.* New York: Russell Sage Foundation.

———. 1998. Social Capital: Its Origins and Applications in Modern Sociology. *Annual Reviews in Sociology* 24: 1–24.

———. 2000. The Two Meanings of Social Capital. *Sociological Forum* 15(1): 1–12.

Portes, A., and J. DeWind. 2004. A Cross-Atlantic Dialogue: The Progress of Research and Theory in the Study of International Migration. *International Migration Review* 38(3): 828–851.

Portes, A., and P. Landolt. 2000. Social Capital: Promise and Pitfalls of Its Role in Development. *Journal of Latin American Studies* 32(2): 529–547.

Portes, A., and M. Mooney. 2002. Social Capital and Community Development. In *The New Economic Sociology: Developments in an Emerging Field*, ed. M. F. Guillen, R. Collins, P. England, and M. Meyer, 3003–3329. New York: Russell Sage Foundation.

Portes, A., and R. G. Rumbaut. 1996/2006. *Immigrant America: A Portrait.* Berkeley: University of California Press.

———. 2001. *Legacies: The Story of the Immigrant Second Generation.* Berkeley and New York: University of California Press and Russell Sage Foundation.

———. 2005. The Second Generation in Early Adulthood: Introduction: The Second Generation and the Children of Immigrants Longitudinal Study. *Ethnic and Racial Studies* 28(6): 983–999.

Portes, A., and A. Stepick. 1993. *City on the Edge: The Transformation of Miami.* Berkeley: University of California Press.

Portes, A., and M. Zhou. 1993. The New Second Generation: Segmented Assimilation and Its Variants. *Annals of the American Academy of Political and Social Sciences* 530: 74–95.

Putnam, R. D. 1993. The Prosperous Community: Social Capital and Public Life. *American Prospect* 13: 35–42.

———. 1995. Bowling Alone: American's Declining Social Capital. *Journal of Democracy* 6: 65–78.

———. 1996. The Strange Disappearance of Civic America. *American Prospect* 24: 34–48.

———. 2000. *Bowling Alone: The Collapse and Revival of American Community.* New York: Simon & Schuster.

Putnam, R. D., with Robert Leonardi and Raffaella Y. Nanetti. 1993. Social Capital and Institutional Success. In *Making Democracy Work: Civic Traditions in Modern Italy*, ed. R. D. Putnam, 163–192. Princeton, NJ: Princeton University Press.

Regnerus, M., C. Smith, and D. Sikkink. 1998. Who Gives to the Poor? The Influence of Religious Tradition and Political Location on the Personal Generosity of Americans toward the Poor. *Journal for the Scientific Study of Religion* 37(3): 481–493.

Remennick, L. I. 1998. Identity Quest among Russian Jews of the 1990s: Before and after Emigration. *Sociological Papers* 6: 241–258.

Rey, T. 2004. Marian Devotion at a Haitian Catholic Parish in Miami: The Feast Day of Our Lady of Perpetual Help. *Journal of Contemporary Religion* 19(3): 353–374.

Richman, K. 2005. The Protestant Ethic and the Dis-Spirit of Vodou. In *Immigrant Faiths: Transforming Religious Life in America*, ed. K. Leonard, A. Stepick, M. A. Vasquez, and J. Holdaway, 165–188. Lanham, MD: AltaMira Press.

Rodriguez, M. 2000. Different Paths, Same Destination: U.S.-Bound Nicaraguan and Cuban Migration in a Comparative Perspective. *Dissertation Abstracts International, A: The Humanities and Social Sciences* 60(10): 3805-A.

Sargeant, K. H. 1998. Religion and New Immigrants: A Grantmaking Agenda at the Pew Charitable Trusts. Philadelphia: Pew Charitable Trusts.

Schrauf, R. W. 1999. Mother Tongue Maintenance among North American Ethnic Groups. *Cross-Cultural Research* 33(2): 175–192.

Skocpol, T., and M. P. Fiorina, eds. 1999. *Civic Engagement in American Democracy*. Washington and New York: Brookings Institution Press and Russell Sage Foundation.

Smidt, C. 1999. Religion and Civic Engagement: A Comparative Analysis. *Annals of the American Academy of Political and Social Science* 565: 176–192.

Smith, H. L., A. Fabricatore, and M. Peyrot. 1999. Religiosity and Altruism among African American Males. *Journal of Black Studies* 29(4): 579–597.

Smith, T. 1978. Religion and Ethnicity in America. *American Historical Review* 83: 1155–1185.

Smith, T. W. 2002. Religious Diversity in America: The Emergence of Muslims, Buddhists, Hindus, and Others. *Journal for the Scientific Study of Religion* 41(3): 577–585.

Stepick, A. 1982. Haitian Boat People: A Study in the Conflicting Forces Shaping U.S. Immigration Policy. *Law and Contemporary Problems, Duke University Law Journal* 45(2, spring): 163–196.

———. 1992. Social, Political, and Cultural Capital: Haitians and Cubans in Miami. Paper presented at the Middlebury College Conference on Immigration, Middlebury College, CT.

———. 1998. *Pride against Prejudice: Haitians in the United States*. Boston: Allyn & Bacon.

———. 2005. God Is Apparently Not Dead: The Obvious, the Emergent, and the Unknown in Immigration and Religion. In *Immigrant Faiths: Transforming Religious Life in America*, ed. K. Leonard, A. Stepick, M. A. Vasquez, and J. Holdaway, 11–37. Lanham, MD: Alta Mira Press.

Stepick, A., and C. Dutton Stepick. 2001. Power and Identity: Miami Cubans. In *Latinos: The Research Agenda*, ed. M. Suarez-Orozco and C. Suarez-Orozco, 57–92. Berkeley: University of California Press.

———. 2002. Becoming American, Constructing Ethnicity: Immigrant Youth and Civic Engagement. *Applied Developmental Science* 6(4): 246–257.

Stepick, A., G. Grenier, M. Castro, and M. Dunn. 2003. *This Land Is Our Land: Interethnic Relations in Miami*. Berkeley: University of California Press.

Stevens, W. D. 2004. "Taking the World": Evangelism and Assimilation among Ghanaian Pentecostals in Chicago. *Dissertation Abstracts International, A: The Humanities and Social Sciences* 65(1): 299-A.

Stewart-Gambino, H. W. 2001. Religious Consumers in a Changing Religious Marketplace Review. *Latin American Research Review* 36(1): 193–206.

Suh, S. A. 2001. *Buddhism, Rhetoric, and the Korean American Community: The Adjustment of Korean Buddhist Immigrants to the U.S.* Seattle, WA: Social Science Research Council Working Group on Religion and Immigration.

Supreme Court of the United States. 1993. *Church of Lukumi Babalu Aye v. Hialeah*. 936 F.2d 586 (CA 11 1991), reversed 508 U.S. 520, No. 91–948.

Szreter, S. 2002. The State of Social Capital: Bringing Back in Power, Politics, and History. *Theory and Society* 31(5): 573–621.

Tiryakian, E. 1991. The Exceptional Vitality of Religion in the United States: A Rereading of Protestant-Catholic-Jew. *Social Compass* 38(3, September): 215–238.

Triay, V. A. 1998. *Fleeing Castro: Operation Pedro Pan and the Cuban Children's Program.* Gainesville: University Press of Florida.

Tweed, T. A. 1995. An Emerging Protestant Establishment: Religious Affiliation and Public Power on the Urban Frontier in Miami, 1896–1904. *Church History* 64(3): 412–437.

———. 1997. *Our Lady of the Exile: Diasporic Religion at a Cuban Catholic Shrine in Miami.* New York: Oxford University Press.

Uslaner, E. 2002. Religion and Civic Engagement in Canada and the United States. *Journal for the Scientific Study of Religion* 41(2): 230–254.

Uslaner, E. M., and R. S. Conley. 2003. Civic Engagement and Particularized Trust. *American Politics Research* 31(4): 331–360.

Vertovec, S. 2001. Religion and Diaspora. Oxford, England: Institute of Social & Cultural Anthropology, University of Oxford.

Warner, R. S. 1997. Religion, Boundaries, and Bridges. *Sociology of Religion* 58(3): 217–238.

Weber, M. [1922] 1963. *The Sociology of Religion.* Boston: Beacon.

———. [1925] 1969. *Economy and Society.* Vol. 3. New York: Benminster.

Wilson, J., and T. Janoski. 1995. The Contribution of Religion to Volunteer Work. *Sociology of Religion* 56(2): 137–152.

Wilson, J., and M. Musick. 1997. Who Cares? Toward an Integrated Theory of Volunteer Work. *American Sociological Review* 62: 694–713.

Woolcock, M. 1998. Social Capital and Economic Development: Toward a Theoretical Synthesis and Policy Framework. *Theory and Society* 27(2): 151–208.

Worsley, P. 1968. *The Trumpet Will Sound: A Study of Cargo Cults in Melanesia.* New York: Schocken.

Wuthnow, R. 1999. Mobilizing Civic Engagement: The Changing Impact of Religious Involvement. In *Civic Engagement in American Democracy*, ed. T. Skocpol and M. P. Fiorina, 331–364. Washington, DC: Brookings Institution Press.

———. 2002. Religious Involvement and Status-Bridging Social Capital. *Journal for the Scientific Study of Religion* 41(4): 669–684.

———. 2004. *Saving America? Faith-Based Services and the Future of Civil Society.* Princeton, NJ: Princeton University Press.

Yoo, J.-K. 1998. *Korean Immigrant Entrepreneurs: Network and Ethnic Resources.* New York and London: Garland Publishing.

Zhou, M. 1997. Segmented Assimilation: Issues, Controversies, and Recent Research on the New Second Generation. *International Migration Review* 31(4, winter): 975–1008.

PART ONE

Charismatic Leaders and Linking Civic Social Capital

2

So Close and Yet So Far Away

Comparing Civic Social Capital in Two Cuban Congregations

SARAH J. MAHLER

In Jesus' time, he recognized that people were suffering and that their necessities and ailments had to be addressed before they were going to have the ability to attend fully to their beliefs. As eloquently communicated in Bible verses from the book of Matthew, he knew that meeting people's material and spiritual needs was an enormous task and that he could not accomplish it alone.

> So Jesus went around all the towns and villages teaching in their synagogues, announcing the good news of the kingdom and curing every kind of ailment and disease. The sight of the people moved him to pity: they were like sheep without a shepherd, harassed and helpless; and he said to his disciples, "The harvest is plentiful but the workers are scarce." Then he called his twelve disciples to him and gave them authority to cast out unclean spirits and to cure every kind of ailment and disease. . . . These twelve Jesus sent out with the following instructions: "Do not take the road to gentile lands, and do not enter any Samaritan town; but go rather to the lost sheep of the house of Israel. And as you go proclaim the message: 'The kingdom of Heaven is upon you.' Heal the sick, raise the dead, cleanse lepers, cast out devils. You received without cost; give without charge." (Matthew 9:35–38; 10:5)

How can people be inspired to help others and not just themselves? This civic as well as spiritual question is one faced by people of faith around the world. Jesus motivated others by teaching, by example, and by deliberately preparing a close set of followers to be his disciples. Together they would shepherd their small flock and prepare more shepherds to watch over it as it grew. To the faithful, to those willing to work according to his plan, Jesus promised no material riches, only eternal salvation.

The issues Jesus faced millennia ago are just as salient today as they were then. This chapter will focus on how two poor and heavily immigrant Hispanic congregations cultivate and deploy civic social capital (CSC). To anticipate, I will show how both churches' pastors try to cultivate CSC through their sermons and actions. Then I will document how each church, despite similar messages from its leadership, takes a different path, one which leads into the greater community and one which circles around home. One congregation has evolved dynamic ministries that serve Miami's neediest people, including drug addicts, sex workers, the homeless, and undocumented immigrants, while the other has developed extensive leadership programs deployed largely to nourish and sustain its own congregants' needs. In the language of the book's introductory chapter, one congregation applies its social capital as much or more civically (i.e., to the greater community) as internally, whereas the other primarily fosters bonding social capital, albeit capital that holds the *potential* for being applied beyond its membership. How did these differences arise, particularly when both churches are situated in the same neighborhood, began their ministries at almost the same time, and serve congregations with similar demographic characteristics, including size, ethnicity, immigration status, and levels of education and skills? There are a number of factors that have shaped these congregations and their missions, not the least of which is the influence of specific individuals, both from the clergy and the laity. One of the most important insights from this study is the mutual influences these clergy and lay leaders have upon one another.

Promoting Civic Social Capital from the Pulpit

Pastor José Moreno[1] gazed out toward his congregation of mostly Cuban Seventh-Day Adventists, leaned his large hands heavily on the massive wood pulpit, and, as if to prepare himself for a protracted ordeal, drew in a long breath while he scanned his flock with his searing ebony eyes. The usual glint of a smile was lost from his face as he asked the congregation, in his Cuban-accented Spanish, to turn to Matthew 13:1 in their Bibles. An immediate rustle stirred the air as several hundred congregants reached for their Bibles, which lay snug against their laps, and turned to the correct page. Moreno began reading the verse:

> Jesus went out and sat by the lakeside, where so many people gathered around him that he had to get into a boat. He sat there, and all the people stood on the shore. He spoke to them in parables, at some length. He said, "A sower went out to sow. And as he sowed, some seed fell along the footpath; and the birds came and ate it up. Some seed fell on rocky ground, where it had little soil, and it sprouted quickly because it had no

depth of earth; but when the sun rose the young corn was scorched, and as it had no root it withered away. Some seed fell among thistles; and the thistles shot up, and choked the corn. And some of the seed fell into good soil, where it bore fruit, yielding a hundredfold, or, it might be, sixty-fold, or thirty-fold."

Pastor Moreno interpreted the passage:

Jesus understood that not everyone who hears the Lord's word will follow it completely. There are different levels of commitment. There is "Brother 100" and "Brother 60" and "Brother 30" and "Brother Zero." Brother 100 is the one who works for God full time through the good times and the bad. He always has time even if he's really busy. But he also has the volunteer spirit. He prioritizes God's needs and name. Brother 100 gives money to the needy even if he doesn't have enough for himself. Brother 60 has not yet reached the level of Brother 100 but God treats him the same because he gives as much as he can. Brother 30 comes to church and shows his appreciation of God. He is usually not very helpful but sometimes God has big plans for him. Brother 30 often tries to avoid commitment but if called by God, he prays to get the strength to do what he needs to do. Brother Zero will do nothing. Often he dismisses others, especially those who seem to be getting ahead. He talks about you if you do something, if you become someone. He always criticizes you to make himself seem above you because he truly is no one. He thinks he can take the spotlight off of you and put it on himself. He avoids responsibility, avoids responsibility for doing the church's work. He always protests everything others do. . . . God sees Brothers 100, 60, and 30 all as fertile ground for sowing his seeds. He sees us as different but we are equally loved. But he doesn't want us to be Brother Zero. . . . Brother Zero, God can still add more zeros to the end of your name and make you into someone. . . . So what type of brother do you want to be? One hundred? Sixty? Thirty? Work for God's glory. And if you are Brother Zero, listen.

Only a stone's throw away but miles distant in many ways from Pastor Moreno's Seventh-Day Adventist Church, Reverend Al González was preparing his sermon for services the next day at the Disciples, a Protestant church belonging to the Nazarene denomination. A jolly, often joking Cuban in his fifties who could, if called, suit up as a convincing Santa, González had been studying his church's finances. Not surprisingly, given the working-class congregation he heads, the news was not good. The air conditioning had to be replaced, the van needed a new water pump, and utilities had skyrocketed. How could he also leverage the church as collateral so the bank would be willing to underwrite a mortgage for the $700,000 building he was renting where the drug and alcohol rehabilitation program is housed? As he would say later, "I knew I could not do it alone." During the next few weeks he dedicated his sermons all toward building stewardship within his largely poor, immigrant, but energetic congregation. The demography of his flock is not the only characteristic that distinguishes it from other Nazarene churches. Its community outreach projects as well as its Hispanic and poor congregation drew the attention of this Protestant denomination's national leadership in hopes of replicating the Disciples' success elsewhere.

Pastor Al began the second sermon in his stewardship promotion series:

In Matthew 9:35 the Bible says that Jesus drew crowds and told his disciples that "the harvests are plentiful but the workers are scarce." God's love is the only thing that can move us. You're here because God's love moves you to come. The past two years have been the hardest in my twenty-three here at the church. Why? I see the needs that people have and the church has grown, but we don't commit ourselves to do the work. I can't do it all by myself. How can I meet so many needs with so few workers? I ask people to give but I can't obligate them, so I feel frustrated. . . . I feel compassion for those who have so many needs. When someone says he's hungry, I believe him. We are not judges, just witnesses. John 3:6 says we are not to judge. A church without compassion is a dead church. The church that is not busy doing good deeds is a church that no one will join. When you have compassion you see others' needs. . . . Those who work are the ones who find that the Holy Spirit fills their hearts. There are some people who are materialist but the church is spiritual. There are millionaire churches here with people who are very well known. But I would tell the pastor that my people will not go into your church because you don't have anything there. I am proud of this church. We don't reject those who don't have any money. We don't publish a list of those who don't give us money on the wall like some churches do. That's materialism; that's egoism—love of money—not compassion. So let us pray to snuff out four evil spirits. Out, religious spirits that teach us only that doing certain good deeds will win us salvation. (He enjoins the congregation to shout "Out," and each time they do.) Out, spirit of conformity! We need to do what God wants and not to be satisfied with who we are. Out, spirit of no commitment! Do you know why our kids don't commit themselves? It's because we don't! Out, stealing spirit! The spirit that robs us of our money, our time and our favor with God.

His voice booms as he leads the hundreds of congregants into shouts of "Out!" González steers the stewardship momentum toward today's most urgent need: "We desperately need $5,000 to buy a used school bus for the church. We need the bus to provide transportation for the *muchachos* [the men in the rehabilitation program] and to bring people to church services. I have only $5,000 now and we have only $8,000 in the bank and we need $20,000 per month to cover expenses. Do you know of anyone who is selling a bus or who will give one away? Ask your neighbors; ask your friends, and please let me know." He asks everyone to stand, offers a prayer of thanks, and ends the prayer with another special appeal for the $5,000 before he asks for God's blessing on everyone present, and the service ends.

The two sermons described here occurred around the same time and were directed toward similar congregations of overwhelmingly Hispanic, particularly Cuban, working-class immigrants and their children, who live in the same municipality of Miami-Dade County called Hialeah. Both sermons express what Max Weber characterized as "exemplary prophecy," leadership that shapes followers' worldviews toward ethical goals. Yet the two congregations show remarkably different responses. While the Disciples, as their name implies, would heed their leader's call by building and extending CSC beyond their church through their deeds (what Weber characterizes as "ethical prophecy"), the Adventists would continue to devote themselves to bonding social capital over bridging and linking CSC. Why? The rest of this chapter develops the explanation by examining the different congregations' histories and modes of leadership development.

Congregations' Histories and Backgrounds

A first step toward explaining why these two congregations take different CSC paths is to compare their backgrounds. These reveal the importance of institutional, contextual, and, particularly, leadership factors.

The Adventists, the "Refugees"

At the time he crafted his "Brother 100" sermon, Pastor José Moreno had been head minister to the Seventh-Day Adventist Church in Hialeah for less than five years. Pastor Moreno was recruited to pastor the Adventist church directly from Cuba, where he served as director of Adventist youth programs for the entire island. A tall dark Black man in his early forties with a medium build and an infectious laugh, Pastor Moreno in many ways is the mirror image of the man who founded the church, the now-retired Carlos Canto. Pastor Canto is a man of commanding height, girth, and mirth who is revered by nearly everyone but particularly by those to whom he ministered at the Adventists' mother church in a poor barrio of Havana. Canto was pastor there in 1980 during the Mariel Boatlift when dozens of his parishioners fled Cuba for greater religious freedom in the United States. Most arrived into Miami and stayed, slowly reconstituting their own sister congregation that Canto would name "the Refugees." According to the church's Web site, he chose this name because "we extend our arms outward, one down to the refugees who arrive into this country and one upwards to heaven." The church, thus, is oriented toward serving the needs of a particular group—refugees whose jarring experience of fleeing their homeland leaves them spiritually as well as culturally adrift. Though the Web site does not say so explicitly, the church's mission is not to minister to all refugees but to target those who have had to leave Cuba. It short, the Refugees serve their own.

The need for refuge experienced by Seventh-Day Adventists arriving during the Mariel Boatlift cannot be overemphasized when trying to explain the current inward orientation of the Refugees' church. Under the Castro government in Cuba and beginning in the early 1960s when official atheism was declared, people of faith have experienced great discrimination. Adventists have suffered arguably more than other Christians because they refuse to work on their Sabbath, Saturday, which is an official workday in revolutionary Cuba. Many also resist the regime's obligatory military service owing to their principles of not bearing arms. Ana Rodríguez, a member of the Refugees' church board, related how this climate affected her while growing up. She had to repeat the seventh grade three times because the final exams were scheduled for Saturdays and she would not break the Sabbath to take them. The school administrators refused to accommodate her by scheduling her exam for another day. Ana said,

> I remember the principal saying that they couldn't understand why my parents would allow me to go through all of this. They suggested writing a letter to my pastor and asking his permission. So, I was trying to tell them that it's not really a pastor's permission. It's about convictions and I was convinced that that was the right thing to do for me, because it was my belief. And even if the pastor said, "It's okay for her to go," it wouldn't be because to me the Sabbath is . . . my day of worship. Of course, I regretted that I was not able to advance in school because I had so many dreams. I wanted to become a doctor or a lawyer or something like that.

Finally, a kind science teacher agreed—at risk of being detected by the Committees for the Defense of the Revolution—to help her take her exams on another day and she passed. With the help of her parents, she escaped the worst during high school, but discrimination against people of faith prevented her from entering college: "When I was on the line to register for college, they saw on my records that I was a Seventh-Day Adventist Christian and they literally told me that they didn't have room for me at the college." The only avenue still open was studying at a music conservatory, a familiar avenue to the faithful in Cuba and one of the reasons why music ministries flourish there.

Each Cuban congregant at the Refugees' church can tell stories similar to Ana's; even Pastor Moreno's family became nearly destitute when his father, a high-ranking member of the Cuban government, converted to Adventism and was stripped of his job, his home, and his privileges. Moreover, those who arrived during Mariel tell harrowing tales of nearly perishing aboard rickety boats that arrived from Miami to rescue them only to be tossed by the seas en route. Tina Pérez recalls that her family was egged and jeered by neighbors in Havana as police took them from their home to the embarkation point in the Port of Mariel. There they had to wait for ten seemingly interminable days with little food, water, and shelter until a boat picked them up. She was eight and had never traveled in a boat before. The horror of traveling the whole night in a storm is etched in her memory. "It rained and it was really terrible. And I just remember people crying and crying and . . . my mom cried the whole night. She cried the whole night and so did my sister. And I didn't want to cry because I thought if I opened my mouth I was going to throw up. Everybody was vomiting everywhere. The seas were terrible. And I've asked my mom if there were any accidents and she told me that somebody did fall off the boat and they never went back for them. They just kept going." The rest arrived safely, but when they stepped off the boat in Key West, they had nothing but the phone number of relatives, which Tina's mother had carefully embroidered into her brassiere, a place she knew the Cuban authorities would not search.

Many of the Refugees endured common experiences of fleeing their homeland with almost no warning, leaving behind all their possessions, and traveling across the tumultuous seas. They left sadly, filled with fond memories of their Havana congregation where the faithful few had endured despite persistent discrimination by devoting themselves to developing a vibrant, enduring faith community. In Miami they would face a new stigma, however. The 125,000 Cubans who fled the island during this brief period in early 1980, the "Marielitos," included thousands of criminals and others, such as homosexuals, who had been jailed on the island. And the Marielitos included a larger proportion of Black Cubans than previous waves of refugees. These traits, though they characterized a minority of the newcomers, cast a negative stereotype over all arrivals and led to different types of social rejection in Miami and beyond (Portes and Stepick 1993; Grenier and Pérez 2002). But experiences of uprooting and new social stigmas also sparked what Ana Rodríguez calls a "flame in our hearts," a powerful urge to cleave together amidst adversity, much as in Cuba. "There were not as many churches in Miami as there are today, so a lot of us felt the need to get together and try to preserve this fervor, this fire, this thing burning in us." But their vision would take years to achieve.

Pastor Canto left Cuba a few years after the Mariel Boatlift and began to search for his scattered flock. For years he gathered as many as he could find for worship in makeshift sanctuaries in different churches, always with the vision of building their own home. Some years later, they purchased a small church on a parcel of land in a predominantly African American middle-class neighborhood of Hialeah. A municipality within Miami-Dade County, Hialeah had been a largely White, middle-class area until it attracted huge numbers of Cuban refugees in the 1960s, which steadily transformed it into the most densely Cuban city in the United States. Why did the Refugees build in one of the few sections of Hialeah populated by African Americans? They would not openly attribute this fact to discrimination, preferring always to elide references to race and racism. However, the preponderance of Black congregants at the Refugees' church stands in stark contrast to all other Cuban-dominant churches our research team visited. The combination of being both Black and "Mariel" no doubt made adaptation for the Refugees within the context of reception in Miami more difficult on personal as well as congregational levels.

The early history of the Refugees' church, then, is reminiscent of the Exodus story in the Bible and evocative of bonding social capital. In the span of weeks, the Refugees were scattered in the aftermath of their hasty flight from Mariel, and they wandered in Miami for several years before the concerted efforts of Carlos Canto gathered them back into a faith community. Given this history of prejudice and sacrifice, then, the fact that Pastor Canto conceived of and gradually constructed the Refugees' new church as a simulacra of the their original church in Havana is not surprising. Not only was the new church created to mimic the original architecturally, its organizational structure and worship style were also copied in expectation that these would provide the congregation with the foundations for regenerating and revitalizing themselves. Not surprisingly, their vision for recreating exactly what they left behind would encounter problems in the new Miami context.

Despite the Refugees' best intentions to unify and solidify, schisms have emerged which draw away energies that might be invested in community projects. Cuban versus non-Cuban, conservative versus liberal, and, most significantly, intergenerational divisions are the major rifts in the church. The Cuban–non-Cuban divide is almost imperceptible except in the ways that people tend to gather outside the church entrance following worship and upstairs above the sanctuary in the fellowship hall. In these spots I have detected cleavages by nationality: Colombians socializing with Colombians, Cubans with Cubans. When I have broached this topic with congregants, they almost invariably deny any national differences, but I cannot help but wonder, given the thick Cuban veil of tradition that drapes over the Refugees' structure and service. During my interview with Irma Castillo, a Mariel Cuban member, she was more forthcoming than most. "A lot of times people kind of get tired of listening to 'When we were in Cuba . . . or 'This happened in Cuba. . . .' So we try to discourage people to even mention this unless, you know, it's necessary. On the other hand, we try to keep a balance with the church officers." By the latter statement she means making sure that the church board has a few non-Cuban members. But "to make sure that everybody's included," she concluded, "is definitely a challenge."

Intergenerational differences, particularly those dividing Cuban-raised parents and their U.S.-raised children, are a growing challenge to church solidarity for the Refugees as, indeed, such differences strain congregations elsewhere (Ecklund 2005; 2005; Stepick 2005; Kim 2006). In the Refugees' case these differences are accentuated by the congregation's deliberate intra-congregational climate emphasizing tradition, specifically, Cuban Adventist tradition. One congregant from the Dominican Republic who has taught Sabbath school to teens for years and who was about to resurrect an Adventist youth service society called the Pathfinders after many years of hiatus explained to me,

> [The youth] speak to me mostly about the fact that their parents were brought up in Cuba, and it was a stricter, totally different environment the way their parents brought them up from the way kids grow up here. And what happens is most of these parents they want their kids to grow up to be like them, and the kids can't handle it or the parents can't handle it. Eventually, somebody has to give in and a lot of the times it's either the kid walking away or just ignoring the parents or just giving them a very hard time. And I tell you from experience because I speak to most of these parents and they tell me, "Look, when I was a kid in Cuba I never disobeyed my parents. I never did what these kids do." And I try to tell them how times have changed. You know, with kids nowadays you just can't pull out your belt and start whipping them. . . . What we try to do in Pathfinders is to teach them to be obedient to their parents. I mean, the Ten Commandments say to honor your father. . . . And what we try to tell them is, "Look, believe it or not, as much as this is going to hurt you, one day you're going to become a parent and you're going to turn out to be exactly the way your parents are today."

Richard Luz, the youth society director who grew up in Cuba and came to the United States in the eighth grade, also senses the generational tensions. He told me that in Cuba people question authority much less than in the United States. "You know that what the [Adventist] Conference says is law. But people born here have a more liberal point of view, and they often feel that as long as they love God it is not so important what their relationship with the church is as compared to their relationship with God. This is the big difference here; people born here ask why things are the way they are and prefer their own ideas even if they are in opposition to the general sentiment."

Richard and other congregants interviewed repeatedly returned to the congregation's conflicts between "conservative" and "liberal" members. Although there are different factors that determine who is conservative versus liberal, the main criteria are desire for change and whether or not elders' authority can be questioned. The more conservative are more resistant to change in all aspects of the church from theological to sociological, and vice versa for liberals. Similarly, conservatives expect obedience toward elders and, especially, leaders, while liberals are more apt to speak their minds regardless of age or position.

Not surprisingly, the generations align quite closely along the same cleavages with the first-generation immigrants (those born abroad) tending to be very conservative while their children, exposed simultaneously to their parents' values and to those of the broader culture such as in school, often lead the call for transformations. This fundamental schism, not unique to the Refugees but experienced widely among immigrant congregations (Stepick 2005), tends to manifest itself in visible but highly symbolic ways. Attire is perhaps the best example. The Refugees pay particular attention to physical appearance, always appearing well groomed and in their Sunday best, men and boys sport suits while women and girls wear nice dresses. At Friday evening youth meetings, however, the dress code is more relaxed, and many of the younger members would prefer that code to carry into the Sabbath. But Pastor Moreno will not permit such transgressions for reasons I return to later.

The Refugees are not only beset by internal issues that siphon off their energy, but also experience difficulties with their immediate neighbors. During the 1990s, the church grew, literally and figuratively, into its structure. In many ways the perfect design for a church in Cuba would prove, unfortunately, ill adapted to Miami. For example, the main sanctuary mimics the old Havana church with its towering interior ceiling rising some thirty feet above the heads of worshipers. In Havana's heat, the space serves to help circulate breezes, lifting the sultry air upward, and it provides acoustical advantages. But in Hialeah, the sanctuary is quickly evacuated after service so the chillers can be cut off because the architects had not factored in the astronomical cost of air-conditioning this gargantuan space. Also, the new structure towers over its neighbors' homes, while the church it replaced had been modest and in tune with the simple but well-manicured homes lining nearby streets. Moreover, on Saturdays the burgeoning congregation, between six hundred and eight hundred strong, drives to service, whereas few owned cars in Havana. The new larger building took up some of the original parking lot, forcing congregants to park along roads and in nearby shopping lots. Pastor Moreno has made great strides to ease the strain between church and neighborhood. He entreats members to be friendly with residents and to respect their property. Indeed, the first item each week on the church's PowerPoint announcements is a reminder to park carefully or be towed. The church has also sponsored events geared to residents and congregants alike, such as health fairs and music concerts. Still, there is an air of incongruity in the vicinity as if somehow this refuge for the Cuban Refugees is still seeking a welcome in its new land. The oversized church structure symbolizes the separation of the Refugees from the greater community around them. The church walls offer protection for those within while erecting barriers to those outside.

There are important clues in the Refugees' congregational history for understanding their inward focus. First, in contradistinction to studies cited in this volume's first chapter that find denomination important (Wilson and Janoski 1997; Brooks and Lewis 2001; Uslaner 2002; Wuthnow 2004), denomination is of little consequence in this particular case. Research I conducted in Cuba on the Refugees' mother congregation as well as on other Seventh-Day Adventist congregations in three different countries where I conducted research showed them to be engaged in many civic activities that extend beyond their sanctuary, supporting soup kitchens and other programs for the needy. And, though Adventists in Cuba are somewhat singled out by the government for refusing to work on Saturdays, their own view is that they suffer most for being practicing Christians than for being Adventists. For the Refugees, rather, the particularly adverse contexts behind their migration and their adaptation to Miami provide an important background to understanding their emphasis on bonding social capital. The question I return to later, after addressing the Disciples' history, is whether or not the Refugees' leadership can stimulate the membership toward development of more outwardly oriented CSC.

The "Disciples"

Less than two miles away from the Refugees' church is the "Disciples" Nazarene church. The Nazarenes are a Protestant denomination of some 1.5 million worldwide whose founding dates to the early twentieth century but whose origins trace back to the Holiness movement of the nineteenth century. Though not Pentecostal, they tend to express their faith with greater emotion than many mainline Protestant denominations. The Disciples congregation is nestled in what used to be one of the most rundown sections of Hialeah. It is now squeezed amidst encroaching two-story condominiums as a result of urban renewal projects. The church was built back when Hialeah was predominantly a White middle-class community, but during the 1970s and 1980s the area underwent ethnic succession. As Hialeah and later most of Miami-Dade County became increasingly populated by Hispanics, Cubans in particular, Anglo residents moved away and their churches often transformed into Hispanic congregations. When Pastor Al González began his ministry in 1979 at what would become the Disciples, he was offered an unpaid position to teach Sunday school to the few people in the congregation who were Spanish speakers. Shortly thereafter, the Anglo minister announced he was leaving, and Al González, though only a lay leader and not yet formally a pastor, became pastor. As he recalls, the first Sunday of his ministry was Easter Sunday. "I invited many different people from a variety of churches to attend that day. They came to support me and we had the first service that Sunday. The next Sunday the only ones who showed were my family and the two who had been in my Sunday School class."

For the next dozen years or so González built the congregation up from this inauspicious starting point. As he himself and others admit, it became a pretty traditional church wherein most members attended services, socialized with each other, and did small acts of community service. In terms of social capital, it favored the bonding variety, in part due to the needs of Spanish speakers for a cultural oasis from the stresses of negotiating the then-White dominant area. Angie Fernández grew up in the church, and now in her twenties she recalls, "It was like a rich people's church, not money-wise but it was full of people who, well they just didn't want to get involved with the community type of thing." González had to work a regular job as well as pastoring because the small, working-class, immigrant congregation could not afford to pay a full-time minister's salary. This left little time for doing good works in the community, but González and his small congregation did pastor to newly arrived Mariel refugees in the early 1980s, and later González began a jail ministry. In short, the early history of the Disciples would not well predict, as in the case of the Refugees, its future CSC.

In 1994, a woman named Flor Roca walked into the church, and her arrival initiated its evolution, its revolution into what the Disciples now refer to as their compassion ministry. "I owe my life to He who saved me," she began, telling her testimony of decline into drugs during one Saturday evening church service. She related growing up in a middle-class home with her mother and two sisters in Cuba. "Then my cousin came to live with us. He was fourteen at the time and he started to abuse me sexually." She had been outgoing but became extremely introverted. Her mother didn't understand the change and laughed at her, as did her friends. Her grades suffered. She left Cuba when she was eleven for the United States, and the cousin stayed behind. For her, emigration was not freedom from the Castro regime but from "another tyranny," her cousin. "You think you can leave your sadness behind but my sadness went on the plane with me. . . . I didn't grow up normally." Flor married her first boyfriend, who turned out to be a physically and emotionally abusive man who beat her repeatedly. Her adult life brought cycles of success and decline fueled by a five hundred to eight hundred dollar a day cocaine habit. Ultimately, the drug got the best of her and she lost everything, her house, all her belongings, and, most painfully, her two children. "My child called Family Services saying that I was a bad mother. I was a monster. I hated myself more than anyone. When they took away my kids I wanted to die." She attempted suicide, but when unsuccessful she hoped someone would put her out of her misery. Misfortune haunted her. She was on the streets and was raped. She was robbed, sometimes for less than fifty cents. "I lived worse than dogs. Why did I wake up, I would ask myself? Why didn't I just die during the night? But my mother had faith in God. I didn't think that a skinny God on a cross would be strong enough to save me. My mother talked to me and said that God is almighty and sovereign. She said that only God can help me and sought psychological counseling for me." Flor began to speak to God and one day felt him communicate with her: "God, did you call me? And he responded right away, 'This is the almighty God.' God wanted to be my personal friend."

Flor entered a substance-abuse treatment program, and after graduating she began her life's mission of reaching out to others like her. God brought her to the Disciples' door she tells assertively, but at first Pastor González was not interested. He had a very ill wife and a struggling congregation. Yet every day Flor would show up with Hialeah's rejects on his doorstep: sex workers, drug addicts, the homeless, the mentally infirm. He told her that there was no program for those people at his church. But she insisted, "God sent me here and He doesn't make mistakes." As Pastor González's son, Abram, recalls, Flor was very passionate about this mission, "so we tried to change. . . . Little by little we started to change the vision of the church as not to think about our own selves but to think about others and helping out others. One of our main goals was 'What would Jesus do?' WWJD. What would Jesus do? And we used to say, well, what would Jesus do? Jesus would not be in the four walls of the church; he'd be out there helping out the needy people. And so today, this is where we're at."

Flor's persistence and her compassion slowly motivated Pastor González and other congregants to transform. Though they, like so many other faith leaders, had tried to be good Christians by appealing to do good deeds for others, their supplications had yielded little fruit. Flor catalyzed the congregation's bonding social capital into bridging and then linking civic social capital with a wider and wider civic radius. In the first program they founded, Rescue with Love, church members would comb Miami's homeless haunts, bring the willing back to the church with them, provide them with showers, a change of clothes, and breakfast, and then invite them to participate in the Sunday service alongside the congregation. When I asked Abram, who became associate pastor of the church, what the reaction of the congregation was to this revolution in the church, he told me, "When I invited them downtown to feed the homeless they didn't want to go. 'No. No. Those are not my people,' they'd say. Mothers were saying, 'Oh. No. My daughter is *not* going to be put in danger. These people are a bunch of delinquents!'" Pastor González, however, knew in his heart that he and his congregation had been called and there was no turning back. WWJD? But the decision, and later González's proposal of marriage to Flor after his first wife died, split the congregation in two. About half of his carefully pastured flock left in the next few years, slashing his workforce and his stewardship base.

But there was no turning back, for the group had become the Disciples. Flor had ignited the church's flame and Pastor González set about ensuring that it would be properly stoked. He would have to craft and sustain a vibrant, complex lay-leadership structure to meet the congregation's ever-growing projects. In the next few years, the church not only aided people to leave the streets on Sundays but found them more permanent shelter when one member offered his vacant apartment. The church's rehabilitation center was born. The church acquired a few more apartments nearby to house recovering addicts, and when the need quickly exceeded supply, the church opened its doors for them to sleep inside.

By the late 1990s, even this space was insufficient, so the church sought to rent or purchase a building to house its growing, faith-based substance-abuse treatment programs, one for women and another for men. A few years later, the church was finally able to secure a mortgage, leveraged by the church property, for a building located at one of the most infamous drug corners in Miami. Refurbished, it is now the permanent home for the men's program, where it houses thirty or more recovering addicts at any one time.

Around the same time that the Disciples began their home for recovering addicts, Pastor González was approached by a congregant from another church who had unsuccessfully tried to start a food pantry in that other church. "He came to me and he proposed that we start the pantry here, and I told him, 'Why not?' though he thought I didn't have much faith in the prospect. But he insisted that people will come to the church for the food, and the food is what Jesus will offer them. It will be the Lord's work; He will do it. And when we started, we gave out twenty boxes of food. . . . That's how it began, and since then we have given out thousands and thousands of boxes of food." The food program known as the Blessings has become so huge that on Thursday evenings when the boxes are distributed, they must be delivered by tractor trailer from a warehouse. People come from all over the Hialeah neighborhoods and even further. They attend a Bible study class followed by a community-oriented service, after which they receive a large box filled with food donated from a variety of local charities and grocery chains.

In less than ten years and through the vision and enormous dedication of the church's leadership, both clerical and lay, and its members, the Disciples have grown their membership and attendance to more than one thousand members, becoming the fastest-growing Nazarene church in the nation. Each time Pastor González looks out at an exuberant crowd filling his pews on Sunday, on Wednesday, on Saturday, and more, he is thankful but he also reminds himself, "The harvests are plentiful but the workers are scarce." Indeed, the Disciples and their community missions generate an enormous demand for volunteers. González, like Jesus and innumerable leaders after him, has had to devise ways of motivating people for community service and building leadership as well as keeping them committed. In the next section I focus on leadership development as a critical difference in the cultivation of CSC in the two congregations.

Comparing Leadership Cultivation in Two Congregations

The Refugees and the Disciples share certain similarities such as their service to the largely poor, immigrant populations in Hialeah and the fact that both operate within larger Protestant institutional structures. But when their CSC is analyzed their differences become quite stark. The Refugees, while certainly called to community service by Christian values and by Pastor Moreno's ethical prophesying, expend most of their energy cultivating and sustaining bonding social capital, both locally and transnationally. Their civic engagement falls into two principal categories: aiding new refugees, primarily Cubans, and managing difficult if not hostile relations with their neighbors. They follow a quite classic model of self-preservation: the immigrant congregation creating a refuge from the outside in order to preserve its traditions (Ebaugh and Chafetz 1999, 2000; Stepick 2005).

Quite in contrast, the Disciples' church down the street transformed itself from a similar, inwardly focused, survival-oriented congregation into an engine of wide-ranging CSC. The Disciples' social capital encompasses both bonding and bridging varieties, the latter overcoming many classic sociological cleavages that frequently inhibit such linkages, differences such as socioeconomic status, nationality, and race. The spark for the Disciples' transformation came, perhaps surprisingly, not from the formal leadership but from the laity. Flor, not Pastor González, is the charismatic persona who wrestled the congregation and its leadership out of their comfortable complacency. She initiated what became a tradition among the Disciples of cultivating lay leadership on a grand scale and deploying their talents toward meeting the needs not only of the congregation (itself a needy population) but also of the greater community around the church. In Weberian terms, Flor pushed Pastor González from exemplary prophesying, from merely exhorting his flock to do God's work in the community, to ethical prophesying, to rolling up his (and his congregation's) sleeves and getting the work done. Flor forced Pastor González to transform his habitus to one more in line with Flor's and bridging CSC. Getting the work done engaged the Disciples with social institutions in the greater society—local supermarkets, food banks, social service agencies, and so on—that broadened their social capital base to include bridging and even linking varieties. As both the church and its outreach ministries have grown, so too have its needs for ever larger numbers of volunteers and leaders to direct them.

Building Civic Social Capital the Refugees' Way: Bonding over Bridging

The founding members of the Refugees' congregation set about rebuilding their lives and their faith community by laying a sturdy foundation and refusing to be budged from it ever since. There are sound reasons for their rigidity. They came from a denomination that for decades survived among the most egregious injustices hurled at any church in Cuba by holding steadfast to their principles and rituals. Churches in general, but the Seventh-Day Adventists in particular, owing to their nonparticipation in the military and refusal to work on Saturdays, became islands of bonding social capital within Cuba. When suddenly uprooted from these tight communities by the Mariel Boatlift, the Refugees' survivors faced hostility in Miami as Black Cubans in a society that discriminated against them and as "Marielitos," laden with that wave's stereotype of being Cuban society's rejects. No wonder that members grasped for their congregation to be a sturdy rudder steering them amidst the turbulent waters of life in Miami, a Miami proving not to be such a welcoming Promised Land. As has been true for other immigrants, they sought to re-create both socially and physically the church and community they left behind. They first had to find their flock, which had been scattered after arrival. Then they slowly but steadily set about re-creating their old congregation socially and structurally; among the greatest symbols of this harmonization and transnationalization of their congregation is the construction of their new sanctuary as a near replica of the original church building. They also focused their ministry on Adventist values and traditions, eschewing much engagement with the wider society. This attention to their own needs inadvertently erected borders more than bridges toward their neighbors, the troubled relationship symbolized by how their soaring sanctuary rises up incongruously amid modest one-story homes and how the first announcement at their services warns attendees not to park on lawns or risk being towed.

The Refugees' emphasis on helping themselves, including addressing the schisms along generational and conservative versus liberal lines, is reflected in their lay leadership selection, self-scrutiny and election processes. Interviews with many church members confirm that this congregation follows Adventists' denominational rules for selecting people to serve as members of the church board and as leaders of its many ministries (called "departments"). The basic procedure is hierarchical but also somewhat democratic. I observed the yearly process of electing leaders as it began during one summer Sabbath service. Pastor Moreno announced the elections and explained the need to put together a commission whose sole job would be to elect the Nominating Committee. The commission could be elected entirely by the congregation (option A) or it could be constituted by the existing church board members plus seven to nine additional members (option B). Pastor Moreno expressed his preference for option B, arguing for its greater efficiency, and the congregation agreed. Then he walked the congregation through nominations from the sanctuary for names of people who might be added. As nominations were suggested, the church secretary noted them but there was no real discussion as to why they were nominated or why they might be good people to serve. When enough names were brought forth, Pastor Moreno closed the process and the commission was set. It would elect members to serve on the Nominating Committee over the next weeks.

The Nominating Committee generates names of individuals who might serve as leaders of the church's departments, such as music, minors, youth society, and women's and men's service organizations. As leadership positions are multiple, each department has a director, associate director, assistant directors, and secretaries, there is ample opportunity for engaging large numbers of congregants in leadership development. At least ostensibly, it is a structure that lends itself to involving a wide variety of people who thus might be in possession of diverse bridging CSC already. In the Refugees' case, however, this potential is thwarted by the next step, when the Nominating Committee must discuss each candidate for each position. The critical insight I gained about the power of the Nominating Committee is the fact that the committee does not interview candidates. Rather, the members of the Nominating Committee utilize only their existing knowledge of the candidates' qualities, religious background, and abilities in their deliberations. Consequently, the more homogenous the committee, the less likely it will endorse unusual candidates. When a congregation opts for option B to form its Nominating Committee, as it did during my fieldwork and as I was told is the congregation's norm, existing church board members dominate and the status quo is favored. With the Refugees this had helped to perpetuate the leadership of the older generation, in this case those who arrived during Mariel as refugees, and their need for bonding social capital. It also frustrates some members, particularly younger congregants, and is fueling schisms. A case in point is leadership development within the Youth Society department.

The selection of leadership for the Refugees' Youth Society illustrates well how this church tries to fill in its fracture lines through the cement of tradition and doctrine. As I interviewed him, Richard Luz, at twenty-one years of age, was just assuming directorship of the Youth Society and was full of ideas for how he would be able to invigorate the group. Richard characterizes himself as "very conservative," as someone who is not interested in changing the culture of the church. He acknowledged that this orientation probably favored his election to youth leader by the Nominating Committee because "the church is interested in forming leaders among the youth since they will become the future church leaders. Now there are those youth who are 'natural leaders' and have stood out as such from the very beginning, and the church is going to then look at how conservative or liberal each of them is. If he is liberal then the church will take a great deal of care deciding what position to give him. Since the church is very conservative, if you put in a liberal leader you will have conflicts. But if you put in an ultra-conservative leader then the youth will not identify with him."

Once elected to his position, Richard was able to suggest names to the Nominating Committee for the Youth Society's other leaders. He recommended Tracey Linares for secretary, a more liberal and outspoken leader who, he felt, would bring a good leadership balance to the organization. This raised some eyebrows because Tracey had left the church for several years, during which time she also had a child out of wedlock. Tracy was not the type of leader the Nominating Committee was interested in endorsing, but she could be someone who might actually serve as a bridge to a broader circle of potential new members. As Pastor Moreno did not know her personally, he, in Tracey's words, "did his homework on her."

> He basically went around asking everyone about me, my past, and trying
> to get background information on me, and he came back to me and he
> said, "Okay, let's finish the conversation. This is what I want you to do

according to what I've learned and what you've told me." And from the very get-go, he told me that he has to represent his church as a whole, and our church is very conservative, but that he will never deny youth needs or any request that we make, you know, to better the youth department or to improve on things or to present issues or anything that would help the spiritual morals and social lives of our youth. That he would always be a big supporter. And I have found that to be true. He's a conservative in a lot of ways. He wants the girls to dress conservatively. He wants the boys to dress neat and clean, no baggy jeans. He wants them to wear ties when they go up on stage. He's a stickler with appearance, both in the way we look to the world as well as the way we look to ourselves.

When questioned why appearances were so important, she responded, "That's just because he's old school. It goes along with 'Cleanliness is next to Godliness.' ... It's because he feels that these little things are not out of the youths' reach and they would make the elders happy, and if he keeps the elders happy it will allow him to let us do more of what we want."

The descriptions from Tracey and Richard serve to illustrate the way that established leaders at the Refugees' church wield power to limit social change and thus to reinforce existing social bonds within their congregation. But the election of multiple leaders for each church department is also a very effective means of generating and expanding leadership. Thus, in the Youth Society case, associate directors and other positions are vetted and selected by the Nominating Committee and filled by individuals who appear to have the potential for leadership but have not had it tested experientially. They are put in charge of organizing events and activities to aid the director and to test their abilities. If they do well, they become candidates for higher positions the following year, and vice versa.

The multi-layered leadership selection and membership involvement process practiced by the Refugees fosters social capital in two fundamental ways: First, it identifies and nurtures leadership. These same processes occur in the church's other departments, generating social capital vertically and horizontally—but always careful, owing to the scrutiny of the Nominating Committee, to choose those who will be loyal to the status quo. Second, it sets people in motion, pulling them into activities that they might not otherwise join. And in doing so it gets them connected. That is, the Refugees are great at cultivating bonding social capital. As explained in the introduction to this volume, we take an expansive view of what makes social capital civic. The Refugees favor one end of the spectrum, bonding, but their leadership development and engagement processes *build capacity for* much broader civic-oriented programs than the Refugees were engaged in during thus study. In this way they are not so dissimilar from the Disciples, at least from where the Disciples stood before Flor lit a fire under that complacent congregation.

Building Civic Social Capital the Disciples' Way:
Informal and Formal Techniques

After only a few visits to the Disciples' church I realized that they had a special way of generating and channeling civic energies, but it took me some time to discover their techniques. Enter the church at any given time, night or day, and there is activity. Trucks with food come and go, recovering addicts sweep the floors, instrumentalists and vocalists rock the sanctuary with inspirational songs, and the phones ring off the hook. A conversation with Pastor González or his son and junior pastor, Abram, is constantly interrupted by the squeal of their walkie-talkie cell phones as volunteers report on shipments en route, projects to be overseen, bills to be paid. Enter during a service and for the first thirty to forty-five minutes the congregation will be standing, jumping, clapping, waving their hands, and singing at the top of their lungs to the Latin beats of the small but energetic band of bass guitar, keyboards, drums, and congas that accompanies the congregation and the three-person backup choir. Abram often grabs a microphone and entreats even more energy from the congregation, running side to side along the front of the sanctuary and singing as if in a night club.

Yes, this church is energetic and, yes, it revs up its members, but how does it commit them to sustained service to others? The Disciples use several formal and informal means to generate and sustain CSC in all varieties, but the approach boils down to three key steps: (1) get people in the door; (2) get them bonded to the church, to their own spirituality, and to others in the church; and (3) get them bridged and linked to community outreach activities.

How do you get people to come to your church? This is the first step and often the most difficult one that congregations face everywhere. Before their revolution into a compassionate ministry, the Disciples evangelized primarily the old-fashioned way. They depended on cultivating a flock slowly through good worship services and some direct outreach, hoping that this would yield word-of-mouth evangelism growth. Once they began their new ministry, however, the Disciples initiated a completely different strategy. Instead of waiting for people to walk through their door, they brought people to their door, and not just any people, nor people who resembled themselves, but people on society's margins. They knew that these people would not come to hear the Lord's word for they felt abandoned by the Lord, but they would come to fill their stomachs and take a shower, particularly when offered a ride. And they came.

As the church grew and became more diverse, the pastors innovated in worship style as well as in outreach strategies. Pastor González tells of leading prayer groups before dawn so that people could participate before going to work. The church also initiated special new services to attract different groups, such as a Sunday evening service for those who have to work on weekends and healing services where the pastors invite the ailing to come forward and have hands laid upon them. Rescue with Love and the Blessings brought hundreds and then thousands to the church for one visit, but the Disciples faced a more uphill battle in order to go from step 1 to step 2, that is, between getting people in the door and getting them connected.

The Disciples employ a number of *informal* techniques to connect newcomers to the church and, by extension, to their own spirituality and to others in the church. This is a necessary step en route to transforming them into the servants who will do the Lord's work on Earth. These techniques, while effective, are not unique to the Disciples and, in general, merely create a friendly, supportive, and welcoming environment that makes people feel good and part of a family. The beginning of the service illustrates this connectedness well. Upon arrival, you are greeted by a lively tune called "Give Me Your Hand," where people more often than not embrace those close by instead of a more-distanced handshake. In contrast to the Refugees' expectation that younger members conform to elders' traditions, the Disciples have adapted their style to accept and welcome a wide cross-section of Hialeah by speaking the different groups' faith languages. For example, Pastors Al and Abram and many of the other established church members walk up and down the aisles hugging women, kissing babies, high-fiving children and adolescents, and extending hearty handshakes to the men. Many people clap, others sway, and a few jump up and down to a series of upbeat Christian tunes played with a Latin beat. There is no dress code, though older members tend to dress up while younger ones make no special effort with their attire.

The band blasts out a series of upbeat songs while the lyrics are displayed on a large overhead screen. There is no liturgy, no structure except singing, moving bodies, and greetings. The mood is joyous, raucous, and, upon reflection, quite liberal in that each person can celebrate and express himself or herself as he or she wishes. Then the lead guitar begins plucking a much more subdued, soulful song that signals a transition into the more sacred and the more unifying. People raise their hands, close their eyes, and often cry as the lyrics are sung:

> You have pardoned me.
> You have saved me from my problems.
> For this I praise you, for this you are my true friend.
> With my hands lifted up to heaven, I bring myself to you today, my Lord
> To receive you, your power and fortitude, to live next to you.
> Fill up my heart with your presence.
> Fill me with your happiness and peace.
> You respond to whatever needs I have because you love me.

This particularly poignant song that recognizes the traumatic backgrounds of a large portion of the congregants is accompanied expressively by Juan, a recovering drug addict who plays lead guitar. Everyone sings the song over and over until tears stream down dozens of faces and others slump over pews as they contemplate both their travails in life and their blessings in the Lord. Pastor González quietly intercedes as the music trails off but nonetheless seizes the spiritual mood and asks, "Who came here seeking something? Who feels something special is happening here? People who've lost hope are open to temptation from the devil, but today we will be nourished by faith." Then he asks people to close their eyes and feel the spirit coming. "Feel free to let the spirit's presence be seen." Though the congregation's eyes remain closed, they "see" the spirit by hearing the rustling of clothes, Bibles, and papers as people's bodies sway and swoon. They know the spirit is moving them.

This mood-setting ritual is followed by an altar call. Dozens come forward to the altar, lower themselves onto their knees, and pray. González continues with prayers of thanksgiving while Abram quietly attends to those at the altar, laying hands on them and giving them individual blessings. Half the congregation of several hundred will walk forward to the altar area seeking a touch, and they will be embraced by senior church members while the pastors slowly make their way from individual to individual offering personal prayers and healing oil on their foreheads. Frequently, the most expressive participants are the recovering addicts from the rehabilitation center who sit in the front pews on one side. One of them told me, "It touches me very much when I hear these songs of praise and I concentrate on worshiping God. God really touches us because you can see us crying, and for us it must be really something because we're so tough. . . . And as we feel God's work in our lives as he is cleansing us we just let go like a little kid and the tears pour down our faces."

Physical touch through hugs and laying on of hands is a bonding language in the Disciples' church, a way of connecting people both physically and emotionally, of making then know that someone truly cares. Juana Díaz, an unpaid staff member and one of the women rescued by Flor, who later became head of the women's program, describes the importance of physical touch: "You come here and you're all destroyed and your own family doesn't want to have anything to do with you. They embrace you here; they make you feel a part of this place, of this church. It's a family and you can feel whole and you can feel a genuine love. There is something that attracts you here and you don't want to leave—and that's Jesus."

Aside from cultivating this emotional, spiritual, and sensual connectedness during and outside of worship, the Disciples get newcomers to take the first steps toward commitment by making them feel, often for the first time in their lives, that they are not outsiders or society's rejects. Dress is casual and no one cares what accent you speak with or what country you are from; you are a child of God and that is all that matters. Additionally, members are knit together through the common practice of giving public testimonies, stories typically laced with horrible histories of child, sexual, and substance abuse, poverty, exoduses from homelands, and illness. Pastor González invites usually no more than one testimony per service, but afterward asks those in the congregation to raise their hands if they have had similar problems and he blesses them all. And finally, the Disciples interject very little denominational doctrine into their service. This has the effect, intended or not, to make it feel less doctrinal and foreign to newcomers.

When a custom specific to the denomination is followed, I note that the pastors use it to bridge established members to the visitors. In the following example, Pastor González combines various techniques to accompany newcomers through their first awkward steps within the church and then to skillfully lead them deeper and deeper into the church community. On this particular summer evening, Pastor González begins the service by warning the congregation, "We're going to offer a prayer, but our visitors tonight may not know it. Don't worry because you will be accompanied by the congregation who knows it." The prayer tells of how life is a struggle and people need the help of the Lord to make it through. After finishing and as people's heads are still bowed, he asks those who prayed this prayer for the first time to raise their hands. He then blesses them individually, assuring each that they now have many brothers and sisters who are here for them. Then he calls them forward to the front of the sanctuary, where several senior lay leaders in the church surround them and place their hands on them while Pastor González prays for them. He then invites the sick to join them and many come forward. More church leaders lay hands on the sick and there is a long, public laying on of hands and prayer for this larger and larger group. González then transforms this de facto altar call into a true altar call by asking those who have not been baptized to raise their hands. Those who are already in front are noted by the pastors, reaching out to touch them; those in their seats are invited forward.

González then asks for volunteers to help distribute the heavy food boxes following the service. They, too, come forward and are blessed for their willingness and the work they are about to do for Christ. At this point half or more of the congregation is squeezed tightly into the front of the church. They are all touching and often holding each other while simultaneously the pastors and lay leaders stretch their embraces over the tops of heads like strands of a safety net. Emotion and energy radiate to everyone in the sanctuary, creating a sensual as well as spiritual communion.

This apparently simple series of public rituals is packed with important constitutive elements that build CSC. Once in the door, people are actually encouraged to take the next steps toward commitment—spiritual and civic. Strangers cement into friends and are invited to acknowledge their own needs. They are assured that they are not alone in their suffering and are offered relief by taking their first step toward healing. In this invitation their physical movement to the altar begins their transformation from passive onlookers into dynamic participants. As they take their first steps, they are accompanied by more seasoned participants who give the newcomers comfort, connection to others, and, at the same time, teach them how to get involved. The final call for volunteers shows the newcomers the expected path they will take as well, the path to service.

As I observed Pastor González during this and many other services, I was curious to find out to what degree his techniques are consciously cultivated or have been learned more through trial and error. So I asked him directly during an interview, and he responded humbly, "The majority of the things I do, I do naturally. They are not written down; they are inspired." He went on to explain that during the service described above he had planned on giving a sermon, but the feeling in his heart at the moment was that "people needed to ask the Lord for help," so he followed that feeling. Pastor González, a man who came to the ministry after many years of hard labor as a Cuban immigrant to Miami, has a genuine gift for reaching people. He assuredly embodies Weber's assertion that some leaders have natural charisma. However, his own abilities, as he well recognizes, would not suffice were it not for the structures that the church has developed as well. The techniques for cultivating CSC that I have just described are largely informal because they proceed, whether intentionally or not, in an unstructured way. There are others that are more formal.

The Disciples create an exceptionally welcoming atmosphere through formal techniques similar to, although better implemented than, those practiced by other churches. These practices, however, are merely the foundation from which the Disciples have developed a series of additional *more formal or institutional* techniques that guide newcomers into deeper and deeper connections to the church and out to the greater society.

The first technique I will discuss involves describing how the Blessings food program brings people not only to the church but inside the sanctuary as well. Under the homeless ministry, Rescue with Love, people's needs for a good meal and shower are attended to first; then, they are invited to worship with the congregation in the hope that they will connect to God and to the church. In short, through meeting people's needs the Disciples, much like generations of missionaries dating back to the original disciples of Christ, hope attendees also meet the Lord. With the Blessings food pantry program, however, the church reversed its strategy. This time people began to be required to attend a religious class followed by a church service, and at the end of the service they would receive a box of food. God first, needs second. When some people figured out the system and would show up just when the service ended for their box of food, the church thwarted the freeloaders by issuing tickets to those people who attended the religious classes. Only ticket holders could redeem the tickets for food. In this way, the Disciples turned their food ministry into a larger missionizing vehicle.

As the church became more widely known for its food and substance-abuse assistance programs, more and more people arrived with other needs. Newer immigrant groups such as Nicaraguans, Colombians, and Argentines began arriving in larger numbers into the neighborhood, owing to its cheaper housing and many small factories. The pastors and volunteer staff would help as they could, learning through requests from these newest waves of immigrants how to connect to agencies that specialize in different social services. Likewise, as different agencies and organizations, governmental and nongovernmental, learned about the Disciples' ministries, they began to refer clients to them, both those in need of services and those offering services (and goods such as donated food). From a small nucleus of very dedicated people, a network of CSC grew that includes bonding, bridging, and linking. Quality leadership thus is capable of transubstantiating bonding into bridging and linking social capital.

Another formal technique among the Disciples for getting people connected to the church is what I call "easy steps to attachment." This technique picks up where the outreach ministries leave off; that is, by getting people to become part of the church through making it easy for visitors to acquire preliminary institutional associations with the church. Other techniques discussed below pick up afterward, serving to transform them into full-fledged members later. The process begins with the welcome. At each service first-time visitors are met at the door, greeted, and asked to fill out a newcomer welcome card. Pastor González revels in reading out their names during service, asking them to stand, blessing them, welcoming them, and thanking them for taking a first step toward the Lord. The newcomers are noted by lay leaders who often approach and embrace them as well. The next opportunity to take a step toward commitment occurs almost invariably after the most emotional parts of the service. The pastor invites the unbaptized to identify themselves and come forward to the altar. Then he encourages them by saying, "You don't have to change your religion, just receive Christ as your savior and you will find new life." His goal is to get them to feel their spiritual void and to desire to fill it, in hopes that they will then consider baptism. Baptism is the critical step, and the Disciples make it very easy. They do not require baptismal candidates to take classes in preparation; everyone is welcome as long as they accept Jesus as savior, which they do in testimonial form just prior to full immersion in the baptismal font located behind the pulpit. There are baptisms at nearly every service and up to a dozen at a time. Baptism at the Disciples is not just a threshold into church membership as it is around the world. It is also characterized as a great personal accomplishment, one acknowledged publicly through the awarding of baptismal certificates in front of the whole congregation.

Indeed, the Disciples love certificates and award them constantly for every rite of passage: completion of leadership and Bible classes, induction into membership, graduation from the substance-abuse recovery programs, and so on. The church frames each certificate to underscore them as enduring symbolic reminders of recipients' achievements and their growing connectedness to the church. Such affirmations are especially significant to many congregants for they have always been underachievers, people who never obtained a diploma or any other recognition in their entire lives. The Disciples' public acknowledgment of every baby step newcomers and members take constitutes an institutionalized yet accessible ladder toward personal achievement as well as CSC.

Baptism is a critical rung of the Disciples' CSC ladder, but sustaining newcomers' connectedness and transforming it into commitment involve steeper steps. The Disciples face two related problems in this area. First of all, as the church has grown—total attendance in any given week approaches two thousand—the sanctuary built for four hundred is over capacity. These numbers strain the ability of the church to retain a small, family feel. Also, a church of this size with as many activities as it sustains needs a steady supply of leaders to assume responsibility for them. Since inception of its compassion ministries, if not before, the Disciples' church has consistently invested resources in programs over personnel. To my knowledge, only Pastors González and Abram receive salaries and modest ones at that.

The church thus depends on volunteers. They are truly its backbone, and the demand for volunteers keeps rising, so how does the church generate enough of them? The principal vehicle developed only a few years ago is a leadership training program that the Disciples learned from another church. Two members were sent to that church's instruction program and were charged with helping the pastors develop and implement it. Its name in Spanish is *Aquí Edificamos Gente* (We Build People Here). The program is visually represented as a baseball diamond, where people advance around the bases, each base representing a higher degree of ministry, commitment, and leadership. As they advance around the bases, graduates are given certificates and more responsibility within the church. Thus, the We Build People Here program not only deepens members' spirituality but also intensifies their connectedness to the church and to its missions. The program fosters leadership as it also teaches Christianity; the more advanced students become the instructors of classes reaching out to newer members. The highest class, home plate in the baseball diamond system, is called Small Groups. In this stage, members are groomed by the pastors to lead small cohorts of people along the model of early Christians. Each small group ideally includes eleven members, called "disciples," and one leader. It is intentionally fashioned along the lines of Jesus' relationship to his own Disciples, common people whom he cultivated into community leaders. As described by Angie Fernández, one of the two members sent to be trained in this new program, "When you have a large church, a small group makes a big difference because you're tending to individuals' needs as opposed to when you have a big church you can't concentrate on individual people. So, that's why they encourage the small group. . . . You know, if someone's sick and you have six hundred people in your church, you might not know. But, if you have a small group and one person out of your ten people is missing, then you'll be like, oh, okay, I need to call that person. So that's how you make it more personal."

The institutionalization of Small Groups has been a major goal of Pastor González recently, and he makes note of them frequently in sermons. They are a critical link in the chain that hopefully will bond those who come to the church for material assistance with those who stay and become disciples for Christ by ministering to others.

As the church implemented its new leadership building program, I noted that those receiving certificates of completion of the Small Groups class were disproportionately graduates of the substance-abuse programs. And as I came to understand more comprehensively the operation of the rehabilitation center, I began to see how it embodies all the principles and techniques of the church as described so far. The substance-abuse treatment program is both the product of the church's CSC *and* a principal generator of new CSC. This brand of new CSC not only bonds people who have been isolated and marginalized for much of their lives, but also bridges them across sociological lines that most of society will not cross and often refuses to even acknowledge. Pastor González provides the moral basis by modeling his charisma on Christ's work two millennia ago with society's rejects of the time: lepers, the mentally ill, tax collectors, and women. Pastor González's model acknowledges that Christ's work was difficult and dangerous; and so, too, is the Disciples' work today.

Recovering addicts are the first to assert that they are a difficult group to transform. During interview after interview, I heard men at the rehabilitation center describe themselves as Mike Martínez did: "I was into the pleasures of the street, which are momentary, and after the high you feel nothing so you try to fill yourself up again, over and over. But no one cares about you; no one loves you. When I came [to the Disciples' drug treatment program] from the hospital I was emotionally destroyed, and when I got here they embraced me and said, 'From today on your life is going to change and you will not be the same. You are not the same because God is going to change you.'"

That the Disciples perceive potential in people who have spent the majority of their lives exploiting others for their own benefit, regardless of the fact that they often have been victims early on in life, just as Flor was, is remarkable. But to turn their lives around so that they become servants to others is, indeed, a miracle. The Disciples have accomplished this miracle over and over. To wit, the church's twenty-third anniversary celebration was attended by hundreds of the recovery program's graduates. No program is 100 percent successful, and the Disciples have not been able to reach everyone equally effectively, but they employ several techniques that merit special attention. I will focus on those techniques that transform the *muchachos* into the Lord's servants. Addressing all the ways people's addictions are treated would go beyond the scope of this book.

The Disciples' formula boils down to the following: (1) forgiveness of oneself, for without this a person cannot attend to anyone's needs but his or her own; (2) structured and disciplined use of time; and (3) service to others. When a new man arrives or is brought to the rehabilitation center after he has been detoxed at a local hospital, he begins his therapy and his involvement in the program and the church by acknowledging his addiction, by being truthful to himself. When he faces the truth, he is taught to forgive himself, for forgiveness is the gift of the Lord, they say. Addicts, overwhelmed by guilt and denial, find forgiveness is hard. As Mike Martínez told me, "At the beginning you feel guilty and that God will not forgive you. The first thing is to forgive yourself. And here atmosphere is important. If you are surrounded by drugs then you love drugs, but if you are surrounded by love then you learn to love."

In the streets addicts learn to bury their emotions by using drugs, and any inkling of vulnerability can cost them their lives. This hard outer shell is difficult to crack, but the Disciples create a culture wherein it is safe to be emotional, vulnerable, and to let the pain out so that the vacuum can be filled with love. Mike explained, "When we come here from our drug lives, we feel this spiritual plunge sometimes. And when we're very active it helps to keep us from plunging too low. Sometimes I get down on my knees and I tell God, 'My God, I can't go on because my burden is too heavy.' But after I speak to God, cry many tears, and then finally get up from praying, I feel my weight lifted, that I am cleansed and renewed so I can go on. The Lord renews me."

To create a safe space for the addicted to heal, the Disciples' rehabilitation program provides both extensive time dedicated to spiritual growth, by structuring prayers and Bible study into each day, and obligatory church attendance at every church service, some half dozen per week. The program's leaders also encourage this environment by showing love though word and deed, including much hugging—an act unimaginable on Miami's drug-infested streets. Men in recovery learn also that they can be supportive of one another; indeed, mentoring is built into the program, but it is not just how-to mentoring, it is emotional mentoring through both hugs and tough love.

In addition to transforming addicts' emotional, spiritual, and social lifestyle, the Disciples introduce extreme order into their disordered lives. This technique is common to other recovery programs but is nonetheless critical to the rehabilitation center's success. The street addict's day is typically chaotic with no set times for eating, sleeping, and working. The recovering addict is subjected to the opposite extreme: a highly regimented day wherein every activity is programmed and during which little free time is permitted. A common refrain among recoverees is "Free time is the Devil's time," or, as a graduate of the Disciples' program told me, "When we have nothing to keep us busy we often get bad thoughts in our minds and we think about the past. So when we are busy it's much more difficult to have these negative thoughts."

Keeping busy does not solve the problem for addicts over the long term because, unless they can learn to apply structure to their time and take responsibility for their actions, they are just as likely to return to old habits after they leave a rehabilitation program. Pastor Abram explained to me that instilling discipline was a key element of recovery that the Disciples learned from another program called Teen Challenge. He noted, "The addict is a manipulative person, so you have to tie him down, not physically, but you have to secure him emotionally. When they do something wrong you have to discipline them." I asked, "Like with kids?" And he responded, "Kind of like with kids. They are kind of like kids because the drug addicts have no discipline. The homeless don't have any discipline. . . . They live their life, but they have no responsibilities, no discipline. They'll sleep the whole day. They'll mess up the whole night, sleep the day, and at night do all sorts of crazy stuff. So now they come to a program where everything changes, and so their mentality has to change. In the morning they have to wake up and at night time they sleep. . . . Some of them have never worked in their life, so you have got to show them how, show them a better way, a better alternative."

Teaching structure and discipline is a conscious effort to adapt recovering addicts to the rhythms of the working life, changes that will be necessary for them to be successful outside the program. But the Disciples' program goes a critical step beyond other substance-abuse treatment programs that structure recovering addicts' days; it requires them to do chores at their facility. The Disciples enjoin the muchachos to provide most of the labor needed for the church's activities. The men in rehab do all the church's janitorial work, but this is just the beginning. As they progress in their treatment they are invited to teach Bible study classes, perform most baptisms, help run the summer Bible camp, prepare church meals, and much more. They even head many of the church's ministries such as transportation, security, parking, and music. The church benefits from their work, but the men told me over and over that they do too. "Working is part of therapy," Abram explained. "It gives them the feeling that they are worth something. See, all of these people have been rejected by society, and now they are lifted up and their self-esteem restored through this work. . . . That's our purpose—restoring them back to society, restoring them back to their family."

The combination of service and spiritual renewal helps rehabilitate the addicts while building their CSC within the extended family atmosphere of the church and its programs. Arguably, the most important mileage on their road to redemption is the work they do for the Blessings food ministry. An enormous and arduous undertaking, the work involves finding, trucking, storing, and organizing tons of food each week into the boxes that are distributed at Thursday night church services. The work is grueling and unpaid, at least in monetary terms. Thus, it is no surprise that newcomers to the program often resent the work. One of the Blessings' program organizers told me,

At the beginning when I started to do all this work I thought to myself, "What am I doing working this hard without earning any money?" And this bothered me at first, and it's the same for many of the new guys. There are many who get over it when we talk to them and tell them that they're doing this work for God and it's also of value to them in the process of improving themselves. But some of them can't take it, and they leave because they're not paid. They don't want to work for free; they don't want to accept that what we're doing is God's work and we do it to change our lives. In the future we will be better men, good workers, and will be ready so that when we look for paid work we'll be able to submit to our bosses. We'll learn to communicate, to be able to work with others in those jobs.

When I asked him if this really resolves the friction, he admitted that many newcomers to the program need additional mentoring, but as they mature "their enthusiasm grows and so does their desire to help others. We give out so much food to so many people that this work makes us participants in the church, and we feel pleased because we are doing something we never did before, we are helping others."

The rehabilitation center is truly the backbone, heart, and soul of the Disciples' community of faith. It also encapsulates the multiple strategies the Disciples employ for bringing people into their community and connecting them to it, preparing them to serve others and then deploying them in the broader community. In many ways the development of CSC among the Disciples is a circle. People outside the church are brought in, transformed, and then sent out to do good deeds in the very communities they are from, and beyond.

The Disciples have a growing reputation for this work in Miami and one that is well deserved. They are an excellent example of how one individual can make a huge difference. In this case I am referring to Flor's early Rescue with Love ministry, but the same words could be applied to hundreds of other church members. Still, more is needed to cultivate and sustain CSC than the energies of one individual, no matter how passionate. The Disciples have learned a variety of ways to multiply their CSC by inspiring others. It is important to ask, however, if there are any negative consequences to the path they have taken, to identify pitfalls that other congregations might encounter as well. In the case of the Disciples, there is one ministry that seems to have withered for lack of attention during the years of building the rehabilitation center and the Blessings food distribution program, the youth group. Several young adults in the church related this history to me, which appears to be largely the diversion of Abram from youth pastor to associate pastor in the church, during which time he assumed much more responsibility for the food and substance-abuse programs. Numerous appeals were made to the congregation to help find a replacement for Abram so the youth program would return to its dynamic status, and toward the very end of my fieldwork these prayers were answered with a new youth pastor.

Conclusion

The Refugees and Disciples demonstrate the importance that religion has for immigrants as they adjust to a new environment. The Refugees and Disciples also illustrate the fluidity of CSC over time and the commonsensical though not often stated fact that different varieties of social capital can and typically do co-exist. For these particular congregations, denomination does not necessarily matter that much in the formation of CSC. The fact that the Refugees are Seventh-Day Adventists from Cuba, where they were discriminated against arguably more than other denominations, can be used to explain their highly inward orientation. However, the Disciples held a similar orientation until inspired to move into a new direction.²

Leadership, not merely professional but particularly lay leadership, its cultivation and its application, does matter in these congregations. The leadership development programs of both the Refugees' and Disciples' churches draw people into webs of interaction. The great difference is that among the Disciples these webs are spun to include diverse individuals *and institutions of the greater society*, whereas the Refugees continue to weave theirs into a shelter, a sanctuary of continuity amidst stormy seas.

What made the difference? I have discussed many factors but save one for the conclusion to highlight. In the United States famous books and films resonate a theme that is very American—the importance of individuals, specifically charismatic leaders. Whether it is the Little Engine that Could, Mr. Smith Goes to Washington, or the Reverend Jerry Falwell inspiring the Moral Majority to jump into politics, hard-working, dedicated individuals are viewed as inspirational. Thousands of sermons calling upon congregants to do the Lord's work, like the "Brother 100" sermon from Pastor Moreno, are preached each week yet inspire little real civic work. But, as in the Disciples' case and, indeed, as in different prophets' cases, the presence and persistence of one real, palpable, inspirational figure, a "charismatic prophet" in Weber's terms, can catalyze and transform an entire congregation or people. Yet even then the Disciples' charismatic prophet had little impact until his woman congregant, Flor, forced him to adjust his habitus to her concerns. Charisma in sync with congregants' habitus can mobilize an extraordinary amount of civic social capital.

NOTES

1. The names of the congregations, pastors, and congregants have been changed to make them more difficult to identify and thus protect them from publicity, despite the fact that their consent to use their real names was obtained. The details written about them, however, are true.

2. This chapter also demonstrates the importance of obtaining historical detail of particular congregations. Time is one important element that is often insufficiently examined when doing research over months and not years. The historical information presented on the congregations in this chapter helps overcome these ethnographic limitations. For example, in the case of the Disciples' history, it documents how the church shifted dramatically from a sole emphasis on bonding social capital to a place

that cultivates all three varieties. Had it been researched at the start of Pastor González's ministry it would likely have resembled the Refugees today.

REFERENCES

Brooks, A. C., and G. B. Lewis. 2001. Giving, Volunteering, and Mistrusting Government. *Journal of Policy Analysis and Management* 20(4): 765–769.

Ebaugh, H. R., and J. S. Chafetz. 1999. Agents for Cultural Reproduction and Structural Change: The Ironic Role of Women in Immigrant Religious Institutions. *Social Forces* 78(2): 585–613.

——, eds. 2000. *Religion and the New Immigrants: Continuities and Adaptations in Immigrant Congregations.* Walnut Creek, CA: Alta Mira Press.

Ecklund, E. H. 2005. The "Good" American: Religion and Civic Life for Korean Americans. *Dissertation Abstracts International, A: The Humanities and Social Sciences* 65(10): 4006-A.

——. 2005. Models of Civic Responsibility: Korean Americans in Congregations with Different Ethnic Compositions. *Journal for the Scientific Study of Religion* 44(1): 15–28.

Grenier, G. J., and L. Pérez. 2002. *Legacy of Exile: Cubans in the United States.* Needham Heights, MA: Allyn & Bacon.

Kim, R. Y. 2006. *God's New Whiz Kids? Korean American Evangelicals on Campus.* New York: New York University Press.

Portes, A., and A. Stepick. 1993. *City on the Edge: The Transformation of Miami.* Berkeley: University of California Press.

Stepick, A. 2005. God Is Apparently Not Dead. The Obvious, the Emergent, and the Unknown in Immigration and Religion. In *Immigrant Faiths: Transforming Religious Life in America,* ed. K. Leonard, A. Stepick, M. A. Vasquez, and J. Holdaway, 11–37. Lanham, MD: Alta Mira Press.

Uslaner, E. M. 2002. Religion and Civic Engagement in Canada and the United States. *Journal for the Scientific Study of Religion* 41(2): 239–254.

Wilson, J., and T. Janoski. 1997. The Contribution of Religion to Volunteer Work. *Sociology of Religion* 56(2): 137–152.

Wuthnow, R. 2004. *Saving America? Faith-Based Services and the Future of Civil Society.* Princeton, NJ: Princeton University Press.

3

Refugee Catholicism in Little Haiti

Miami's Notre Dame d'Haiti Catholic Church

TERRY REY AND ALEX STEPICK

On October 27, 1983, a Polish American Catholic priest named Thomas Wenski led 140 Haitian immigrants in somber procession beneath the majestic oaks that grace the churchyard of Notre Dame d'Haiti Catholic Church in Little Haiti, one of Miami's most depressed inner-city neighborhoods. There they joined hands in a circle and prayerfully erected a large wooden cross in their center to commemorate the 33 Haitian refugees who died when their sailboat, *La Nativité*, capsized just off the South Florida coast at night exactly two years and one day before. Horrifyingly, their bodies had washed up on Hillsboro Beach by the following morning. "This wasn't only for those who died aboard *La Nativité*," noted Wenski. "It's for the hundreds whose bodies were never found" in other unsuccessful attempts to reach the United States (Vaughan 1983b).

In the fall of 1999, Monsignor Gérard Darbouze, a Haitian priest who became pastor of Notre Dame upon Wenski's investiture as auxiliary bishop of Miami in 1997, oversaw the erection of a foreboding black iron fence around the lush ten-acre churchyard. For years, homeless people, drug dealers, and sex workers had made free use of the leafy space at night, prompting Darbouze to raise the fence. This was his first major undertaking upon inheriting Notre Dame's pastorate from Wenski, whose liberal politics had irked Darbouze since they founded the church together in 1981. Fortunately for the neighborhood's needy Haitian immigrants, Notre Dame and the Haitian Catholic Center continue to offer vital social services, thanks to a healthy dose of institutional inertia that resulted from a confluence of Wenski's rich personal stock of civic social capital and the rise of liberation theology in popular Haitian ecclesiology. This confluence created one of the most successful, socially engaged ethnic parishes in contemporary North America.

The juxtaposition of the wooden cross and the iron fence speaks symbolically about the crucial role that clerical religious leadership plays in any religious community's service to the poor and the downtrodden. As S. N. Eisenstadt notes: "the test of any charismatic leader lies not only in his ability to create a single event or great movement, but also in his ability to leave a continuous impact on an institutional structure—to transform any institutional setting by infusing into it some of his charismatic vision, by investing the regular orderly offices, or aspects of social organization, with some of his charismatic qualities and aura" (1968, xxi). The vibrant survival, behind the iron fence, of Notre Dame's social service agencies, which continue to receive some one thousand beneficiaries each day, is thus testimony to the "ethical charisma," to use Weber's term, that Wenski infused into Notre Dame.

This chapter has two main objectives. First, by exploring Weber's classic concept of charisma and its implication for religious-based service to immigrants in Miami, we trace the history of Notre Dame and the adjoined Pierre Toussaint Haitian Catholic Center to illustrate how ethical charisma, embodied in this case by Wenski, is transformed into civic social capital. We are especially interested in understanding the decisive fused influence of individual clerical religious leadership and popular ecclesiology on the establishment and sustenance of humanitarian services for needy inner-city immigrants, in this case Haitians in Miami. Although humanitarianism is clearly at the heart of the Christian gospel, not all religious leaders give it the same degree of importance. Weber's notion of charisma helps explain why this is.

Our second objective is to demonstrate that Notre Dame d'Haiti Catholic Church, far from being merely an insular ethnic parish whose social action is limited to assisting refugees in their myriad struggles in Miami, is an integral part of the transnational Haitian religious field. In the words of one journalist, "Notre Dame has not only been a place of worship, but a place to build strength and solidarity within the Haitian community. It is an education center, a community center, protest center, and celebration center—the spiritual headquarters of Haitian Miami" (San Martin 1991a). Just as Haitian Miami is a transnational community, its "spiritual headquarters" is a transnational locus with important and longstanding connections and commitments to the struggle for justice and human rights in the Haitian homeland. This struggle has itself also gone far in shaping the very nature of Notre Dame d'Haiti.

The Prehistory of the Haitian Catholic Mission in Miami: 1972–1982

Haitian refugees began arriving in South Florida in significant numbers in the early 1970s and by the end of that decade numbered around fifty thousand, most of them residing in Miami, a modern American city just seven hundred miles from Haitian shores. In response, the Catholic Archdiocese of Miami,[1] then under the stewardship of Archbishop Coleman Carroll, commissioned an

African American priest named Charles Jackson, a native of Jacksonville, Florida, to say the first Haitian Mass in the city in 1973 at the Church of Corpus Christi in Miami's Allapattah neighborhood. The first African American to pastor a Catholic parish in Florida (Taft 1986), Jackson had served for a time as a missionary in Martinique, where he learned the French Eucharistic liturgy. In 1973 he delivered a Mass in French for the fifty or sixty Haitians gathered at Corpus Christi, some of them directed to Jackson's parish by clergy from other parts of the city. Within five years the Haitian population's further growth in Miami led Archbishop Carroll to request a priest from the Oblate Fathers of New England and Eastern Canada, who had for several decades been active as missionaries in Haiti. The Oblates sent Father Joseph Hamel, who said the first Catholic Mass in Haitian Creole in Miami at the Cathedral of St. Mary in 1978 for some four hundred communicants. By the end of that year the Roman Catholic Archdiocese of Miami added a second weekly Haitian Mass at the Church of St. Bartholomew in Miramar, some twenty miles north of downtown Miami.

In 1978, Archbishop Edward McCarthy, Coleman's successor as of 1977, established the Pierre Toussaint Haitian Catholic Center to provide numerous much-needed social services to the area's twenty thousand Haitians, most of them refugees. A second Oblate, Father Marcel Peloquin, arrived the following year and was named director of the center. Peloquin had served for twenty-seven years as a missionary in the Haitian Catholic Diocese of Les Cayes, where he founded the rural Mission of Chantal. The archdiocese also in 1978 assigned a recently ordained native Floridian, Father Thomas Wenski, to serve at Corpus Christi.

Being the son of Polish immigrants, Wenski was especially sensitive to the concerns of South Florida's newly arriving Haitians: "I've always considered myself an ethnic. As a kid, I was always the Pollack. I wore my Polishness as a badge of honor. That sense of ethnicity always helped me when I learned Spanish to identify with the Cuban community and also when I learned Creole to identify with the Haitian community" (quoted in Schaffer 1989). The first Creole that Wenski learned was the Eucharistic liturgy, later gaining proficiency through coursework at Florida International University and during a three-month ministerial residency in southern Haiti, where he replaced a vacationing priest in the village of Ducis. Soon Peloquin and Wenski were also ministering to Haitians outside of the cathedral at the Krome Detention Center, where interdicted Haitian migrants were detained, and in Fort Lauderdale, Belle Glade, Immokalee, Delray, and Lantana.[2]

The four year period from 1978 to 1982 was decisive for Haitian Catholicism in South Florida. Deeply impressed by the intense spirituality with which the sixty Haitians would sing Creole hymns during his ministry at Corpus Christi, Wenski successfully petitioned for a tri-lingual Mass at the parish, and soon he was saying Mass in Haitian Creole each Thursday night. Two years later, in response to Archbishop Carroll's plea to the Catholic Church of Haiti for clergy to help serve Miami's swelling Haitian population, Father Gérard Darbouze, a native of Les Cayes who had been a priest of the Haitian Diocese of Jérémie, joined Peloquin and Wenski in Miami (by now Hamel had returned to Canada). The year prior (1979), Wenski was chosen to lead the newly consecrated Notre Dame d'Haiti Catholic Church, which was still without a home independent of the cathedral. He was also named director of the Archdiocesan Haitian Apostolate. The three priests, Wenski, Peloquin, and Darbouze, were thus the founding fathers of both Notre Dame and the Haitian Catholic Center, which was housed across the street from the Cathedral of St. Mary in what was then its rectory. By 1980, they were every morning saying Masses in Haitian Creole in the cathedral, and other Creole Masses less frequently in Allapattah, Pompano Beach, Belle Glade, and Fort Lauderdale. The Haitian Catholic Center of the Archdiocese of Miami had thus established itself as the mother ship of Haitian Catholics in South Florida by the early 1980s, precisely when the largest single wave of Haitian refugees to reach the United States crested.[3]

To Wenski, 1981 was a year of "Divine providential timing" for the Haitian Catholic Mission in Miami.[4] May of that year witnessed the last graduating class of girls from Notre Dame Academy at the corner of Northeast Sixty-second Street and Northeast Second Avenue.[5] Then the school merged with Archbishop Curley High School because of dwindling enrollment, and the archdiocese decided to cede the campus to the Haitian Catholic Mission. Because more than twenty-five thousand Haitian refugees had arrived in South Florida the year prior, Wenski naturally perceived the hand of providence in the transfer of the school grounds to the Haitian Apostolate. Notre Dame d'Haiti was thus established as a "quasi parish," with Wenski as its pastor.[6] Masses in Creole were immediately said in the church that August for the mission's one hundred members, though Notre Dame's official consecration was not made until November 15 by Archbishop McCarthy.[7] By 1982, Notre Dame had absorbed Corpus Christi's weekly Creole Masses and the Cathedral of St. Mary's daily morning Creole Mass, offering in the new quasi parish two Creole Masses per day.

The school cafeteria was transformed into the church, while the two stories of classrooms were used to house the multitude of social service programs offered by the Haitian Catholic Center: English as a Second Language and Creole literacy classes, job placement counseling, health screenings, legal assistance, etc. Almost immediately, the center's service programs were drawing hundreds of beneficiaries. Meanwhile, Haitian Masses continued to be said at the cathedral, just two miles north, as they do to this day, largely because Wenski realized that some Haitian Catholics would be reluctant to make a former school cafeteria their spiritual home. Ultimately, Haitians with such ecclesiological predilections were relatively few, however, and Notre Dame became the *axis mundi* for thousands of Haitian Catholics in Miami.[8]

Henry Wieman and Regina Wescott-Wieman argue that during any "period of deeply disturbing transition . . . religion feels the need of leadership in ways and degrees not recognized before" (1935, 46). In the late 1970s and early 1980s, thousands of Haitian refugees arrived by boat to the shores of South Florida as part of one of the most "deeply disturbing" transitional experiences ever known by immigrants in the United States. Despite their flight from some of the worst poverty and oppression in modern times in the Haiti of the Duvaliers, the American "melting pot" was uncharacteristically xenophobic toward poor Haitians. Because Haitians traditionally turn with great respect to priests and pastors in times of need, desperate refugees in Miami were especially open to being swayed by charismatic religious leadership. In them, Wenski found a flock: "The masses were my market."[9] For these masses Wenski served quite effectively as an "ethical prophet," in Weberian terms: "an instrument for the proclamation of a god and his will, be this a concrete command or abstract norm" (Weber [1922] 1963, 55). Wenski effectively, and quite naturally, transformed his ethical charisma into civic social capital, which was concomitantly richly nurtured by the popular ecclesiology of his flock, whose church in Haiti was then in the midst of being radically transformed by liberation theology.[10]

From the time he became director of the Haitian Apostolate for the Archdiocese of Miami in 1979, Wenski began lobbying for the establishment of an ethnic parish for Haitians. Although the U.S. Catholic Church had achieved marked success with ethnic parishes during the late-nineteenth- and early-twentieth-century waves of immigrants, support for such parishes had largely waned by the 1970s as immigrants assimilated and as their neighborhood enclaves became more ethnically diverse. For many ecclesiologists, the ethnic parish was thought to have served its purpose and was thus obsolete. Archbishop Carroll, for one, opposed the idea, arguing that when Cubans first immigrated in significant numbers to Miami they had no ethnic parish; since this had not negatively affected the Cuban apostolate, why should the archdiocese do any differently for Haitians? Undeterred, Wenski pressed on, arguing for a Haitian ethnic parish: "Immigrants integrate into American society best from positions of strength, which is precisely what the ethnic church fosters. . . . Establishing an ethnic parish was key to giving Haitians a sense of identity, and a sense of belonging. . . . The whole idea was to make the Church visible to Haitians and to make Haitians visible to the Church." In the end, Wenksi won and an ethnic parish for Haitians in Miami became a reality at Notre Dame d'Haiti. "From then on," comments Wenski, "they [the archdiocese] basically let me do whatever I wanted."[11]

Transnational Prayer and Protest: Haiti and Little Haiti in an Era of Radical Change, 1982–1994

There is a modern Haitian American proverb that Monsignor Wenski has been known to quote from time to time over the years: "When Haiti sneezes, Little

Haiti catches a cold." Because it was so closely attuned to, and created by, the social and political upheaval that rocked Haiti in the 1980s, the Notre Dame community in Little Haiti cannot be soundly understood without focusing careful attention on the remarkable events that brought to an end thirty years of brutal dynastic dictatorship in Haiti under the Duvaliers.[12]

As it had throughout Latin America, liberation theology took firm root in Haiti in the late 1970s, creating a new breed of Catholic priests in the country who envisioned the church as the prophetic "Bride of Christ," who should exercise a "preferential option for the poor." For the first time in Haitian history, the Catholic Church confronted the poverty and injustice that had forever plagued Haitian society,[13] the very forces that drove thousands of Haitians to seek asylum in Miami in the late 1970s and early 1980s. Many of the first generation of congregants at Notre Dame thus brought this new conception of church with them, and their expectations of a socially and politically engaged church resonated harmoniously with Wenski's own ecclesiology, hence its actualization at Notre Dame d'Haiti.

After four centuries of fairly uniform complicity in the sociopolitical oppression and injustice that have always characterized Haitian history, the Haitian Catholic Church completed a remarkable 180-degree turnaround by 1980 from being a major source of legitimation for the dominant, its traditional *raison'être*, to being an effective catalyst of hope and change for Haiti's impoverished masses. The Conference of Haitian Religious (Conférence Haïtienne des Religieux—CHR) was formed by a group of progressive Haitian clerics as "the collective conscience of the Haitian Church during the Jean-Claude presidency" (Greene 1993, 106). A December 4, 1980, CHR communiqué boldly proclaimed, "The hour has come where we must make a choice that will bring the Haitian Church to a new turning point. The choice is clear: it is the preferential option for the poor." The Haitian Catholic Church must thereby "break with a past infamous for its complicity with the powerful" (Conférence des Religieux Haïtiens 1990). The CHR represented the collective voice of the flourishing base church communities that were springing up in Haiti beginning in 1976.[14] In Haiti, Tilegliz, or TKL (*Ti kominite legliz*, "little church community"), was the equivalent of the base church communities that were the concrete result of liberation theology in Central and South America. By the early 1980s, there were over five thousand church-based communities in Haiti. They were inspired by the liberation theology and ethical prophecy of priests like Jean-Bertrand Aristide and driven internally largely by women, who rose to the fore of politics in the Tilegliz movement like never before in Haitian history.

The visit of Pope John Paul II to Port-au-Prince on March 9, 1983, greatly encouraged Tilegliz to push forward in the anti-Duvalierist struggle. Much to the chagrin of Baby Doc, who had hoped that the pontiff's visit would have a stabilizing effect for his already shaken regime, John Paul II's speech to thousands of enthusiastic Haitians made an unmistakable plea for an end to the oppression upon which the social inequalities in Haiti have always depended. The pope declared in French, "*Il faut que quelque chose change ici*" (Something has to change here), words that would forever have a resounding echo for Haitians. Among John Paul's most forceful exhortations was this: "a deep need for justice, a better distribution of goods, more equitable organization of society and more participation" (Juan Pablo II 1986, 192–193).

The pontiff's historic visit to Port-au-Prince was closely monitored by Haitians in Miami, where the Notre Dame community was especially overjoyed to hear their pope denounce the abuses of the Duvalier regime. Wenski himself was in Haiti for the occasion, where days later he managed to interview Gérard Duclerville, a Catholic lay activist who had been imprisoned and tortured by the Haitian government (Martinez 1983).[15] Wenski's recording of the Duclerville interview was played on Haitian radio in Miami, with one hundred copies made and sold at Notre Dame. The flip side of the cassette was John Paul II's homily at the Port-au-Prince airport. Wenski later published the interview with photos in *Lavwa Katolik*, Florida's only Creole newspaper, which he founded and edited. In response, the Haitian government lodged a formal complaint to the Archdiocese of Miami, recognizing that although located abroad, Notre Dame d'Haiti was clearly integral to the popular struggle against the Duvalier regime (McCarthy 1985a). It also served to establish a harmonious rhythm between Wenski's ethical charisma and his flock's liberation ecclesiology: "That's probably when I proved to the Haitians here that I'd paid my dues. . . . I was saying Mass in Creole every week. Whenever something happened in Haiti, we said Mass for the victims. I think that gave us credibility in the community" (quoted in Viglucci 1995).

Emboldened by its pontiff, the Haitian Catholic Church, especially progressive, courageous members of the clergy, both Haitian and foreign, like Fathers Hugo Triest, Antoine Adrien, Jean-Bertrand Aristide, Jean-Marie Vincent, Gilles Danroc, Max Dominique, and Bishop Willy Romélus (all of whom at one point in time have visited and/or said Mass at Notre Dame in Miami), "played an important leadership role" in the events of late 1985 and early 1986 that precipitated and ultimately resulted in the departure of Jean-Claude Duvalier (Greene 1993, 191).

Haitian Catholic protest against the Duvalier regime took on transnational form, especially at Notre Dame in Miami, where Wenski's sermons often criticized the regime's human rights abuses. At a special Wednesday morning Mass and prayer vigil called for by the six bishops of the Haitian Catholic Church on February 9, 1983, for example, the Notre Dame pastor employed a Haitian proverb to express his view of the deteriorating political situation in Haiti: "If the bull knew its force, it would not let the little boy tie a rope around its neck . . . and it seems the bull is recognizing its force" (Wenski, quoted in Balmaseda 1983). The bull was symbolic of the rising popular Catholic Church in Haiti, while the boy symbolized none other than Baby Doc, Jean-Claude Duvalier, *Président à Vie* (President for Life). A local Duvalierist radio station, WGLY (widely believed to be financed by the Haitian government), accused Wenski of inciting violence with such preaching and aired threats to the Notre Dame pastor (Vaughan 1983a). Notre Dame's own radio broadcast, *Chita Tande* (Sit, Listen), responded simply and indirectly by keeping Miami Haitians abreast of political developments in their homeland.

Meanwhile, in the summer of 1985, the teetering Duvalier regime deported three Belgian Catholic priests for criticizing its government: Fathers Hugo Triest, Ivan Pollefeyt, and Jean Hostens. One week after being expelled from Haiti, Pollefeyt and Hostens came to Miami to say Mass in Little Haiti at Notre Dame on August 4, 1985. In preparation for their visit, on the day prior Wenski encouraged a day of fasting and led a candlelight procession as a gesture of support to the church in Haiti, explaining it to be "a gesture of solidarity with the church in Haiti, and a way of giving moral support to the priests to show them that the Haitian people, if not the government, are with them" (quoted in McCarthy 1985b).[16]

On the eve of Duvalier's fall, hundreds of Haitians were gathering daily in celebration before Notre Dame d'Haiti, chanting, "Duvalier is gone. Praise the Lord!" At times their joyful anticipation of the regime's fall was dramatic, such as on January 30, 1986, when about one thousand people took to the streets to stage a mock funeral procession, "stuffing a straw man with newspapers and parading through the streets, playing bongo drums and singing a Haitian funeral dirge" (Fisher 1986). On February 7, 1986, their prayers were answered when Jean-Claude Duvalier was whisked off by the U.S. government to exile in France. Two days later, on the first Sunday after Duvalier's departure from Haiti, an extraordinary Mass was held in Miami at Notre Dame d'Haiti. Archbishop McCarthy recalled that he "woke up early Friday and heard a lot of happy horns tooting. Haiti is free—hallelujah." McCarthy said Mass for over three hours before two thousand ecstatic Haitians in the Notre Dame churchyard, proclaiming in English on behalf of the archdiocese that "we will be with you in your joy and your anxiety. We love you and admire your pilgrimage to freedom." In an outpouring of religious and political faith, the chants of thousands of Haitians of "*Libete! Libete!*" (Freedom! Freedom!) echoed from Notre Dame and throughout Little Haiti (Cottman 1986).[17]

With the Duvalier dictatorship toppled, a new Haitian Constitution was ratified in 1987, and hopes abounded for a renaissance of justice and human rights in the homeland. Haitians on both sides of the Straits of Florida were cautiously optimistic when elections were called for November of that year, finding it difficult to place any trust in the Haitian army, who remained in control of the country under General Henry Namphy. In the days leading up to the elections, Haitians in Miami were praying "practically around the clock" for the peace at the polls in the homeland. "For this thing to come off," noted a realistic Wenski, "it will need a miracle" (quoted in Gaither 1987).[18] Prayers for a peaceful vote in post-Duvalier Haiti went unanswered, however, and the Notre Dame faithful were once more transformed into protestors after soldiers and paramilitary agents opened fire on voters in Port-au-Prince, killing at least thirty-four on election day, Sunday, November 29, and causing the abortion of the elections. Six days later, some six thousand Haitians gathered in Little Haiti around Notre Dame to embark on a march of protest against the Namphy regime (Evans 1987). Nothing had changed. Whatever joyous smoke still wafted in the transnational Haitian air following Jean-Claude Duvalier's ouster the year before and whatever exuberant hope remained for a new era of justice and human rights in Haiti were cleared away on "Bloody Sunday" in 1987. Almost naturally, a series of constitutionally illegitimate regimes proceeded to exercise state power in Haiti, the nation's rigid class structure remained in tact, the poverty of the masses somehow worsened, and leading observers began to speak of Haitian politics as "Duvalierism without Duvalier."[19]

Led by Aristide, Tileglis nonetheless continued the struggle for justice in the same uncompromising spirit embodied by the CHR's 1980 communiqué and the pope's 1983 speech in Port-au-Prince. The Haitian Catholic bishops, meanwhile, were widely believed to have been exhorted by the Vatican to tone down their church's political activism. Excepting Bishop Romélus, they endeavored to silence Aristide, eventually having him banished from the Salesian Order and ordering him transferred to a rural parish far from the politically explosive shantytowns of the capital. Now bereft of the support of the church hierarchy, Aristide became the target of a number of orchestrated attacks because of his outspokenness against the abuses of the Haitian army and a series of corrupt regimes that succeeded the Duvaliers. Among these acts of violence, the September 11, 1988, attack during Mass on Aristide's parish church, St. Jean Bosco, located in one of the capital's poorest neighborhoods and long an epicenter of Tileglis activities, represents "one of the most lurid crimes ever perpetrated against the church in Latin America" (Farmer 1994, 185). Thirteen of Aristide's parishioners were left dead.

The plan to devitalize Aristide, however, proved a total failure because, as Paul Farmer writes, the church hierarchy's mistreatment of Aristide only made him seem more prophetic to the Haitian masses: "Aristide himself, shorn of his church, had already become something much larger than a radical priest. White-robed, hands outstretched Christ-like as he preached, he had become pure symbol: the righteous leader in a nation shorn of them, the pure-hearted bringer of Justice" (1994, 60). The faithful at Notre Dame in Little Haiti, along with their pastor Father Wenski, were similarly tremendously inspired by Aristide. *Miami Herald* columnist Andreas Viglucci explained: "In 1983, Wenski came across the writings of a young seminarian named Jean-Bertrand Aristide in a Creole church monthly, biblical commentaries that had a lot of applications to Haiti. Wenski reprinted the articles in a Creole newspaper that he published at the time. For many Haitians in Miami, it was their initial exposure to the priest who was to become the first democratically elected president of the country" (1995).

Following the 1988 massacre at St. Jean Bosco, rumors reached Miami that the Vatican had ordered Aristide's transfer to Montréal. In response, Father Gérard Jean-Juste, a radical Haitian Catholic priest who was director of Little Haiti's Center for Haitian Refugees, organized a protest calling upon Archbishop McCarthy to intervene and combat Aristide's transfer. In the words of Jean-Juste, the people of Little Haiti knew well that "Aristide is the heart of the liberation movement in Haiti. Take the heart and you kill the body" (quoted in Dibble 1988). To their relief, the transfer never transpired, and Aristide remained in Haiti, destined for the presidency.

Aristide's enormous popularity culminated with his election to the Haitian presidency in late 1990, in the first truly democratic election in the history of the Republic of Haiti. The attempts on his life and his treatment at the hands of the Catholic hierarchy served only to enhance his status in the eyes of the popular masses. And on December 16, 1990, the thirty-seven-year-old "Titid" (Little Aristide), as he was affectionately called by his supporters, garnered more than 67 percent of the vote, with Marc Bazin, the second-place finisher among the twelve candidates, winning little more than 10 percent.

The election of Jean-Bertrand Aristide sparked jubilant celebrations in Little Haiti and throughout the Haitian diaspora. On February 7, 1991, the day of Aristide's inauguration, Notre Dame d'Haiti was packed with jubilant worshippers for a Mass to celebrate the occasion. Following the Mass, a young acolyte named Dorcély Jean hoisted an eighty-pound, nine-foot wooden cross upon his shoulders and led a procession of several hundred people from the church eight blocks to a central intersection in Little Haiti, Northeast Second Avenue to Northeast Fifty-fourth Street, where the crowd had blossomed to a sea of red and blue, Haiti's national colors. Jean's words summed up the collective hope of the Haitian faithful: "I'm so happy. The cross is very heavy, but I don't feel it because we have a new life. That's why I carry the cross. To thank God" (quoted in San Martin 1991a).[20]

Jean's joy and that of millions of disenfranchised Haitians in the homeland and the diaspora was once again short lived. It was of little surprise to anyone at all familiar with Haitian history when Aristide was overthrown in a coup d'etat led by General Raoul Cédras with the backing of important elements of the Haitian economic elite on September 19, 1991, a mere nine months after the former parish priest's historic election as president. Because they took Aristide's vision of a new social order to be little more than incendiary Marxist promotion of class warfare, the traditional lords of the Haitian world did away with the menace. Aristide would spend the next three years in exile in Washington, D.C., where he became the target of a multifaceted character assassination. An Organization of American States' economic embargo and later a much broader United Nations' embargo were imposed on Haiti. But the traditional Haitian power sectors maintained their social posture of domination relatively unencumbered by the sanctions. The poor, meanwhile, took the brunt of both the economic hardship caused by the embargo and the bloody wave of politically motivated violence unleashed by the junta against the pro-Aristide left.[21] What reaction did the Catholic Church, once so instrumental in the ouster of the very powers which Aristide's ethical prophecy trumped, have to the 1991 coup? "Although the Church was not an active participant in the overthrow of the president, it is unlikely to have shed many tears at the departure of its increasingly hostile Brother" (Greene 1993, 246). In fact, the Vatican would become the only nation-state to recognize the government that toppled Haiti's first truly democratically elected president.

Within days of the coup a new wave of sea-faring refugees began to flee Haiti as the Cédras regime committed some of Haitian history's most unspeakable brutality against Aristide supporters. By early December 1991, the U.S. Coast Guard had interdicted over six thousand Haitian migrants who were detained at the U.S. military base in Guantanamo Bay, Cuba. As part of an appeal by the United States Catholic Conference, a special offering collected one thousand dollars at Notre Dame, which Monsignor Wenski used to purchase 250 Creole hymnals to bring to Guantanamo, where he made a pastoral visit celebrating Mass in all six refugee camps, teaching military chaplains the Creole Eucharistic liturgy, and recruiting assistants for them from among the refugees (David 1991). He returned to Little Haiti with more than six hundred handwritten notes from the refugees, notifying family in Miami of their whereabouts. Some of the notes supplied phone numbers of relatives for Wenski to contact. Others he read at Mass and on Creole radio. One of them read, "Tell mommy not to cry. I am still alive" (Markowitz 1991).

Hundreds of others in Haiti were not so fortunate and fell victim to the murderous junta. Among those who did manage to flee were some Tilegliz leaders like Father Gilles Danroc, who was driven from his parish in Haiti's Artibonite Valley by the Haitian military. With some of them residing at Notre Dame for weeks while awaiting word that it was safe to return to Haiti, the Little Haiti church became something of a command center for Tilegliz in the diaspora. As *Miami Herald* reporter Harold Maass described it: "Danroc and a handful of others have been able to stay involved in their struggle by running an underground communications network, of sorts, out of a church office in Little Haiti. . . . They use the office's fax machine, phones, and computer to exchange dispatches on conditions in Haiti with activists back home and religious and human rights organizations throughout Europe and North America" (1992).

Over the ensuing three years of junta rule in Haiti, Notre Dame remained engaged in the struggle spiritually, politically, and socially. Not only were frequent Masses said for victims of the coup, but funds were raised to aid them.[22] Wenski, meanwhile, regularly used both the radio and the pulpit to denounce the illegitimate junta in Haiti.[23] The summer of 1994 was especially taxing on the community, as the Clinton administration heightened its efforts to oust the junta, which responded by ramping up its oppression, driving a massive exodus of over twenty thousand refugees to sea. In a gruesome parting shot, the junta assassinated longtime Tiegliz leader Father Jean-Marie Vincent on August 29, 1994, just weeks before the United States finally occupied Haiti and sent Cédras and other members of the Haitian army's high command into exile and restored Aristide to power. At Notre Dame a memorial Mass was said that September for Vincent and the thousands of others who were murdered in Haiti from September 1991 to September 1994 (Casimir 1994).

The Changing of the Guard: Notre Dame d'Haiti in the Post-Wenski Era

With Wenski no longer at Notre Dame, up went the black iron fence, for which Darbouze had by 1999 raised seventy thousand dollars, more than twice the amount that the church had raised in 1992 to aid victims of the coup in Haiti.[24] As Little Haiti is a densely populated urban neighborhood with little public park space, the churchyard is the largest, greenest vista in the area. Typical inner-city problems like drug abuse, prostitution, and homelessness became increasingly acute in Little Haiti as its poverty worsened and population increased in the 1990s, and the churchyard regularly drew the homeless and others onto the church's property. Wenski's response to the problem was not to build a fence but to pressure the city and county governments to foot the bills for the clean up: "It's not like we're generating the trash; this is a social problem that we have nothing to do with" (quoted in Casimir 1996). By the mid-1990s, the problem was so bad in the ten-acre churchyard, home to some of the city's most majestic oaks, that every year before its carnival the church was paying upwards to three thousand dollars to have the all of the mattresses, clothing, boxes, and trash removed.

The Archdiocese of Miami invested Monsignor Thomas Wenski as auxiliary bishop on September 2, 1997, in a moving ceremony before twelve thousand people at the Miami Arena.[25] His move from Notre Dame to the archdiocese office, where among other things he became director of Catholic Charities, and his move out of the ghetto rectory to a posh house on Biscayne Bay, left Monsignor Gérard Darbouze to pastor Notre Dame d'Haiti, a position that he took on officially at the beginning of 1999. Then sixty-nine years old, Darbouze was about to celebrate his twentieth year of service to Miami's Haitian Catholic

Apostolate. He made it clear that he had no intentions of carrying on Wenski's indefatigable commitment to social and political activism: "My concern is not to have an impact outside my parish, but model Haitian unity here. . . . I'm not a politician. I'm not an activist. I'm a minister. That's it" (quoted in Witt 1998).

Having served as a priest in the Haitian Diocese of Jérémie for twenty-five years prior to arriving in Miami, Darbouze may be described as a scrupulous "old school" Haitian Catholic priest, one trained before liberation theology transformed Haitian Catholicism in the late 1970s and early 1980s. Prior to that, the Catholic seminary in Haiti trained priests primarily for pastoral service and education. Then, the ultra conservative Haitian archbishop François Wolff Ligondé, who had close ties to the Duvaliers, would not tolerate any liberationist tendencies among his clergy. He raised no objection, for instance, when Papa Doc had the Jesuits deported from Haiti in 1962 upon suspecting the order of inciting popular discontent with his dictatorship. A graduate of the Haitian Catholic seminary of that era, Darbouze thus views pastoral service as the church's true mission, and so he was often irked by Wenski's high-profile political and social activism. In 1983, in fact, when the Haitian government complained to the Archdiocese of Miami because of Wenski's publicizing on radio and in the press his interview with Gérard Duclerville, who had been beaten by the Haitian army, Darbouze also lodged a complaint about Wenski to Archbishop McCarthy.

Ten years later, in 1993, with the junta now in power for more than a year with no sign of relenting, Miami's Creole radio programs consistently expressed outrage at the political and human rights nightmare that Haiti had once again become. In an expression of objection to the political activism of Wenski and other Catholic clerics in Haiti and the Haitian diaspora, Darbouze commented to one reporter on the eve of inaugurating his own pastoral broadcast, "They [Haitians in Miami] are sick of that. They expect to get something better from priests, and they will" (quoted in Maass 1993).

Monsignor Darbouze thus exemplifies what Leo Grebler, Joan Moore, and Ralph Guzman (1970, 454) describe as a "priestly" as opposed to a "prophetic" cleric, one who demonstrates a "pastoral orientation."[26] Predictably, therefore, Notre Dame would change somewhat under its first Haitian pastor, who explicitly gave primacy to pastoral concerns over social concerns. For one thing, the longstanding monthly all-night vigils were cancelled out of security concerns. For another, Catholic Charities, which Wenski was then directing for the Archdiocese of Miami, took over the direction of the various social programs offered at the Pierre Toussaint Haitian Catholic Center. And then, of course, there is the fence.

But this reorientation of parish goals at Notre Dame cannot be understood merely in terms of Darbouze's style of leadership and ecclesiology anymore than Notre Dame's political posture can be understood by consideration of Wenski's ethical charisma alone. As noted above, the social and political success of Notre Dame d'Haiti Catholic Church resulted from a confluence of Wenski's leadership and the deep influence of liberation theology on his Haitian flock, who had become accustomed in Haiti to a church engaged in the struggle for justice and human rights. By the time Darbouze took the helm at Notre Dame in 1999, the Tilegliz movement in Haiti was all but dead. It is essential to remember that Notre Dame is not merely a parish in the Archdiocese of Miami but a leading Catholic institution in the transnational Haitian religious field.

For all of its brilliance and wide-ranging influence, the limitations of Weber's theory of charisma prohibit sound appreciation of the interplay between religious leadership and the needs of the faithful. Pierre Bourdieu, for one, criticizes Weber's "psycho-sociological theory of charisma" for regarding charisma merely as "as a property attaching to the nature of a single individual" (1987, 129), hence ignoring the religious needs and expectations of the laity in the effectiveness of religious leadership. In his classic study of Melanesian cargo cults, Peter Worsley anticipates Bourdieu's criticism: "To achieve this [charisma], the leader must strike responsive chords in his audience. The charismatic leader, that is, is a catalytic personality. His catalytic function is to convert latent solidarities into active ritual and political action" (1968, xvii).[27]

The coup d'état that ousted President Aristide from power in 1991 also toned the death knell for liberation theology in Haiti. Correctly recognizing such grassroots initiatives as the lifeblood of any opposition it might encounter to its illegitimate authority, the Cédras junta orchestrated a massive and effective campaign of terror against them. Hundreds of Tilegliz members were murdered, while hundreds of others took to the seas in attempts to seek political asylum in Miami. By the time Aristide returned to power in 1994, the movement had been quashed. As a result, newly arriving Haitian immigrants filling the pews of Notre Dame in Miami were not as expectant of a prophetic church as were earlier immigrants, whose solidarities were once readily converted into active ritual and political action by Wenski's catalytic personality.

Though hastened radically and violently by the brutality of the Cédras junta from 1991 to 1994, the decline of liberation theology in Haiti was actually part of a regional depoliticization of the popular Catholic Church in Latin America.[28] And being very much a transnational church, Notre Dame was bound to be affected by this, regardless of the social and political leanings of its pastor. Yet undeniably, leadership is one of the determinants of any congregation's civic social capital, as explained by Grebler, Moore, and Guzman in their study of the Catholic Archdiocese of San Antonio: "The conditions that militated against the Church's orientation toward social-action goals were stress on pastoral functions within the operative teaching of the Church at this time in Texas [1920s and 1930s]; a continuing shortage of priests and financial resources; a climate of laissez-faire in the larger society, reflected in emphasis on the individual in local interpretations of Catholic social teaching; and a population of Mexican immigrants and previous settlers considered woefully in need of the pastoral essentials. Given these conditions, it is highly unlikely that priests would assume the role of social reformers" (1970, 456). The final condition implies that a clergy's perception of its laity's pastoral needs chiefly shapes its congregation's social posture. Haitians have long been among the most devout Catholics in the world, although historically many, if not most, Haitian Catholics have also practiced Vodou without misgiving. In response, the Haitian Catholic hierarchy has resisted any social-action orientation among its clergy, whose main concern, it was determined, should instead be keeping the flock on the straight and narrow way. Objection to Vodou's persistent and widespread appeal to Haitian Catholics has always been central to the Catholic Church's pastoral mission in Haiti, hence its three "anti-superstition campaigns." The last of these campaigns waged from 1941 to 1942 and employed the Haitian Army to demolish Vodou temples, drums, and all kinds of ritual paraphernalia.

One might therefore expect in diasporic Haitian Catholicism much clerical discouragement of such syncretic deviations. Yet, despite his rather strict interpretation of Catholic Canon Law, Monsignor Wenski cultivated a rather hands-off approach to the question of Vodou, in part because of his awareness of his outsiderhood, however Haitianized he may have become over the years: "People don't appreciate being told they're s—. They have to realize things on their own. Also, I have to remember that I'm not Haitian. They might not accept certain things from a white guy. . . . A guest can't go and rearrange the furniture. I've felt that advice serves me very well" (quoted in Viglucci 1995). As an insider, meanwhile, Darbouze is at home militating against Vodou, something that most Haitian Catholic priests have always done.[29] When Halloween approaches, for instance, he discourages trick-or-treating because it hearkens to Vodou's Feast of Gede (the spirit of the dead). Communally, this is Vodou's most important liturgical ceremony, as it seizes the occasion of the Catholic All Saints and All Souls Days to commemorate the distant and tragically anonymous ancestors of Africa. Still, it is furniture that needs rearranging.

A Bicentennial Conclusion

Haiti celebrated its bicentennial in 2004. In preparation, red and blue banners were hung on lampposts throughout Little Haiti, where on New Years' Day thousands of Haitians flocked to Notre Dame d'Haiti for a colorful and emotional outdoor Mass and jubilee. It was an extraordinary occasion, even by Notre Dame's standards. The joy would last just two months, however, as on the last day of February Haitians in Miami awoke to learn that a rebellion in their beloved homeland had driven President Aristide from power and that he was being whisked off to exile for the second time in recent history. Haiti once again sneezed and Little Haiti caught another cold, meaning that hundreds of Miami Haitians dropped whatever they were doing and flocked to Notre Dame. They came, as they always have, to pray for Haiti and to try to gain some sense of meaning amid the upheaval. In a moving expression of solidarity with Haitian Catholics, a group of Cubans made pilgrimage from the Shrine of the Virgin of Charity del Cobre (the patron saint of Cuba) to Notre Dame, led by the spiritual father of the Cuban exile community, Bishop Augustín Romero. Journalists also came, knowing that if Haiti is anywhere in Miami, it is at Notre Dame.

Conspiracy theories were quick to hit the city's Creole airwaves and circulate via *telejòl* (word-of-mouth) that fateful morning. The one with the greatest currency had it that Presidents George Bush and Jacques Chirac had initiated a Franco-American coup d'etat in Port-au-Prince to please the Haitian economic elite and foreign investors, among Aristide's most vociferous opponents. By 8:00 a.m., the pews of Notre Dame were filled with sobbing people overcome with an all-too-familiar sense of disbelief in the seemingly inevitable. Some of them had heard the rumors on the radio that morning and came to find out what had really happened and/or to protest. With Monsignor Darbouze having retired, a young and dynamic Haitian American priest named Father Reginald Jean-Mary was now the chief cleric at Notre Dame, and he took to the pulpit to offer solace to his flock. During his stirring impromptu sermon, a woman in a rear pew cried out, "*Aba George Bush! Aba George Bush!*" (Down with George Bush! Down with George Bush!), evidently believing the leading rumor about the forces behind Aristide's fall. Jean-Mary seized the opportunity to place emphasis on the dire need for Haitian unity, which is one of the most common themes that we have heard preached in Haitian churches over the years: "Madame! Madame! That is not it! That is not what we need right now at all! It is not the time for blame and division, but for unity, prayer, and healing!" For Haitian Catholics in Florida, there is no better place to turn for these things, along with the worldlier things in its treasure trove of civic social capital, than Notre Dame d'Haiti, where their faith and spirituality have transformed a drab high school cafeteria into one of the most moving religious sanctuaries in the U.S. Catholic Church.

NOTES

1. In 1958, Pope Pius XII created the Diocese of South Florida out of the sixteen southern-most counties of the Diocese of St. Augustine, which had previously comprised the entire state of Florida. Ten years later, Pope Paul IV decreed the Diocese of Miami an archdiocese, also naming Monsignor Coleman Carroll its archbishop. Upon Carroll's death in 1977, Monsignor Edward McCarthy became archbishop of Miami, until his retirement in 1994, when he was succeeded by Monsignor John Favalora. By 1983, the archdiocese had over one million Catholics. http://www.miamiarchdiocese.org/ip.asp?op=A155000&lg=E.

2. By the end of the 1970s, there were roughly five thousand Haitians in Palm Beach County, where Peloquin, Wenski, and Darbouze, or sometimes the Rev. Mr. Emile

Ambroise, a Haitian deacon who relocated from New Jersey to direct an outreach program for Haitians in Palm Beach County, were saying weekly Masses at St. Philip Benizi Catholic Church in Belle Glade and at Lantana's Holley TB Hospital, where Haitian refugees diagnosed with tuberculosis were held and treated. Every other week they were also saying Mass at Our Lady, Queen of Peace in Delray, where around two thousand Haitians had settled. In Broward County, weekly Masses were also said by this time at St. Clement Catholic Church in Ft. Lauderdale and at San Isidro in Pompano Beach. Wenski and the other priests would also make monthly visits to minister to and say Mass for the one thousand farm workers settled in Immokalee in Collier County, at Our Lady of Guadalupe Catholic Church.

3. "As the U.S. government and advocates for Haitians fought over the rights of Haitians to remain in the United States, a South Florida Haitian community emerged in the 1980s. Its focal point, known as Little Haiti, lies just north of downtown Miami and has become the geographic center of Haitian life in the United States. . . . According to the 1990 U.S. census, nearly two-thirds of the foreign born Haitians in Miami arrived in the United States during the 1980s, with nearly 40 percent arriving between 1980 and 1984" (Stepick 1998, 5–6).

4. Bishop Thomas Wenski, interview with authors, September 26, 2000, Miami.

5. These streets are also named Martin Luther King Jr. Boulevard and Felix Morisseau LeRoy Boulevard, respectively, the latter after the renowned twentieth-century Haitian poet.

6. In Catholic canon law a quasi parish (sometimes called a mission church) is "a definite community of the Christian faithful, entrusted to a priest as its proper pastor but not yet erected as a parish because of particular circumstances" (Beal, Corden, and Green 2000, 516).

7. The cover of the program for the consecration of Notre Dame features a drawing of a large, overcrowded boat leaving a tropical bay, obviously in Haiti, as well as a portrait of Pierre Toussaint and Our Lady of Perpetual Help, patron saint of Haiti. These images also adorn the inside of the Notre Dame Church: Perpetual Help and Pierre Toussaint in stained glass behind the altar, and the depiction of "boat people" in a large mural on the northern wall. In addition to the boat, the mural also depicts a departing "Haiti Air" flight.

8. Mircea Eliade coined the term *axis mundi* (axis of the world) to designate a people's geographic centering in the sacred, giving them a sense of grounding and direct reference to the sacred: "around this cosmic axis lies the world (= our world)" (Eliade [1957] 1987, 36).

9. Thomas Wenski, interview with authors, September 26, 2002.

10. Wenski also notes the influence on his ecclesiology of Silvano Tomasi and Joseph Fitzpatrick, two Catholic priests and scholars who worked extensively with Italian and Puerto Rican immigrants, respectively, in New York City. See Tomasi 1987; Fitzpatrick 1971.

11. Thomas Wenski, interview with authors, September 26, 2002.

12. Known popularly as "Papa Doc," Dr. François Duvalier ruled Haiti from 1957 until his death in 1971. He was succeeded by his son, Jean-Claude Duvalier ("Baby Doc"), who was ousted by rising popular discontent in 1984. The human rights record of the Duvaliers' is one of the worst in Latin American history, with much of their abuses orchestrated by the notorious paramilitary organization known as the Tonton Makouts (Diederich and Burt 1986).

13. The Jesuit missions of the eighteenth and twentieth centuries are important exceptions to this norm, for which reason they were expelled from Haiti both in 1762 and 1962.

14. The first TKL in Haiti was established by Father Gabriel Charles at Mont Organisé in Haiti's Northeast Department in 1976 (Father Gabriel Charles, interview with Terry Rey, August 10, 2002, Trou-du-Nord, Haiti).

15. Duclerville was probably targeted not for his work in a Catholic literacy campaign, but for his protests against the Duvalier regime's bustling homeless people off of the Port-au-Prince streets before the arrival of Christmas tourists in the capital.

16. In October 1985, Father Wenski hand delivered a message of thanks to Pope John Paul II for his inspiration and support for the Haitian people's struggle against oppression that was most manifest in his 1983 stop in Port-au-Prince. The message was signed by a group of Haitian Catholic priests in Miami, along with Wenski and scores of Little Haiti residents. It was also read repeatedly over Miami's Creole-language radio (McCarthy, 1985c).

17. Significantly, Monsignor Willy Romélus, bishop of the Haitian Diocese of Jérémie and the most outspoken opponent to the Duvalier regime among Haiti's six bishops, visited Miami a few weeks after the regime was finally toppled, saying Mass to more than two thousand people over several days, both at Notre Dame and at Corpus Christi, where Florida's Haitian Catholic Mission was born just over ten years prior (See McCarthy 1986; Dejean 1995).

18. See also Thompson 1987; Lee 1988.

19. For discussion on politics in Haiti during the years immediately following the ouster of Duvalier in 1986, see Trouillot 1990; Mathieu 1990; and Wilentz 1989.

20. Support to the new president by Little Haiti's Catholic community went beyond the symbolic and moral, as in early April 1991, Notre Dame held a fund-raiser for the Aristide government (Herald staff 1991).

21. For analysis of the brutality of the Cédras junta against Aristide supporters, see Commission Justice et Paix du Diocèse de Gonaïves 1995; Marotte and Razafimbahiny 1997.

22. In August of 1992, for example, more than fifteen hundred people responded to Notre Dame's call to donate toward the victims' pressing medical needs and daily subsistence. On one day over $30,000 was raised from a crowd of several thousand who gathered at Notre Dame (Herald staff 1992).

23. See, for example, Kollin 1993.

24. "Early last year, church officials hired Rich Iron Company to put a $70,000 fence" (Mardy 1999).

25. See Witt 1997; David 1997.

26. "In saying Mass, preaching, administering the sacraments, in assisting those in his parish who are ill, especially those who are near death," the "priestly" priest is carrying out his fundamental pastoral mandate, set down in Canon Law and sanctioned by Church tradition (Grebler, Moore, and Guzman 1970, 454).

27. For a fuller discussion of this "interactionist" model of charisma, see Rey 1998.

28. For discussions of the demise of liberation theology in Brazil, see Nagel 1997; and for Latin America more generally, see Chesnut 2003.

29. Although Vatican II, Puebla, and Medellín inspired some measure of enculturation of the Catholic Mass in Haiti, homiletic denunciations of "superstitions" and "the ancestors" remain common in the Haitian Church (Rey 1998).

REFERENCES

Balmaseda, L. 1983. Prayer Vigil Is a Protest for Haitians. *Miami Herald*, February 10, 1C.

Beal, J. P., J. A. Coriden, T. J. Green, eds. 2000. *New Commentary on the Code of Canon Law*. New York: Paulist Press.

Bourdieu, P. 1987. Legitimation and Structured Interest in Weber's Sociology of Religion. In *Max Weber, Rationality, and Modernity*, ed. S. Whimster and S. Lash, 119–136. London: Allen and Unwin.

Casimir, L. 1994. Support Urged for Honoring Slain Haitian. *Miami Herald*, September 18, 2.

———. 1996. Little Haiti Church Wants Homeless Out; They've Taken over Carnival Site. *Miami Herald*, January 11, 2.

Chesnut, R. A. 2003. *Competitive Spirits: Latin America's New Religious Economy.* New York: Oxford University Press.

Commission Justice et Paix du Diocèse de Gonaïves. 1995. *La répression au quotidien en Haïti.* Paris: KARTHALA, 1995.

Conférence des Religieux Haïtiens. 1990. *Communiqué.* December 4 press release.

Cottman, M. J. 1986. Miami Mass Celebrates New Haiti. *Miami Herald*, February 10.

David, J. D. 1991. Catholics Assist Haitians, Volunteers Sought to Help Refugees. *South Florida Sun Sentinel*, December 11.

———. 1997. Call of Two Shepherds. *South Florida Sun Sentinel*, September 3.

Dejean, P. 1995. *Willy Romélus: l'évêque—courage.* Montreal: Hurtubise.

Dibble, S. 1988. Archbishop Asked to Oppose Transfer. *Miami Herald*, October 17.

Diedrich, B., and A. Burt. 1986. *Papa Doc and the Tonton Macoutes.* Port-au-Prince: Deschamps.

Eisenstadt, S. N. 1968. Introduction to *Max Weber, On Charisma and Institutional Building*, by Max Weber, ix–lvi. Chicago and London: University of Chicago Press.

Eliade, M. [1957] 1987. Translated by William R. Trask. *The Sacred and the Profane: The Meaning of Religion.* New York: Harcourt.

Evans, C. 1987. 6,000 Protest Haiti Election Turmoil. *Miami Herald*, December 6.

Farmer, P. 1994. *The Uses of Haiti.* Monroe, ME: Common Courage Press.

Fisher, M. 1986. Little Haiti Exiles Celebrate Too Soon. *Miami Herald*, February 1.

Fitzpatrick, J. P. 1971. *Puerto Rican Immigrants: The Meaning of Migration to the Mainland.* Englewood Cliffs, NJ: Prentice Hall.

Gaither, D. 1987. " '. . . to See a Born-Again Haiti.' " *Miami Herald*, November 27.

Grebler, L., J. W. Moore, and R. C. Guzman. 1970. *The Mexican American People* New York: Free Press.

Greene, A. 1993. *The Catholic Church in Haiti: Social and Political Change.* East Lansing: Michigan State University Press.

Gremillion, J., ed. 1976. *The Gospel of Peace and Justice: Catholic Social Teaching since Pope John.* Maryknoll, NY: Orbis.

Herald staff. 1991. Local Fund-Raisers Scheduled today for Haiti's New Government. *Miami Herald*, April 7.

———. 1992. Church Raises Funds to Help Haitians. *Miami Herald*, August 20.

Juan Pablo II. 1986. *Mensajes sociales de Juan Pablo II en America Latina.* Bogota: CELAM.

Kollin, J. 1993. Mass Mourns Ferry Casualties, Priest Rips Haitian Government. *Miami Herald*, February 22.

Lee, F. R. 1988. Haitians Urge End of Regime. *Miami Herald*, January 2.

Maass, H. 1992. Haitian Priests in Dade Stay Involved with Struggle. *Miami Herald*, January 19.

———. 1993. Creole "Voice of Calm" is Heard above Political Din. *Miami Herald*, January 21.

Mardy, H. 1999. Festival Has a New Purpose: Raising Cash to Fix Up Church. *Miami Herald*, January 14.

Markowitz, A. 1991. Priest Back with Haitians' Notes. *Miami Herald*, December 31.

Marotte, C., and H. R. Razafimbahiny. 1997. *Mémoire oubliée: Haïti, 1991–1994.* Montréal: CIDHICA.

Martinez, G. 1983. A Catholic Lay Worker Is Beaten in Haiti Jail. *Miami Herald*, March 24.

Mathieu, S. M. 1990. The Transformation of the Catholic Church in Haiti. PhD diss., Indiana University.

McCarthy, K. 1985a. A Newspaper for the People. *Miami Herald*, July 4.

———. 1985b. Expelled Catholic Priests to Lead Little Haiti Mass. *Miami Herald*, August 4.

———. 1985c. Haitians Send Pope a Message of Thanks. *Miami Herald*, October 17.

———. 1986. Bishop Urges Local Haitians to Return to Help Rebuild Country. *Miami Herald*, March 16.

Nagel, R. 1997. *Claiming the Virgin: The Broken Promise of Liberation Theology in Brazil*. London: Routledge.

Rey, T. 1998. The Virgin Mary and Revolution in Saint-Domingue: The Charisma of Romaine-la-Prophétesse. *Journal of Historical Sociology* 11(3): 341–369.

———. 1999. Junta, Rape, and Religion in Haiti: 1991–1994. *Journal of Feminist Studies in Religion* 15(2): 73–100.

———. 2004. Marian Devotion at a Haitian Catholic Parish in Miami: The Feast of Our Lady of Perpetual Help. *Journal of Contemporary Religion* 19(3): 353–374.

San Martin, N. 1991a. Miami's Haitians Rejoice. *Miami Herald*, February 8.

———. 1991b. Power of Payer. *Miami Herald*, September 5.

Schaffer, G. 1989. Priest Uses Ethnicity to Reach Out to Flock. *Miami Herald*, February 16.

Stepick, A. 1998. *Pride against Prejudice: Haitians in the United States*. Boston: Allyn and Bacon.

Taft, A. 1986. Black Catholics: Their Numbers Are Small; Their Devotion Is Steady. *Miami Herald*, January 31.

Thompson, M. D. 1987. Haitians Pray for Peace in Homeland. *Miami Herald*, November 26.

Tomasi, S. 1987. *Piety and Power: The Role of Italian Parishes in the New York Metropolitan Areas, 1880–1930*. New York: Center for Migration Studies.

Trouillot, M.-R. 1990. *Haiti, State against Nation: Origins and Legacy of Duvalierism*. New York: Monthly Review Press.

Vaughan, C. 1983a. Radio Unites, Divides Haitians. *Miami Herald*, June 9.

———. 1983b. Tribute Stirs Memories of Haitians Who Drowned. *Miami Herald*, October 28.

Viglucci, A. 1995. God's Man in Little Haiti. *Miami Herald*, February 26.

Weber, M. [1922] 1963. *The Sociology of Religion*. Translated by Talcott Parsons. Boston: Beacon.

Wieman, H., and R. Wescott-Wieman. 1935. *Normative Psychology of Religion*. New York: Crowell.

Wilentz, A. 1989. *The Rainy Season: Haiti since the Duvaliers*. New York: Simon and Schuster.

Witt, A. 1997. 2 Popular Priests Ordained as Bishops. *Miami Herald*, September 4.

———. 1998. A New Era at Notre Dame d'Haiti. *Miami Herald*, February 27.

Worsley, P. 1968. *The Trumpet Shall Sound: A Study of Cargo Cults in Melanesia*. New York: Schocken.

4

Politics and Prayer
in West Perrine

Civic Engagement in the Black Church

SU OLTMAN FINK

One day in November 2001, some sixty people packed the small satellite police station in the Black neighborhood of West Perrine, Florida, where a community meeting sponsored by the Neighborhood Resource Team (NRT) was about to begin.[1] Police officers, social workers, representatives from government agencies such as the Florida Department of Children and Families, pastors, businessmen, landlords of low-income housing projects, and other citizens talked together in the meeting room and outside in the hallway. Suddenly, Miami-Dade County commissioner Dennis Moss arrived. The people in the hallway grew quiet and moved aside as the commissioner made his way through the crowd in the hallway and into the meeting room, shaking hands and making his greetings. Soon, everyone entered and was seated. At one side of a very large round table that took up much of the room sat one contingent of the Black leadership of West Perrine: Rev. Walter Richardson, pastor of the large Sweet Home Missionary Baptist Church of West Perrine; Commissioner Moss; Ed Hanna, developer and head of the Community Development Corporation (the CDC); and Police Officer Ron Tookes, the coordinator of the meeting and director of six Neighborhood Resource Teams that operate in government and private housing projects in south Miami-Dade County. Sitting in two rows at the back of the room was the other contingent: other pastors and lay leadership that made up the West Perrine Christian Association (WPCA), a group to which Commissioner Moss affectionately referred as his "pastor leaders."

Reverend Richardson opened the meeting in prayer:

Let us pray, letting God know how appreciative we are today for life. . . .
Thank you this morning for these concerned and caring citizens who
have gathered, that we might lend our voice to your voice to make this

community and others like this a place where justice prevails and peace resides. Help us to continue to have the courage of our convictions to face people insistent and people whose objects and objectives are to destroy what you have made. We come against anything that would seek to tear down your kingdom. And we pray for your presence. Thank you for our police department. Thank you for our commissioner, for those that give leadership. Thank you for men and women of God whose job it is to proclaim righteousness. We pray now, Lord, that all that we do as we work together will make this world and, indeed, this community a better place to live. Help us; we need your help. We pray for the thousands upon thousands of victims around this world who are suffering because of warfare, because of unjust systems, because of the threat of anthrax. We pray for the families, the victims of the 9/11 incident, to provide continual healing. . . . Bless us now. We'll be so careful to give you all the honor and all of the credit. And we ask of you, the most powerful name. Amen."[2]

The group responded with a hearty "Amen." Many who had been calling out responses throughout Reverend Richardson's invocation now relaxed and began to joke with each other, having enjoyed the prayer. After a few minutes, when the banter began to die down, a series of "Amens" signaled that the next part of the meeting was about to commence.

Commissioner Moss then addressed the gathering, thanking Reverend Richardson for his prayer and recognizing his "pastor leaders." Next, Ed Hanna stepped up, and someone quipped, affectionately, "Here's the Mayor of Perrine." The room exploded in laughter. This was unincorporated Miami-Dade County, so there was no mayor of Perrine, but if there were, it undoubtedly would be Hanna. Through the West Perrine CDC, Hanna had implemented much of Perrine's redevelopment and cleanup efforts. He reported on the worst slum landlords in Miami-Dade County, whose Perrine properties had finally been demolished. He predicted that when these properties were redeveloped twenty million dollars would come into the county. He also reported that the number of building code enforcement violations was decreasing due to the joint efforts of the police department, the commissioner's office, and community pressure. Finally, Police Officer Ron Tookes introduced members of the NRTs and explained work they were doing to improve housing, standards of living, and employment and to eradicate crime.

This chapter historically and anthropologically explores the accumulation and expenditure of civic social capital (CSC) by Black churches in West Perrine, Florida, a Black neighborhood in south Miami-Dade County (formerly Dade County).[3] Specifically, I am interested in how churches in Perrine use religious resources and networking skills to generate CSC, to activate stored CSC, to accumulate more of this capital, and to invest it in the community. In West Perrine,

CSC has generally developed in "zones of conflict" between the neighborhood's Black churches and South Florida's dominant society.

During the first half of the twentieth century, Perrine's churches struggled with a dominant society that blatantly and formally discriminated against Blacks.[4] CSC in this context was directed toward the self-governance of a separate Black community. It constitutes a case of bonding social capital emerging in response to not only legalized segregation, but also economic exploitation and outright violent repression. Later, in the 1980s, Perrine's churches shifted their civic focus to the internal causes of the community's devastating social ills. In this second context, Perrine's churches spent their CSC in an effort to eradicate crime, clean up their neighborhood, and win back its youth. In the process, because of changes in the broader social structure, the bonding social capital could be transubstantiated into bridging and linking CSC that gave access to federal resources, including the U.S. attorney general.

Drawing on the work of David Chidester, I propose that CSC is often generated through "zones of conflict" (1988, 7–9). A zone of conflict is a situation of social tension between two or more power systems. This chapter examines two large zones of conflict in which Perrine's churches have engaged. The first conflict was set in the historical context of the American racist system of the first half of the twentieth century. On an institutional level, the zone of conflict occurred as Black churches struggled with the dominant political system to obtain services and opportunities denied to them as members of an oppressed ethnic group: for instance, Perrine's churches struggled to obtain funding from Dade County's school board for a colored public school, and they established an alternative police department because the county did not provide them with adequate protection against the Ku Klux Klan. The second zone of conflict emerged in the 1980s as one faction in Perrine, represented by its churches, waged a battle against a second faction, Perrine's drug dealers, and against the "secular influences" of a dominant society that Perrine's fraternity of churches believed was destroying their community.

CSC and the Black Church

The Black church has been a vehicle par excellence for the development of CSC, having from the time of slavery generated and applied Black power. It was largely through their churches that enslaved Africans and their descendants constructed both an African American identity[5] and the solidarity that assured their survival in the two-tiered racial political system of the United States. At least from the time when Black slaves were imported to the New World, they looked to religion to explain and understand not only the spiritual aspect of their lives, but also the secular and political aspects. C. Eric Lincoln writes that African American religion addresses all the needs of its community, both the private and the public. It encompasses two realms, "the 'spiritual' and the 'public,' or the 'private' and the 'communal'" (Lincoln 1999, 230). Lincoln and Lawrence Mamiya identify the "Black sacred cosmos" as a worldview that is particular to the African American religious experience. "The Black sacred cosmos or the religious worldview of African Americans is related both to their African heritage, which envisaged the whole universe as sacred, and to their conversion to Christianity during slavery and its aftermath" (Lincoln and Mamiya 1990, 2).[6] From the time the first slaves were brought to America until today, potential political power has been accumulating in the Black church. The history of Black political power is in large part also the history of the movement toward the actualization of this potential through the consolidation by churches of this stored power and the use of it to achieve political and social change.

The Black church has long functioned as an alternative social system for its people, who were until recently otherwise shut out altogether in a racially hostile America. This has been so much the case that Lincoln can maintain that "to understand the power of the Black Church it must first be understood that there is no disjunction between the Black Church and the Black community. The Church is the spiritual face of the Black community, and whether one is a 'church member' or not is beside the point in any assessment of the importance and meaning of the Black Church" (Lincoln 1999, 96). The Black leadership of Perrine, including the commissioner, the Community Development Corporation head, businessmen, and police officers, are all active church members. They speak for and represent their entire community, even including the large numbers of "un-churched" individuals from the projects and crack houses.

The NRT meeting described above thus represents one moment in a long history of African American confrontation, through its churches, of the dominant political system in America that has historically denied Blacks the rights, privileges, and opportunities extended to Whites. It also illustrates the intersection of religion and politics in a broad-based coalition. The meeting opened, like other meetings involving the Black church, by "having church," illustrating how in the African American community religion and politics are so deeply integrated. Here was a public meeting in a government building with a primary focus of community improvement that opened with the public worship of God, a religious ritual central to the African American religious experience. Such ritual affirms that in the African American community, civic engagement is seen in large part to be a religious commitment out of which emerges its leadership, its meaning, its goals, and its optimism. The public ritual of prayer is a way for the community to empower and define itself, in particular, because of its perceived raison d'etre to serve God. As God's partner, the community gains ultimate status not only in the local context, but in the global and sacred ones, too. The use of prayer in a government building by a prominent pastor, and with the sanction of government officials, legitimizes the message that these leaders want to impart to the wider community: the belief that God reigns supreme, that in God's kingdom there is no separation between church and state, and that in the kingdom this community is God's partner.

Early Black Settlement in Perrine: 1896–1919

Perrine formed originally as an agricultural community in 1903, when Henry Flagler, who sought to extend his Florida East Coast Railroad (FECRR) southward from Miami, made it the location for the general supply depot for the Key West extension of the line. Perrine was one of many villages that developed alongside the railroad. Miami had just been incorporated as a city seven years earlier in 1896. The arrival of the railroad in Perrine initiated the beginning of a century of rapid growth in population and development in the South Florida wilderness. As they settled in Perrine, Bahamian Blacks and African Americans from northern Florida and Georgia organized churches, which were as driven as much by political as religious motives.

For most of the first half of the twentieth century, Perrine's Black churches were forced to nurture the development of their community in almost complete racial segregation. Excluded from the social, economic, and political life of broader Dade County, Black church leaders took care of communal affairs in the absence of any formal or other governmental support. Church leaders developed a kind of "invisible government" for their Jim Crow, segregated community that paralleled the official Dade County government. Its governing body, the Negro Council, provided the kinds of services one would expect from a municipality or county government: education, a type of police protection, the building and lighting of roads, and garbage removal.

South Florida was one of America's last frontiers. Until Henry Flagler, the latest in a long line of visionaries aspiring to develop South Florida, decided to bring his railroad to South Florida, the area surrounding the village of Perrine was wide open to settlers, many of whom squatted on the lands that Congress had once thought "too sickly and sterile" to warrant efforts at surveying and selling (U.S. Congress 1838). In the latest attempt to stimulate the economic development of Florida, the state offered free land to anyone who would help finance construction of the railroad line. Flagler, in securing the rights to extend his railway, had obtained vast amounts of land adjoining the rail line itself. In 1896 he created the Model Land Company (MLC) to manage his expanding real-estate holdings in Florida and the Perrine Grant Land Company to sell the valuable farmlands located along Biscayne Bay, eighteen miles south of Miami and extending six miles west from the coastline. Flagler's companies played a major part in the settlement and the development of southern Dade County, including Perrine (Brown and Hudson 1996, 47).

In platting the village of Perrine, the MLC implemented the Jim Crow practices of racial separation adopted throughout the South in the early twentieth century (George 1979, 438–445). A 1903 MLC plat of Perrine shows a section designated "for Negroes" on the east side of the railroad tracks. This plat set the general parameters for settlement in the village of Perrine: Whites would be permitted exclusive settlement on the east side of the tracks. On the west side of the tracks the land would be divided, with one section for Blacks and the other for Whites, and, as MLC sales records show, throughout the first four decades of the century, Blacks and Whites lived in close proximity to one another on the west side of the tracks. Several large parcels of land were sold to White growers, who built living facilities there for their workers. These were one-room wooden shacks with shared outhouses for their year-round Black laborers and separate boardinghouses for seasonal workers of both races. Other lots in the "Negro" section were sold to Blacks who began to settle in the village itself. Yet despite this early attempt by the MLC to organize Perrine's social structure according to the norms dictated by Jim Crow practices of the American South, the continuing biracial settlement of the lands in the vicinity of Perrine and the nature of farm life itself resulted in only a partial segregation in Perrine during its first fifty years.

In 1896, although there were only two families squatting specifically on the land that would soon become the village of Perrine, both Black and White squatters had already settled in the surrounding area (Taylor 1986, 55). In spite of legal struggles over the land, squatters continued to settle in the general vicinity of the village of Perrine well into the teens of the twentieth century and beyond (Model Land Company n.d.). The two groups of Blacks who settled in Perrine, Bahamians and American Blacks from northern Florida and Georgia, brought two very different cultures with them, and these largely determined their relationships to the land, their living arrangements, and their interactions with Whites. Generally, during Perrine's early history, Bahamian Blacks lived almost entirely separately from Whites. American Blacks had more contact. Some of the American Blacks developed positive relationships with Whites, leading to substantial levels of trust between the two races.

Perrine's first church was organized by Bahamians at the Ramsey-McCrimmon sawmill on the Tropico Lumber Company grounds in 1912, with the company providing a building for the church.[7] Some of the ancestors of today's most prominent leaders and families of the Perrine community founded this church, and the membership increased steadily throughout the first half of the century, as Bahamian immigrants continued to arrive. Robert Bruce Ingraham, a Bahamian immigrant, founded Perrine's first Holiness Church, Hurst Chapel, in 1919. Ingraham lived on a thirty-five-acre parcel of land and employed his own workers in agriculture. A prominent community leader, he had a deep conversion experience that convinced him of his calling to establish a church based on righteous living "everyday and not just Sunday," one that would preach "real salvation, the Holy Ghost, the Spirit of God."[8]

One prominent plantation owner, Robert Kerr, employed many Black farm-workers, mostly Americans. In the 1920s he provided them with a hut for their church services. They organized two churches, one Methodist and another Baptist, which met on alternate Sundays in this building.[9] The fourth church to be established in Perrine, Mt. Moriah Missionary Baptist Church, was founded in the residential quarters of the Peters plantation by American Blacks in 1919.

The Black Church and CSC in Postwar Perrine

During Perrine's first fifty years, as it moved from a rural outpost into a town of thirty-five hundred by 1948, a certain degree of trust and reciprocity had developed between the races, albeit within the confines of a segregated society. Chidester's theory that "political power may be generated by the competition between mutually exclusive social interests" (1988, 7) suggests that both the zone of conflict that the interaction between this Black community and the dominant White society represented and an emergent collaboration between the races contributed to the production of CSC.

Numerous zones of conflict throughout the first fifty years of Perrine's history, especially between its churches and the dominant White system, have led to the accumulation of CSC in Perrine's Black churches, such as when the Perrine community clashed with the Dade County School Board over the education of Black children. This struggle was undertaken in the context of the larger struggle in America concerning the rights and privileges that should be afforded Blacks in a society dominated by Whites. Despite the apparent resolution of this dispute in 1896 by the landmark U.S. Supreme Court case of *Plessy v. Ferguson*, which mandated equal but separate treatment for Blacks and Whites, it soon became evident to Blacks in south Dade County that the Dade County School Board was ignoring the mandate of the Supreme Court and that the treatment of White and Black children was far from balanced. Church leaders finally succeeded in obtaining a salaried teacher from the county in 1920, on the condition that a church be provided for use as a classroom (Taylor 1986).

A second example of CSC in Perrine emerging out of a zone of conflict was the growing demand for municipal services by farmers in South Dade, whose population increased significantly during the 1930s and 1940s (Mohl 1989, 28–29). Residents of Perrine formed two governing councils, one White, the other Black, to try to procure needed municipal services from an overburdened county government. The Negro Council represented the interests of Perrine's Black community. It effectively raised money from the community to install streetlights, to provide for garbage collection, and to press to have roads built. A partial list of Negro Council members shows that they were pastors, deacons, and lay leaders of Perrine's churches, an outgrowth of the church leaders who organized Perrine's first school. Some worked on the large farms of White growers, holding responsible positions. Others, like Robert Ingraham and Doc Coleman, pastors of Holiness churches, were self-employed. The Negro Council was effective in getting the county to build roads in their neighborhood by enlisting the help of the MLC and County Commissioner J. Lamar Paxson, Robert Kerr's former business partner who now represented District Four, South Miami (Model Land Company n.d., box 96, folder 1715, file 2166).

Until 1948, when the community's first police officers (one White and two Black) were hired, Perrine's Black community had no way to officially confront threats made by the Ku Klux Klan, and even the eventual presence of this small police force would not be sufficient to provide protection to Blacks, especially since Black police officers were not permitted to arrest Whites until 1963.[10] To fill this security vacuum, Perrine's Black Freemason chapter acted as a de facto Black police force. The Black Freemasons functioned in many ways like the Black church in that they represented the Black community in both spiritual and civic matters. Their parades through Perrine were spectacular events, featuring music and high pomp and circumstance that attracted the entire community. One member, Archie Finkley, described the Freemasons as "a religious organization. It's supposed to take care of the down and out, the troubled, the blind, the crippled." Indeed, one of the central communal services provided by the Eastern Star, the woman's branch of Freemasons, was a burial society that provided funerals for people too poor to afford them. The Eastern Star had its own building, where the women held dinner parties and other social gatherings. They also helped provide assistance for churches in need.

By the end of World War II, changes occurring in Miami due to population increases, an expanding county power base, and increased development which was encroaching on farms in South Dade fueled the desire of Perrine's White growers to reorganize themselves politically to maintain control over their economic interests. There were more Blacks living in Perrine than Whites, and Perrine's White growers knew they had to enlist Black participation in forming their new government. Initially reluctant to get involved in "White people's business," Perrine's Negro Counsel members were eventually persuaded to support incorporation by Robert Barfield, a long-time White Perrine grower and business man who was well respected among both Blacks and Whites.

On March 15, 1948, Perrine's citizens voted to incorporate. Barfield was sworn in as mayor the next day, and the election for a new set of elected officials was set for the following November. Church leaders, including Rev. Doc Coleman, a prominent Republican, registered enough Black voters (there were 316 Black voters to 278 White voters) to ensure that the Black president of the Negro Counsel, Ben Shavis, would be elected as commissioner, and then would have enough votes to become the first Black mayor of Perrine.

On the eve of the election, the Ku Klux Klan announced that they would be riding through Perrine in an effort to discourage the biracial government.

Bishop Ingraham, then a teenager, was at home alone and in charge of watching his younger siblings; and he watched as a state trooper pleaded with his next door neighbor, Doc Coleman, to leave with his children, saying that the police could not offer him protection from the Klan. Ingraham remembered, "And they said, 'You had better leave here because they are getting ready up there, and they are coming after you.'" Coleman sent his children to stay with family and friends outside of Perrine, but he refused to leave. He told Ingraham, "I remember seeing White people kill my daddy in Georgia. I'm looking at 'em. [He said] I'm not going one step. I'll be right in that house there." Ingraham himself was terrified.

Ben Shavis got the message and he left town for a few days. When he returned he dropped out of the mayoral race. Barfield was voted mayor instead of Shavis. The failed attempt to put together a legally sanctioned integrated government based on interracial cooperation fomented a bitterness in the hearts of Blacks and Whites who had worked together. When Shavis withdrew from the race, so did four White candidates. Two months later, Barfield, along with three other commissioners, offered their resignations. Barfield was quoted in the *Miami Daily News* (1949) as saying, "I want to get out of the city of Perrine and I want to get my property out." Indeed, by May, the town had been abolished. The next decade would find most of the farms in Perrine sold.

This example illustrates that Perrine's Black community possessed enough CSC to entice the White growers to try to work with them at a time when Whites rarely appealed to Blacks for support. It is unlikely, given the existing social climate of the period, that the White growers would have been motivated by social considerations (i.e., a desire to improve the social and political conditions of the Blacks) to form a biracial government. The Whites obviously believed that the Blacks had an amount of political and social power necessary to assist them in achieving their own political goals. Their apparent willingness to share power with Blacks was a result of the solid relationships that Whites had formed with many of the Black citizens of Perrine. That the Black community had developed important relationships even with the state police was demonstrated by the expressed regret of the police not being able to protect the Perrine community from the Klan.[11]

The failure of Perrine's incorporation and the sell-off of farm land primarily by Whites meant a dismantling of the biracial network that had served to hold Perrine together for a half-century. This led in turn to a decline in CSC over the next thirty years. When Perrine's Whites pulled out, Black Perrine's ties to White society were severed. Forced to rely on "strong ties," the community became more insular and isolated. Black Perrine was now called West Perrine, its isolation reinforced by the widening of U.S. Highway 1, which had been built alongside the railroad some years earlier and which had served to separate Black from White Perrine throughout the century. Ironically, Blacks in Perrine were becoming more isolated at a time during which Blacks across the country were beginning to experience greater inclusion into the wider society.

Dealing with Desegregation, Drugs, and Generational Conflict: 1966–1990

When integration reached Perrine, its youth encountered a White culture that was in the midst of great social change itself. In the wake of the "1960s revolution," White youth were expressing new attitudes concerning freedom, rebellion against authority, sexual liberation, and drug use. Perrine's churches were slow to understand what was happening to their youth because of their isolation from White society.

When schools in South Dade were desegregated in 1966,[12] Perrine's church-oriented community, one that had long maintained a protective watch over its youth, was particularly concerned with the safety of its children. Shirley Green, a Black woman of Bahamian descent, was sixteen years old and a member of the first class to attend a White high school after desegregation. She related how her Black teachers had tried to prepare her class for the White world: "White people, they don't talk loud. Okay? And if you talk loudly, you are going to frighten them. And then they'll think you're acting bad. . . . And the Whites didn't want you to look them in the eye. So we had to be re-taught." This last point was directed mostly toward the Bahamians, for, according to Green and others, "the Bahamians are known to be more assertive, more aggressive than the American Blacks. So in most situations Bahamians tend either to get into trouble, or to be more successful." According to oral histories, in the mid 1960s, there were still clear distinctions between Bahamian and American Blacks in Perrine.

Looking back at the churches' response to school desegregation in the turbulent 1960s and early 1970s, some pastors and elders later suggested that the church was unaware that long exposure of its youth to secular values they encountered in the public schools would lead to their abandonment of the church, which in turn would cause many of the social ills that came to plague Perrine in the ensuing decades. Perrine's children, in attending public school, spent the majority of their waking hours in an environment far removed from the religious foundations on which they were raised at home. Delores Alexander, now a pastor at a Pentecostal church in neighboring Goulds, grew up in Perrine and graduated from high school in 1966. She gave voice to a widespread belief that public schools were indoctrinating children with secular views. She said that churches did not realize this was happening until it was too late. She noted, "It was so subtle that we never expected it. And so when we wake up one morning and you realize that your kid has been going to a public school that has preached secular humanism . . . and they have been going for six to eight hours a day, five days a week." The result, explained Finkley, the

Freemason quoted above, was that young "people quit praying, quit going to church" because "the devil got in them."

By the 1970s, Perrine had become a site of Black male youth engaged in selling drugs and many females supported by welfare. Later, church leaders would accuse many of Perrine's youth of adopting the "new" materialism and "get rich quick" values of White society, and of finding the lucrative drug trade a quicker way to get ahead than the more legitimate avenues that their parents had pursued. Some of Perrine's older generation accused their adolescent daughters of materialistic incentives in getting pregnant, complaining that these girls believed they could achieve a much-desired independence from their parents by becoming beneficiaries of new social welfare programs that provided a single mother with a free apartment and food stamps. The encounter many youth had with secular values was blamed for a generation of young girls raising another generation of children who would grow up "un-churched" and resulted in a deepening generational rift. As young people stopped going to church, Perrine's very cohesion and identity were threatened as the transmission of its church-based values to its youth became gravely endangered.

Generally, churches responded to this emerging generational crisis by becoming more inwardly focused. They concentrated on saving souls, intensifying their participation in prayer groups, and by exhorting against sinners, practices that their increasingly un-churched youth viewed as irrelevant. Furthermore, theological differences between churches became more pronounced as congregations became more insular.

Another challenge to the cohesion of the community was its growing population. Many newcomers lived in new rental properties made available as slum landlords, both White and Black, built apartment buildings and cheap duplexes and bought and rented out the old one-room shacks that had served as quarters for farmworkers, some of them dating to the 1920s. Some of these newcomers were relocating from other Black slum areas closer to the city. The growth in rental housing stock encouraged transience. The pride the community once had in building and owning "good solid homes" and in making sure the community was physically cared for was eroding. Many of the older generation of community leaders who took care of looking after West Perrine's physical needs were aging and dying.

Ethnic diversity further complicated Perrine's community cohesion. In the late 1970s and 1980s there was a large influx into Perrine of Black immigrants largely from Jamaica, although a few were from other West Indian Islands, South America, Africa, and Asia. In the late 1980s and early 1990s they would establish two Protestant Jamaican churches, a Muslim mosque, and a Hindu temple, but these institutions would remain separate from about thirty churches that made up the one-square-mile area of Perrine, now an all Black community. They would not join Perrine's older and more established churches in their civic activities.

By the 1980s West Perrine was one of the most crime-infested areas in Dade County. Its original residents, those who had bought their property, built their homes, formed their churches and schools, and raised their families, bemoaned the decline of their community. Abandoned dwellings were transformed into crack houses by the drug lords who took over West Perrine's streets. Teenage gangs terrorized the area with shootings, assaults, car thefts, armed robberies, and drug dealing. Residents were now afraid to leave their homes, and police were reluctant to go into the neighborhood. In the early 1980s race riots had erupted in Black neighborhoods in Miami, and there was concern that West Perrine could be next.

West Perrine, a community that encompassed only sixteen square blocks, had become a dangerous neighborhood, even as it remained rich in churches, with almost forty in all. There were the four historic churches, two Methodist and two Baptist, that were formed by the 1920s. There were two additional Baptist churches, Sweet Home and St. Peters, both of which had begun as breakaway churches over internal disputes. The others were mostly small independent Pentecostal, Apostolic, Holiness, or Sanctified churches. Many had total memberships of no more than fifty, some of which comprised entirely of a single extended family, while others were founded by pastors from other communities who felt called to serve in West Perrine. Breakaway churches, also referred to as "bastard churches," were common and reflected schisms in the community, some of which occurred over doctrinal disputes and others as a result of personality clashes or power struggles, or because of some pastor's questionable morality. Orientations were often reflected in their names, such as Holy Faith Tabernacle Deliverance Center of Apostolic Faith, Christian Converts for Christ Ministries, Triumph Church and Kingdom of God in Christ, Evangelist Mission Church of God in Christ, Community Church of Christ Written in Heaven, and Pentecostal Church of Our Lord and Savior Jesus Christ. However, these churches were ill-equipped to handle the destructive issues facing the West Perrine community at large, such as drug abuse, teenage pregnancy, single-parent homes, poverty, and school dropouts.

Its power base eroded, Perrine was at the mercy of a range of individuals, from slum landlords to drug lords, all of whom sought individual profit at the expense of the community. Into this power vacuum stepped church and business leaders from Richmond Heights, a middle-class Black community just to Perrine's north, who offered their help. By the 1980s these Black community leaders had transplanted to Perrine a social service model that had been successful in maintaining the Richmond Heights community. The Jaycees, the Masons, and the Community Action Agency were used to delivering services to the community, but the most influential social action group was the Richmond Perrine Optimist Club. It was made up of business people, school principals, teachers, and pastors from Richmond Heights and chaired by developer

Ed Hanna, who was working to improve real estate values in Perrine by replacing slum housing with single-family homes and by helping residents, many of whom lived in government-subsidized projects, to qualify for mortgages so they could move into those homes. His partner, Dennis Moss, who would become the area's first Black county commissioner in 1993, focused on crime prevention and youth. Moss ran a last resort school for teenagers expelled from the Dade County Schools and a crime prevention program. In 1983, the Rev. Walter Richardson joined this group when he became pastor of Sweet Home Missionary Baptist Church in West Perrine. The immediate goal of this group of Black community leaders was to restore West Perrine as a viable Black community; their long-term vision was the empowerment of the community as an allied political force.

In the hopes of rehabilitating West Perrine, the group devised the Seventeen-Point Plan, which became known as the Moss Plan. The issues addressed in this plan were remarkably similar to those addressed by the Negro Council thirty years earlier: street lighting, housing, schools, police, crime, and garbage pick up. They centered their efforts on the improvement of housing, which included the eradication of crack houses, nightclubs, and liquor package stores. Eradication of the local street drug trade would soon be added to their list.

A charismatic preacher, Reverend Richardson became the spokesman for this new group of community leaders, and he brought a new type of ecclesiology to Perrine, one dedicated *primarily* to social justice and civic engagement. Brought up in a housing project and third in his family's line of Pentecostal pastors, Reverend Richardson set upward mobility as a personal goal. He had left the Pentecostal Church for the Baptist Church, much to the dismay of his family, in order to gain a wider exposure for what he came to believe was his mission, that of social activism and the struggle for justice for Blacks in America. When he took the position at Sweet Home Missionary Baptist Church in 1983, he was an accomplished musician, had attended seminary, had a well-paying job as an executive at Sears and Roebuck, and lived comfortably in Richmond Heights with his family. His education would eventually include two master's degrees and a PhD.

Richardson undertook the task of mobilizing community support for the Seventeen-Point Plan, knowing that effecting any concrete social change would require changing the attitudes of an entire community that seemed mired in what he called the "generational curse" of poverty and hopelessness. He preached the value of home ownership to his congregation, but his success was kept in check by class bias. He observed, "Some complained that there are people who don't like Sweet Home because we keep our yard clean. And we paint our church. And we have nice cars in our parking lot on Sundays. There are people who say, 'I can't go to that church; that's upper crust.' And here we're trying to empower the community and say, listen, 'What we are is what you can be.'" Although Reverend Richardson attracted some members from Perrine, his message had greater appeal to the more upwardly mobile and more highly educated

Black middle class who resided outside of Perrine and who responded to his dynamic teaching and exegesis because he spoke about their struggles, hopes, and ambitions. Nor was Reverend Richardson successful in attracting the Perrine pastors to join his cause. The large number of churches in West Perrine bespoke disagreements among them. Seemingly irreconcilable theological and social divides, as well as power struggles between pastors, impeded collaboration between the churches.

One such divide was the classic dispute between the Pentecostals and the Baptists. As one church leader explained, "If you have a Pentecostal and you have a Baptist, if you just listen to their sermon, you will say, oh well, it sounds fine. They are reading the same Bible, they are preaching the same sermon. However, as far as living it, the Pentecostal will say, 'I have to live everything that is in the Bible.' Whereas the Baptist would say, you know, 'If I want to have a little woman on the side, that'll be okay. And you know, if I go to nightclubs and really do it up one night or so that'll be okay.' We have some Baptist ministers around here who have like five or six kids out of wedlock."

By 1986, Richardson realized that the community's most immediate threats, such as the generational rift and other social divisions, came from within it and that unless the drug culture could be eradicated, the redevelopment of Perrine would never happen. Not to be discouraged by the different factions in the community and knowing that he would not be able to fight the drug dealers alone, Richardson attempted to build church solidarity by marching through the streets of Perrine on Saturdays and Sundays after church, with as many supporters as he could muster. He described the effort as a "compassionate confrontation" to show drug dealers that there is an alternative lifestyle available, but that if they were not interested in adopting it the community would not allow their behavior to continue. Richardson said that the marchers walked "away down the streets, and we sing and we pray and we stop in front of crack houses and all that." His efforts drew some support from the community, but the new power wielders, the drug dealers, were not put off.

It would ultimately take the tragedy of multiple shootings over a two-day period in May 1989 that culminated in the murder of a prominent Black businessman to convince Perrine's churches that the community was in dire trouble. Lee Arthur Lawrence had been marching with Reverend Richardson's group for a couple of years but had become impatient with the lack of progress being made to rid the community of the drug lords. He decided to take matters into his own hands and called the police in repeated efforts to get drug dealers off his property. As a result, he was murdered. The murder, in which Lawrence was shot forty-seven times by a drug gang member, shocked those who knew him and delivered a wake-up call to many of the older members of Perrine's community, those who had retreated into their small church circles and closed their eyes to how far their community had deteriorated.

In an almost immediate response to the murder, the community formed the West Perrine Christian Association (WPCA), a coalition of pastors, with Richardson as its president. In one fell swoop, Perrine's churches put aside their differences and came together in common cause, thereby expressing a unified commitment toward the reclamation of Perrine as their community. Bishop Ingraham of Community Church of Christ Written in Heaven was one of the first to join the WPCA, explaining that Lawrence's murder inspired him to combat the social ills that led to the tragedy. He related, "When the ministers got out and said we have to form something, we got to invite all the churches, and then we got together to form the Christian Association. And, we made a promise to the community at his [Lawrence's] burial that this would not be him alone, but it would be us from here on in."

Using the WPCA to engender an abundance of CSC through this critical zone of conflict, Richardson went even further to enlist churches in the wider Miami area, both White and Black, to participate in the marches. Soon, so many people were marching that the police had to provide personnel to divert traffic and ensure protection. The weekly marches attracted media attention, and with much community support, liquor stores were closed, crack houses boarded up, and drug dealers driven out of the neighborhood, demonstrating anew the same faith-based courage that once enabled the community to stand off the Ku Klux Klan.

The Pastor, the Businessman, the Cop, and the Attorney General: Perrine's Present and Future

In time, West Perrine's struggle would be understood to be less one against racism and more one against the harmful secular values promoted and endorsed by the dominant society. Pastor Delores Alexander expressed this view when she noted that churches were involved in a "war of religion," that "the religion of secular humanism has been at war with the faith as we knew it." The Sanctified Church tradition, of which the Pentecostal, Holiness, and Apostolic churches are a part, embodies these anti-secular sentiments. But these are unlike other religious traditions that mandate separation from secular society as a prerequisite to living a holy life. Elder Bennett reminds the people of Perrine that they "can live holy" in this world and that they can and should live a life of full civic engagement. The problems in society, the teen pregnancies, shootings in schools, juvenile delinquency, and problems in the government and in the churches, are seen, according to Pentecostal doctrine, as stemming from one cause: People don't live holy lives. In this view, God must be put back into people's lives. Indeed, as Elder Bennett proclaims, "God is the solution to the problem."

The churches' battles with "secular" society are zones of conflict that are often generative of CSC for pastors and their congregations, as the following example demonstrates. Bishop Watson, as president of the West Perrine

Christian Association, attended Commissioner Dennis Moss's monthly round-table meeting at city hall and related the following:

> I went to the commission, Dennis Moss. I went to the round-table meet-ing. And I came in there, and they come to me and they say, 'Bishop Watson, we'd like for you to pray today. And by the way, you don't men-tion Jesus.' I say, 'By the way, I don't pray them kind of prayers.' He said, 'Okay, do what you want to do.' So when Commissioner Moss, when they gave him my name to pray, they say, 'Bishop Watson, we gonna have you to pray. Now you know we don't do that.' And I hollered back out to them, 'Commissioner, I don't pray them kind of prayers.' He said, 'Go ahead, Bishop.' And when I got through prayin', you know, the way I supposed to pray, you'd be surprised that Washington was there.[13] Well they come to me and say, 'Praise the Lord. 'Bout time you got someone here to pray.'

The resources that Commissioner Moss brought to the community clearly demonstrate the impressive amount of CSC that Perrine's new political power base accumulated in just a few years. Arguably, Commissioner Moss's greatest achievement in improving Perrine's quality of life has been tied to a larger plan for community improvement that incorporates aspects of the earlier plans that he had helped to design. This large plan is spearheaded by Ed Hanna, executive director of the West Perrine CDC, with the support of others leaders (including Reverend Richardson and Police Officer Tookes) in the original Richmond Heights group of community leaders. One of Moss's first accomplishments upon being elected to office shortly after Hurricane Andrew devastated South Florida in 1992 was an appropriation by the Federal Emergency Management Agency (FEMA) of 73 million dollars for the Moss Plan, a comprehensive revitalization plan for the long-neglected communities in his district, which stretched nearly twenty miles from Richmond Heights to Florida City at the southern tip of the Florida Peninsula. On behalf of his local group, Moss secured 4.5 million dollars from the state of Florida to build a health center and a youth facility on West Perrine's historic Homestead Avenue.

Hanna's efforts to tear down crack houses and eradicate slum landlords also have the backing of Moss's office and the county police department, which enforces code violations against landlords. Hanna's redevelopment efforts, backed by the WPCA, aim to lower crime by destroying crack houses and encour-aging home ownership over renting. Hanna and Reverend Richardson try to convince residents to replace their old plumbing and septic tanks with a mod-ern infrastructure to attract developers. Because Hanna's group has been suc-cessful in the past in improving conditions in Perrine, the government has confidence in his ability to lower crime and increase tax revenues for the county (by raising property values). The WPCA, for its part, has succeeded in its requests to Commissioner Moss, which in turn augments Commissioner Moss's own stock of CSC by adding to his influence at city hall, for as Perrine's crime rate falls, its ability to attract development and to increase tax revenues strengthens.

One of the WPCA's most significant achievements, one that would have national implications, in fact, was its collaboration with Janet Reno, then Dade County state attorney. Richardson's marches, the formation of the WPCA, and the increased media attention to Perrine attracted the attention of the state attorney, who began attending the meetings of the WPCA. Miami had been beset by riots throughout the 1980s and into the 1990s. There was concern that West Perrine might be next in line. Reno was attracted to West Perrine because of its strong history of community involvement and because it enjoyed a better relationship with police than did other communities elsewhere in the county.[14] She already had strong relationships with individuals in Perrine, including Ethel Beckford, whom she called the "heart and soul of the community." Reno had often accepted invitations to speak about crime at Beckford's church. Reno sensed Perrine's abundant resources and believed that she could play a role in connecting them to governmental resources.

Reno approached several local Black pastors with whom she had long-standing connections to try to come up with a plan to lower crime in South Dade. As state attorney for Dade County, Reno knew that the traditional use of a police force to fight crime in lower-income areas was not effective because of the underlying problems of inadequate housing, education, and health care, and underemployment, unemployment, and poverty. She also knew that relations between the police and Black communities were usually poor. The "Team Police" approach, already in place in other inner-city parts of the county, was supposed to improve relationships between police and community. In this approach, police were supposed to refer people with social problems, such as health, housing, and family issues, to an appropriate government agency, but their main emphasis remained law enforcement, and often social issues were lost in the bureaucracy.

Reno saw her role as bringing governmental agencies in line with the needs of the community and then devising a plan for the community to access these governmental resources. Sitting in on the WPCA meetings, she listened to pastors and other citizens share their frustrations over not being able to meet basic living requirements, hearing how the welfare programs were preventing families from being able to afford to live together, how they were encouraging further dismantling of the family by giving incentives for single teenage girls to qualify for housing by having babies, and many other examples of failed government programs. She listened to pastors complain that welfare programs were destroying the African American family unit, that children were being raised without male role models, and that the church, long the heart of the Black community and an institution crucial to the existence of African Americans, was being abandoned. After attending many of the weekly meetings over a two-year period, Janet Reno assembled the NRT, a multi-agency resource umbrella agency that brought together HRS (the State Department of Health and Rehabilitative Services, which administered health, welfare, and juvenile delinquency programs in Dade County), HUD (the county's Housing and Urban Development), MDPD (the Dade County Police Department), and the Dade County School Board under one roof.

Key to the success of the new agency would be the team coordinator, that individual who could organize the disparate elements of community and government. State Attorney Reno appointed Ron Tookes, a Black police officer and community leader from Coconut Grove whom she had known for more than thirty years, to head the NRT. Tookes had a longtime commitment to community service, joining the police force in the late 1980s because he believed that a closer relationship between the police and community would prevent race riots. After his appointment he moved to Richmond Heights and joined the efforts of Reverend Richardson, Commissioner Moss, and CDC director Hanna. He also became a member of Richardson's Sweet Home Missionary Baptist Church.

Tookes was an excellent choice to lead the NRT in Perrine, as attested by his marked success in uniting different factions and sectors of the Perrine community, in garnering support for Perrine's efforts in the outside community, and in connecting people in need with appropriate services, all of which contributed to a reduction in the local crime rate. Above all, Tookes was successful because he was a member of the larger governmental organization and he was Black, religious, and active in the church. These characteristics allowed him to become something like a central electronic relay station through which Perrine connected with the outside community. The connection effectively facilitated the further accumulation of CSC and its deployment.

Reflecting on his own moral development, Tookes admitted, "The one thing that kept me straight as a youngster, and all of us straight as a youngster, was the fact that we feared God. And it wasn't so much that our parents had to see us do wrong, but we felt that God was looking." Tookes echoed the feelings of the ministers in the West Perrine Christian Association that church guidance was essential to the delivery of social services when he said, "Government cannot do it alone. Government needed community input. It needed input from the clergy, from the church. I know what really prompts my Afro-Americans to move in the right direction. And it's nothing that's generated by government influence. It's generated by religious influence."

The team concept extended beyond government agencies to include private organizations such as churches, social clubs, businesses, and nonprofit organizations. The NRT became a clearinghouse and referral service for connecting persons in need with the persons or agencies that could help them. Part of Tookes's job was establishing relationships with these different organizations in order to form a network for his support system. He became adept at going into the White community to access their resources for his programs. He explained, "It's important for us to continue to educate the people we call the 'haves,' meaning the east side of U.S. 1, the Palmetto Bay folk, the Pinecrest folk, to let them know how much I need them as a partner. In order to be able to help ease the economic crises we're having on this side." Through his partnering efforts, Tookes received Thanksgiving baskets and toys for Christmas from these more affluent, predominantly White organizations just across the highway. He convinced a fishing store to take one hundred of his kids on an annual fishing trip, and the University of Miami to contribute football tickets for his Join a Team and Not a Gang program.

Tookes deftly employs the WPCA as moral authority before the county commission and to back him up in conflicts with local police departments. The WPCA is, indeed, his power base and a source of much CSC that Tookes invests quite profitably at city hall. As he noted, "I consider the Christian Association as my board of directors. . . . Wherever you set up shop, we really would love to have the clergy being our spokes-mechanism. In other words, they're the ones that we can basically become cohesive with and they can see our needs. And one of the good things about working with the clergy and working with the ministers is that they don't have the restrictions of not being able to, where they can't go down and talk to the commissioners. And they can do all the things that—a lot of things I can't do."

The success of the NRT approach, particularly in the hands of Police Officer Tookes, indeed demonstrates how CSC can increase in purchasing power when the storehouse of such capital (here, the churches and church-based groups) is connected with other wells of power in the community in a direct and efficient way. The NRT's efforts to combat crime led to the creation of five more teams in other crime-ridden public-housing projects and low-income private apartment buildings in other Miami neighborhoods. It also led to the Family Preservation Program, which operated like a mobile NRT unit that dealt specifically with family-related problems.

So effective was Tookes's approach that he steered away from a traditional law enforcement approach. Sometimes, instead of arresting drug pushers, he tried to find them a job; but when he does, it is on the condition that they go to church, any church. He explained,

> Every person in the area is on crack or has a drug problem, or they got any kind of problem. All the ex-offenders, the heads of households, all the welfare mothers, all have our cards in their purse or in their pockets. If a guy's stopped on the street a lot of times, I send mixed signals to the police department because a guy who's running from the police, they stop him. He's got my card on him. So they say, well, how you involved

with Tookes. You know, well, he was trying to help me find a job. He was-
n't able to get a job, so he's out doing whatever. So now that relationship
has developed where the police officers now understand what's really
happening here. They're liable to see me in the middle of a dope hole,
just sitting there talking to the guys. And I'm not arresting him, or trying
to pat 'em down for drugs, any of that kind of stuff. But what I'm trying to
do is to convince them to get off drugs. Stop selling drugs.

Tookes then tells them that he will be happy to help them, but they need to
come back to see him on a Monday, but only if they have Sunday's church program. He tells them, "Sunday morning I want you in church with your mother.
I don't care what church. You go. If you don't want to go to your mother's
church, go to anybody's church. So then Monday morning for me to help you,
you gotta come in here and tell me you went to church and bring the program."

This approach can be seen not simply as an attempt to give "religion" to
those he seeks to help, but to connect the church to the governmental organs of
social services, to create and access more effective mechanisms of social
improvement. It is through such connections that CSC moves in Perrine. In
making such connections, Tookes went so far as to actually locate the Family
Preservation Program in churches years before the Bush administration's faith-
based initiatives were launched. In fact, Tookes even labeled his approach "my
own faith-based initiative," that of "taking families to church, taking youngsters
to church." He elaborated, "About three or four years ago I developed a system
where if a guy comes in here or a family calls me and tells me that they have a
family member who's on drugs, and he needs some help, I need to call Reverend
Sumpter, or call one of the ministers and say, 'Listen, I need you to counsel this
person. I'm about to send them down to the HAC [Homeless Assistance Center]
but I need you to counsel them for me and talk to them about church and that
sort of thing.' . . . I'd say it's better than methadone. . . . For the crack user it's
one of the best things that we can do for them."

Such an alliance lends greater credibility to the churches in the community, as the un-churched population is, they hope, drawn back into the pews,
where ministers can also seek to reorient them spiritually. It also allows the
county's law enforcement agency to establish new connections with pastors and
to reinforce collaborative networks that potentially could connect needy people
to appropriate service providers, an end result of which Tookes an others envi-
sion as a decrease in crime and, in the language of this volume, an increase in
the local churches' store of CSC.

Some West Perrine churches have concerns about involving the government so directly in their affairs; they are fearful, for instance, of the potential
strings attached to government funds. Unlike Officer Tookes, Reverend
Richardson, and Commissioner Moss, some pastors would prefer a stricter

separation between church and state to safeguard religious freedom. These pastors thus tend to be opposed to the faith-based initiatives championed by the Bush administration. Rev. Joseph Sumpter, past president of the WPCA, for instance, believes that government funding will interfere with the churches' ability to preach the word, while Shirley Green believes that tax auditors will coerce churches to vote for Bush if they have not kept their books in proper order. Yet by now, most of Perrine's churches have learned how to access government money, thanks in large part to Officer Tookes's strong support and lobbying efforts. He has convinced many pastors that it is an opportunity to transfer the responsibility for administering to the needs of the local community from the government to the church. Tookes has gone so far as to bring in people to teach the church leaders how to write grants to access government funds. There are now churches in Perrine with memberships of no more than forty members that have grant writers.

The successful returns on Perrine's churches' investment of CSC in Tookes's NRT initiative have had national ramifications. When President Bill Clinton appointed Janet Reno U.S. attorney general in 1993, her agenda as the nation's leading law enforcement officer was shaped by her experiences in West Perrine. Using Perrine's NRT model as an example of successful synergism between community and government, Reno encouraged law enforcement agencies around the country to adopt similar models according to their particular local needs, and she invited Ron Tookes and other members of South Dade's NRTs to the Department of Justice in Washington, D.C., to explain to a nationwide assembly of government officials how their program worked.[15] Reno's office assisted Clinton in drafting his Welfare Reform Bill, which was passed by Congress in 1996 as the Personal Responsibility and Work Opportunity Reconciliation Act, otherwise known as the Welfare Reform Act. In 1996, a "Charitable Choice" section was added to the Welfare Reform Act, establishing new rules for collaboration between government and religious institutions. The law prohibits public officials from discriminating against religious social-service providers who seek to compete for government contracts, and it protects the religious integrity and character of faith-based organizations. These ideas were taken up by President George W. Bush, who, in one of his first major initiatives, established the Office of Faith-Based and Community Initiatives in an effort to overcome some of the bureaucratic obstacles to the participation of faith-based organizations (Streeter 2001).

Linking Social Capital through Prayer and Politics

Perrine and its Black churches constitute an extreme case of religion being the source of CSC, particularly linking CSC. Indeed, most of Perrine's Blacks appear to fuse the civic sphere with religion. Even the Pentecostals, who prefer an individualistic approach to social issues (see Kniss and Numrich 2007), have been at times integrated. The Black churches of Perrine have been independently engaged in their own faith-based initiative for nearly a century. From local efforts among Black Freemasons to take up arms to confront the Ku Klux Klan to the initiatives of church leaders to destroy crack houses, the history of West Perrine's civic engagement is a legacy that has had both local and national impact, a recent powerful example of the CSC sown and reaped by the Black churches in the struggle for social justice and improvement in America. The combination of bonding, bridging, and linking social capital emerges fundamentally from conflict within a society that originally legally sanctioned segregation. Led by its Black religious institutions, Perrine struggled with a dominant society that blatantly and formally discriminated against Blacks. CSC was directed toward self-governance. It was based squarely upon bonding social capital, yet linking social capital to the local White power structure occasionally provided resources, although not as often as it threatened violence, at least until the post–civil rights era. By the end of the twentieth century, Perrine's leaders were integrated in numerous ways. In response to a social crisis provoked by drugs and associated neighborhood decline, Black religious leaders overcame denominational differences and bonded into a unified group. The opening of the political system to Blacks provided new opportunities for linking social capital, first, to county officials and, eventually, to federal programs. Throughout this community's history, the ostensibly secular organizations that coordinated and administered the new resources brought by these links remained self-consciously and thoroughly infused with religion.

NOTES

1. "West Perrine" is not an official place name, but rather a popular label for the Black section of Perrine, an unincorporated area of southern Miami-Dade County located on the west side of the railroad tracks and U.S. Highway 1. Though "West Perrine" and "Perrine" are used interchangeably throughout this chapter, the focus here is on West Perrine. In 2002, the more affluent and primarily White section on the east side of U.S. 1, formerly a part of Perrine, was incorporated and named the Village of Palmetto Bay.

2. All of the ethnographic descriptions and quotations are from work done by the author in the context of this fieldwork. The names of people and places in this chapter, with the exception of one person who is identified with a pseudonym, are actual names. These individuals gave permission to use their names in association with the information gathered by the author. A fuller description can be found in Fink (2005).

3. Dade County officially changed its name to Miami-Dade County in 1997. Most of the events reported in this chapter occurred when the official name was still Dade County.

4. For a history of Blacks in the greater Miami area, see Dunn 1997.

5. As Peter Berger and Thomas Luckmann maintain, "Identity is formed by social processes. Once crystallized, it is maintained, or even reshaped by social relations. The social processes involved in both the formation and the maintenance of identity are determined by the social structure." (1966, 159).

6. Mechal Sobel originally developed the concept of the "Black Sacred Cosmos" as a melding of African religions with Christianity (1979, 3–22).

7. This church was originally named Pine Grovers. A year after its formation it affiliated as an AME (African Methodist Episcopal) church after Bishop Hurst of the Southern District AME in Jacksonville, Florida, sent a pastor to conduct a revival meeting in Perrine in 1913 (Taylor 1986, 56). A Hurst Chapel Sunday church program describes the formation of this church: "a newly arrived group of Bahamians, accustomed to worshiping God on the Sabbath, realized that, next to finding lodging for their families, they must have a place of worship" (Taylor n.d.).

8. According to Bishop Joseph Ingraham, his grandfather acquired this property through squatting.

9. These churches were Mt. Sinai Baptist Church and the Methodist church, which would eventually be named Kerr Memorial.

10. Miami may have been the first city in the South to hire Blacks as members of its permanent police force. In 1944, under extreme secrecy, five Black men were sworn in as police officers of the Miami Police Department (Dunn 1997, 172–173).

11. Elsewhere in Miami, the police were not as supportive of the Black community and at times even sanctioned the Klan's activities. See George 1979.

12. Although school desegregation was mandated by federal law in 1954, it took an additional twelve years to reach Perrine.

13. Bishop Watson is referring to government officials from Washington who attended the meeting.

14. A report on the 1980 McDuffy riot in Miami concluded that poverty, boredom (caused by the lack of recreational facilities in Black neighborhoods), and immigration, which was perceived to be the cause of job displacement from Blacks, may have been contributing factors to feelings of discontent among Blacks. However, the number one cause of the riot was that Blacks felt they were treated unjustly by the police and by the criminal justice system. The Perrine community, on the other hand, did not feel this immediate sense of injustice. Blacks had been on the police force in Perrine since the 1940s, and there was a communal memory of fairness in dealings with Whites within the limits of socially imposed racism (Porter and Dunn 1984; Dunn, 1997, 245–267).

15. Reno called Boston's program (in the 1990s) the country's best example of successful synergy between the government and the Black community, citing an excellent police chief, mayor, domestic violence court, public health component through the Boston hospitals, and an effective Black clergy, headed by the Rev. Eugene F. Rivers III. Rivers's "Ten Point Coalition" has been written about extensively (Dionne and Chen 2001).

REFERENCES

Berger, P., and T. Luckmann. 1966. *The Social Construction of Reality: A Treatise in the Sociology of Knowledge.* Garden City, NY: Doubleday.

Brown, W., and K. Hudson. 1996. Henry Flagler and the Model Land Company. *Tequesta* 56: 46–78.

Chidester, D. 1988. *Patterns of Power: Religion and Politics in American Culture.* New York: Prentice Hall.

Dionne, E. J., Jr., and Ming Hsu Chen, eds. 2001. *Sacred Places, Civic Purposes: Should Government Help Faith-Based Charity?* Washington, DC: Brookings Institution Press.

Dunn, M. 1997. *Black Miami in the Twentieth Century.* Miami: University Press of Florida.

Fink, S. O. 2005. Politics and Prayer in West Perrine, Florida: Civic Social Capital and the Black Church. Masters thesis, Florida International University.

George, P. S. 1979. Policing Miami's Black Community, 1896–1930. *Florida Historical Quarterly* 57(4): 434–450.

Granovetter, M. 1973. The Strength of Weak Ties. *American Journal of Sociology* 78(6): 1360–1380.

Kniss, F., and P. D. Numrich. 2007. *Sacred Assemblies and Civic Engagement*. New Brunswick, NJ: Rutgers University Press.

Lincoln, C. 1999. *Race, Religion, and the Continuing American Dream*. New York: Hill and Wang.

Lincoln, C., and L. Mamiya. 1990. *The Black Church in the African American Experience*. Durham, NC: Duke University Press.

Model Land Company. N.d. Records. Archives and Special Collections, University of Miami, Coral Gables, Florida.

Mohl, R. 1989. Miami's Metropolitan Government: Retrospect and Prospect. *Florida Historical Quarterly* 63(1): 24–50.

Homer A. Plessy v. Ferguson. 163 U.S. 537; 16 S. Ct. 1138; 41 L. Ed. 256; 1896 U.S. LEXIS 3390.

Porter, B., and M. Dunn. 1984. *The Miami Riot of 1980*. Lexington, MA: Lexington Books.

Putnam, R. 1993. *Making Democracy Work*. Princeton: Princeton University Press.

———. 2000. *Bowling Alone: The Collapse and Revival of American Community*. New York: Simon and Schuster.

Sobel, M. 1979. *Trabelin' On: The Slave Journey to an Afro-Baptist Faith*. Westport, CT: Greenwood Press.

Streeter, R. 2001. *Charitable Choice as Historical Phenomenon and Future Reality*. Washington, DC: Hudson Institute.

Taylor, J. 1986. *The Villages of South Dade*. St. Petersburg, FL: Byron Kennedy.

———. N.d. Research Papers. Historical Museum of South Florida, Miami.

United States Congress. 1838. *Report to Accompany Bill S. No. 241*. Twenty-fifth U.S. Congress, 2nd sess., March 12.

Woolcock, M. 2004. Why and How Planners Should Take Social Capital Seriously. *Journal of the American Planning Association* 70(2): 183–189.

PART TWO

Service and Volunteerism and Bridging Civic Social Capital

5

Unidos en la Fe

Transnational Civic Social Engagement between Two Cuban Catholic Parishes

KATRIN HANSING

Since 1959 over a million Cubans have migrated to the United States; the majority today live in the greater Miami area, also known as the capital of the Cuban exile. Unlike many other immigrant groups in the United States who have and continue to maintain ongoing transnational ties to their countries of origin, the dominant image of the relationship between Cubans on both sides of the Florida Straits has been one of two communities in a state of cold war with few, if any, ties but many animosities. Decades of anger, bitterness, and distrust have, in fact, dominated the official discourse and image between the two sides, as was witnessed in the Elián Gonzalez episode in 2000, which focused national attention on the divisions between Miami's Cubans and the broader U.S. population (Lizza 2000; McQueen 2000; De La Torre 2003; Stepick et al. 2003).

Despite the very real political rifts, economic embargo, and deep-seated emotional wounds that exist between both sides, the two Cuban communities have been and continue to be much more closely connected than is usually publicly acknowledged. Especially since the mid-1990s, a wide range of transnational ties and activities has emerged of which family visits and the sending of remittances are among the best documented (Eckstein and Barberia 2001, 2002). In addition, numerous social, cultural, and religious ties have developed which are slowly but surely transforming the relationship between this otherwise divided nation (Tweed 1997).

This chapter examines the transnational ties between the Catholic Church in Cuba and the Archdiocese in Miami. Although not entirely new, these ties increased enormously after the beginning of the 1990s economic crisis in Cuba, a result of both the demise of Soviet subsidies to Cuba and the prolonged U.S. embargo. Since then a host of Miami exile-led religious initiatives toward Cuba have been pioneered, each with varying intentions and influences. Apart from examining the general nature, characteristics, gradual development, and transformations of these ties, this chapter will specifically focus on the relationship and linkages fostered by two Cuban Catholic communities, one in Miami and the other on the island. By focusing on this particular case study, this chapter hopes to bring to light some of the more subtle and detailed nuances of the slowly but surely changing relationship between Cubans on both sides of the Florida Straits.

In terms of civic social capital (CSC), this chapter reveals the complexities and ambiguities of distinguishing between bonding social capital and bridging CSC. The Cuban Revolution dissolved the bonding among Cuban Catholics, sowing distrust. between those on the island and those in exile. This chapter describes how those bonds are being re-established through nearly invisible bridges to the island and with careful concern for not undermining the intense bonding among Miami Cubans that presumes no contact, no bridging with Cubans in Cuba.

Overview of Ties between Cuban Catholics in Cuba and Miami since 1959

Miami and Cuba have been joined by the hip ever since the Cuban Revolution in 1959. Like Siamese twins, in fact, the one does not breathe without the other. Pushing hundreds of thousands of Cuban exiles to Miami, the Cuban Revolution not only profoundly changed Miami socially, linguistically, politically, and economically but also tremendously transformed the city's religious, particularly its Catholic, landscape.

As discussed in this volume's first chapter, the Miami Catholic Archdiocese has been coterminous with that of the Cuban exile. From the very start the church played a major role in the welcoming, integrating, and resettling of Cuban refugees. In fact, of the seven hundred thousand Cubans who entered the United States between 1961 and 1973, the Catholic Church resettled 70 percent of them.[1] This active engagement continued throughout the 1980s with the Mariel Boatlift and subsequent *balsero* (rafter) crisis of the mid-1990s. Over 60 percent of all newly arriving Cubans continue to be resettled by the Catholic Church. Over the past four decades the church has also welcomed many Cuban priests, some of whom were expelled from the island.

Despite the intense involvement of the Catholic Church in the nearly fifty-year-old Cuban drama, the actual ties between the archdiocese and the Catholic Church in Cuba were weak, especially in the first three decades after the revolution. This situation can mainly be attributed to the difficult political situation between the United States and Cuba as well as the politicized atmosphere in both communities. In Cuba, the Catholic Church, like all religious expression, was faced with enormous pressures and prejudices from the Communist-led government and forced into a position of marginality and silence, while the church in Miami became a powerful and outspoken anti-Communist space and voice. These very different realities and political pressures lived by both churches, as well as the omnipresent hostility between the two countries, created an environment of mutual distrust and caused the churches to drift apart.

Since the mid-1980s, but especially since the economic crisis and opening of the religious realm in Cuba in the early 1990s, more active and ongoing transnational ties have developed between the two churches. Today, in fact, a number of transnational ties exist. For the most part these include informal religious ties, such as unofficial clergy visits, sister church links, as well as a series of lay initiatives, most of which have a humanitarian character. Apart from bringing badly needed material aid to Cuba these linkages are also creating important people-to-people ties between an otherwise still largely divided nation. Among the existing ties is the case of the relationship between the parish of St. Agatha in Miami and the diocese of Guantánamo-Baracoa, situated in the eastern part of Cuba.

Since 1998, these two religious communities have been officially connected through a formal sister church–diocese relationship. Despite the growing number of religious links between Cuban Catholics on both sides of the Florida Straits, these formal institutional ties are still weak. St. Agatha was for a decade the only church in Miami that had such an official tie with a diocese on the island.

How did this transnational religious link develop, how does it manifest itself, and what have some of its effects and consequences been? These are some of the questions I propose to examine in this chapter. Given the fact that the two communities' relationship is predominantly based on material aid that is sent from St. Agatha to Guantánamo-Baracoa, I will mainly focus on the dynamics involved in the development of St. Agatha's long-distance civic social engagement toward the Cuban diocese. In so doing, I will particularly look at the mobilization and use of CSC among St. Agatha parishioners in raising the necessary funds for the Catholic Church in Cuba as well as highlight some of the subtle yet complex power relations in which these two communities' unusual relationship are embedded.

The Parish of St. Agatha in Miami

St. Agatha Church is nestled in the neighborhood of Westchester, a predominantly middle-class Cuban residential neighborhood in Miami-Dade County. According to Father Rolando Garcia, the current parish priest, roughly 80 percent of the church's over thirty-eight hundred registered members[2] are Cuban, while the rest are from various other Central and Latin American countries. Only a small number of members are Anglo-American, and almost all members are White. Among the Cuban congregants, many were born and raised in Cuba and came to the United States for political/ideological reasons in the 1960s and

1970s or are second-generation Cuban Americans. As a result, the parish is politically conservative, especially with regards to Cuban affairs.[3]

Social ties between the Cuban congregants tend to be fairly strong. While some of these relationships were formed through the parish, a large percentage of people already knew each other long beforehand. Some, for instance, went to Catholic school together in Cuba, were or are members of the same apostolic groups, or know each other because they are originally from the same town or province in Cuba. Based as much on their common faith, exile fate, and Cuban identity, these networks have produced an extensive amount of social capital that has greatly benefited the parish on a material as well as ministerial level. St. Agatha, for example, is one of the most socially active churches in the Archdiocese of Miami with an unusually high number of fifty-four ministries, almost all of which are Cuban lay led and run. Despite this active parish life, the majority of St. Agatha's ministries have tended to uphold the more general Catholic parish principle of primarily supporting the needs of the parish, and thus have maintained an "inward focus." In other words, rather than reaching out and focusing on wider community issues, which are predominantly dealt with by the archdiocese, St. Agatha's ministries reach inward and mainly concentrate on the religious, spiritual, and personal needs of their own parishioners, i.e., on bonding social capital. The one exception is St. Agatha's long-distance sister relationship with the diocese of Guantánamo-Baracoa in Cuba, a case of transnational bridging CSC.

In January 1998, Pope John Paul II undertook his historic visit to Cuba. Among the large entourage of clergy and pilgrims who accompanied him to the island were several Miami-based clergy, both Cuban and Anglo-American, including Miami's Archbishop John Favarola. During his five-day visit the pope delivered a message of peace, love, and hope to the Cuban people and called on Cuba to "open itself up to the world and the world to open itself up to Cuba." Inspired by the Holy Father's words and well aware of Cuba's dire economic crisis, Archbishop Favarola returned to Miami with the idea of creating formal ties of support between certain parishes in Miami and the fourteen dioceses in Cuba. Apart from raising badly needed funds for the Catholic Church on the island,[4] it was hoped that these church-diocese ties would also act as a means of communication and potential solidarity between an otherwise divided nation and people.

Despite the archbishop's good intentions and the large number of Cuban-dominated parishes and clergy in Miami, the idea was met with much resistance on the part of most Miami-based churches. In fact, of the dozens of Cuban-dominated parishes, St. Agatha was the only church that committed itself to supporting the archbishop's idea. Most other churches responded by stating that they had too many other needs and commitments in their own parishes and, therefore, could not reach out to the church in Cuba. According to a number of

St. Agatha congregants, however, the reason had more to do with Cuban exile politics than a lack of resources. As one woman explained, "Most people automatically assume that by helping the church in Cuba one also helps Fidel and his regime stay in power. They are blinded by a mentality that equates everything Cuban with Fidel Castro, including the church. So when the church-diocese plan was announced many just rejected it out of fear."

Being a politically conservative parish, St. Agatha's initial reaction to the church-diocese idea was not much different from the rest of the Cuban churches in Miami. Most congregants, in fact, reacted with skepticism and hesitation. Given these circumstances, what made St. Agatha end up responding affirmatively to the archbishop's call?

According to Gabriela Rodriguez, a St. Agatha parishioner and the lay leader of the Guantánamo-Baracoa ministry, several coinciding factors influenced the parish's willingness to reach out. First and foremost was the leadership and personality of St. Agatha's former parish priest, Monsignor Felipe Estévez. Known for his open-mindedness and strong, ongoing relationship and support of the church in Cuba, he embraced the archbishop's plan wholeheartedly. Well aware of the biases among his congregation, Father Estévez repeatedly mentioned the idea in his homilies and other church events. Each time, he emphasized Christian values of love and fraternity and he encouraged his parishioners to reach out and get involved with the church in Cuba. In addition, he had the foresight to create a ministry that would specifically dedicate itself to the planned church-diocese partnership.

In need of open-minded lay leaders who could and would be willing to see beyond the dominant exile politics, Father Estévez approached Gabriela Rodriguez and asked her to take over the new ministry. Known for her intense devotion to the Cuban church and strong belief in dialogue with the island, Gabriela accepted the challenge and in turn recruited several other fellow Cuban parishioners to help her. All of these individuals were born and raised in Cuba and were closely connected to the Catholic Church on the island before coming to Miami. Despite living in exile they have all remained committed to the church in Cuba; and, although only Gabriela and one other member have returned to the island, all have maintained close personal ties with their former parish and clergy. It is precisely this open-minded and supportive attitude that was needed to start the ministry. If Father Estévez can thus be credited with sowing the seeds and paving the ground for the church-diocese link at St. Agatha, Gabriela Rodriguez and her organizational committee must be credited with turning the idea into a viable and successful ministry. Crucial to both, however, was the timing of the archbishop's appeal, which almost immediately followed the papal visit to Cuba in 1998.

Having experienced and struggled against Communism in his native Poland, Pope John Paul II was seen and praised by many exiled Cubans as a fellow anti-Communist. This not only roused hope and confidence, but also helped break certain mental barriers on the part of some exiled Cubans. As Gabriela explained, "The visit of the Holy Father [to Cuba] really opened many doors. You see, people thought, 'If he goes, then it is ok for us to go, too.'" Besides prompting more Cubans in Miami to visit the island, the papal visit also encouraged some to start helping the church, as in the case of St. Agatha.

St. Agatha's choice to link up with the diocese of Guantánamo-Baracoa, the youngest and arguably most economically needy diocese on the island, was completely arbitrary. As a result, however, St. Agatha parish's new ministry adopted the diocese's name and came up with the slogan: St. Agatha–Guantánamo-Baracoa, *Unidos en la Fe* (United in Faith).

The ministry's main aim is to support the diocese in Cuba with an annual contribution of at least six thousand dollars. In order to raise this money Gabriela and her team organize a series of fund-raising activities each year, which include several garage sales, domino tournaments, tamales and empanadas sales, in addition to the main money-making event, Noche Cubana, a banquet dinner at which Cuban food and entertainment is provided. Selling tickets at ten dollars per person, the ticket sales for this event have raised between twenty-five hundred and three thousand dollars per year. This event's annual success has mainly been due to volunteer support and participation in its preparations as well as in the actual event itself. Fundamental to both the volunteerism and attendance, however, have been the strong social ties and capital among the parishioners as well as the wider Cuban community in Miami.

The Making and Manifestations of Transnational Civic Social Engagement: Noche Cubana

Like every year, Noche Cubana 2001 took place on a Saturday night in early November. The event was supposed to commence with a special Mass at 7:00 p.m., followed by the gala dinner at 8:00 p.m. At around 6:30 p.m. the church compound was still dark and deserted. That is except for a handful of yellow-clad women who kept darting in and out of the parish hall. Inside the hall's sweltering kitchen Gabriela and seven other women from the Guantánamo ministry were working like busy bees. Catering for about 250 people, they hurriedly worked in tandem, carrying in cakes and canisters of soda, fetching extra plates and glasses, and heating up large aluminum trays of delicious-smelling *yuca* (sweet manioc), *congris* (rice and beans), and *puerco asado* (roast pork).

Just beyond the kitchen, inside the parish hall, over twenty large round tables had been set up and modestly decorated with plastic ware and flowers. Above each plate a little picture had been placed featuring a Guantánamo landmark, most often the cathedral or another church, while a whole series of larger, blown-up photographs, posters, and banners featuring images of Cuba were hung up along one of the walls.

Preparations for Noche Cubana had started long beforehand. Since September, Gabriela and the rest of the Guantánamo-Baracoa ministry had been meeting every couple of weeks to discuss and plan the evening and co-ordinate who would be in charge of what. Like every year, food and beverages, cups, plates and cutlery, napkins, candles, and flowers would have to be bought; and tables, chairs, microphones, and the entertainment would have to be organized. Although Gabriela and the other ministry members usually buy and pay for a large percentage of these items from their own pocket and do most of the preparatory work, they also rely heavily on the support of others. Dozens of people, including congregants, relatives, and friends, pitch in and donate their time, effort, and material support. Reflecting on the collaborative nature of Noche Cubana's preparations, Gabriela commented, "Here everyone helps out. We have people who donate bread, others who cook, others who make coffee, etc. This is the beautiful thing about this ministry; it is about participation. This isn't Gabriela helping or so and so helping but an entire ministry, an entire parish helping the church in Cuba. It is really a group thing." Based on strong social ties, this "group thing," as Gabriela called it, or civic social engagement does not restrict itself solely to parish members and their families, but reaches far beyond parish borders, into the wider Cuban community in Miami.

In late September 2001, the Guantánamo-Baracoa ministry met at one of the member's homes near St. Agatha to co-ordinate the upcoming Noche Cubana. After a prayer and short welcome, Gabriela plunged into the heart of the matter: food. How would the eight of them supply food for over 250 people or more? To keep their own costs low, Gabriela suggested that they contact several local Cuban-owned and Cuban-run businesses and ask them to donate food and party ware. Everyone agreed that this was a good idea, but as the proceeds of the event would be sent to Cuba this would surely disturb certain politically conservative members in the community. In other words, some business owners might not be able to separate their exile politics from charity and thus opt out of supporting this transnational form of social civic engagement. Despite the possible polemic, various Cuban-owned supermarkets, bakeries, and restaurants were approached and asked to contribute to St. Agatha's good long-distance cause.

When it came to choosing and contacting these businesses, the ministry members relied heavily on existing social ties and capital based on their Cuban ethnicity. As Iliana Alvarez, a ministry member, explained, "I called a few people and asked if they knew anyone who worked in a supermarket or restaurant. I mean, who has the time to go from one business to another asking for donations? By the end of the day I had the names of four people, all relatives or friends of friends. I called them, told them who I was and what we were doing, and within a few days I received packets of paper plates, cups, and even some food."

Unlike Iliana, Magy Fernández, another ministerial member, went in person to two Cuban-owned establishments, a bakery and a supermarket with which she had no prior ties but from which she received donations, too. According to Magy, the managers pitched in, partly to support a good cause, but mainly because they were Cuban. As she put it, "Look, both of the managers I dealt with were Cuban and one of them was even from my home province. This opens doors and creates solidarity. I mean, it helps when you know people, but even if you don't, just being Cuban does."

Cubans in Miami are well known for their strong social capital and ethnic solidarity (Portes 1987; Portes and Stepick 1993). What is notable is that Iliana and Magy and the others from the Guantánamo-Baracoa ministry consciously mobilized and made use of the Cuban community's strong CSC, colloquially known as *palanca* (literally, leverage). In fact, it was precisely this CSC that underpinned much of the event's organization, both for material donations and for volunteer help. Based on the principle of knowing people who know people or having connections, doors were opened. Existing social ties were activated and new ones formed along the same exclusive ethnic lines. As a result, the already strong solidarity among Cubans in Miami was not only reinforced but also augmented. The importance of palanca or CSC did not, however, limit itself to the organization and co-ordination of Noche Cubana, but was also a crucial component during the event itself.

Mass had just ended and streams of predominantly elderly, elegantly dressed people made their way from the church to the parish hall, where the banquet dinner was about to start. Amidst loud "hellos" and "how are you's," smaller groups of people could be heard chatting about their health, families, and the Mass. Inside the now brightly lit hall much of the same lively activity was taking place. Many, if not most, people seemed to know each other, partly from St. Agatha but also because many were originally from the Guantánamo-Baracoa area and had grown up, gone to school, and even been confirmed together in Cuba. Many of these Guantánameros were not even St. Agatha parishioners but had heard about the event from other Guantánameros and Baracocense.

In the Miami exile community scores of political, religious, entrepreneurial, and social groups, committees, and organizations have been formed within such geographical identities, which in turn have recreated powerful sources of CSC. Similarly, most people who attended Noche Cubana were in large part there to both support their towns and the Cuban diocese and to reunite with their fellow Guantánameros.

Although housed, hosted, and in large part organized at St. Agatha and by its parishioners, Noche Cubana was thus not an exclusive parish event. It also attracted and greatly depended on the support of the wider Cuban community. Rather than being a purely congregational activity, it built upon already established ethnic and provincial ties. In this, St. Agatha and the Guantánamo-Baracoa ministry acted as the primary spaces and agents in and through which these ethnic, social, and human ties and capital were brought together and mobilized.

As such we have the case of Marta Vega, a Guantánamera in her early sixties who left Cuba shortly after the revolution. Although Marta is a member of a neighboring parish, she takes part in almost every Guantánamo-Baracoa ministry event organized by St. Agatha. "I come to be with my people from Guantánamo," she explained. "I know many of them from before." Pointing to her right, she said, "Look, Emilia over there. I have known her since I was seven; and Carlito, the one in the white shirt, he and I received our first communion together. We are like family, you know."

In addition to the strong social ties that draw Marta to these types of events, she also comes to support her church and province in Cuba. Pointing to one of the little photocopied pictures on the table, she exclaimed, "Look, that was my church, the cathedral in Guantánamo. She was so beautiful! Now she is pretty run-down. But before she was the most beautiful church. I wish you could have seen her." Speaking as if she had just returned from Guantánamo, Marta, like so many others in the parish hall that night, has never been back to Cuba since she left the island over forty years ago. Nevertheless, she feels as attached to her hometown and church as the day she left.

It is people like Marta, predominantly middle-class, elderly Cubans, who make up the backbone of support, both moral and material, of the Guantánamo-Baracoa ministry. These are people who for the most part have never returned to Cuba but who have come together on the basis of their common past, strong local identity, and common Catholic faith. In so doing, they develop and reinforce a shared sense of civic social engagement toward the church in Cuba. Through this long-distance charitable support many Cubans in Miami have been able to re-connect with the church in Cuba and with their own pasts. In fact, many people's motivation to participate and support such events as Noche Cubana stems from a strong yearning to reach out, participate, and feel connected to a Cuba that once upon a time was theirs.

Most people who attended Noche Cubana were born and raised in Cuba and have clear memories of what they left behind when they came to live in exile in Miami. The attendees carry painfully wonderful memories of an idealized past when almost everything seemed better, brighter, and more beautiful than in today's Cuba. "You didn't get to know the Cuba we had, the Cuba of before [la Cuba de antes]," remarked Marta. "Everything was different then. The people, the buildings. We had wonderful places to go out to, parks, restaurants. But all of that is gone now."

Certain sectors of the Cuban exile community in Miami, especially those who came in the first waves of exile, are well known for their culture of nostalgia. This is visible in the names of many businesses, churches, organizations, streets, schools, and the many Cuban-themed restaurants and cafés that have tried to recreate an atmosphere of pre-revolutionary Cuba through old pictures, music, and other memorabilia. La Cuba de antes is omnipresent in the Cuban exile capital, i.e., Miami. Perhaps more than anywhere, however, la Cuba de antes exists in people's minds and everyday, lived experiences. Rooted in pain and loss, it is a place and time they miss and mourn, and one to which they constantly make reference. Defined by their exiled existence, many people's realities and much of their everyday lives are focused on re-creating and connecting with that which they once had. Noche Cubana is one of many exile spaces in which familiar faces, memories, and shared experiences come together and a piece of the past is brought to life. Moreover, through the event's actual connection to the diocese of Guantánamo-Baracoa and the fact that most of the money raised in Miami goes toward helping the Cuban diocese and restoring old churches in Guantánamo-Baracoa, a space and relationship has been created in which its contributors in Miami can feel both intimately and concretely connected to the process of reconstructing what they feel once upon a time was theirs.

Noche Cubana 2001 was deemed a success. Thanks to the St. Agatha– Guantánamo-Baracoa ministry members' hard work and dedication as well as the mobilization and use of the Cuban community's strong social capital, over two thousand dollars was raised. The money would go a long way in Cuba; probably toward further restoration or even construction of a new church. The material objectives of the ministry had once again been achieved. What can we say about the social and human consequences of this church-diocese relationship?

There is no doubt that the St. Agatha–Guantánamo-Baracoa connection has helped overcome certain barriers between these two religious communities while also building new bridges between an otherwise divided nation. Hearts and minds on both sides, but especially in Miami, have been opened and softened. Due to the economic imbalance between the two communities and continued lack of person-to-person ties, however, it has been very difficult for the two sides to create and foster a solid fraternal relationship. Instead, most of the reconnecting is not only geographically and unilaterally happening in Miami, but also on very specific Miami-Cuban-centric terms.

Transnational Power Relations toward "*Los Pobrecitos*" in Cuba

The economic crisis in Cuba, which became acute in the early 1990s when the Soviet Union cut off the island from its massive subsidies, created a change in attitude and relations on the part of many exiled Cubans toward their fellow countrymen on the island. Stories of constant blackouts, lack of water and gasoline, and, most of all, food and medicine shortages engendered a strong sense of compassion among many, which has in turn led certain people to reach out and help their families and friends on the island. As a result a growing culture of charity has developed, which is most notably manifested in the large amounts of family remittances that are sent to Cuba each year and also through such events as Noche Cubana, which aim to raise money to support specific projects on the island. Each year millions of exile dollars enter Cuba in this manner, making this one of the main sources of hard currency on the island, surpassed only by tourism. As a result, Cuba and Cubans today are as dependent on foreign investment, tourism, and its enemy's currency, the U.S. dollar, as in pre-revolutionary times. Although this economic crisis has ironically brought the divided peoples of this nation closer together, it has not done so on equal terms. Instead, this renewed economic dependency has given rise to a series of attitudes, mentalities, and social relations that are deeply embedded in unequal power relations.

Most people had finished their dinner and were enjoying their last drops of *café cubano* and morsels of cake when Gabriela's voice resounded from the microphone, announcing that the entertainment was about to begin. Standing on a podium at the front of the parish hall, she asked everyone to extend a warm welcome to "Guantánamo's one and only Bebe Espino," a woman over eighty years old who used to be the Guantánamo Cathedral's choir's pianist before the revolution. Gabriela had barely finished her last sentence when Bebe began playing the well-known and popular song "Guantánamera." The loud chatter that had filled the room suddenly stopped and, as if taking a collective trip down memory lane, everyone joined in to sing this and half a dozen or so other songs that followed, most of which dated back to the 1940s and 1950s.

Humming along to the music, Maria Cárdenas was trying to sell the last batch of raffle tickets, which she and several other women were vending in order to raise a few extra dollars for the Guantánamo-Baracoa ministry. "I do this for my church," she said, referring to the Catholic Church in Cuba. "I also painted these paintings as prizes for the raffle tickets," she said, pointing to two colorful abstract pictures. Moments later she was called on stage together with Father Garcia to hand out the raffle prizes. Before drawing the winners' numbers Maria thanked everyone who had contributed to the fifty-three dollars' worth of raffle tickets she had sold. She acknowledged that although it was not a huge sum of money, it would at least be able to buy some food and medicine for "*los pobrecitos*" (the poor little ones), as she referred to Cubans living on the island. "They have nothing," she continued, "absolutely nothing. They are barely living, just surviving." Overcome with emotion she went on to denounce Fidel Castro, whom she called a "*salvaje*" (savage) and "*un monstro*" (a monster).

While Maria caught her breath, Father Garcia started telling jokes. "Before the start of the Special Period (economic crisis in Cuba)," he began, "there used to be a sign at the Havana Zoo that read, 'Please do not feed the animals.' When the Special Period began the sign was changed to 'Please do not eat the animal food.' Today the sign reads, 'Please do not eat the animals.' " The hall echoed with laughter and several more jokes in a similar vein followed.

When speaking about Cuba and Cubans on the island, Father Garcia's tone was, like Maria's, compassionate and critical, but also slightly patronizing. Despite the well-intentioned objectives of Noche Cubana and the other Guantánamo-Baracoa ministry's fund-raising events, much of the compassion and charity that fuels these activities is tinged with a complex view of and attitude toward Cubans on the island that is based on empathy and pity as well as paternalism. Although captured in such expressions as Maria's "los pobrecitos," this attitude is more commonly expressed through people's tone of voice, which camouflages and envelops in niceties a more subtle but equally potent form of paternalism. Although rooted in pity and pain and enveloped in the best of intentions, this paternalistic attitude marks my Cubans' attitudes and behaviors toward their compatriots still in Cuba.

Conclusion: Uniting across Borders through Faith

Religious ties between Cubans on both sides of the Florida Straits are increasingly rapidly. What once was a presumed bonding among Cuban Catholics became severed by the Cuban Revolution and is now being bridged and may become bonded CSC again. The tense political climate between Miami and Cuba forces most of these links to be informal, unofficial, and often even secretive in nature. The St. Agatha–Guantánamo-Baracoa link was first and for quite a while the only official church-diocese tie between Cuban Catholics on the island and in Miami. The ministry's development and success are largely based on the Cuban community's already existing strong CSC. What has made Miami Cubans engage in supporting the Guantánamo-Baracoa initiative is as much based on a culture of nostalgia as it is on solidarity with the Catholic Church on the island. Despite the presence and potential danger of the above-mentioned paternalistic overtones, the actual link between the two communities is a major achievement, especially given the still-dominant antagonistic discourse between the United States and Cuba. These kinds of ties and exchanges not only demonstrate an increasing willingness to reach out, but also represent one of the few legitimate arenas for rapprochement and reconciliation between Cubans on the island and those in the United States. The evolving relationship also reveals how the distinction between bonding social capital and bridging CSC is both mutable and embedded in particular historical relationships. Leaders such as Fidel Castro, the pope, the archbishop of Miami, and the priest of St. Agatha can all make a difference. For some, however, such as the priest of St. Agatha, it takes considerable skill and allies with parish lay leaders to re-establish bonds that anti-Castro exiles would prefer to remain unbridged.

NOTES

1. The church was also involved in the Pedro Pan Operation, in which over fourteen thousand Cuban children were secretly brought to the United States (Triay 1998; Conde 1999).

2. In the Catholic parish system the definition of a member is a nuclear family. St. Agatha's 3,800 members are thus, in fact, 3,800 nuclear families.

3. On differences in Cuban political opinions, see Pérez 2001; Diaz Fernandez 2001; De La Torre 2003; Stepick and Dutton Stepick 2002; Eckstein and Barberia 2002; and Grenier 2006.

4. In order to secure a certain level of commitment and economic aid, the archdiocese decided that each participating parish in Miami should raise a minimum annual amount of six thousand dollars for their sister diocese in Cuba.

REFERENCES

Conde, Y. 1999. *Operation Pedro Pan: The Untold Exodus of 14,048* Cuban Children. New York: Routledge.

De La Torre, M. A. 2003. *La Lucha for Cuba: Religion and Politics on the Streets of Miami.* Berkeley: University of California Press.

Diaz Fernandez, M. 2001. Intergenerational Dynamics in the Cuban Community in Southern Florida: Identity and Politics in the Second Generation. *Cuban Studies* 31: 76–101.

Eckstein, S., and L. Barberia. 2001. Cuban American Visits: Public Policy, Private Practices. *Report of the Mellon-MIT Inter-University Program on NGOs and Forced Migration.* Cambridge, MA: Massachusetts Institute for Technology, Center for International Studies.

———. 2002. Grounding Immigrant Generations in History: Cuban Americans and Their Transnational Ties. *International Migration Review* 36(3): 799–837.

Grenier, G. J. 2006. The Creation and Maintenance of the Cuban American "Exile Ideology" in Miami. *Circunstancia, Revista de Ciencias Sociales del Instituto Universitario de Investigacion Ortega y Gasset* 10: 1–14.

Lizza, R. 2000. The Miami Herald's Cuban Problem: Between the Lines. *The New Republic Online,* http://www.tnr.com.

McQueen, M. 2000. In the Cauldron. *American Journalism Review,* December 4, 28

Pérez, L. 2001. Growing up in Cuban Miami: Immigration, the Enclave, and New Generations. In *Ethnicities: Children of Immigrants in America,* ed. R. Rumbaut and A. Portes, 91–124. Berkeley: University of California Press.

Portes, A. 1987. The Social Origins of the Cuban Enclave Economy of Miami. *Sociological Perspectives* 30(October): 340–371.

Portes, A., and A. Stepick. 1993. *City on the Edge: The Transformation of Miami.* Berkeley: University of California Press.

Stepick, A., and C. Dutton Stepick. 2002. Becoming American, Constructing Ethnicity: Immigrant Youth and Civic Engagement. *Applied Developmental Science* 6(4): 246–257.

Stepick, A., G. Grenier, M. Castro, and M. Dunn. 2003. *This Land Is Our Land: Interethnic Relations in Miami.* Berkeley: University of California Press.

Triay, V. A. 1998. *Fleeing Castro: Operation Pedro Pan and the Cuban Children's Program.* Gainesville: University Press of Florida.

Tweed, T. A. 1997. *Our Lady of the Exile: Diasporic Religion at a Cuban Catholic Shrine in Miami.* New York: Oxford University Press.

6

La Catedral del Exilio

A Nicaraguan Congregation in a Cuban Church

ISABEL DEL PINO-ALLEN

Suyapa Velazquez remembers the day she re-joined Ms. Adela Jaramillo's after-school class at San Juan Bosco's Catholic Church's Religious-Civic-Patriotic School.[1] With a hint of embarrassment and a bit of bewilderment, the Central American teen recalled, during her interview held at recess time in the afternoon, "I was out for a few months to help care for my little brother, and when I came back the other students had already finished studying the geography of Cuba, the meaning of Cuba's coat of arms, and other important things." In an effort to catch up to her classmates, Suyapa searched the Internet and proudly produced a report on Cuba's geography, including the name of the country's fourteen provinces. Much to her chagrin, she discovered her efforts were unappreciated and she was also mildly chastised for bringing to school current information whereas the school only teaches pre-Communist 1958 facts about Cuba. "No, we don't teach any of the changes that [Fidel Castro] has made in Cuba," Angelita Esparraguera, the director and founder of the school, responded when asked why the school teaches out-dated curricula. "We use our own books. Our students need to learn our realities."

Welcome to San Juan Bosco parish, also known as *la catedral del exilio* (the exiles' cathedral). While the church's official name in the Miami Catholic Archdiocese is in English, Saint John Bosco, I never heard anyone refer to it in this way. Everyone refers to it in Spanish, San Juan Bosco. The parish has been the heart and soul of Cubans' Little Havana's Catholic community in Miami since the early 1960s, when thousands of Cuba's faithful fled during the early years of the Castro revolution, particularly as the government shut churches, religious schools, and other faith-related institutions. Originally nestled in a White, working-class area, the parish experienced a dramatic change in demography and leadership during the 1960s. Cuban exiles became its priests and lay leaders as their distinctive Cuban community grew. They dedicated themselves to both the cultivation and preservation of Cubans' Catholic identity. Cubans in Miami are well known for being tight-knit, for their dense bonding social capital that has been used to aid them economically and to promote their political views on the national and international screen (Pedraza-Bailey 1985; Portes 1987; Portes and Stepick 1993). Their unity derives from shared ideas and cultural traditions—*cubanía*—as well as deep antipathy for Castro. Cultivation of their faith, in contrast, was necessary for Cubans are among Latin Americans least-churched populations, a fact true even before the 1959 revolution (Tweed 1997). The Catholic Church preserved the exiles' identity by promulgating anti-Castro sentiment and action as well as fidelity to the church.

This chapter examines how one key Cuban parish in Miami generates civic social capital (CSC) with a distinctive anti-Communist spin. There is a twist, however. San Juan Bosco has remained firm in its ideology and techniques for social capital formation despite a major process of ethnic succession. No longer a parish preaching solely to Cubans but one still overwhelmingly financed by wealthier Cubans who have relocated to more affluent areas of South Florida, San Juan Bosco's catchment area now is home to large numbers of Central Americans along with older Cubans too poor to move to the suburbs and more recently arrived Cubans. Because the recently arrived Cubans lived for decades in Cuba under Castro and have families there still, among other factors, these Cubans tend to hold different perspectives than the original exiles (Grenier and Pérez 2003; Grenier 2006). In short, the parish is experiencing a succession that challenges the bonding social capital that established San Juan Bosco. What lessons does this parish teach about handling demographic change and its effects on parish identity?

History of the San Juan Bosco Parish: The Making of a Cuban Parish in Exile

To appreciate how the parish is dealing with succession, it is important to tell the history of the creation of the parish as a distinctly Cuban ethnic parish. San Juan Bosco Catholic Church was founded in 1963 by the first bishop of Miami, Coleman Carroll, to establish a church to cater to the burgeoning Cuban influx. The bishop opted to name the nascent church after a nineteenth-century Italian saint, Don Giovanni Bosco, who enjoyed a large following of devotees in Cuba and after whom several churches on the island were named. The parish joined many other transposed landmarks, powerful institutions in Cuba that were shut down by Castro and reconstructed in Miami by the very same people, now exiles, who had directed them on the island (Garcia 1996; Grenier and Pérez 2003). Giving the parish the name San Juan Bosco, the Spanish translation of the original Italian, immediately established it with name recognition. It already felt like "home" to exile Cubans even though at first the church enjoyed no formal location for worship.

"We first started Mass at the Tivoli Movie Theater on Sundays," recalled Monsignor Emilio Vallina, longtime senior priest at the parish, remembering the early days when the Miami Diocese had not yet approved the conversion of an auto repair shop into the church that would become San Juan Bosco. "We had three Masses on Sundays and during the week I would visit door to door," said the seventy-six-year-old Cuban priest. Vallina, an extremely prominent figure in the Cuban exile community, fondly recalls how the early parishioners and he proudly scraped burned oil off the floors and collected used chairs to create the makeshift church. "In our own Cuban exile we also had neighborhood missions. Back then we could go out at night. In the parking lots, I would park a small truck and bring loud speakers to attract people and invite them to our church." The priest's recollection is an example of how the then Diocese (later Archdiocese) of Miami tasked the clergy with reaching out to the displaced exiles and bringing them into the church community.

The Struggle for Religious as well as Ethnic Unity

The diocese faced greater challenges than merely incorporating hundreds of newcomers into its modest facilities; it also encountered a population that, though overwhelmingly Christian and usually Catholic, was also typically un- or under-churched. Centuries of minimal investment by the Vatican in evangelizing Cuba, particularly the rural areas, resulted in the fact that the vast majority were "cultural Catholics," people who identified as Catholic yet had had limited exposure to church doctrine and traditions (Crahan 1989; Kirk 1989; Mahler and Hansing 2005). To this day, priests in Miami's Cuban parishes lecture congregants on such basic customs as fasting prior to receiving communion. Another indicator of the effort to solidify doctrine in a region overwhelmingly populated with immigrants is the fact that catechism classes for children run two years, a timeframe that shocks many Latin American immigrants who recall classes in Latin American homelands typically running for six to twelve months. Deacon Diego Chávez, one of San Juan Bosco's longest-serving elders, admits to not having been particularly religious when he was a police sergeant in pre-Castro Cuba. Indeed, he spoke about how the practice of *religión a mi manera,* or "religion my way," is still common among Cubans in Miami. The parish's Pastoral Council president, Emiliano Bonet, explained this phenomenon by drawing a comparison between the practicing religious person and a spiritual religious person: "The practicing religious person goes to church on Sundays, but there is also the person who never goes to church yet is a believer. I do not feel that the person who is always in church is more religious or has a better value system or feelings toward others [than the person who practices religion his/her way]. We Cubans are as religious as all others, we just express it differently." Perhaps Bonet could be interpreted as arguing that Cubans are people of faith on par with others, but they are less religious, certainly less participatory than the Central Americans who now predominate in the parish.

Cuban priests throughout Miami have long campaigned against religión a mi manera; they prefer schooling Catholics "properly." They also fight against Cubans' common practice of worshiping Santería and other African-based syncretic faiths, faiths that gained great popularity throughout Cuba during slavery, owing to the predominance of Africans in the population and the scarcity of Catholic religious teaching to instill and uphold doctrine, particularly in the countryside (Portuonda-Zúñiga 1995; Hearn 2004). Miami's Cuban priests view such practices with great disdain and as "contaminating" their flocks. But observations of key Cuban religious festivals, particularly the patron saint days of September 8 (Our Lady of Charity) and December 17 (St. Lazarus), and the dotting of Miami's landscape with *botánicas* (shops selling Afro-Cuban/Catholic religious paraphernalia) illustrate clearly that Afro-Cuban faith and practice are very much alive and well in Miami.

Cultivating Political and Class-Based as well as Religious and Ethnic Social Capital

As Little Havana became Miami's surrogate capital for Cuban immigrants during the early days of their exile, the San Juan Bosco parish became its heart, its *axis mundi*. Cuba's upper class left the island starting in the late 1950s as the country headed into political and economic turmoil, followed by the middle class in the early to mid-1960s, and by increasing numbers of the working class in the 1970s (Boswell and Curtis 1984; Grenier and Pérez 2003). Most settled initially in Little Havana. They proceeded to turn the neighborhood into a microcosm of the country they left behind by replicating (albeit in scaled-down fashion) institutions that had been integral to their middle- and upper-class origins. From private schools to department stores and funeral homes, not to mention communities of faith, Little Havana recreated cubanía (Portes and Stepick 1993; Grenier and Pérez 2003).

The parish of San Juan Bosco has served as Little Havana's prime agent for solidarity and cultural preservation among Cuban exiles; it is also keeper of the anti-Castro flame. In the words of Father Vallina, "The church served the purpose of being a house of worship to God and a gathering place for the brethren. At the same time we started having civic activities, we had cultural and patriotic events because one can never forget that everything is based on one thing: love to God *and love to the motherland* (emphasis added)." The last words of this quotation reveal well the marriage of religion and patriotism in exiles' rhetoric and in actions. The church molded itself into a reservoir of memories of the early Cuban exile and a repository of pre-Castro Cuban traditions and values. "San Juan Bosco is the place Cuban exiles come for special occasions," said Isabel

Espinola, the long-time secretary to Father Vallina. "For us Cubans, this is the mother church, the place you come when you feel sad or when you feel happy. You should see this place during our festivities."

Special occasions celebrated by the church not only commemorate important religious days but also mark key dates that have civic and patriotic significance for Cubans. One of these special occasions is May 20, the day pre-Castro Cuba celebrated the moment in 1902 when the United States, after winning the Spanish-American War, liberated Cuba from Spain and granted the island conditional sovereignty. Not recognized by the current Cuban government, which considers that the date does not represent true freedom but merely one colonial power supplanting another, the parish's commemoration of this date closely aligns it with exile politics.

In addition to mobilizing the church around Cuban patriotic holidays, San Juan Bosco's leadership celebrates additional dates that held particular significance in pre-Castro Cuba, especially among professionals. For example, prior to 1959, it was customary for members of the professions to honor their peers once a year. December 3 was physician's day and there were similar dates for honoring accountants, engineers, etc. San Juan Bosco keeps these class-specific traditions alive even though their intended audience is now largely retired. What purpose can this serve? The parish leaders recognize that they are reinforcing and reconstructing the class divisions imported from Cuba. "We have always supported the professional classes—attorneys, physicians, and so on—even though most have moved to other areas. They all continue to commemorate special occasions here," responded Father Vallina to the question. The priest explained that when professional groups celebrate their festivities with meals at local restaurants or reunions at banquet halls, a Mass at San Juan Bosco is de rigueur. "These are traditional things that cannot be forgotten. The parish has values, values that must be retained." The church is a magnet that draws exiles in and helps them remember and celebrate their history, traditions, and culture. From a CSC perspective, however, it is easy to see that dedicating the parish to celebrating dates and professionals important in pre-Castro Cuba serves to bind together individuals who under the normal dislocating conditions of exile might have drifted away from church and cubanía. It also raises the question of how working-class Cubans and non-Cuban parishioners, who now constitute the majority of the congregation, relate to so much peculiarly Cuban ethnic cultural and historical emphasis.

The larger tapestry San Juan Bosco has long helped to weave, however, is a singular Cuban exile community, one where the racial, economic, social, and even geographic strata that clearly cut across social life in Cuba were muted while everyone has been expected to unite for the greater cause of removing Fidel Castro (Portes 1987; Portes and Stepick 1993). Racial issues were easy to forget since most exiles until the Mariel Boatlift of 1980 were White. Early exiles promoted the belief that there had never been racial prejudice in Cuba (Masud-Piloto 1996; Grenier and Castro 2001; Grenier and Pérez 2003; Stepick et al. 2003). Poverty was also easy to overlook since many of the early arrivals who had been wealthy prior to exile experienced marked hardships as they fled their homeland with mere pennies in their pockets and landed in Miami to find a monolingual and monocultural environment where at least some were hostile to their arrival (Pedraza-Bailey 1985; Portes and Stepick 1993; Masud-Piloto 1996).

The societal mores that had ruled Cuban culture in the old country were replaced by new ones. Exile, with its capital in Little Havana, became a leveling field where *"De qué familia es?"* (What family do you come from?) was no longer so important. *Santiagueros* (natives of Santiago) were as good as *matanceros* (natives of Matanzas); peasants (*guajiros*) were no longer incomparably inferior to *habaneros* (those from the capital city of Havana). Even *batistianos* (people who had sympathized with the last Cuban dictator, Fulgencio Batista) mingled and befriended *priístas* (people who had sympathized with the last Cuban constitutional president, Carlos Prío, the man Batista overthrew in a coup d'etat). Former political, geographic, and, to a lesser extent, family and class factions dissipated *if* they opposed Fidel Castro and affirmed that pre-Castro Cuba was infinitely more civilized and better than post-Castro Cuba. Cubans developed profound bonding social capital based in what scholar Alejandro Portes has labeled as enforceable trust (1987), i.e., if you were not anti-Castro and anti-Communist you were ostracized and even subject to terrorist retribution (Foment 1989).

The Religious-Civic-Patriotic School: Generating Cuban Civic Social Capital

The development of San Juan Bosco interwove parish and politics. To build and congeal CSC around hatred of Fidel Castro was a potent formula for the first generation, but could the animosity continue as the social glue among the second generation? Exiles' greatest response to this concern was to construct their own schools where they could control the curriculum. For example, in 1961 Belén Jesuit Preparatory School was re-opened in Miami. The premier high school for wealthy Catholics in Havana dating back to 1854—and even the alma mater of Castro himself—Belén Jesuit turned exile into opportunity. Parishes such as San Juan Bosco that lacked funding to open full schools in the early years often opted for developing after-school programs.

The Civic-Patriotic Parochial School at San Juan Bosco (*La Escuela Religiosa, Cívica y Patriota*) began at the start of the 1967 academic year. Angelita Esparraguera, the founder and principal, recalls that in 1965 Father Vallina called a few people and alerted them about a problem Cuban families were facing. "He told us that working families needed a safe place to have their children

wait for them from the time the children finished school until the parents finished worked," she recalled. "What's more important, these children were for-
getting their Spanish and losing their culture." She noted that Vallina was
inspired to start a school in homage to Don Giovanni Bosco, the saint after
whom the church was named and whose own ministry had revolved around
children and their education. Vallina pursued the idea of the after-school ministry with the diocese and heard about an innovative program with the same
objectives in San Antonio, Texas, in which Mexican-American students received
religious education in Spanish and learned about American culture by examining their own. "We flew to San Antonio to see how this church implemented the
program," related Esparraguera, adding that San Juan Bosco's leadership drew
ideas from the Texas program but created something unique to fit the needs of
the Cuban community in Miami. "Monsignor Vallina feels poor children should
have the same rights and advantages as children whose parents have financial
means. It occurred to us to offer a series of vocational subjects so that our students could develop their God-given talents. We incorporated Spanish to maintain the values of the motherland because we realized that these could be lost.
We saw that in the future we would run the risk of losing patriotic sentiments
among our youth. Children inevitably assimilate to American culture, which is
good, but it is also good not to lose one's own culture. You gain nothing if you
assimilate to a foreign culture but lose your own."

San Juan Bosco would overcome the forces of assimilation in regular school
by teaching children to speak, read, and write proper Spanish at the parish's
after-school program. More importantly, the school would promote cubanía,
teaching children Cuban identity, middle-class values, and ethics through a
subject taught in all schools, public and private, in pre-Castro Cuba: *Moral y
Cívica*. This civics and morals class would help turn children "into moral persons
and productive members of our society," Esparraguera explained.

A return to the Moral y Cívica curriculum was deemed critical to instilling
in second-generation children pre-Castro Spanish-influenced Cuban cultural
and moral traditions. Among these were love of country and culture (especially
traditions and conventions derived from Spain) and an acceptance of social
stratification that ranked people according to their family and racial background and economic status. White Cubans of European background held the
highest social standing while those with African and/or Asian heritage were presumed to be socially inferior. This entrenched social order called for those at the
lower strata to look up to and emulate those in the strata above them.

The road to upward social and economic mobility in pre-Castro Cuba began
with the adoption of "correct" values and perspectives. In the words of
Esparraguera, "When people have the right values they automatically do the
things that would eventually lead to economic prosperity and social respectabil-
ity. They study, they work hard, they marry at the right time and raise a family

properly, and they respect the law." In the radically different environment of their 1960s exile, where the newly arrived had lost their social status, Cubans' reach for *Cuban* high moral and civic ground through specialized parochial school programs made sense.

In Miami the parochial schools and their after-school programs that served public as well as parochial students endeavored to preserve this cultural capital among younger Cubans so they would be ready to resume their role in Cuba upon return. Return was believed to be so immediate among Cuban exiles in the early years that many exiles made no long-term plans or investments. As months turned into years and then decades, the dream of return still burned brightly in the older exiles' imagination and they still prepared for it, even as they overwhelmingly abandoned Little Havana for more prestigious zip codes distant from the axis mundi.

Addressing Succession

The Little Havana neighborhood that surrounds San Juan Bosco is no longer the Cuban enclave of the 1960s and '70s. Over the decades, as Cubans experienced greater socioeconomic success they moved to more affluent areas and were succeeded by incoming immigrants, both later-arriving Cubans and Central Americans. Based on demographics, Little Havana today might be renamed Little Tegucigalpa (after the Honduran capital) or Little Managua (after the Nicaraguan capital). However, the Cuban legacy endures. Many elderly Cubans (and Cubans have the highest average age of any U.S. Hispanic group) still reside there, the ones too poor to move to the suburbs. Little Havana is still called Little Havana. It still has the monument to the failed Bay of Pigs invasion. While Cubans are no longer a majority in the neighborhood, they remain the most influential.

There are similarities and differences in the immigration experiences of Cubans versus the Central American newcomers. Since 1959, Cubans have consistently been treated differently from all other foreigners entering the Unites States. Overwhelmingly, they are conferred refugee status and given attendant services and benefits from the U.S. government. In the early years, this aid was substantial, including funds to help defray costs for basic needs such as housing and food, assistance with having their educational and professional credentials accepted, and small business loans (Pedraza-Bailey 1985; Stepick and Grenier 1993; Grenier and Pérez 2003).

Central Americans entering South Florida have encountered much more varied hospitality. During the 1980s, tens of thousands of Nicaraguans were welcomed, and often assisted by Cubans, because they were fleeing a socialist regime (the Sandinistas) in their homeland. After a political struggle many received political asylum though far fewer social benefits than Cubans (see Portes and Stepick 1993, chapter 7). "Time passed and our exile was followed by that of the Nicaraguans," recalled Monsignor Vallina, "and I would tell you, I feel I am a Nicaraguan too. I feel very happy with them. I don't have any complaints about them. More than anything I have always advocated for their respect and their consideration." Vallina's comments reflect the Cubans' overall embracing of Nicaraguans as brothers fleeing Communism. Marlaly Reyes, a fifty-two-year-old Nicaraguan who has been a parishioner for thirteen years and leads a Thursday prayer group, echoed this acceptance, "We have been welcomed by Monsignor Vallina. This church has been a place of refuge for us." Jairo Amador, a thirty-year-old Nicaraguan parishioner who has been in charge of the charismatic music ministry, shares the same sentiment of gratefulness to Cubans for their help when he stated, "We have received much more than we have given."

Unlike the Nicaraguans, Central Americans from Honduras, El Salvador, and Guatemala arrived into the United States fleeing right-wing regimes or civil wars, natural disasters, and/or economic instability in their homelands. Though some benefited from "temporary protected status," a form of temporary asylum accorded by the U.S. government to undocumented immigrants from countries experiencing different types of turmoil, many remain undocumented and have little likelihood of regularizing their status. Additionally, unlike the first wave of Cubans who, although they arrived with almost nothing but the shirts on their backs, hailed from the most educated strata of Cuban society, Central Americans who settle in Little Havana (as opposed to the more middle-class suburbs) usually arrive with lower levels of education and skills, not atypical for their homelands. They thus face more challenges than Cubans in bettering their socioeconomic situation and leaving the neighborhood. Indeed, as South Florida has for some years been the nation's hottest real estate market, with the median price of a home rising from one hundred thousand to nearly four hundred thousand dollars in the first few years after 2000, the odds of Little Havana's residents escaping to the suburbs are stacked against them. Another difference between the senior and junior inhabitants of Little Havana is race. Most Cubans, particularly the earliest arrivals, are light skinned whereas the Central Americans have much darker, sometimes indigenous or mixed-race features. Both groups derive from societies where racial hierarchies are important, much as in the United States, and light skin more valued. All of these combine to mark Nicaraguans who now live in Little Havana and attend San Juan Bosco as different from the early-arriving Cubans who founded the church and still run it. Accordingly, the bonding social capital that the church produced for the early Cubans is more difficult to create for the current parishioners.

Deeper than Demographics: Devotional Differences

The Nicaraguan and other Central American newcomers also express their religion differently. The Catholic Church in Central American has historically been a more powerful and prominent institution than in Cuba, and this is reflected in the degree of religious devotion and commitment as well as in the worship styles expressed by the newcomers. Priests continue to school Cuban parishioners in catechism and protocol, but not Central Americans for the latter are viewed as true and devoted believers. Consequently, the parish leadership has tolerated Central Americans' wider array of worship styles.

At San Juan Bosco there are thriving charismatic and music groups with more upbeat, animated, and expressive worship styles bordering almost on Pentecostal services, a noted departure from the staid format of most U.S. and Cuban Miami Catholic Masses. Such celebration styles are especially popular among the Central Americans for whom expressive worship is more customary. Mario Guerrero, a Nicaraguan in his twenties, explained that when worshipping God, Nicaraguans enjoy loud singing and praising. Indeed, the celebration of Nicaragua's patron saint on the eve of December 8, Our Lady of the Immaculate Conception, is called la gritería (the shouting). Nicaraguan faithful travel from door to door singing praise to the Virgin Mary and are welcomed with refreshments. To Cuban parishioners, outbursts of emotion in a traditional and solemn place like a church are seen as vulgar. But Cuban elders at San Juan Bosco have learned to accept Nicaraguans' and other Latin Americans' distinctive forms of expression. "It is important to recognize they are truly Catholics," stated Vallina when discussing the differences between Central American and Cuban parishioners. Deacon Rodolfo Padrón, a Cuban who arrived with the first wave of exiles, admitted that Central Americans surpass Cubans when it comes to religious zeal. He said Nicaraguan parishioners want to be useful to the church in simple ways that relate directly to God. They join prayer groups, charismatic groups, and other informal religious organizations because they look for ways to be useful and to communicate with God. In contrast, Cubans join more traditional and subdued organizations at the parish such as the Legion of Mary and the St. Vincent de Paul Society.

San Juan Bosco's accommodation of its diverse congregations fulfills the roles of both neighborhood church *and* niche church (Ebaugh, O'Brien, and Chafetz 2000). The parish serves the varied worship needs and styles of its membership while tailoring some services, both secular and religious, to the specific needs and desires of distinct groups. "We have certain Masses that attract Cubans from before. There are people who have left the neighborhood but come back to go to Mass here," said Vallina. "The 10:00 a.m. Mass on Sunday is mostly Cuban, the afternoon Masses are mostly Nicaraguan." There is even a Latin-language Mass given at 4:30 p.m. on Sundays for the most traditional worshippers. For this Mass, the parish hired a European-trained organist, choral director, and arranger with a vast knowledge of Baroque music who stresses he wants nothing to do with the church's more charismatic music ministries. "The Latin Mass attracts not only traditionalists, but people who enjoy good music," said Alfredo Fernandez, the choral director for the Latin Mass, pointing out that opera singers and other trained vocalists often sing. "Monsignor Vallina is a lover of fine music and a true patriot," Fernandez affirmed. The parish, like many others in the archdiocese, also caters to its ethnic congregants by offering special Masses on days important to them spiritually (such as patron saint days) and nationally (such as independence and other key holidays). Moreover, clearly visible are the different figurines of the Virgin associated with immigrants' homelands, such as La Caridad for Cuba and La Purísima for Nicaragua.

A Dose of Politics

The process of succession that San Juan Bosco faces is not at all atypical for parishes all over the United States. The alchemy of immigration and exile politics in Miami, however, is quite distinctive from that of other major immigrant-receiving cities such as Los Angeles or New York. Cubans have risen from marginalized minority to empowered majority; in no other city does a group of immigrants predominate *both* demographically and politically (Portes and Stepick 1993). The parish faces the challenge of sustaining its prominence as its original parishioners age and move away to be replaced by larger and larger numbers of non-Cuban Hispanics along with Cubans who do not share the class background of the parish's founders.

The aging of the Cuban population and the entrance of hundreds of thousands of newer immigrants from Central and South America and the Caribbean are shifting Miami's demographic and political center, a phenomenon already palpable at San Juan Bosco. Yet despite some accommodation of newcomers to their religious worship styles, the church leadership and orientation remains decidedly first-wave Cuban. In fact, participant observation within the parish reveals that the pressures to assimilate exhibited within encourage non-Cuban newcomer immigrants to Cubanize, not always as if in opposition to Americanization, but as a form of assimilation that inculcates newcomers with Cuban beliefs and values that harmonize with American values. For example, the church consciously teaches that hard work and dedication can overcome poverty and sorrow. The leadership also encourages immigrants to be pro-American, arguing that an inherent handicap within non-Cuban Hispanic cultures is that the immigrants arrive from countries where there has been animosity toward the United States. "Many [Latin American immigrants] don't see the United States favorably," explained Deacon Chávez, "especially Mexicans because they say the United States stole half of Mexico. . . . But they are learning."

Through its institutions and political orientation, the parish teaches loyalty and patriotism with a distinctive Cuban accent. "Well, they come to Miami and they have to learn from us," Isabel Espinola, secretary to Monsignor Vallina, explained. "We Cubans are a major part of Miami, so even if they [Nicaraguans and other Latin Americas] don't want to, they have to learn our ways. I think it is just part of their being here, especially in this area [Little Havana]." Espinola added that even though Nicaraguan and other Central American parishioners are willing to absorb and adapt to the ways dictated by the Cuban community, they are not completely acquiescent. Rather, they accept the Miami Cuban ways because they see how successful Cubans have become. "Cubans have helped us a lot and we owe a lot to them. They are always there to help us gain our rights and to support what we do," said Alba Morales, a twenty-seven-year-old Nicaraguan, pointing to the political and economic structures that Cubans have firmly established in Miami. "We should be a little bit more like them. We are fortunate that our country got rid of Communism, that we can go back if we want to. Cuba is still not free; that is a sorrow we also carry in our hearts." Alba's comments reflect the view that current Nicaraguan parishioners expressed regarding the "moral authority" bestowed upon Cubans by their long suffering and "magnanimous deeds" toward other Latin Americans when their own homeland is still "enslaved."

Cubanization through Social Service Delivery

"Our parish is noted for dispersing, first of all, guidance. . . . [Spiritual] assistance alone is easy to give out but does not meet material needs," explained Monsignor Vallina when asked about the parish's missions. "We strive to help people and not just disperse consolation, but also material assistance. What we offer is geared to the needs of the people." Indeed, San Juan Bosco provides an array of critical social services to the neighborhood: a job referral service, a medical clinic, the after-school program, a food delivery program run through the St. Vincent de Paul Society, a free or reduced meal program for seniors operated with Florida state funds, English-language and vocational programs through Miami-Dade County Public Schools, and a legal assistance office to aid people with immigration-related issues. Some programs are funded by the state or local governments, but the parish also raises funds internally. The senior church deacon, Chávez, indicated that the church receives a steady stream of small-scale donations: "There are former Cuban parishioners who have moved and continue sending donations of ten or fifteen dollars a week, but steadily." He added that other individuals and firms give large donations of money or goods. "We have an insurance company that donates bags of foods for whoever needs them; they don't ask about nationalities." He attributes this generosity at least in part to the fact that when Cubans arrived, Miami lacked social services providers who could speak Spanish, but now successful Cubans fill that gap.

During the early days of the Cuban exile, Chávez recalled, when a Cuban immigrant prospered and was able to purchase a new television set, that immigrant would immediately donate his old set to another Cuban. When an early

Cuban immigrant received monetary help from the parish, many times the same recipient would double the amount given to him and return it to San Juan Bosco with a thank you note. Chávez says that such actions, which can be viewed as evidence of bonding social capital, are infrequent among Nicaraguans and other new immigrants who, even if they are religious and behave properly out of love for God, don't seem to have a sense of community responsibility, of CSC. He attributes this to the fact that they can rely on Cubans' CSC: "They have an advantage because there is a larger support group. Back then [when Cubans first arrived] people who didn't speak English were not able to function. Today that is not the case."

Deacon Chávez's words reveal ambivalence toward non-Cuban neighbors and parishioners. There is sympathy but also superiority; Cubans identify with the newcomers since they once walked in the same shoes, but the Cubans see themselves as having achieved success with little assistance. The record clearly shows that Cubans, particularly as Cold War refugees, received a great deal of aid from the United States (Pedraza-Bailey 1985; Stepick and Grenier 1993), but this has not translated into popular perception. Cubans also view themselves as culturally superior. They point to the rise in crime rates that appears to have accompanied the demographic shifts in Little Havana to substantiate their position. Additionally, newcomers are viewed as less community-minded and less trustworthy. At San Juan Bosco such perceptions have spurred the parish to protect its charitable programs from fraud. The parish has hired a man who was an undercover police detective in pre-Castro Cuba to catch people suspected of requesting services they don't really need. Recounting how this church detective caught a man who had dressed as a pregnant woman to elicit help by unexpectedly showing up at the person's home, Deacon Chávez argued that San Juan Bosco's charitable reputation serves as a magnet for con artists. He alleged, "We have mothers who claim their husbands have been deported when in reality the husbands live with them; people who claim they were robbed; even people who say they need funds (from the parish) to help them buy a house. We have all types." In addition to screening people to fend off the con artists, the parish has established geographic boundaries to delimit its beneficiary pool.

The Medical Clinic: Gatekeeping Civic Social Capital

Nowhere does the parish screen the beneficiaries of its charity more than at San Juan Bosco's medical clinic. Unique among all other parishes in Miami, the clinic began providing services to indigent and undocumented immigrants in 1991, shortly after Little Havana became overwhelmingly Nicaraguan. The project that culminated in the medical clinic began when Monsignor Vallina solicited the help of Dr. Manolo Reyes, an executive with a local Catholic hospital who had been a television anchorman on an English-language station in

Miami as well as an actor in pre-Castro Cuba. Doctor Reyes, who is not a physician but likes to be addressed as "doctor" owing to his law degree from Cuba, invited his employer, Mercy Hospital, to partner with San Juan Bosco and equip a clinic for the needy. Vallina and Reyes contacted other influential Cubans and with their help began to recruit physicians to donate their time to the clinic on a regular basis. Among the influential Cubans who were instrumental in setting up the clinic is Dr. Pedro Greer, a highly esteemed Cuban physician known as the "doctor of the homeless" for his early work in bringing medical services to the homeless in Miami.

The clinic underwent an upgrade when the parish built a new sanctuary several years ago, freeing up the old sanctuary for the clinic, which is now more spacious and better equipped. Open for three days a week, featuring three examination rooms and a waiting area, the clinic is staffed by three volunteer physicians. If a physician examining a patient deems that a specialist is needed or that a patient's care requires services that cannot be provided at the clinic, the attending physician refers the patient to a network of specialists who also donate their time and services and see patients in their private offices. Whenever possible, the clinic dispenses drugs free of charge to patients, and if the drugs are not available the clinic refers patients to Navarro Pharmacies, a chain of Cuban-owned drugstores. In many cases Navarro either provides the drugs free of charge or at considerable discount.

The clinic patients are grateful to receive services and have no objection to waiting to see a physician. Maria Jimenez, an unemployed Argentinean in her early sixties who visits the clinic for stomach problems and attends Mass at San Juan Bosco whenever she has "the opportunity to do so," was cheerful after waiting for hours to see a physician. The other thirty-four patients, who were calmly waiting their turn the day Maria visited the clinic, chatted amicably and offered laudatory comments about the clinic, its physicians, and its overall services. Maria Eduarda, a Nicaraguan woman in her seventies, said she was particularly impressed when she was given a referral to go to the clinic's affiliated hospital to have tests done free of charge.

The clinic clearly helps fill a need for medical care among some of Miami's poorest and least insured residents. Additionally, the Little Havana area, with its relatively low housing costs and large number of Spanish-speaking small businesses, is a magnet for undocumented immigrants. When the clinic was founded and until it moved to its new quarters, all walk-ins were seen, diagnosed, or treated by physicians without having to present any documentation. But the increasing number of patients and the suspicion that many of them were abusing the charity prompted San Juan Bosco and Mercy Hospital to adopt new rules. These rules specify that the clinic diagnose and treat only residents who live in the vicinity of the church. Moreover, prospective patients now must bring proof of financial need and proof of their immigration status in the United States.

The medical clinic's restrictions on access can be viewed merely as an organization's legitimate interest in making sure that scarce resources reach only
the most needy. Observation of the waiting area and interviews with clinic staff,
however, indicate a subtle air of paternalism by the Cuban benefactors toward
their non-Cuban beneficiaries. A stronger dose of paternalism is evident in the
parish's after-school program and not merely because the subjects are children.
In each case, benevolence is accompanied by a dose of cubanía, the message
that the (pre-Castro) Cuban cultural and historical traditions are superior and,
as such, merit reproduction even among non-Cubans. Thus, a parish located in
a neighborhood that is decreasingly Cuban in terms of nationality still generates
distinctly Cuban CSC. Nowhere is this more evident than in the parish's after-
school program.

Reproducing Civic Social Capital among Non-Cubans

The Religious-Civic-Patriotic School continues to function today as it did nearly
forty years ago, though its student population has changed dramatically and
hardly any Cuban students remain. "We try to mold our students to be civic-
minded and patriotic so that they love their roots and also the United States. We
have been doing this for thirty-five years," said Esparraguera, adding that if it
were not for the after-school program, the children of Central American immigrants in the area would have no place to go after their regular school. Through
this after-school program students still learn three basic subjects: religion,
Spanish language, and Hispanic culture. The latter includes the history and
geography of Cuba as well as cultures of other Latin American countries to
accommodate the current student body made up of Nicaraguans, Hondurans,
Salvadorans, Ecuadorians, Peruvians, Panamanians, and others. All classes are
taught exclusively in Spanish. In addition to the required classes, the students
have a choice of electives. These include arts and crafts, drawing and painting,
ceramics, chess, sewing, computer skills, and manners and etiquette. The
school used to teach separate "grooming" classes so students would learn
proper etiquette, manners, and hygiene, but the principal says few students
now register for these courses. Consequently, the contents have been incorporated into the civics curriculum to assure that students know such things as
table manners and allegedly essential hygiene. In all classes, students receive
grades for discipline as well as for effort and academic improvement.

Tuition is a very modest forty dollars a month, much less than similar programs run through public schools. There are five female teachers, a Nicaraguan,
a Honduran, an Ecuadorian, and a Guatemalan, in addition to the Cuban director, Esparraguera. The teachers are paid a low salary for their part-time positions, but the fringe benefits package includes health insurance provided by the
Archdiocese of Miami. When a teacher is hired, she is required to learn about

Cuban culture and traditions in order to teach them. In addition, she must keep accurate records of all her assigned students and report to Esparraguera regarding their academic as well as social progress. "The students are graded on their progress in all the areas that we deem important, and certainly civility and social adaptation are two of them," Esparraguera said.

Though classes start much earlier, the civics part of the curriculum begins at 4:15 p.m., when the students assemble for prayer. Afterward they go to their respective classrooms. "We teach children to celebrate the twentieth of May [Cuban Independence Day as celebrated in pre-Castro times]; we teach the Cuban national anthem to all children, and to the Nicaraguan children we teach the Nicaraguan national anthem as well. We maintain those [Cuban] values because that is the origin of the program," added Esparraguera. In addition to learning about Cuban symbolic icons, students learn "Cuban values as they relate to the reality today. First of all, we develop their consciousness that they live in the United States and they need to be aware of news events. People comment about what is happening in the world. The child needs to know what Cuba is, why Cuba is in the news, what is the significance of the Cuban embargo. We show them a map of the Gulf of Mexico and show them why so many people die trying to reach the United States by rafts. . . . We explain to them the context in which they are living and this draws their attention. It is very nice to mold their consciousness. . . . Children here don't know about their neighborhoods, about the nation; we locate the child within an international scope," affirmed Esparraguera, commenting that the civic instruction they receive in the after-school program will help them advance in society.

"They [Nicaraguans and other Latin Americans who reside in Little Havana] want to move up socially and economically. They want to leave their apartments and buy a house. They have the same aspirations as we do," maintained Esparraguera. She and other parish leaders believe that by learning the proper values Nicaraguans and other Central Americans will be able to achieve as much as the Cubans have achieved. However, they fear such mobility is hampered by a difference in Central Americans' attitudes toward education and careers. Esparraguera recalls that in the old days when Cubans were the majority of the students at the after-school program, parents aspired to have their children earn good grades in their regular schools, to receive scholarships, and eventually graduate from college. Nicaraguan parents, on the other hand, want their children to join the armed forces. She attributes this desire to the parents' low educational level and social and civic "deficiencies." Esparraguera compared success stories among Cuban alumni of the program, which has produced attorneys, a judge, a state representative, business leaders, and other professionals, against the likely future of her new students. She is not confident that the next generation of alumni will fare as well, since only one Nicaraguan graduate of the Religious-Civic Patriotic program has gone to college from the thousands who have been students there. She feels students' parents are at fault because she believes they lack the social skills, the education, and the civic awareness (proper value system) necessary to transmit the appropriate values to their own children and help them progress. Their shortcomings are manifested in their limited achievements as a community, she said.

San Juan Bosco's after-school program administration attempts to remedy these Central Americans' deficiencies by teaching civics and religion to children and by involving their parents in this part of their children's education. Parents are constantly invited to meetings and events to expose them to the same social and civic ideas and skills that will allow them to progress. The school celebrates achievement in these areas through a traditional technique. It publicly bestows trophies, plaques, and medals on students (with parents watching) to mark every achievement. Virtually all students receive a trophy for something, marking their progress toward becoming righteous and productive citizens, just as the students are taught that Cubans have become.

How do non-Cubans feel about being crafted into the Cuban mold? Jairo Amador, the head of the charismatic ministry, is positive and his views are typical of many other Central Americans in the parish. He characterizes his homeland, Nicaragua, as backward and thus in need of guidance in order to prosper: "Nicaragua is a country whose people have been subjected to suffering. We have endured earthquakes, wars, catastrophes, dictatorship, communism, liberalism, everything. We are an uneducated people due to what we have gone through, our people have not been allowed to prosper. . . . We receive Cuban culture and then we apply it." However, for Amador and other Central American parishioners their brightest guiding light is God and family, not cubanía. "Our values and principles come from God and we learn them from our parents. Only parents can teach those values."

What Kind of CSC?

Not only is San Juan Bosco a microcosm of Miami, but it is also illustrative of more far-reaching social realities affecting twenty-first-century America and, indeed, other countries. The parish was founded to minister to the needs of a new immigrant group, Cuban exiles, as they navigated the turbulent waters of being a recently arrived minority in a land dominated by an established majority. Over time, however, the combination of the exiles' high human capital and unprecedented U.S. government support propelled the Cuban exiles to transform Miami. Cubans rose to the top not only demographically but also economically and politically. San Juan Bosco both benefited and lost during this transformation. Its original Cuban congregation grew wealthier but also moved away from the working-class neighborhood. At least some of the original parishioners maintained their bonds to San Juan Bosco and contributed money or time that enabled the parish to bridge to newcomers from Central America and Cuba. Because of reduced federal support for the newcomers, they received less assistance and in many cases a rejection from the U.S. government. Many also had lower levels of human capital than the first wave of Cubans who established the church. The newer arrivals have not prospered to the same degree as the Cubans, yet they are powerful in their faith and devotion to God.

While San Juan Bosco has accepted the different worship styles of the new arrivals, it persists in thinking that the new arrivals can socially and economically replicate the successful earlier Cubans. It finds the morals of the Central Americans lacking, however, and seeks to inculcate them by policing their free health services and teaching the new arrivals' children "proper" values in the after-school program. In the process, the Central Americans are expected and generally seek to become specifically Cuban Americans. San Juan Bosco uses multiple forms of pressure to assimilate Central Americans *not* to a White middle-class American mainstream model, but to a Cuban exile pattern. As the Cuban population ages and is not demographically reproducing itself, it clearly is reproducing cubanía through socializing non-Cubans into the Cuban mold. The long-term consequences of this unique mode of CSC remain to be seen, but the frustrations that the San Juan Bosco leaders express and the Central Americans' relative lack of economic success compared to the early-arriving Cubans are not encouraging. San Juan Bosco, in accepting the Central Americans' more expressive worship styles, clearly has produced bridging religious CSC, but it apparently has not produced effective linking social and political CSC.

NOTES

1. Velazquez is not her real name to protect her identity. All other names in the chapter are accurate.

REFERENCES

Boswell, T. D., and J. R. Curtis. 1984. *The Cuban-American Experience: Culture, Images, and Perspectives*. Totowa, NJ: Rowman and Allenheld.

Crahan, M. 1989. Catholicism in Cuba. *Cuban Studies* 19: 3–24.

Ebaugh, H. R., J. O'Brien, and J. S. Chafetz. 2000. The Social Ecology of Residential Patterns and Membership in Immigrant Churches. *Journal for the Scientific Study of Religion* 39(1): 107–116.

Foment, C. 1989. Political Practice and the Rise of an Ethnic Enclave: The Cuban American Case. *Theory and Society* 18: 47–81.

Garcia, M. C. 1996. *Havana USA: Cuban Exiles and Cuban Americans in South Florida, 1959–1994*. Berkeley: University of California Press.

Grenier, G. J. 2006. The Creation and Maintenance of the Cuban American "Exile Ideology" In Miami. *Circunstancia, Revista de Ciencias Sociales del Instituto Universitario de Investigacion Ortega y Gasset* 10: 1–14.

Grenier, G., and M. Castro. 2001. Blacks and Cubans in Miami: The Negative Consequences of the Cuban Enclave on Ethnic Relations. In *Governing American Cities: Interethnic*

Coalitions, Competition, and Conflict, ed. M. Jones-Correa, 137–157. New York: Russell Sage Foundation.

Grenier, G. J., and L. Pérez. 2003. *Legacy of Exile: Cubans in the United States*. Needham Heights, MA: Allyn & Bacon.

Hearn, A. H. 2004. Afro-Cuban Religions and Social Welfare: Consequences of Commercial Development in Havana. *Human Organization* 63(1): 78–87.

Kirk, J. 1989. *Between God and the Party: Religion and Politics in Revolutionary Cuba*. Tampa: University of South Florida Press.

Mahler, S. J., and K. Hansing. 2005. Myths and Mysticism: How Bringing a Transnational Religious Lens to the Examination of Cuba and the Cuban Diaspora Exposes and Ruptures the Fallacy of Isolation. In *Cuba Transitional*, ed. D. Fernández, 42–60. Gainesville: University Press of Florida.

Masud-Piloto, F. R. 1996. *From Welcomed Exiles to Illegal Immigrants: Cuban Migration to the U.S., 1959–1995*. Totowa, NJ: Rowman and Littelfield.

Pedraza-Bailey, S. 1985. *Political and Economic Migrants in America: Cubans and Mexicans*. Austin: University of Texas Press.

Portes, A. 1987. The Social Origins of the Cuban Enclave Economy of Miami. *Sociological Perspectives* 30(October): 340–371.

Portes, A., and A. Stepick. 1993. *City on the Edge: The Transformation of Miami*. Berkeley: University of California Press.

Portuonda-Zúñiga, O. 1995. *La Virgin De La Caridad Del Cobre: Símbolo De La Cubanía*. Santiago de Cuba: Editorial Oriente.

Stepick, A., and G. Grenier. 1993. Cubans in Miami. In *In the Barrios: Latinos and the Underclass Debate*, ed. J. Moore and R. Rivera, 79–100. New York: Russell Sage Foundation.

Stepick, A., G. Grenier, M. Castro, and M. Dunn. 2003. *This Land Is Our Land: Interethnic Relations in Miami*. Berkeley: University of California Press.

Tweed, T. A. 1997. *Our Lady of the Exile: Diasporic Religion at a Cuban Catholic Shrine in Miami*. New York: Oxford University Press.

7

Black Churches and the Environment in Miami

EILEEN M. SMITH-CAVROS

In the beginning of the summer of 2001, my summer job was mapping churches with the Religion and Civic Life in Miami Project at Florida International University. It seemed I was biding my time until I began my "real" academic research on my chosen research subject, the interplay between people and the natural environment. The mapping project, emphasizing social capital and religiosity, seemed unrelated to my research interests. However, in the Black urban and semi-urban neighborhoods where I was assigned to do my fieldwork, I found churchgoers connecting with nature through their engagement in various projects linked to the environment, ranging from neighborhood cleanups to re-vegetation and greenway creation.

The goals of these community activists varied from social to environmental to spiritual-stewardship. While rarely labeled exclusively "environmental goals," the activists' civic engagement revealed important environmental connections and priorities among congregants in Black churches across projects and across denominations. These shared concerns and goals generated civic social capital (CSC), inspired by religion, to benefit the threatened natural ecosystems and the challenged Black neighborhoods of Miami, both of which seem equally beleaguered. This CSC was not only directed toward goals considered by many to be unusual for African Americans, but also entailed bridging with unusual allies, White environmentalists. As in Su Oltman Fink's chapter on African Americans in West Perrine, the environmentalist African Americans I met deployed their CSC directly in formal politics.

"Environmentalism" has long been seen as a movement appealing to economically stable Whites (Mohai 1985; Humphrey and Buttel 1982). For those who equate membership in "mainstream" environmental groups with level of environmental interest, this has led to a stereotypical view of Blacks as "nonenvironmentalists." Early research suggested that social issues like community crime took precedence over environment (Howenstine 1993; Kreger 1973). These findings, however, have been re-examined by recent research suggesting that Blacks are as pro-environment as Whites. William Arp and Christopher Kenny (1996) suggest that some earlier studies did not examine environmental issues of particular and immediate interest in Black communities. Judi Anne Caron describes Blacks interacting with the "New Environmental Paradigm" that emphasizes "stewardship and harmony" with the environment (1989, 25). Several studies suggest that Blacks are more concerned than Whites about select environmental issues (Cutter 1981; Burby and Strong 1997; Newell and Green 1997; Bunyan and Mohai 1992; Mohai and Bunyan 1998).

Why might Blacks be more concerned with some environmental issues than Whites? Part of this could be linked to environmental justice issues which abound in Black neighborhoods (Bullard 1990). Many researchers have found indirect discrimination in which Blacks and other minorities are more likely to reside near highly polluted Superfund sites (Hogan and Hogan 1998) and toxic waste sites (Bunyan and Mohai 1992). Arp's research (Arp and Llorens 1999) supports the interpretation that environmental justice issues such as these can be linked to a greater degree of local concern among Blacks. Bullard (1990) connects the degradation of land in poor and minority areas to the exploitation of people.

Land and "place" must not be underestimated in the willingness of people to consider and address environmental issues. Liam Kennedy explains, "Place, understood as a space of provisional self-definition or communal definition, remains powerfully affective in urban culture. Places are charged with emotional and mythical meanings; the localized stories, images and memories associated with place can provide meaningful cultural and historical bearings for urban individuals and communities" (2000, 7). He further notes that the "centrality of race to the configuration of contemporary urbanism is rarely acknowledged" (Kennedy 2000, 4). In the recent past, Blacks in the United States were restricted to particular spaces and places which now have special meanings for them, both negative and positive.

Since Black churches have a history of activism, they seem to be logical points from which to examine environmental issues. Hans Baer and Merrill Singer (1992) describe how African American religions historically provided strength for a people challenged over and over again by turbulent times. Carlyle Stewart credits "the pivotal role of black spirituality in shaping the consciousness, identity, and values of African-American people" (1999, 1). He adds, "This model is not contemplative as other models of spirituality, but is dynamic, active and reflective" (Stewart 1999, 123). And Robert Franklin further states, "The Black church tradition emphasizes that personal conviction, moral renewal, and sanctification should manifest themselves in acts of justice, charity, and service in the wider world" (1997, 34). Scholars have noted that "the

Black church provides a cultural blueprint for civic life in the neighborhood" (Patillo-McCoy 1998, 767). Melvin Williams (1974, 133) draws connections between this activist church and nature. He describes the strong influence of the natural world in a Black Pentecostal church: "A familiar reaction to disenchantment with the urban American competitive way of life is the extolling of the virtues of 'mother earth' and the search for some means of 'going back to nature.'"

This chapter examines the two largest environmentally related projects comprised primarily of Miami Black churchgoing volunteers and the ways in which they embodied civic engagement that provides social capital *and* environmental capital. One of the case studies examined was a planting of more than six hundred native trees, spearheaded by community, church, and environmental groups in Richmond Heights, Florida; and the other was a task force effort in Miami, Florida, to restore and renew Virginia Key Beach, which during the days of segregation was the designated "Black beach" in south Florida.

Although both projects varied in content, outcome, and some participant demographics, they shared several elements. Most project volunteers were urban Blacks over sixty years old, who attended predominantly Black churches and whose attitudes about nature were rooted in spirituality and their rural youth. The participation of several distinct charismatic individuals motivated the groups. Both projects were propelled forward by participants' shared sense of the importance of history, of place, of stewardship, and of future (Smith-Cavros 2006). Both projects were successful because of the leadership of the church-based Black activists as well as their development of bridging CSC through coalitions with complimentary groups on the respective projects, and, perhaps most importantly, their faith in youth and the future.

Virginia Key Beach Restoration

The beach at Virginia Key, Florida, is a windswept, seemingly endless shoreline fringed by swaying coconut palms and the turquoise blue ocean within view of Miami's skyline. On this beach, one might see a loggerhead sea turtle, sea beans from Latin America, medical waste, or sea glass in a rainbow of colors. Its dunes have eroded and been invaded by exotic plants which have created havoc with the natural environment. Virginia Key is also home to a sewage treatment plant and landfill. During segregation, this beach on a barrier island was the only one available to Blacks in greater Miami. It was accessible only by boat until the 1950s. Marvin Dunn details the important role of beaches to the history of Miami Blacks: "In early May 1945 Miami blacks began agitating for a permanent bathing beach in Dade County. The goal of the agitation was not to integrate the County's white beaches, but to pressure the County to open a beach exclusively for blacks. To press home the point, a group of blacks, led by Father Theodore R. Gibson of

Coconut Grove's Christ Church, tested their right to use County-owned beaches by swimming at white's-only Baker's Haulover Beach on May 9, 1945. With this event, the civil rights movement in Dade County began, more than a decade before it did in other cities in the South" (1997, 160).

On August 1, 1945, Virginia Key Beach was designated the "colored beach" in south Florida, and it became an important gathering spot for Blacks for recreation and even religious services. Under the model of the Supreme Court's 1896 *Plessy v. Ferguson* decision (which sanctioned segregation through the idea of "separate but equal"), Virginia Key was "improved" in the 1950s in a similar way to nearby White beaches. However, only Virginia Key had a sewage plant and waste dump added, both located in close proximity to the beach. The effects of this on the beach are still undetermined (Virginia Key Park Civil Rights Task Force, 2000). Complaints about odors and possible deleterious health effects from the sewage plant have been voiced by a diverse spectrum of area activists and residents. In 1958, Miami Blacks, led by "preeminent civil rights leader" Father Gibson (1915–1982), successfully insisted on the use of facilities at nearby Crandon Park (Dunn 1997, 192). With opportunities for recreation beyond Virginia Key, many Blacks took advantage of newfound freedoms and frequented other local beaches.

Community activism regarding Virginia Key began in "1979 when concerned citizens responded to County plans to lease 33 acres of Virginia Key to the Goodyear Corporation as an aerodrome for blimps. The group was successful in blocking the lease, relying heavily on the principle of public access to public land" (Paddon and Suman 1995, 159). By the 1980s, Virginia Key Beach Park was switched from county to city ownership in a land swap, then closed to the public for several years, until windsurfers were allowed back in the mid-1980s. In 1985, Miami Commissioner Joe Carollo called Virginia Key "wasted" and "proposed . . . that Virginia Key be developed as a major boating and tourism site combining aspects of a theme park, beach recreation and California's Marina del Rey (Fiedler 1985, 7). But "when Dade County conveyed the 85 acres of Virginia Key land to the City of Miami in 1982, it specified that the land was to be used for public park purposes" (Paddon and Suman 1995, 164). Despite this, in the 1990s the City of Miami attempted to develop the public land portion of Virginia Key as a privately operated venture labeled an "eco-campground." A public referendum defeated this. Kirk Nielson notes, "Ironically, a group of whites originated the proposal to preserve the Virginia Beach area as a civil rights park. Most of them are members of Sierra Club Miami Group, Friends of Virginia Key, and the Urban Environmental League"; though he added that "Enid Pinkney and artist Gene Tinney are trying to rally other blacks and Miami City officials behind the cause of preserving Virginia Key as a public park. In a recent letter to Mayor Carrollo, she [Pinkney] wrote: 'Keeping Virginia Beach as a public beach could be a memorial to those brave African-Americans who stood up for the right to enjoy God's ocean, sand and sun'" (1999, 27).

FIGURE 1 Bishop Augustín Román was born, grew up, and was ordained in Cuba. He was expelled from Cuba in 1961 along with another 130 priests. In 1987 he negotiated a peaceful end to uprisings at two federal prisons where Cuban refugees were being detained. When he was appointed auxiliary bishop in 1979, Román became the first Cuban in 200 years to be appointed bishop in the United States. He was the central figure in the construction and subsequently became director of Miami's Shrine of Our Lady of Charity, Cuba's patron saint.

Photo by Jerry Berndt.

FIGURE 2 Giant mural approximately thirty feet high behind the altar at the Shrine of Our Lady of Charity, Cuba's patron saint. The small statue of the Blessed Virgin, brightly lit toward the bottom, was smuggled out of Cuba in 1961. The mural tells a particularly Catholic and nationalistic history of Cuba. Our Lady of Charity is the only religious icon to be recognized by the Catholic Church with two official shrines, this one in Miami and the original one in Cuba.

Photo by Jerry Berndt.

FIGURE 3 Sign on car at the Shrine to Our Lady of Charity. The sign indicates the close link for many in the Cuban community between Catholicism and anti-communism. It says, "Honk your horn for peace and democracy. Down with communism and terrorism."

Photo by Jerry Berndt.

FIGURE 4 Women are registering for the Disciples' food program. On the wall is a large poster that outlines the Disciples' leadership training program.

Photo by Jerry Berndt.

FIGURE 5 Passing it on: A man in the Disciples' rehabilitation center passes out food to a woman in need.

Photo by Jerry Berndt.

FIGURE 6 Valuing music and formality at the Refugees Seventh-Day Adventist Church. On the table in front are tablets with the Ten Commandments.

Photo by Jerry Berndt.

FIGURE 7 Haitian woman at Notre Dame D'Haiti Catholic Church with a T-shirt that has a picture of the church's founder, Father Thomas Wenski, now bishop of the Orlando Diocese. Above the picture on the T-shirt it says, in English and Haitian Creole, "Here is our Bishop. Mother Mary, he is in your hands."

Photo by Jerry Berndt.

FIGURE 8 Youth at Notre Dame d'Haiti, each with an image of Our Lady of Perpetual Help, the patron saint of Haiti.

Photo by Jerry Berndt.

FIGURE 9 Father Reginald Jean-Mary, the third leader of Notre Dame D'Haiti, whose leadership has re-emphasized the development of civic social capital.

Photo by Jerry Berndt.

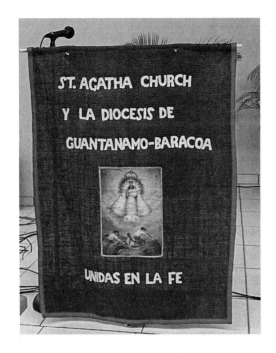

FIGURE 10 Podium at St. Agatha's Noche Cubana (Cuban Night) fund-raiser for their sister parish in Cuba, Guantánamo-Baracoa.

Photo by Katrin Hansing.

FIGURE 11 Women and St. Agatha's Father Rolando Garcia singing nostalgic Cuban songs at the Noche Cubana (Cuban Night) fund-raiser for their sister parish in Cuba, Guantánamo-Baracoa.

Photo by Katrin Hansing.

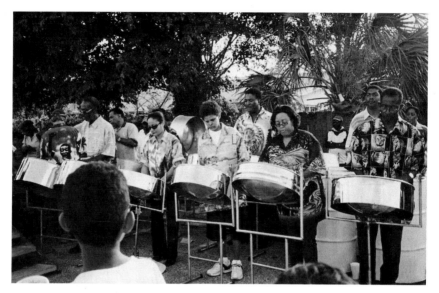

FIGURE 12 Twenty-first Century Steel Band performing at the Church of Ascension Carnival. This Episcopal Church serves primarily a West Indian community. It is located directly opposite Christ the King Catholic Church, which has a congregation of Trinidadians. Both churches are on the edge of Perrine, a historically African American community.

Photo by Christine Ho.

FIGURE 13 Emmanuel Apostolic Church, a small storefront Jamaican Pentecostal church that is next to a small supermarket. In spite of its modest appearance, as described in chapter II, the congregation is full of energy and does an excellent job of incorporating its youth.

Photo by Christine Ho.

The Miami City Commission formed Virginia Key Park Civil Rights Task Force in 1999 through a resolution accompanied by "a moratorium on issuing any Requests for Proposals on consideration of private development on Virginia Key during the one-year period that the Task Force would be in effect" (Virginia Key Park Civil Rights Task Force, 2000, 9). Over the Martin Luther King Holiday weekend in 2000, a public planning hearing was held to determine priorities for the future use of Virginia Key. These included environmental concerns, historical restoration, park and recreation use, and cultural emphasis (Virginia Key Park Civil Rights Task Force, 2000). The Civil Rights Task Force became the Virginia Key Beach Park Trust (VKBPT) in 2000. Its board of directors is made up primarily of Blacks, most of whom have lived in the Miami area all of their lives and can remember visiting Virginia Key as children. They have garnered millions of dollars in funding and grant support for preservation and restoration (*Miami Times* 2000b). Some whom I interviewed made guarded, careful political comments as plans for Virginia Key were still evolving and depended on local political situations and alliances. In order to protect the best interests of all concerned and of the project itself, all names in the following section are pseudonyms. These comments also reflect that the participants' CSC included an awareness of the precarious, embedded nature of CSC.

Before I spoke with any members of the task force, I interviewed a locally prominent Black environmental professional, Robert Grayson, who observed: "Virginia Key is being pushed from a political perspective, not an environmental perspective. And it's a political, historical kind of issue that even now is not being addressed from an environmental perspective." He added that if Virginia Key were really an "environmental issue," the fact that a sewage plant and sewage outflow pipe are located so close to the beach would be a prominent issue. Grayson admits, however, that it is not politically or economically feasible to relocate the plant. He commented that he would personally never swim there, although many others do. I next spoke with a White environmentalist and long-time educator who has been involved in the Virginia Key issue for years, Ms. Helen Brown. Brown discussed the unlined landfill and the sewage treatment plant. While agreeing with Grayson that it was not realistic to discuss moving these, she noted that "the technology [of the treatment plant] someday will improve." In contrast to Grayson, Brown absolutely saw activism at Virginia Key as both an environmental issue and a Black heritage issue.

With these two somewhat contrasting opinions in hand, I began to attend Virginia Key Park Civil Rights Task Force meetings in the summer of 2001. It was very easy to meet the VKBPT members through my acquaintances in the Miami environmental community. I interviewed seven Blacks who are active in the Virginia Key Trust and who are also churchgoers. I also interviewed one Black trust member who is not active in a church and two White environmentalists.

The single Virginia Key activist I interviewed who is not a churchgoer is Roger Emmett, a Black male over fifty years old. Emmet saw Virginia Key as an environmental and historical issue, explaining, "People are as much engaged with the beauty of the place and what it meant and how valuable it is as a free and open space as they are with the history." He continued later: "We see [Virginia Key] as a place where history, environmental appreciation, recreation, culture can all happen. . . . The fact that within an urban environment there is a place that people can go with their families and not have to see tall buildings and enjoy nature the way it is and can commune with previous generations. . . . I think that can very much be Virginia Key's gift to the world."

The other eight interviews I had with Blacks active on the Virginia Key issue included men and women ranging in age from their fifties to their eighties. All have or have had leadership roles in local churches. One interviewee is a pastor, one is co-founder of a church, and another is the historian of a different church. This particular group of interviewees represents four local churches, from small independent churches to larger internationally affiliated denominations. All eight activists stressed the importance of Virginia Key in preserving local Black history as well as the environmental and public access issues.

Public access to public land was mentioned by interviewees as a key motivating factor for their activism. One noted, "[If Virginia Key had been developed] there would be a very fine hotel there, and we knew immediately that if a hotel were put on Virginia Key Beach that there would be some method of excluding the general public from Virginia Key Beach." Another explained, "We didn't agree with what they planned to do, which was to develop it [as] a commercial place. . . . [W]e needed to get involved in the preservation of Virginia Beach so that it could be for the public . . . for which it's supposed to be. So that everybody in Miami would have access."

A pastor, who has spoken before the City of Miami Commission on the issue, also emphasized the importance of public access as a broader issue: "When we lose that waterfront [including Virginia Key] to the private interests, then the public is the worse for it. I think we have to carve out a niche so our children and grandchildren will be able to benefit from this, not just some wealthy developer. This [waterfront] is something that should be shared by the entire community and not just the wealthy." Another Virginia Key volunteer commented on public access: "My greatest pet peeve is that . . . all this water around [Miami], you can't see it . . . most of it. It's blocked off by tall buildings, hotels, everything that you could think of. So in order to maintain access to that, to help an organization do that is paramount. It helps families, to keep families closer together, by being able to have a place where they can go that they don't have to pay, where they can enjoy nature, watch the kids, they can have great fun . . . just everything encapsulated into one." In the words of one of his fellow activists, this is clearly a "public park issue that would be depriving citizens of what we own."

All of the volunteers expressed concerns about the environment and its preservation, the "nature" of Virginia Key. One woman noted, "And looking at it [Virginia Key] as an environment point of view, there is a need to preserve the beauty of the beach, the nature," a notion echoed by many: "I think it's very important to have the beach remain . . . the natural beauty and foliage that we have on Virginia Key. And I think that should go on." For several others, stewardship of nature resulted from an appreciation of the "beauty" of the Key: "I think that you just simply call it stewards of nature. And I take that to mean that stewards take care, that they [take] care of what is there. As far as a great appreciation for nature, I don't know whether we look at it from that perspective or not. I think that we just see it, the beauty of it, and we want it around us and we take care of that which we see."

Many of the churchgoing interviewees expressed the moral position that preserving Virginia Key is simply the "right thing to do," not just a scientifically, historically, or environmentally correct approach. This was illustrated in the expressions of the inherent fairness of public access. The preservation of this beach is a moral-value issue for them. Volunteers perceived preservation of the beach for the many as being civic-minded, hence their civic engagement.

All of the people I interviewed had memories of visiting Virginia Key Beach as children or young adults during segregation, and these personal memories were interwoven with their notion of nature and the recurring concept of beauty that ought to be protected. Several people related stories of how they took the ferry to Virginia Key Beach before a causeway was completed at the end of 1947. Their nostalgia and affection for the place was evident in the tone of their voices and their smiles as they told their stories. One reminisced, "We were happy, that was our beach, we enjoyed it, we took care of one another, and there were picnics galore. . . . I loved the balmy palm trees. . . . I loved that. We would just sit on the beach, play in the sand, and pick the shells. You know, we would pick the shells and some of the snails, and we would build little castles with the sand and let the water come and just, you know, let it wash away. So we enjoyed it as a group of people who were actually . . . we were people who were restricted from the other part of the world in Miami, Florida."

I asked one pastor if Virginia Key was a stewardship issue for him, and he paused for a moment and answered, "At a gut level, hey, this is a part of what I knew as a child and I'd like to see it preserved for others to have the same opportunity and be able to enjoy it as much as I did. Honestly, I hadn't thought of it as stewardship, but I can see it as that. I think leaving Virginia Key in its natural habitat is the way to go." Other memories that surfaced about Virginia Key were related to connections between nature and the spiritual, as evidenced by the following recollection of a Virginia Key Trust member:

My father was a minister. And . . . he would take people out there [to Virginia Key] after they had been converted and saved and they'd joined the church. And they had to be baptized, so he would take them out in the water. They would have on a white robe, white headpiece, and then he would have on a robe with a sort of sash belt around him, and they would go out and he'd go out in the water. And he would say, "I baptize you in the name of the Father and the Son and the Holy Ghost." And then he would put them body and soul in the water [laughs] and bring them up. They would come up rejoicing and praising God and the Holy Spirit. And you know, those are some of the memories in addition to just going out there for fun and for swimming and for that type of thing. The religious aspect of it was an important part to me.

This importance of the religious aspect to the civic engagement at Virginia Key is accompanied by other factors. One Black female volunteer explained how children who viewed the preserved Virginia Key in the future should learn several messages, including their own history as members of the Black community, the natural history of the area, and the fact that those who came before them cared enough to preserve Virginia Key. Another Black female activist commented: "You know, that original plan [for Virginia Key], they were thinking about building concrete buildings again. That's, the saddest thing on that. Seventy-seven acres. I believe that's what they would have done. . . . Condos would have been right there on Virginia Key Beach and history would have been lost. And it's like . . . it's almost like we were never there. That's it. It would have seemed as if we never existed as a group in a restricted area, with our own culture." This idea that history could be "erased" from Virginia Key was also brought up by a pastor who claimed, "It's an important issue, and what the city [was] trying to do [was] lease that property out, to build condos . . . just wiping out the historical significance of that for Black folk. As they have sought to preserve other historic markers around the county, they should also be mindful that this is an important issue for Black folk."

All interviewees saw themselves as "working with others" rather than working singly or working only with other Black activists. These others included environmentalists, but also sportspersons concerned about the physical preservation of the beach. Several Black activists mentioned what they had 'learned' from the 'environmentalists, "So as we [members of Virginia Key coalition] share information . . . [with] the Army Corps of Engineers . . . so all of us are learning because we don't know everything about the whole project, you see. . . . I listened to [a White environmentalist] who was there the other night and she knows all about the vegetation [on Virginia Key]. What's foreign and what's native. You know, I don't know that. So I think it's an educational process and we all need to learn different aspects. . . . I know the history. . . . And so we put what we know together and share it to educate the whole."

While some Black volunteers gained understanding through the Virginia Key process about natural resource management and botany, it is important to note that this augmented their already-existing ideas. Even before they were "introduced to" the vocabulary and techniques of environmental scientists, they felt that the natural beauty of the place had to be preserved. Therefore, this episode should not be construed as White environmentalists simply teaching Miami Blacks an appreciation for nature. Nature was a part of the consciousness of Miami Blacks long before the Virginia Key issue arose (Smith 2003).

The coalition that was formed to preserve Virginia Key was comprised of Black activists who were concerned about preserving the place, environmentalists who wanted conservation of nature, and sportspeople such as windsurfers who desired active recreation and also valued the space itself. Miami is a notoriously difficult place for community activists to move their agendas forward; yet, as is demonstrated by the Virginia Key Park Civil Rights Task Force, when seemingly diverse groups unite, they often become more effective. I asked one leader of the trust about this coalition and why she thought it was better with several divergent groups, and she responded, "Because there's strength in a group and . . . more people . . . supporting what you're trying to do, I feel that you make a better case for getting the kind of response that you want from the government, especially from the City of Miami. And when they see that they will have to deal with people from all walks of life, I think the group gets more respect than it would if it were just one single group. I think there's more power in a coalition of people than in one group of people. . . . I'm glad that there are the environmentalists, that there are people interested in sports, people interested in Black history. We're all working together."

Most of the Black activists on the trust seem to view themselves as separate from the environmentalists despite the fact that the groups share many similar goals. Several activists described the two groups with different labels, nonetheless noting how they "came together," or, in the words of the social capital literature, they bridged. Many of the Black volunteers are very active in Black churches, some with current ties to Bahamian congregations, and many of their parents migrated from the Bahamas to Florida. One member of the trust's board of directors had ancestors who arrived in South Florida from the Bahamas early in the twentieth century. She and other volunteers described this Bahamian American heritage and an ensuing appreciation for nature stemming from a tradition of island beaches, growing plants, beachcombing, digging for shellfish, boating, fishing, and crabbing. One explained, "We are carrying on because we saw what our parents did. And many of our parents came from the Bahamas. . . . It was such a strong heritage, even with the food." Virginia Key Beach and its preservation tied into their own Bahamian American identities (Smith-Cavros 2006).

The importance of the church in fostering environmental activism is central among most of the Black activists. I asked one Black churchgoing member of the trust if spirituality influenced the fight for Virginia Key, and she unhesitatingly responded, "You know, of course it has!" Another volunteer noted how her church is a "teaching church," where education is important, and that Virginia Key functions to educate area people about the environment.

Emmet, one of the few non-churchgoing Black activists working on Virginia Key, also felt that spiritual issues were important: "Well, of course, as you've probably ascertained by now, when the beach was happening—and I wasn't here then, I'm not from Miami—it was the hub of life, and church life was very much a part of that. And you know, you saw the picture of the baptism [on Virginia Key]. The church has a history of being the center of organizing more than just religious activities. So, I think, that's probably something you'll find across the board. Maybe a little more pronounced in the Black community because, you know, spirituality is always kind of up-front. . . . So yes, I would say it's not really coincidental. . . . I think it's a pattern you see fairly commonly."

The churches of those Virginia Key volunteers who belong to organized religions act as a conduit for the activity of trust members and volunteers. All of the churches promoted social activism as a way of "doing God's work" and emphasized the importance of preserving Black history and church history. In addition, several pastors and church leaders who were not trust members testified at city government meetings about Virginia Key or wrote letters on its behalf. Other churches announced Virginia Key–related meetings and relayed information to their congregations. While some churches did less to *act* on their environmental and preservation ideals, many of their individual congregants and pastors actively supported the Virginia Key movement.

Because Virginia Key has importance in the history of segregation as well as being a sacred space, its preservation has multiple meanings. The preservation of Virginia Key's environment is different from the abstract idea some environmentalists have of saving the tropical rainforest, a place many of them will never visit. Virginia Key is a highly personal issue that has historical, spiritual, and environmental significance for Blacks in Miami.

The civil rights movement and the environmental movement have impacted and influenced what is happening at Virginia Key. Several of the Black churchgoers involved in the Virginia Key Trust were active in Miami's civil rights movement and fought for the integration of beaches, schools, and politics. At least two Black participants and several White activists in the Virginia Key movement have also been members of environmental groups like Greenpeace and the Sierra Club.

Key charismatic leaders have also played an important role in the Virginia Key project. Many of the volunteers are ex-educators and current community leaders. Several are quite comfortable speaking in front of large groups and entered the project with both a network of political connections in Miami and the proven ability to motivate and inspire others around them. Many of the volunteers I spoke with were also retired and had, as a result, leisure time to devote to this and other local causes. Most, but not all, volunteers were solidly middle class and thus were able to afford to devote extra time to an unpaid cause.

The restoration efforts at Virginia Key Beach itself have begun and are visible. These include native plantings of trees and shrubs and the construction of nature trails. Black cultural and historical events have been held there, including an Easter Sunrise service (like those held there in the 1950s), a Bob Marley memorial event, a reggae festival, and an African passage commemorative remembrance. Rastafarians have organized beach cleanups at Virginia Key, and plans are underway for a civil rights museum and natural history displays. After several decades of neglect, the beach is regularly open and is staffed by lifeguards.

The CSC that has been and will be produced by this project can be measured in several ways. It is the restoration of a natural area from an environmental standpoint. It is the restoration of a piece of the soul of the Miami Black community from another. The civic engagement and investment of social capital by the Virginia Beach Park Task Force and its volunteers were made with full awareness of the implications. It is an investment in the restorative power of both the nature of the beach and its history that volunteers hope and believe will influence the generations of children who will visit the beach in the decades to come. It emerged from the intense racial bonding enforced by segregation that combined with contemporary bridging to the White environmental movement. It is firmly rooted in the particular historical geography of Blacks in South Florida and has hidden origins in the immigration of Bahamians, who now are perceived as and portray themselves in the political arena as African Americans.

Tree Planting in Richmond Heights

A tree-planting project in a Black middle-class residential community shares many features with the Virginia Key Beach project in that its principals, Black churchgoers, have invested significant amounts of CSC in initiatives that benefit Black communities through environmental activism and stewardship. Richmond Heights is a community in south Miami-Dade County whose population is about 97 percent Black. It is a tidy neighborhood, with many retirees, some of whom consider themselves pioneers of this area. According to Lucille Heinrich, their houses were first built "in the late 1940s [by], Captain Frank C. Martin [who] decided to build a quality housing development for African American World War II veterans" (1997, 2). Martin, a White Pan-Am pilot, may never have envisioned that his development project would grow to its current population of "over 2,300 single family homes, and a population of about 10,000+ persons" (Luckie 1997, 8). One thing that was left out of the development was trees. One of the volunteers on the tree-planting project explained, "We really didn't have trees out here in Richmond Heights on the street. When these homes were built, what trees there were, the pine trees, they cut all the trees down. And the only trees that was out here was what people planted in their yards. There was no trees along the streets and the sidewalk."

In an attempt to remedy this situation, several tree plantings of native tree species took place in Richmond Heights in the middle to late 1990s. The largest of these was partially funded by a grant from the Cool Communities Program through American Forests, a national not-for-profit environmental organization. Two of the project organizers in Richmond Heights were Black church deacons, and many of the volunteers were Black churchgoers. The technical advisor for the Cool Communities Program in Miami-Dade County was Dr. Jack Parker, a White faculty member in the Environmental Science Department at Florida International University in Miami. Parker recounted for me how his "relationship with Richmond Heights actually started much earlier than [the tree planting in 1995]. I think it was before Hurricane Andrew [August 1992] when I came into the community. Somebody invited me in and I talked about the need for trees in Richmond Heights." In targeting neighborhoods in the mid-1990s with Nancy Masterson, an American Forests project coordinator, Parker returned to Richmond Heights and met Deacon George Baldwin. According to Parker, Deacon Baldwin "became the key person to make that [tree planting] happen" at the neighborhood level.

Baldwin is an outspoken man of tremendous energy. At the time of this research, Baldwin was president of the Richmond Heights Neighborhood Crimewatch, Inc. (RHNC), which played a major role in the planting of trees. The organization's mission statement reads, "Our mission is to recognize the historical significance of this predominantly African American neighborhood, and to develop Richmond Heights into a model neighborhood whereby other minority neighborhoods can learn how to organize their neighborhoods and work toward improvement of their quality of life" (Richmond Heights Neighborhood Crimewatch 2001). Emphasis is also placed on the environment by the organization, which lists goals that include "beautification and cleanup" and "plant[ing] trees in the neighborhood to help reduce power consumption and beautify the neighborhood." The section on fostering neighborhood pride expands to include Black history by "establish[ing] a 'Pioneer' committee comprised of the original settlers in the community in order to gain their full support of the programs" and to "promote African American history and awareness" (Richmond Heights Neighborhood Crimewatch 2001). Several people connected with the Crimewatch believed that the planting of trees would actually reduce crime. Deacon Tommie Daniels mentioned:

> It makes a difference when you can walk out or walk down the street and walk in shade. It makes a difference and in some theories, shade trees keep down violence. Because when the kids go out to play, the parents can go out and sit under trees. If they're sitting under the trees, the kids

ain't gonna fight. . . . This was an actual case study, cause I lived in
Milwaukee. Milwaukee is ninety miles north of Chicago and . . . so what
happened is we did some studies in Chicago at the playgrounds. And I've
always been a visionary person. . . . [W]e found that where [not] a tree
was planted and that was a playground, many people did not want to sit
out there in the sun, so consequently, what happened is kids got into
arguments and fights more, cause there was no adults there. Then, we
went to another park where trees were and the kids did not fight. So tree
planting cuts down on violence.

Baldwin took me on a driving and walking tour to see the magnitude of the
project. Over six hundred trees have been planted in Richmond Heights, on
the swales, in school yards and parks, and in residential yards as well. It had
been over five years since the initial plantings, and the results were stunning.
Richmond Heights, an area that is only about two square miles in total, was full
of greenery. The trees planted were of a modest size. Deacon Baldwin said that
no trees were planted over ten feet tall so that "people could handle [them]. We
wanted the residents to handle trees. We could've gotten the county to plant
them, but that's not what we wanted."

The leaders of the tree-planting project all had prior environmental volunteer work experience. They were also part of a project in which they sought to
create a "pioneer monument" to honor the early settlers of Richmond Heights.
This effort also has an environmental aspect, because the monument will feature plantings around it, continuing the theme of "greening up" Richmond
Heights. Several volunteers were performing the arduous task of transcribing
the names of all Richmond Heights pioneers from the 1940s and 1950s from city
records for the monument. I asked one of them why this was so important, and
she answered, "The children can go there and say, 'That's my mother; that's my
grandmother; that's my great-grandfather.' And this is the only community that
we know about . . . that has a monument [like this]. And like I said, we're proud
of this community, very proud of this community. And we want to keep it this
way. . . . God Bless Captain Martin . . . when he went out [with] a dream for these
homes for the veterans. Yes, there's a lot of history right here in Richmond
Heights." The past, then, as at Virginia Key, is remembered both for its intrinsic value
and for its validation of the present. Stevens continued: "There will be plants all
around [the monument] . . . lighting and plants all around. . . . The lighting and the
structure and the planting and the watering . . . it's gonna take that." Baldwin
wrote a successful proposal and received a forty thousand dollar grant from the
Miami-Dade County Commission for the monument itself. He showed me
the monument site at Lincoln Boulevard and Madison Street and explained his
ideas for extensive plantings. In November 2001, Baldwin began a drive to raise
a million pennies, or ten thousand dollars, to augment the monument fund.

Church is also a critical element for these leaders of the tree planting. Deacon Baldwin travels outside of Richmond Heights to church at the New Way Fellowship Church in Opa Locka, where he often teaches Bible classes. However, we met for the first time at his wife's church in Richmond Heights, where I attended a service. This is the Macedonia Church of God in Christ. This church is the next project that Baldwin has set his sights on. He explained: "[For] this church, I obtained a grant to plant trees all around the perimeter. They're building a new 1.3 million dollar edifice. We're going to be highlighting this church. All eleven thousand members of the community will be invited [he pointed to a large field]. All this space belongs to them. We're going to plant trees here and in the swales."

His goal was to inspire various ministers and congregants across denominations. When I asked him if this was stewardship, Baldwin reasoned, "There is no doubt about that. See, when you look at the environment, every church should have trees planted in that churchyard ... so people can know that they're part of nature. That's my way of looking at it. . . . I'm sure somebody is going to pick up on it. I know it. There are six churches in this community and I'm going to start with one." The deacon emphatically explained to me how the church community needs to "wake up" and seek resources to draw people in, and to actively do more and show that to the wider world. At another point in the interview he commented on the tree planting: "The purpose of the church is to reconcile God and man. . . . How can you do that in four walls if you don't reach out? I planted trees to make sure the community reached out." Baldwin intertwined religion and the environment again when he described a book that he is writing, to be entitled "Man's Inhumanity to God": "As long as I'm alive, I'm going to be doing. . . . It's a shame for God to let the sun go over Florida and people don't plant trees. To me, it's like a sin to not do that [plant trees]. You help your own self and you help the environment. . . . The next generation that comes after me is going to do it. Richmond Heights is a beautiful model. Maybe I won't make a difference, but I think I will."

Deacon Daniels has attended a church that is located outside of Richmond Heights for over fifty years, the Greater Israel Bethel Primitive Baptist Church in Overtown, in the heart of downtown Miami. I asked him if he believed that his church influenced him in how he thought about the environment and nature, and he replied, "I think it does. See, it said in the Bible, we learned about creation and how God created, and the purpose of everything He created. I think it affects your life, the environmental part of it anyway. You learn to treat things, and you know the purpose of them and everything has a purpose." In response to the same question about whether church had an influence on her volunteer work, Scavella, who attends Christ Episcopal Church in Coconut Grove, explained, "If you're a real Christian, you want to give, you want to do, you want to improve everything that is around you ... [and] that's the Christian spirit.

You want everything to eventually be beautiful, or try to make it so . . . try to." Stevens, who attends Bethel Baptist Church in Richmond Heights, echoed these sentiments: "Yes, in a way . . . yes," the church had influenced her feelings about the environment and nature. She explained how the church encouraged people to be active: "To tell you the truth, in the first place it [the tree planting] created some jobs for the young people; it gave beautification to different communities. . . . [T]hat's the way I feel about the churches."

Baldwin emphasized the benefits of the tree-planting project in relation to the ecosystem and human inhabitants:

> We planted trees here; anyplace we can, we plant trees. We did it because we want not just Miami-Dade County to know, but we wanted the nation to know that tree planting naturally and automatically cools the community. . . . The rationale was we wanted to see a cooler community because this heat island is something people don't think about. But we [also] needed places, habitat for birds, you know. And it just makes it look nice. It makes the community look nice. . . . Now, what we want these trees to do is grow like these [he gestured] and we want them to overshadow the road. . . . [I]t's going to take awhile. I probably won't be on the scene. And the purpose of it really is to have a cooler community. What we did is, we [also] planted trees in the yards of eighty-five families and we were trying to show a reduction in the use of energy by 35 percent.

The results of the tree planting were quite evident. It was obvious that the plantings had been watered and well taken care of. Residents that I spoke with beamed proudly as they pointed out trees that they themselves had planted or helped to plant. Everyone I spoke to talked about the idea of planting more trees in the future, as if their original tree planting, though a completed project, were only a beginning. Everyone I talked with in Richmond Heights shared a deep pride in the projects they worked on and the positive CSC they believed would result in future generations.

Environmentalism, the Black Church, and CSC

The Virginia Key and Richmond Heights projects reconfirm the general finding that Black CSC arises as a response to American racism (see, for example, Harris 1999). Virginia Key beach was cherished because it was once the only local beach for Blacks, and Richmond Heights similarly had its origins as the first middle-class subdivision for Blacks. The two projects also confirm the importance of the Black church in generating and implementing CSC. The projects embodied spiritual motivations, and the Black leaders who advanced them were firmly rooted in churches. In both case studies, the place was also seen as a *sacred* space, particularly, an African American *sacred space* embedded in

Miami's legacy of segregation. Virginia Key had a very direct correlation to the sacred. Religious services and baptisms, recreating biblical holy waters, were frequent on its shores. Pastors brought first boatloads then busloads of African Americans to church picnics on Virginia Key's beaches. It was both de facto church space and religious recreation area, and it was in great part for this that some activists sought to save it. Much emphasis has been put on the spiritual renewal of the beach, as evidenced by the rebirth of traditional Easter Sunday services as a capstone alongside the physical and environmental restoration (*Miami Times* 2000a).

In Richmond Heights, for Deacon Baldwin and others, it was about creating and expanding sacred space beyond the four walls of the church through the tree planting and a homage to pioneer spirit and equality. Richmond Heights, another legacy of Miami's segregation as a Black middle-class development, adopted sacred space status for some participants. It reminded them of places in their youth that were deeply connected to their spirituality and values with which they hoped to reconnect local children.

How much CSC was generated and of what nature? The African American activists behind the Virginia Key and Richmond Heights initiatives engendered bonding social capital based on a sense of belonging and of community identity inspired by their memories of segregation. The bonding that emerged through racism and religion were thus necessary elements of these projects, but they were also insufficient. To succeed, both projects also had to bridge and link beyond the Black community. To accomplish their goals of preserving the history of Virginia Key and producing a tree canopy in Richmond Heights, the projects required bridging CSC to White environmentalists. At Virginia Key, the strength of the Black activists was greatly enhanced as they joined with recreational windsurfers and White environmentalists. Richmond Heights' volunteers facilitated their tree plantings because of their relationships with nonprofit American Forests and Crimewatch.

The Virginia Key and Richmond Heights projects, furthermore, each addressed the issue of local public land as valuable CSC. At Virginia Key the political issue of public access to public land was framed as a fundamental right. In Richmond Heights, the social and environmental importance of shared public land was demonstrated through median plantings, park and school plantings, and the idea of uniting neighbors for the joy and even safety of the community.

The bridging and framing that made these projects successful was done by leaders raised in the era that spanned segregation to desegregation. They knew how to create social links to outsiders who had complementary resources, and they knew how to frame their issues in ways that drew upon their roots in the church and appealed to those who could help but were outside their churches.

Both projects also contained an element of concern for African American youth. Although youth were not the fundamental motivation for these projects, the adults still articulated a motivation to advance these projects so that the youth would have a knowledge of local African American history. Both projects connected youth with the older generation, utilizing nature, from trees to beach, as a tool to assist and inspire. Bridging generations is a powerful form of CSC for community and environmental re-investment.

Describing these projects as resulting in CSC, however, doesn't reveal the entire story. It seems, then, that the CSC that was sought by most activists could also be described as a social-*environmental* capital that benefits the community and the natural environment. Both Black communities and urban environmental issues are often low among the priorities of those who broker power and funds at the local, state, and national levels. However, as shown in these two case studies, what is good for these communities and for the environment is often similar or the same. The power of a bridging coalition between diverse interest groups, volunteerism, spirituality, historical conservation, commitment to place, excitement for the future, and environmental awareness and stewardship are crucial to inspire and enact change. If these elements of community engagement are coupled with a goal of CSC and social-environmental capital, the combination may be what it takes to pull Blacks and nature back to the bargaining table with a new sense of empowerment, with the Black church at the center of the encounter.

REFERENCES

Arp, W., and C. Kenny. 1996. Black Environmentalism in the Local Community Context. *Environment and Behavior* 28(3): 267.

Arp, W., III, and J. Llorens. 1999. Environmental Justice for Black Americans: A Question of Fairness. *Western Journal of Black Studies* 23(2): 125–131.

Baer, H., and M. Singer. 1992. *African-American Religion in the Twentieth Century: Varieties of Protest and Accommodation.* Knoxville: University of Tennessee Press.

Bullard, R. 1990. Waste and Racism: A Stacked Deck? *Forum for Applied Research and Public Policy* 8(1): 29–35.

Bunyan, B., and P. Mohai. 1992. *Race and the Incidence of Environmental Hazards: A Time for Discourse.* Boulder, CO: Westview Press.

Burby, R., and D. Strong. 1997. Coping with Chemicals: Blacks, Whites, Planners and Industrial Pollution. *Journal of the American Planning Association* 63(4): 469–481.

Caron, J. 1989. Environmental Perspectives of Black Acceptance of the New Environmental Paradigm. *Journal of Environmental Education* 20(3): 21–26.

Cutter, S. 1981. Community Concern for Pollution: Social and Environmental Influences. *Environment and Behavior* 13: 105–124.

Dunn, M. 1997. *Black Miami in the Twentieth Century.* Gainesville: University Press of Florida.

Fiedler, T. 1985. Carollo: Let's Develop Virginia Key Land. *Miami Herald*, April 11.

Franklin, R. 1997. *Another Day's Journey: Black Churches Confronting the American Crisis.* Minneapolis: Fortress Press.

Harris, F. C. 1999. Something Within: Religion in African-American Political Activism. *Journal of Church and State* 42(winter): 189.

Heinrich, L., ed. 1997. *The Story of Richmond Heights, Miami.* Miami: Florida Commission on Community Service.

Hogan, P., and M. Hogan. 1998. Environmental Justice: An Analysis of Superfund Sites in Florida. *Social Problems* 45: 268–287.

Howenstine, E. 1993. Market Segmentation for Recycling. *Environment and Behavior* 35(2): 86–102.

Humphrey, C., and F. Buttel. 1982. *Environment, Energy, and Society.* Belmont, CA: Wadsworth Publishing.

Kennedy, L. 2000. *Race and Urban Space in Contemporary American Culture.* Edinburgh: Edinburgh University Press.

Kreger, J. 1973. Ecology and Black Student Opinion. *Journal of Environmental Education* 4: 30–34.

Luckie, A. 1997. Richmond Heights—Then and Now. In *The Story of Richmond Heights, Miami,* ed. L. Heinrich. Florida Commission on Community Service.

Miami Times. 2000a. 3,000 Revive Easter Tradition on Virginia Key Beach. May 3–9, 2B.

———. 2000b. Editorials: Virginia Key Beach Trust. December 20–26, 6A.

Mohai, P. 1985. Public Concern and Elite Involvement in Environmental Conservation Issues. *Social Science Quarterly* 66: 820–838.

Mohai, P., and B. Bunyan. 1998. Is There a "Race" Effect on Concern for Environmental Quality? *Public Opinion Quarterly* 62(4): 475–505.

Newell, S., and C. Green. 1997. Racial Differences in Consumer Environmental Concern. *Journal of Consumer Affairs* 31(1): 53–70.

Nielsen, K. 1999. A Historic Dip. *Miami New Times,* April 8–14, 23–27.

Paddon, J., and D. Suman. 1995. The Virginia Key Campground. In *Urban Growth and Sustainable Habitats,* ed. D. Suman, M. Shivlani, and M. Villanueva, 155–169. Miami: University of Miami.

Patillo-McCoy, M. 1998. Church Culture as a Strategy of Action in the Black Community. *American Sociological Review* 63(December): 767–784.

Homer A. Plessy v. Ferguson. 1896. 163 U.S. 537; 16 S. Ct. 1138; 41 L. Ed. 256; 1896 U.S. LEXIS 3390.

Richmond Heights Neighborhood Crimewatch, Inc. 2001. *Mission Statement.* Publicity brochure, Miami.

Smith, E. 2003. Black Churchgoers, Environmental Activism, and the Preservation of Nature in Miami, Florida. PhD diss., Florida International University.

Smith-Cavros, E. 2006. Black Churchgoers, Environmental Activism, and the Preservation of Nature in Miami, Florida. *Journal of Ecological Anthropology* 10(1): 33–44.

———. 2008. Environmental Attitudes of Modern Black Churchgoers: Place, Nature and Memory. *Journal for the Study of Religion, Nature and Culture.* Forthcoming.

Stewart, C.F.S., III. 1999. *Black Spirituality and Black Consciousness.* Trenton, NJ: Africa World Press, Inc.

Virginia Key Park Civil Rights Task Force. 2000. *Report.* Miami-Dade County, Miami, FL: Virginia Key Park Civil Rights Task Force. January 17.

Williams, M. 1974. *Community in a Black Pentecostal Church.* Prospect Heights, IL: Waveland Press, Inc.

PART THREE

Religious and Spiritual Activities and Bonding Social Capital

8

Youth and Charity in a Sweetwater Parish

Our Lady of Divine Providence Church

AIDIL OSCARIZ

On a typically hot and humid Miami day in 2003, bulldozers, forklifts, and construction workers moved busily about the Our Lady of Divine Providence churchyard, erecting a twenty-thousand-square-foot church. The new edifice, completed late the next year, replaced a squat red brick structure less than half its size that was built there a quarter-century prior, just as the congregation was about to open its doors to the waves of refugees from Cuba and, somewhat later, from Nicaragua, then crashing on Miami shores. From the time that Archbishop Coleman F. Carroll designated the parish in June of 1973 until the parish's first building was dedicated in December of 1979, the congregation gathered in a trailer about fifteen blocks away from its present location in Sweetwater, a small municipality a few miles west of downtown Miami. The construction of the first church was soon followed by the construction of the parish school, which in 1979 began housing after-school programs and Catholic religious education classes,[1] all administered by the Theatine Sisters of the Immaculate Conception, who joined the parish that same year. By 1986, over two hundred children, kindergarten through third grade, were enrolled in the school, which added a grade each year thereafter, and by 1991 was offering classes from kindergarten through eighth grade. The timing of the construction of both the church and the school was nothing short of auspicious, theologically speaking, as between May and September of 1980, the Mariel Boatlift brought "more than 125,000 unscreened and undocumented aliens" from Cuba to the United States, the vast majority to Miami (Sandoval 1985, 11). The church had become a haven for hundreds of *Marielitos*, as the new Cuban refugees were called.

In the early 1980s Our Lady of Divine Providence's congregation was thus heavily Cuban, with a sprinkling of other Latin American immigrants. But soon enough, political turmoil in their homeland drove an unprecedented number of Nicaraguans to seek refuge in the United States, many of them settling within the boundaries of the Our Lady of Divine Providence parish (Fernández Kelly and Curran 2001; Portes and Stepick 1993). The 1990 U.S. Census reported that 74,244 Nicaraguans then lived in Dade County, which is likely an underestimation (Konczal 2001). The parish's growth was commensurate with Nicaraguan immigration to the city, and within a few years the congregation's ethnic demographics had shifted considerably. By the end of the 1980s, 70 percent of members were Nicaraguan, rendering the once-predominant Cuban parishioners a minority.

According to Orlando Aleu, a Cuban American who joined the congregation in 1982, initially this demographic shift did not result in any discord between the new group and the Cuban exile community, who could themselves relate all too well to the refugee experience. During an interview he indicated, "There was a solidarity because we knew, we came from a Communist country, of people who are fleeing the same system." Nicaraguan immigrants, however, did not find the United States to be as welcoming as had the Cubans before them. The U.S. government was reticent to consider them to be "political refugees," thereby denying them asylum, and thus many settled in the area as illegal immigrants. Moreover, the Cuban exiles' warm reception of the new Central Americans was short-lived, and soon a power struggle emerged in the neighborhood and in the parish. In short time, though, the parish's Nicaraguan majority and the significant number of Cubans and other Hispanics appear to have settled their differences in the local Catholic community, which they have each infused with their own unique cultural traditions. While Nicaraguans come to Divine Providence from all over Miami for a taste of their homeland culture and a sense of national pride, people from all different countries join them December 8 to celebrate the Feast of La Purísima,[2] Nicaragua's patron saint, which is the highlight of the year at the church. The feast days of the patron saints of other "sending" Latin American countries are also celebrated at the parish, making the church an important part of Miami's vibrant popular Catholic cult of the saints. Such devotions issue from, just as they reproduce and augment, the rich stores of religious capital at Our Lady of Divine Providence, religious capital understood here as "the degree of mastery of and attachment to a particular religious culture" (Stark and Finke 2000, 120).[3]

As is the case in much of the Catholic world, however, popular saint devotions among immigrants in the United States, while contributing to the maintenance of cultural identity, do not automatically generate civic social capital (CSC). This is certainly true at Divine Providence, where only intermittently has any significant social or political activism resulted in concrete gains for the parish's poor immigrants, especially Nicaraguans. The two most significant exceptions to this generalization occurred in 1980, when the church generously availed itself to hordes of *marielitos*, and during the years 1982 through 1986, when it did the same for Nicaraguan refugees. These periods transpired while Our Lady of Divine Providence was pastored by Father Ernesto Garcia-Rubio, a Cuban priest who joined the parish in 1975 and became its pastor in 1978. Some Nicaraguans parishioners today speak of him with much gratitude and nostalgia, disbelieving several charges of sexual abuse levied against him by men who were once teenage refugees at the parish. But, some of the allegations were sufficiently substantiated that the Vatican defrocked Garcia-Rubio in 1999, and the Archdiocese of Miami paid settlements to two of his alleged victims as part of a class-action suit in 2003. The shock of the allegations deeply divided the parish.[4]

As difficult as it is to admit in light of the sex abuse scandal, Garcia-Rubio's record at Our Lady of Divine Providence did have a positive side. The fruitful social ministry for Nicaraguans that he led was in part motivated by his personal history, which engendered in him a sense of deep indebtedness to Nicaragua; he was himself a political prisoner of the Castro regime. His own parents also sought refuge abroad and, as fate or divine providence would have it, settled for a time, prior to the Sandinista Revolution, in Nicaragua.

During the crucial years for Miami's Nicaraguan immigrants in the early 1980s, Garcia-Rubio responded to their imminent needs by, among other things, recruiting volunteers to aid them with the arduous and lengthy process of filing for work permits and legal resident status. The parish also provided an array of vital services such as psychological counseling, job placement, housing assistance, food distribution, and economic aid. For some time, every evening the massive electric sliding accordion doors that divided the church building into four different sections in the form of a cross were closed to divide the space into makeshift dormitories for hundreds of Nicaraguans. By day, the church was transformed again into a day-care center for the refugee children. Behind the church, there was an old shack made out of tree limbs, sticks, and straw, where some Nicaraguan immigrants also slept, while still others, weather permitting, would sleep outside in the churchyard. They bathed in an adjacent lake.

All of this served to enhance the Nicaraguan immigrants' dedication to the parish. Eduardo Gonzalez, for one, would become the parish's director of Music Ministry, a post that he has held now for over ten years. Several members of his family had gained work permits thanks to the immigration services provided at Divine Providence from 1982 to 1986.

When the sex abuse scandal embroiling Garcia-Rubio became public, the archdiocese had little choice but to remove him from the Sweetwater parish in 1988, sending him on sabbatical to Colombia and insisting that he not return to Miami to celebrate the twenty-fifth anniversary of his ordination (Weaver 2004). For reasons unknown, his replacement was not named until 1992, when a Nicaraguan priest, Father Oscar Brantome, was designated Our Lady of Divine Providence's new pastor.

In 1997, the Nicaraguan Adjustment and Central American Relief Act (NACARA) finally granted Nicaraguans the opportunity to apply for permanent legal residency status in the United States. However, the application process was anything but easy for Our Lady of Divine Providence's Nicaraguan immigrants, who once again turned to their church for assistance in negotiating the process. Under the leadership of their Nicaraguan pastor, they were offered spiritual and moral support, prayers, and letters endorsing their residency applications. Space was also made available to volunteers who helped complete the convoluted paperwork and steer them through the process. Under Father Brantome's stewardship, the church also held prayer services in support of the cause.

When Father Brantome became seriously ill and was forced to retire in the late 1990s, the congregation was anxious to learn who would replace him and traversed a difficult transitional period that one parishioner characterized as "disequilibrium." But soon their concerns would be allayed and stability restored, as the archdiocese assigned Father Luis Ramon Rivera to pastor the parish. Rivera soon won over the now largely Nicaraguan congregation, despite being a second-generation Hispanic American of Puerto Rican descent from New York. The support mechanisms to immigrants filing procedures with the Immigration and Naturalization Service were quickly revived, and Father Rivera was always willing to write letters of endorsement for members of his flock. He also secured the occasional pro bono services of immigration attorneys and income tax specialists to help poor immigrants apply for legalized immigration status and file their income tax returns. But the mandate of constructing a large new church for the growing parish became so all-consuming of their pastor that some parishioners mistook him as distant to their social concerns. Retrospectively, however, it is easy to see how the pastor's necessary absorption in the massive construction project, which was charged to him by the archdiocese when it appointed him to shepherd the parish, may have been mistaken by some as disinterest when, in fact, as he related in his interview, "Because of the construction we had to stop a lot of things. Time-wise, we were very limited. But . . . we're beginning to start up some of the regular routine." With roughly five million dollars in debts and forty thousand dollars due each month to repay them, much attention clearly is needed to oversee parish finances.

Religious Capital versus Civic Social Capital

Catholic theology teaches that there are seven Corporal Works of Mercy, the first six of which are based upon the Gospel of Matthew 25:31–46: (1) feeding the hungry, (2) giving drink to the thirsty, (3) welcoming the stranger, (4) clothing the naked, (5) visiting the sick, and (6) visiting the prisoner. The seventh work, burying the dead, is extra-biblical. Additionally, the Catholic Church teaches that the Spiritual Works of Mercy are also seven: (1) to teach the ignorant, (2) to counsel the needy, (3) to chastise the sinful, (4) to comfort the sorrowful, (5) to forgive enemies, (6) to suffer tribulation, and (7) to pray for all fervently. These fourteen principles provide the Our Lady of Divine Providence parish, as they do all Catholics, with the theological foundation for charity on both the individual and congregational levels. In general, however, it may be said that the Divine Providence parishioners' strongest commitment in regards to service is pastoral rather than social, and that the social services in which they do engage are usually parish-specific, and hence definable as bonding rather than bridging forms of social capital. Furthermore, such forms of social capital are only civic insofar as they aid immigrants in completing the legal processes for becoming American permanent residents. The resultant limited level of CSC at Our Lady of Divine Providence is thus far outweighed by the considerable stock in religious capital that the parish enjoys. Here, service is defined as spiritually and internally focused, mostly confined to religious services and events held by and for members of the church community. Most ministries and groups at Divine Providence, in effect, concentrate on the Spiritual rather than the Corporal Works of Mercy. As one of the members of a prayer group which meets daily to pray the rosary explained, "The Legion of Mary exists for the purpose of spreading the Spiritual Works of Mercy." She identifies St. Vincent de Paul as the parallel organization within the church that is responsible for the Corporal Works of Mercy.

Our Lady of Divine Providence's deacon, Rev. Eduardo Panellas, explained that the parish's mission is no different from that of the wider Catholic Church: "To deliver the gospel to everyone, serving as a missionary, bearing witness to the gospel wherever one may go." While clergy and congregants alike recognize the difficult financial conditions of many of their parishioners and residents of the surrounding area, their material needs are secondary to their spiritual needs and to improving the quality of their lives by virtue of the strength and endurance afforded by their faith. The means to achieve this main objective are to evangelize and set an example to follow, to spread the Word, and to live within the guidelines established by the faith. Several congregants and groups refer to the unofficial mission of the parish, as articulated by its current pastor, Father Rivera, as "to work primarily on the spiritual aspect of the congregation, forming one community." In other words, Father Rivera self-consciously has chosen to emphasize bonding social capital over bridging social capital. The CSC generated within the church, then, is likely to be among fellow congregants rather than reaching out into the broader community. Consistent with this dictum, most activities are only advertised and held within church walls, thereby attracting mostly those who already comprise the congregation. Of course, it can be difficult to recognize the needs of the wider community without either aggressive outreach programs or the community's own petitions being addressed to the parish. Yet, even in the rare instances when such petitions are brought to the parish's attention, they are seldom addressed, as one parishioner opined during an interview: "[The pastor] is of the mentality that says, 'Why are you gonna go help outside when you can help your community.' . . . Actually, he never agreed on that, you know, feeding the homeless. Well, he's kind of like, 'Why are you gonna feed the homeless if the trailer park next to the church [is right here]? We have a lot of poor people [right here] who are hungry and [why should] you go to downtown? You know, just come, come to this trailer park.' "

This powerfully testifies to the critical role of religious leadership in any congregation's administration of CSC. Our Lady of Divine Providence, for example, holds very little of this bridging or linking CSC because its leadership has deemed such prerequisite investments in social ministries to be of secondary importance to pastoral investments and to the massive construction project. Consequently, out of the parish's eighteen groups and ministries, it is usually only the St. Vincent de Paul and the Knights of Columbus groups that consistently provide material assistance to parishioners as well as to local organizations and individuals beyond the parish. Yet even these ministries are chartered largely at the pastor's discretion, as he oversees parish functions and thus determines what types of services are provided and the eligibility requirements for beneficiaries.

The raison d'etre of these groups under Father Rivera has become almost solely spiritual. As one young member of the community commented, "There's God knows how many prayer groups," groups or ministries that devote most of their time to prayer, expanding their theological knowledge and their understanding of the Bible and the faith. This is even the case with most of the groups who *do* extend their services to the wider community; for example, those who visit the sick or incarcerated do so primarily to offer them spiritual solace and to evangelize. The Respect Life Ministry, a pro-life group, distributes literature (often extremely graphic) at busy intersections throughout the city with the purpose of informing people of the stance of the Catholic Church on abortion. The Neo-Catechumenal Group makes door-to-door visits around the vicinity in order to evangelize. Most of the activities that take place at the parish throughout the year are devotional observances, vigils, processions, and other traditional celebrations and ceremonies such as patron saints days, *Via crucis* (stations of the cross), and Christmas plays. Other events include the annual festival and weekly garage sales, where food, clothes, and a variety of items are donated and, in turn, sold to raise funds for the parish, which the parish, in turn, allocates to any of its other projects.

Representing an important exception to this rule, the proceeds of the Feast of La Purísima have been sent to a different church in Nicaragua each year since the devastation wrought there in 1998 by Hurricane Mitch. The earnings from the weekly parish garage sale, meanwhile, go toward preparations for upcoming events, such as cooking traditional Nicaraguan dishes for festivals such as La

Purísima. These fund-raising events represent opportunities to connect with the outside community and uninvolved churchgoers, which Orlando Aleu and other parishioners consider to be constructive experiences. He explained,

> We also build community because, for example, we sell coffee, we sell donuts, we sell the typical foods of which country, and people come and stay for a while and share. And that's where we start becoming aware of many of the needs in the community that we are unaware of. For example, when first arriving, one is disoriented. Immigrants who just arrive, you know, when one gets to a new place and sees everyone and says, "*Coño,* here I feel . . ." Then they begin to gradually get closer, and then one knows, one senses, the same way when one is traveling as a tourist, they say, "He's a tourist." Well, here we do the same thing and we try to find out about the necessities, if the kids are attending catechism, if they are attending school, if they have some problem with Immigration. Then you give them different types of guidance to try to help them. . . . Sometimes we don't see the problems that exist in society, and they are inside the church; they reach the church. Because people come looking for two things, spiritual comfort and looking for material assistance.

Aleu's commentary reflects the difficulty that many congregations face in balancing investments in both religious capital and CSC. It is worth recalling here that one of the crucial insights of Bourdieu's theory of practice as it pertains to religion is that religious capital can be "transferred into other fields and transformed into other forms of capital" (Rey 2004, 333; Robison, Schmid, and Siles 2002). This book contains numerous examples of this phenomenon or, more specifically, of religious capital being transformed into CSC. Moreover, in most of these examples, the hand of either a cleric or a lay leader can be seen as the guiding force behind such a "transubstantiation" of capital, to use Bourdieu's term, whereas at Our Lady of Divine Providence the laity are largely expected to accumulate CSC on their own.

Spirituality and Service in the Nueva Alianza/Young Adult Group

As stated on the Web site of the Catholic Archdiocese of Miami, the objective of its Office of Youth and Young Adult Ministry is to help young Catholics "reach their full potential and to participate in the total mission of the Church: to build the Kingdom of God" (www.miamiyoungchurch.com). The Our Lady of Divine Providence young adult group, Nueva Alianza, also developed its own Web site, which was entirely in Spanish and contained news, events information, and links to other Catholic sites.[5] It also had an e-mail link for those who wanted to make a request for prayer. The archdiocesan mission statement for its Office of Youth and Young Adult Ministry resonates with the opening words of the Nueva

Alianza home page: "Our objective is to guide and help young adults to walk in
Jesus Christ's path and through those who willingly do so, also evangelize other
young adults who have not yet known the Love of God."[6] On the Web site, the
members collectively introduced themselves as "young people who have known
the Love and Mercy of Love and for this mercy, we wish to live our lives following Our Lord Jesus Christ" and invited other youth with a desire to explore that
love and the Catholic Church to visit. "If families tried for the youth to become
more incorporated into the parish, that would bring one of the main things to
the community. The thing that moves any place is the youth," opined one
parishioner.

Because Our Lady of Divine Providence is a relatively large parish with
roughly thirty-five hundred registered families, there are many youth who are
registered as members of the church and who attend services regularly. The
8:30 p.m. Sunday Mass is devoted to the youth and was initially intended to help
recruit members for the parish's youth group and its young adult group, Nueva
Alianza, and to attract potential Eucharistic ministers, altar servers, and chorus
members.[7] Our Lady of Divine Providence's catechism classes are central to
parishioners' lives, preparing children for the different sacraments and generally making important investments in their religious capital. Catechism is
offered from Monday through Thursday evenings and on Saturday morning.
Fifty-five volunteers teach the different classes, and the program is directed
by a Theatine sister. More than one hundred adolescents completed their theological and liturgical preparation toward the Sacrament of Confirmation in
2002 alone.

Two adults oversee the weekly meetings of the candidates for Confirmation.
The adults additionally meet once a month to formulate an agenda and select
leaders for this group and for the larger Nueva Alianza youth group. Nueva
Alianza is comprised of two subgroups, one of young adults between the ages
eighteen and thirty-five and the other whose members are all teenage minors.
Leaders for Nueva Alianza are identified at the beginning of each school year,
which is when the group begins to convene again. Those whose leadership
potential is recognized are invited to attend a three-day training workshop.
Leaders for the younger subgroup are then chosen from that group of teenagers
and are asked to attend an additional course in youth leadership that is offered
by the archdiocese. Aleu, the current director of the Knights of Columbus group
in the parish, is one of the adult leaders for the younger group of teens, a role
that he described as a "spiritual" one that is "only to accompany you, support
you during your time, but you will perform all your own work." He also seeks to
cultivate members of the group to take on leadership roles themselves, something they generally feel ill-equipped to do.

Although Nueva Alianza members prefer to speak English over Spanish,
Nueva Alianza discussions are usually bilingual. Spanish is occasionally spoken

to include those newly arrived immigrants who have yet to learn English. In addition to regular recreational activities such as picnics and retreats, the group joins with youth groups from other parishes in the archdiocese for an annual trip to either Disney World or Busch Gardens, upstate in Orlando. Besides serving as occasions to deepen one's spirituality through fellowship and to make new friends, such events and the more routine prayer meetings make the youth group a forum in which members feel relatively free to discuss some of the challenges that confront most adolescents and young adults in urban America. Some establish a bond with the adult leaders and confide in them, often letting off steam about their parents' indifference or inability to understand or take them seriously. In some cases, enough trust is fostered in these relationships for youth to disclose their drug abuse or sexual histories. Yet, despite their deep appreciation of such benefits, upon turning eighteen most of the members from the younger subgroup do not stay on to become members of the young adult subgroup, and they generally do not remain active in the church after their tenure with the youth group.

Several of the young adults from Nueva Alianza are among the most active members of the Divine Providence parish. Established circa 1989, it is the oldest continually running young adult group in the Catholic Archdiocese of Miami. Open to anyone between the ages of eighteen and thirty-five, initially the group counted about forty members. With such a large weekly turnout, they had to gather in a suitable locale, and so their first meetings were held in the parish hall that was located on the first floor of the school.[8] Because its size was not conducive to the kinds of conversations the group desired, the young adult division was further divided into subgroups based on age and gender. This made discussions after Bible readings or lectures more manageable and facilitated the interaction of people of the same age groups. Friendships were made, and social lives were cultivated beyond parish walls. But in time, some members went off to college, got married, became disinterested with the group, or otherwise simply moved on. With few reinforcements from the teen subgroup, the young adult group began to weaken, eventually dwindling to half its original membership. As one member recalls, "No matter what we did, the group was just not going. We would pray, we would do services, we would do so many things, you know, retreats, and the young people are just preferring to go dancing, you know, than staying over here."

Nueva Alianza thus experienced a level of attrition that threatened the once-vibrant group's existence. Discouraged by the futility of their efforts to attract new people, and now down to eight members, they turned to the archdiocese for support in the summer of 2001. They then learned that most youth groups throughout the archdiocese had altogether disbanded, making theirs something of a lone survivor. Even the once popular Power Night, the monthly fete hosted by the archdiocese for youth group members from all of its parishes, was discontinued. But suddenly, and paradoxically, the Our Lady of Divine Providence's youth group's quandary became a source of inspiration. As one member related, "We're like the group that has continuously, nonstop, existed, you know, for all this time, for thirteen years, you know. It's God, you know, because otherwise, you know, it would just disappear."

In an effort to reinvigorate the group, its leaders requested that its original spiritual guide be permitted to reassume his position, a request that the pastor denied. Instead, he appointed Doña María Martinez and her husband, a middle-aged couple, to steer Nueva Alianza. In addition to serving as spiritual guides, the Martinez's were also appointed as liaisons between the group and the pastor, effectively cementing the pastor's control over the group. Yet, after three years as coordinator, Doña María decided she was not giving her best and, as she reflected in her interview, she "just needed to step away and let others come and bring their new ideas." Occasionally attending the meetings and participating in their activities, she slowly transitioned out of the group, which was still struggling to regain momentum; it was, she explained, a "cycle where everybody was in a low."

About a year later, there were approximately twenty young adults, fifteen of whom regularly attended weekly meetings. Some members of the group did not consistently attend meetings or other activities because they were away at college for months at a time, while others were prohibited from attending regularly by jobs or school-related commitments. Aged between eighteen and thirty-three years, most current members were new to the youth group and unaware of its history of struggle. Some were new to the parish, and most joined on the invitation of friends or family members, as has historically been the case. Given that all current members of the group are first- or second-generation immigrants from Latin America (most were first generation), and because some did not yet speak English fluently, Spanish became the language of choice during meetings and for most conversations outside of the meetings.

"The people I found—a new kind of friendship and the brotherhood that existed kept me here," noted one member. For young recently arrived immigrants, Nueva Alianza is especially appealing, providing them with an immediate space of belonging and with mentorship for negotiating American society. In this regard, members of the group have intervened on behalf of several young women whose concerned parents, fearful of what they view as the insidious customs of American youth, were strongly restrictive of their social interactions. Many youth group members echo the sentiments of one member who explains, "I felt that I was in my country," when referring to why she moored at this particular parish after drifting through others in her search for a spiritual home.

Clearly, the potential for making friends is one of the youth group's main attractions. As a newcomer, one gets a sense of collective unconditional friendship and acceptance. While the leaders regard those in the group as their close friends, they also, of course, maintain friendships outside of the parish. Still, Nueva Alianza members broadly attest that their deepest and longest-lasting friendships are those forged in the group. Some even become romantically involved with one another. Loyalties to friends outside of the group, moreover, are sometimes supplanted when youth group members begin to deem some of these outside friends' behavior, such as drinking and nightclubbing, to be immoral. As a result, greater "friendship space" opens up in group members' lives, and they become more integral to one another's worlds, attending one another's birthday parties, bridal showers, and weddings and vacationing together. Although most people join the group for a couple of years and then move on, possibly to other groups in this or another parish, they generally do not abandon the social networks built during their membership.

Nueva Alianza'a current leaders have made a concerted effort to stress the religious focus of the youth group, discouraging socializing of a more secular nature. This has not, however, negatively affected group solidarity because all members are quick to agree that the main purpose of their gathering is, after all, spiritual fellowship. They all remember a time not too long ago when people "would come just to socialize." One of the leaders recalls his own experience, "I was coming just for the friendship, you know, to be with the guys and every-thing." In some cases, the group began to be seen as little more than a "social club." To distance themselves from that reputation and to sharpen the group's spiritual focus, core group members refrain from socializing with one another beyond their parish meetings. Thereby they eliminate the possibility of people attending "only for the going out part," explained the oldest leader, who is thirty-three years old. Instead, it has become customary to hang out outside the church building, talking and joking around for an hour or so after each meeting. But some members outside of the core group will occasionally go out to dinner or films, for, as group leader Walter Silva puts it, "We're not people only for pray-ing, we're also, you know, to socialize." Thus, although it is not the central focus of the youth group, building friendships and feeling social acceptance and sup-port is one of the benefits that its members seek. Still, deepening one's spiritu-ality is the group's main attraction. As one of the members related, "I guess I looked to spirituality, you know, not necessarily the group but people from the group who, you know, like help you grow spiritually."

Such contacts formed within the youth group obviously represent a founda-tional level of strong bonding social capital among group members. As group members age, move out of their parents' homes, and pursue their own profes-sional career paths, they reap the benefits of the various forms of bonding social capital that they accrue while members of Nueva Alianza. Even if developments in their personal lives, such as moving away or taking on employment that con-flicts with hours of Mass or group meetings, make it difficult or impossible for them to remain active members of the Our Lady of Divine Providence parish, they still have the bonds formed in Nueva Alianza. Yet even in such cases, which clearly place departing parishioners at risk of losing social capital (Stark and Finke 2000, 118–119), those who leave take with them the handsome sum of religious capital that they garnered through participation in Nueva Alianza.

Including Nueva Alianza, Our Lady of Divine Providence has eighteen groups and ministries.[9] Whereas one might expect a high level of interaction between and among the groups, Nueva Alianza members generally do not participate in any other group. The only significant exception is the Temple of God Charismatic Group, which, although not an age-specific group, is comprised mostly of adults. Members of the charismatic group have actively reached out to the youth group more than any other parish entity, sometimes leading discussions at youth group meetings, providing assistance at retreats, and including the youth in their own activities, such as picnics and prayer meetings. Other ministries and prayer groups also sometimes invite youth group members to participate in their social activities, but they seldom accept such invitations, further cementing Nueva Alianza's preference for spiritual over social concerns.

Nueva Alianza's spiritual focus and its parish-bound notions of service are consistent with those of the broader parish and its leadership. Although some members of the group are explicit about wishing to extend services to the wider urban community, the general attitude is echoed by one Nueva Alianza leader,

> It's like in your house; in your house you have to help in something, wash the dishes, clean the bathroom, you know. Here you also have to help in something; you have to take some responsibility to help the church. . . . I think [the congregation should] first concentrate more on its own needs and if it has like immediate things to fix; you know, if you're like limping from one leg and you need to fix it, fix that before and then go; go and help the community. . . . I think they're both as important because if you're fine right now, you know, spiritually and emotionally and all of that, and then you just go out for like three months and go out and help people and forget about, you know, keeping yourself, you know, well, then at some point you're just gonna burn out and you're not gonna be able to either help other people or, you know, you're gonna come back to yourself and you're gonna be like burned out.

Thus, to Nueva Alianza members, and for Our Lady parishioners at large, Christian belief and practice may certainly aspire to acts of charity, but this is of secondary importance to personal spirituality and to the spiritual life of the parish.

In a congregation with thirty-five hundred registered families from cultures that greatly prize children, why the youth group is so small is a valid question. Some members of Nueva Alianza attribute this to the "lack of [spiritual] growth in the community." Other Nueva Alianza members point out that this age group is by its very nature "unstable," confronting sudden life changes and options such as attending college, choosing a career, and following the temptations of secular distractions. Another Nueva Alianza member contends that young immigrants feel pressured to assimilate and keep up a fast-paced American lifestyle. Parents are also blamed for being disinterested in their children's spiritual lives, for not bringing their children to the church, or for not providing proper "formation" at home. Some Nueva Alianza members are hopeful that once the new church is finished, the group might flourish anew if the parish leadership would then propagate more CSC by providing greater support to its groups and ministries. For now, however, as Deacon Panellas acknowledges, "There is no active youth. Maybe we can say *mea culpa* for not trying to engage them; you understand, we are a bit slack in that sense." Noting that resources such as music instruments and a volleyball court on church grounds could be used to lure the youth to participate, the leader of the thirteen-to-eighteen-year-old youth group concurs that parish leaders are "not giving them the attention of having people to help them, for example, who have the time so that they will come."

Economic, political, and cultural factors also contribute to the relative weakness of the youth group and the low output of CSC at Our Lady of Divine Providence. As one youth group member explained, "People [might] be too occupied trying to subsist, that they forget everything else and don't want to commit themselves [to rendering any services]." Nicaraguan congregants explained that for cultural reasons they rely very little on anyone outside the household for material assistance or economic advancement. "In our culture, usually parents or—we are raised, you know, not to look for help, you know," notes a Nicaraguan young adult parishioner. This self-reliance makes it difficult to gauge the scale of people's needs and, conversely, to perceive the importance of offering aid to others. Although Divine Providence is a very large congregation, it consists mostly of recent immigrants of limited financial means, many of whom are undocumented and thus forced to accept menial jobs, sometimes working two or three of them at once. The young adults are not exempt from the brunt of their families' economic difficulties. Many struggle to pay steep out-of-state college tuitions because they are not recognized as legal residents, regardless of how long they have been living in Florida. Often unable to obtain legal employment for the same reasons, many rely on their parents' financial support, while others take on minimum-wage jobs. This often creates serious time constraints for the youth, who juggle both school and work-related responsibilities, making any additional commitment seem overwhelming, especially when recreational activities are already elusive. As one twenty-two-year-old explained when interviewed, "It's hard to give up other fun things. It's hard to not go dancing, it's hard to not go to the beach on a Sunday instead of going to feed the homeless." But as hard as it may be, Jenny has spent the last five years of her life doing just that, shunning these "temptations," as members of the youth group often refer to secular distractions and entertainment.

Parish leaders do accept some responsibility for the youth's relative inactivity. But is this merely a symptom of a traditionally disengaged and inactive leadership with a preference for spiritual nurturing and inwards assistance, or is it inherent to Catholic ecclesiology? Deacon Panellas expresses a dislike for "being on top of people," correctly pointing out that the bishops at the Second Vatican Council asserted doctrinally that "the layman must discover his responsibility; the layman must discover his charisma, his gifts. And if we don't give them opportunities for them to discover all that they can do, we suffocate them."[10] Father Rivera concurs, "It is more the leadership than the individuals. If the leadership [within the group] is open and willing, the group will flourish and become more social" in its ministry. In principle, each group is autonomous in terms of service and what they choose to do in the community, pending the pastor's approval. Nevertheless, no one was able to furnish an example of the leadership encouraging the supposed autonomous groups and congregants to initiate any form of community service, whereas there are plenty of illustrations to the contrary. The pastor's stern management style, moreover, can be intimidating, especially for young congregants. "We're all like always careful, you know, not to upset him," admits one member of the youth group. An astute and perceptive man, Father Rivera is perfectly aware that his leadership style sometimes rubs certain parishioners the wrong way: "There are parishioners in the parish that say that I'm very heavy-handed, that I am, in Spanish, *prepotente* [arrogant]. And yet everybody enjoys the parish, likes the parish, and wants the parish. With leadership, you have to know when to say yes, and you have to know when to say no. Unlike a democracy—this is not a democracy. If it was a democracy, nothing would ever get done here."

Father Rivera's position typifies the Catholic approach to administration from the Vatican on down to the local parish level. Democracy is hardly a common feature of administrative power in the church. At Our Lady of Divine Providence, there is no question who is in charge. One member of the youth group explained that even Father Fermín Solana, the associate pastor and only other permanent priest, "always recognizes that Rivera is the one in charge of the parish, so if we come to him [Father Solana], we will ask [for something and he will reply], 'Well, let me talk to [Father Rivera] first and then, you know, I'll get back to you on that.'" Information generally trickles down from the top, though sometimes it is safeguarded even from the most active laypersons. During all the research done at this church, it was impossible, for instance, to find anyone who could provide specific information regarding the ongoing construction, an activity that obviously greatly affected parish resources and other activities. People repeatedly said that only the priest and his inner circle were "the ones who would know," while the parishioners were largely kept in the dark, especially concerning financial issues.

Although both the clergy and the laity at Our Lady of Divine Providence do express the need to broaden the parish's scope of its social services, a culture of power is entrenched at the parish in which any move toward doing so would require the pastor's directive. Financial resources would be required for Nueva Alianza to expand its civic portfolio, but the youth are left to themselves to secure such resources. When they fail to do so, any initiative they have taken has to be abandoned. Nueva Alianza has proposed initiatives such as reading to young cancer patients in local hospitals and visiting elders at nursing homes, but none has ever been actualized. On the other hand, when several hundred dollars were needed for the purchase of a keyboard to be played at its charismatic prayer services, the group managed to come up with the money, which is yet another reflection of the preference for religious capital over CSC in the parish, a preference that has effectively trickled down from on high.

Members of Nueva Alianza are somewhat apathetic about their status. They are explicit about the need to extend social services much more broadly. They realize that their relative weakness in this regard is chiefly a structural problem at the parish, a lack of resources because of construction and the church leadership's emphasis on spiritual over civic concerns. However, the youth are loath to voice this notion. No dissent or disapproval about the organization, administration, or orientation of the parish was ever conveyed by any of the members either during interviews or during any meetings that I attended. The most overt criticism lodged was the admission by one youth group leader that the parish provided them with inadequate leadership training.

But hope springs eternal; in recognition of the critical importance of self-reliance and the cultivation of an indigenous leadership, Nueva Alianza has taken measures to secure its future and to better enable itself to achieve its objectives. At one point when all of the group's three leaders became engaged to be married, meaning that they would be leaving the group, each lame-duck leader was assigned to one of three groups. In alternating weeks, the groups were each responsible for conducting a religious teaching, and each of its members had a designated task pertinent to the topic. This program lasted for several weeks and gave many members their first opportunities to lead a religious discussion or lead prayer and worship, to read Bible passages, and to enact short skits about biblical themes. The hope was to engender confidence in those who might take on leadership roles, to prepare them better than previous leaders had been prepared, and to deepen the entire group's spirituality, which members unanimously affirm as a necessary investment toward the cultivation of CSC. Or, as one member put it, "The group itself has been trying to educate itself [for the past few months] and then prepare ourselves to go out there and help, you know, not necessarily like something physical but more like spiritual, spiritual preparation, and then go out and help."

The current leaders have a short-term plan to actualize "service more in the church," but they also contemplate other members' plans of engaging in regular service such as visiting the elderly and retired priests. Most of the activities in the youth group remain parish-specific, such as serving as Eucharistic ministers, ushers, fund-raisers, and organizers of special events. There is also the annual retreat, at which adult congregants are asked to give speeches and members of other churches are invited to participate, and the Feast of La Purísima, for which Our Lady of Divine Providence is renowned in South Florida. Over the years, the youth group has been very active in decorating the church for this beautiful event and in preparing Nicaraguan cuisine to sell at a booth that they manage. This entails collecting donations to buy and prepare the food as well as cooking and serving it. The youth group also plays an important role in processions and in theater productions performed during Holy Week and Christmas, and they are also called on to perform random tasks such as sleeping in the church to guard rented chairs on the eve of Good Friday. Finally, and contrary to his previous stance, on Father Rivera's initiative, Nueva Alianza has become involved with the archdiocesan Angel Tree Program, which collects Christmas gifts for children of incarcerated parents.

Leadership and the Face of Charity

Our Lady of Divine Providence historically was a focal point of enormous bonding social capital and bridging civic social capital (CSC) that focused on service provision on top of cultural and religious CSC activities. However, the Catholic sex scandal deposed the church's charismatic priest who led these service CSC initiatives. The church is now led by a priest who has narrowed CSC activities to favoring spiritual concerns that emphasize bonding among congregants. Whatever stores of CSC the parish acquired when they did bridge and link to Mariel Boatlift refugees and then Nicaraguan refugees in the 1980s have been reinvested in service to its own congregants, chiefly and only intermittently in their negotiation of the legal processes involved in becoming U.S. permanent residents, and a few of the concomitant needs that new immigrants have in urban America, e.g., acquiring job placement, learning English, accessing health care, etc. In CSC terms, the parish exemplifies bonding and has almost no examples of bridging or linking.

The Nueva Alianza young adult group of Our Lady of Divine Providence is mainly comprised of first-generation children of impoverished immigrants from Nicaragua. They exemplify challenges typical of immigrant youth who are becoming Americanized and whose parents apparently do not understand or communicate with them. The Nueva Alianza provides them with a forum where they can express and discuss these concerns with both each other and the Nueva Alianza's older leaders. Yet the parish's focus on spiritual activities means that the youth have no bridging or linking mechanisms to further address their concerns. The adult leaders are not provided with training or access to other organizations that address these issues. Nor is there a forum where their parents can learn about and respond to their children's concerns. Instead, nearly all the youths' attention is focused on spiritual activities. In general, they are deeply spiritual, but they also recognize that the Christian calling includes some measure of social engagement beyond evangelization. In a parish that provides the current youth congregants with little in the way of bridging or linking CSC, the youth groups are adrift and thus fail to thoroughly address the challenges associated with Americanization or actualize their ideals of charity, either as inspired by the Corporal or Spiritual Works of Mercy or by their own ideas of service to the needs of others.

Although congregants, young and old alike, quite broadly agree that the parish should have a higher degree of civic engagement and humanitarianism, the current parish leadership, distracted by building a new church, ignores their initiatives. As one female member of the youth group, explained, "I think and hope and ask God that those who are currently leaders, those who have access to Father Rivera and speak with him and have access to him listening to them—I hope; I hope for the good of the church that they have their minds where it needs to be and are willing to do all those things that are needed [in the community]." Aleu, who fits this description, speaks on behalf of the Knights of Columbus and other congregants when he describes the wish to reinstate many of the services once offered to the community, such as counseling and job placement services, admitting that the parish "needs to emphasize more service towards others."

The occasional bridging CSC initiatives such as the Angel Tree Program notwithstanding, the electrical sliding doors that once enclosed the space shared by throngs of Latin American refugees now serve as little more than a reminder of the crucial role that the parish once played in the lives of hundreds of immigrants and as testimony of their plight and the endurance of their spirit. The abandonment of the many social services offered previously underscores the critical role of leadership in creating and maintaining bridging and linking CSC activities. Our Lady of Divine Providence's change in leadership, occasioned by the sex scandal, undoubtedly transformed the focus of CSC activities at Divine Providence from bridging service CSC plus bonding social capital culture and religion to almost exclusively bonding through religious activities.

NOTES

1. These are officially known as Confraternity of Christian Doctrine, or CCD, classes and generally are referred to as catechism classes.
2. This festival is also known as *La Inmaculada Concepción* (The Immaculate Conception) and *El Viejo* (The Old One).
3. It should be noted that Stark and Finke (2000) define religious capital much more broadly than Bourdieu (1987), whose limitation of religious capital production and possession to the clerical body of an institutional religion has been criticized by several scholars (Rey 2007, 86, 125, 135).

4. On sex abuse allegations against Garcia-Rubio and related litigations, see Weaver 2004 and the Survivors Network of Those Abused by Priests 2005. The *Miami Herald* describes the allegations and their fallout as having "deeply divided" the parish. One parishioner wrote of the pain that it caused in a letter to the editor in the *Patriot News*: "I attended Catholic school, and throughout my adult life continued very involved with my church Our Lady of Divine Providence in Miami. I used to visit the terminally ill on Saturdays to provide comfort and strengthen their faith before passing to a better life. My children were baptized and confirmed by the priest at my church. The community truly believed that he had been blessed by God to speak to our hearts and reach out to the community, until one day he appeared on the cover of *The Miami Herald* for sexually abusing refugee children from Cuba and Nicaragua. I was shocked and saddened by the news, and later became enraged to learn that the church knew about the incidents and eventually helped him leave the country. He never faced the law. The pain and fear kept me and my children away from any church for many years" (quoted in Canizares 2004).

5. Accessed in 2001 for this research, this Web site is no longer in existence as its host, www.catholic-forum.com, ceased providing free Web hosting for Catholic organizations.

6. Author's translation.

7. The school, although part of the parish and under the same administration, is largely irrelevant to Our Lady parishioners, most of whom cannot afford the relatively steep tuition and other fees that are in excess of $4,500 per year.

8. The St. Raphael Parish Hall was converted into much-needed classroom space in 1997.

9. Prior to 2004, the groups and ministries at Our Lady of Divine Providence were the Knights of Columbus, St. Vincent de Paul Society, Exodus Group for Confirmed Youth, Nueva Alianza Youth Group, Adult Bible Study Group, New Life Ministry, Temple of God Charismatic Group, Confraternity of Worshippers of the Blessed Sacrament, Neo-Catecumenate Journey Group, Small Church Communities, the Divine Will Group, and a group that renders aid to the ill led by Father Solana (Our Lady of Divine Providence 2004). In a 2006 interview, Rivera indicated that three more groups have been added.

10. Pope John XXIII convened the Second Vatican Council in 1962. Over the next three years, the world's Catholic bishops worked to bring Catholic doctrine and liturgy "up to date" (*aggiornamento*), and, indeed, the laity were encouraged to take a much more active role in the church than ever before. *Lumen gentium*, the council's chief ecclesiological statement, devotes its fourth chapter to the laity, strongly emphasizing their "noble duty of working to extend the divine plan of salvation to all men of each epoch and every land" (www.vatican.va/archive/hist_councils/ii_vatican_council/documents/vat-ii_const_19641121_lumen-gentium; accessed December 29, 2005). Consistent with this call, as noted in a parish document, "At the core of Father Rivera's philosophy is the firm conviction that personal commitment is to lead to responsible action by the use of one's time, talent, and treasure, and that many of the talks of church activity and ministry are not the exclusive domain and burden of the ordained and religious, but rather can be shared with an involved, caring, and thriving laity" (Our Lady of Divine Providence Catholic Church 2004).

REFERENCES

Bourdieu, P. 1987. Legitimation and Structured Interest in Weber's Sociology of Religion. In *Max Weber, Rationality, and Modernity*, ed. S. Whimster and S. Lash. London: Allen and Unwin.

Canizares, G. 2004. Rhetoric on How to Vote Distresses Catholic. *Patriot News*, November 23, A13.

Fernández Kelly, P., and S. Curran. 2001. Nicaraguans: Voices Lost, Voices Found. In *Ethnicities: Children of Immigrants in America*, ed. R. Rumbaut and A. Portes. Berkeley: University of California Press.

Konczal, L. 2001. The Academic Orientation of First and Second Generation Nicaraguan Immigrant Adolescents. PhD, Florida International University, Miami, FL.

Our Lady of Divine Providence Catholic Church. 2004. History of Our Lady of Divine Providence Catholic Church. Church document, Miami, FL.

Portes, A., and A. Stepick. 1993. *City on the Edge: The Transformation of Miami.* Berkeley: University of California Press.

Rey, T. 2004. Marketing the Goods of Salvation: Bourdieu on Religion. *Religion* 34: 331–343.

———. 2007. *Bourdieu on Religion: Imposing Faith and Legitimacy.* London: Equinox.

Riesebrodt, M. 1999. Charisma in Weber's Sociology of Religion. *Religion* 29(1): 1–14.

Robison, L. J., A. A. Schmid, and M. E. Siles. 2002. Is Social Capital Really Capital? *Review of Social Economy* 60(1): 1–21.

Sandoval, M. C. 1985. *Mariel and Cuban National Identity.* Miami: Editorial SIBI.

Stark, R., and R. Finke. 2000. *Acts of Faith: Explaining the Human Side of Religion.* Berkeley and Los Angeles: University of California Press.

The Survivors Network of Those Abused by Priests—SNAP. 2005. Miami Clergy Abuse Victim Wins Court Battle. Press release, October 11. See http://www.snapnetwork.org/snap_press_releases/2005_press_releases/101105_miami_victim_wins_battle.htm.

Weaver, J. 2004. Church Suspected Priest It Defended. *Miami Herald*, September 13.

9

Faith in the Fields

Mexican Marianism in Miami-Dade County

NOEMÍ BÁEZ, MARÍA DE LOS ANGÈLES REY, AND TERRY REY

Upon a stage in the yard of St. Ann Mission Catholic Church in rural southern Miami-Dade County stand six Mexican American youths costumed as Aztec warriors, performing act 1 of the play *El Más Pequeño de Mis Hijos* (The Least of My Children). On an altar before them lies a pretty, young, motionless woman dressed in white. Before a backdrop of mountains and pyramids, and to the sounds of war drums, the chief warrior recites a series of incantations before kneeling beside the woman. He next plunges a knife into her chest and rips out her heart, standing and raising the extracted organ to the sky to propitiate his pagan gods. The cruelty does not subside in act 2, as several young Mexican American men portraying Spanish conquistadores storm the stage, raid an Aztec community, and proceed to torture and kill everyone in their path of "discovery" and conquest. It is a cruel world, indeed, although all of this suffering is abated by the middle of the play when Our Lady of Guadalupe appears miraculously to Juan Diego.

Reenacted here are the miraculous events of 1531 that are so well known to all Mexicans, the apparition of the Virgin Mary, as Guadalupe, to a poor Indian farmer. So integral is Guadalupe to Mexican national consciousness that nineteenth-century Mexican novelist and journalist Igancio Manuel Altamirano claimed, "The day in which the Virgin of Tepeyac is not adored in this land, it is certain that there shall have disappeared, not only Mexican nationality, but also the very memory of the dwellers of Mexico today. . . . In the last extreme, in the most desperate cases, the cult of the Mexican Virgin is the only bond that unites them" (quoted in Brading 2001, vii).

El Más Pequeño de Mis Hijos was written by José Miguel Roja, a Mexican immigrant who swam across the Rio Grande into Texas and eventually made his way to Homestead, Florida, in search of work in the fields. Roja is deeply devoted to Our Lady of Guadalupe, assured that she watched over him during his dangerous and difficult journey and enabled him to eventually settle and thrive in Florida.

Among the two thousand people who saw his play that evening in 2001, most had similar stories to tell. They also shared the depth of Roja's faith in Guadalupe. They have all made St. Ann Mission Guadalupe's a home away from home, just as they have made it their own spiritual home away from home, exemplifying quite forcefully how religions "do more than situate embodied persons in domestic space and familial history," as notes Thomas Tweed (2006, 10).

The social capital produced by St. Ann Mission is almost exclusively *bonding*. The only *bridging* is between Mexicans who attend the church regularly and other Mexicans who only infrequently attend. While St. Ann Mission does offer some social services, the primary form of social capital relations is religious and spiritual.

Mexicans in South Florida

At the end of the twentieth century more than half of the foreign-born population of the United States was from Latin America, totaling over 36 million people. Of these, more than 20 million were from Mexico, the majority of them living in the southwestern United States, especially California, Texas, New Mexico, Nevada, and Arizona. In Florida, the 2000 U.S. Census counted over 350,000 Mexicans, making them a minority in the Sunshine State among Hispanics, most of whom originate from the Caribbean and Central and South America. The rapid growth of Miami-Dade County's Mexican population notwithstanding, Mexicans still ranked only sixth, as of 2000, among the county's Hispanic groups, behind Cubans, Puerto Ricans, Columbians, Nicaraguans, and a collectivity called in the census "Other Hispanic." However, Mexicans are the fastest-growing Hispanic group in Florida, as they are in Miami-Dade County, many drawn by opportunities for work in agricultural fields and plant nurseries.

Although it is true generally, as Portes and Rumbaut explain, that "Mexicans are the *only* foreign group that has been part of both the classic period of immigration at the beginning of the twentieth century and the present movement" and that "this geographical contiguity has facilitated both labor recruitment and subsequent mass labor displacements, mediated by social networks" (2001, 277), Miami-Dade County is an exception. In fact, there was no Mexican community of demographic significance in Florida during or immediately following "the classic period of immigration" in the late nineteenth and early twentieth century. It was only in the 1950s that Mexicans were driven by increasingly stiff competition for work in the fields of the southwestern United States to come in considerable numbers as itinerate laborers to harvest the winter crops of South Florida, mainly beans, tomatoes, squash, and potatoes (Aguirre, Schwirian, and LaGreca 1980). Many of the families with whom we became acquainted at St. Ann Mission had lived for some time in Texas before arriving in Miami-Dade County. Plant nurseries have since flourished in the area along with the region's burgeoning service and construction industries, all of which have also drawn a large Mexican immigrant labor force. With the advantage of year-round work, southern Miami-Dade County has seen the establishment and growth of a permanent Mexican community.

Miami-Dade County's Mexican population thus grew to an official count of just over thirteen thousand by 1980. This figure nearly tripled over the next twenty years to a total of more than thirty-eight thousand (Miami-Dade County 2003). The vast majority of Miami-Dade's Mexican immigrants have always been clustered in and around the fields in the rural south of the county, in municipalities like Naranja, Leisure City, and Homestead.[1] Homestead's total population is roughly thirty thousand, a slight majority of which is Hispanic. Official county statistics (Miami-Dade County 2000) estimate that as of the year 2000 just over seven thousand Mexicans were residing in Homestead, though thousands more settle in the area seasonally as migrant field workers. Naranja, which is the actual location of the St. Ann Mission, then counted just over four thousand residents, 27 percent of them Hispanic; while Leisure City, adjacent to Naranja, had over twenty-two thousand residents, 65 percent of them being Hispanic. Although the county census does not, unfortunately, provide a further breakdown of Hispanic ethnicities for these latter two municipalities, it is easy to assert that Mexicans comprise the majority of Hispanic immigrants in the collective area of Homestead, Naranja, and Leisure City, an area that many people in South Florida simply call "Homestead" (as we do in the rest of this chapter). And everyone in Miami knows that Homestead is where you find the best Mexican food around.

Just as their compatriots have done in the southwestern United States, Mexican immigrants in Florida have established devotional centers for Our Lady of Guadalupe, patron saint of Mexico and, as decreed by Pope Pius XII in 1946, patroness of the Americas. Although Mexicans in Homestead generally reject the term "Chicano" and seek to distance themselves from what they perceive as the negative aspects of the Chicano southwest (e.g., gangs, drugs, tattoos, and low-riders), they nonetheless share the same conviction that their journey to and settlement in the United States is overseen maternally and divinely by Our Lady of Guadalupe. Just as Guadalupe has served as "spur, solace, and expression of identity, both national and transnational, to migrants" (Hall 2004, 275) of Mexican origin in the southwestern United States, where her cult is as old as any in Catholicism, so, too, has she served her faithful devotees in the fields of Homestead. South Florida's Mexican community is, of course, much younger than that of, say, El Paso or Los Angeles. Yet "contexts change," as Hall explains, "The ways in which the Virgin seems to operate change, too, and human interactions adjust as well. These, however, seem to me to be the overarching constants: strength, power, and connection" (2004, 300). We now turn our attention to the context of Mexican immigrant devotion to Guadalupe and its "overarching constants" in south Miami-Dade County.

Saint Ann Mission: Pastoral Dimensions

Primarily to serve the growing community of Hispanic farmworkers in the Homestead area, on November 5, 1961, the Diocese of Miami established St. Ann Mission.[2] As such, in addition to the mission church in Naranja, there is a chapel in each of the three labor camps in the surrounding agricultural fields. Demographically, the mission's neighborhood is largely comprised of lower-income African Americans, some of whom live in the nearby public housing projects. In spite of this, people of African descent rarely attend Mass at St. Ann Mission,[3] surely in part because all Masses here are said in Spanish, though some do partake of the mission's limited social services, such as its weekly food and clothing distributions. This is one of the few instances of bridging civic social capital (CSC) at the mission that goes beyond the boundaries of Mexican ethnicity, whereas most other charitable initiatives at the mission generally attract only Mexican beneficiaries, which are thus more appropriately labeled bonding social capital.

St. Ann Mission would be easy for a first-time visitor to miss were it not for a sign on the corner of its yard that reads in Spanish, "Mision Santa Ana." Approaching the mission, one is often greeted with the tempting smell of bar-beque wafting from the parish hall, where usually the youth group sets up grills, tables, and chairs to sell the food that they have prepared to raise funds: *carne asada*, tamales, tortillas, and other quintessentially Mexican fares.

The church itself is not very distinct, resembling a rather squat old white house complete with a front lawn and backyard surrounded by a metal chain-link fence. A large cross adorns the church façade and just above on the roof sits a modest statue of St. Ann, where a steeple would be if the mission had one. Off to the right of the church is the rectory, while to the rear is a separate long white building that serves as something of a parish hall. Between it and the church, outside is a shrine to Our Lady of Guadalupe, featuring the Virgin's statue facing a bench, where often people pray and meditate. Commonly they leave at her feet white and red carnations, beseeching and prayerful notes, rosaries, and votive candles. Inside the church is small and almost square. Toward the back is an elevated floor space, on which stand the altar and a wooden table covered by a handmade white tablecloth embroidered with the Mexican flag. The pews are made out of wood and are devoid of kneelers. In the corners and around the altar are small potted trees, and off to the left is a large icon of Our Lady of Guadalupe.

Father Pedro García, a middle-aged Cuban Catholic priest, pastors St. Ann Mission. He resides here and says the one weekly Mass at the mission each

Sunday at 11:00 a.m. He also says Mass each Sunday morning at 8:00 a.m. at the Redlands Labor Camp and at 5:30 p.m. at the Everglades II Labor Camp, followed by a 7:30 p.m. vigil at the South Dade Labor Camp. During the week, Mass is said once more at each labor camp, home to itinerate Mexican farmworkers. Each camp has a small chapel, and these are overseen by the mission religious leaders, namely Padre Pedro, the occasional seminarian in residence, and three Mexican nuns from the Guadalupan Order who also lead the mission and camp choirs, among other things. Thus, for migrant workers in the fields who might otherwise find it difficult to get to the mission for Mass on their one day off of the week, St. Ann Mission's ministry in the camps is the bedrock of their faith.[4] For all other sacraments besides the Eucharist, though, they must venture to the mission.

The mission faithful warmly embrace Father García as one of their own, even though he is not Mexican. They realize that his own people have also suffered a great deal in their immigrant journey and have worked hard to improve their families' lives in Miami and contribute to their families' incomes back home, just like them. Just like them, too, they are Latinos. Quietly, Father García has become one of the most effective spiritual leaders for immigrants in the Archdiocese of Miami, and he is highly respected by leading figures in the Catholic Church. When he celebrates Mass, he pauses before consecrating the Eucharist to call all the children in attendance up to the altar. They join hands and form a circle around the table for the blessed event, a gesture that endears him to the children's parents, who are often moved to tears.

The Mass follows the liturgical pattern that Catholics everywhere would recognize, though the celebration at St. Ann Mission is evocatively Mexican. Our Lady of Guadalupe serves as a "translocative" and "transtemporal" symbol par excellence for Mexican immigrants throughout the United States, as she allows her devotees to move "symbolically between the homeland and the new land" (Tweed 1997, 138) and between the past and the present, all the while being central to their maintenance of a Mexican and a Catholic identity in a foreign land. More importantly, in their minds, she is the reason why they have made it to Florida in the first place. Of this, the congregants of St. Ann Mission are unwaveringly convinced. The hymns also serve translocative and transtemporal functions, being derived from hymnals used commonly in the Catholic Mass in Mexico.

Overall, Mass at St. Ann Mission is a joyous and festive occasion that strongly evokes Mexico in sound and vision. The twenty-four pews each hold ten persons, more or less, and they are always full. Most arrive as families, often in pickup trucks, and usually dozens of children (a few of them in wheelchairs) and seniors are in attendance. Many of the faithful dress in traditional Mexican-style clothes, like cowboy hats and boots for men, and long white embroidered dresses for women. Others reflect the working-class status of the congregants with the same faded and soiled clothes that they wear to work in the fields. Their stories of struggle and hard work are told in the men's calloused hands and in the women's sun-burnt faces and tired eyes. However they may be garbed, in addition to coming as faithful communicants, many of them also come to express their gratitude to the mission for its material as well as spiritual support. It is to these dimensions that our attention now turns.

Social Dimensions

On August 24, 1992, Hurricane Andrew—until Hurricane Katrina it was the greatest natural disaster in recent U.S. history—roared across South Florida, leaving in its wake twenty-three dead and an estimated 26.5 billion dollars in damages.[5] Homestead was ground zero, and the area's devastation was stunning. In response, with 40 million dollars in funding, Catholic Charities transformed five religious sites in South Florida into service centers for hurricane victims, with St. Ann Mission joining forces in one of the most significant domestic church-based relief efforts in U.S. history. The site was transformed into a veritable internal refugee camp, with over three hundred displaced persons taking up temporary residence under tents that were erected for the cause. A day-care center was also established, and the mission distributed over 16 million pounds of food (Davis 2002). The mission was equipped with solar panels to provide light, which was especially needed for a makeshift medical clinic in what the U.S. Department of Energy heralded as a model of energy use during disaster relief (U.S. Department of Energy 1994).

Fortunately, events like Hurricane Andrew are relatively rare, and eventually the tent city was dismantled, regular power was restored, and St. Ann Mission regained some semblance of normalcy, though not without first demonstrating quite powerfully its readiness and willingness to give the highest priority to charity and social service in times of need. Although one might have expected the mission's emergency service program to hundreds of non-Mexicans to generate for the mission a handsome yield in bridging CSC, such has not been the case. All the same, after the tragedy of Hurricane Andrew abated, charity would remain integral to the mission's ministry because the majority of its regular communicants are poor Mexican immigrants who face many difficulties in their daily lives. Serving them, in turn, contributes to the mission's rich store of *bonding* social capital that focuses on endearing the faithful to the mission and ensuring their fidelity, and in many cases that of their children.[6]

Understanding anything sociologically about the community at St. Ann Mission requires paying careful attention to the extraordinary struggle that many of the Mexican immigrants there face in their daily lives. In this regard, their lives mirror those of their compatriot migrant farmworkers in South Florida's other major Mexican immigrant center, Immokalee, the focus of a recent study by Phillip Williams and Patricia Loret de Mola: "For most migrant farmworkers, limited social capital, combined with their undocumented status and weak social networks, undermines their opportunities for social mobility" (2007, 234). In addition to struggling to find and keep jobs, feed their children, obtain green cards, learn English, and generally make meager ends meet, many men in the community struggle with alcoholism. A number of youths with whom we have spoken at the mission noted to us almost nonchalantly that their fathers are alcoholics, something to which the local police also attest as being a major problem in Homestead's Mexican community. Often bred by this, domestic violence occurs at an alarming rate here, too. Adding to these social crises is the recent emergence of gangs among the area's youth, and the proliferation of drugs in local schools.

Given its people's problems and its modest budget, the mission is thus forced to make troubling decisions concerning where to begin to help and how to help. Because many of its congregants are uninsured, one priority is health care. Toward this end, "Padre Pedro," as García's loving flock call their pastor, has successfully solicited the services of a couple of local physicians who provide pro bono medical consultations at St. Ann Mission. A doctor is available at the mission on two Saturdays of each month in this capacity, and prescribed medications are provided either free of charge or at considerable discount, much less than an uninsured patient would pay at a pharmacy. The few other social service programs, such as the weekly food and clothing distributions, are much needed and greatly appreciated by their beneficiaries, but in reality these are but drops in an ocean of need. Everyone here wishes, of course, that they could do more to serve the needy, yet whatever the will of St. Ann Mission's faithful to serve the Mexican community of Homestead, daunting obstacles stand between potential and actualization in this regard. For one thing, St. Ann Mission enjoys no major endowment and operates under tight fiscal restraints. And for another, most of the mission's congregants are poor despite their working a great deal, sometimes holding two or even three jobs, hence prohibiting them from volunteering for the mission's various social service programs or pastoral events. Padre Pedro knowingly attributes the lack of volunteerism to "a lack of time—their main priority is work and trying to survive." For reasons such as these, the possibility for amassing any level of *bridging* CSC through outreach to other ethnic communities in the area is thus very minimal. St. Ann Mission is not alone in this regard, however, as, generally, immigrant "churches facilitate 'bonding' social capital but often neglect 'bridging' social capital" (Williams and Loret de Mola 2007, 233).

Having considerably more free time and flexibility than their beleaguered parents, the youth are the mission's most active cohort, and they comprise a few different groups or task forces. The youth groups demonstrate a great deal of enthusiasm, bolstered by the confidence and blessing of their pastor. In addition to raising funds for several important mission events, which they also orchestrate, they are the mission's main agents of pastoral and social outreach. Some of them are active members of the ten or so *communidades* that Padre Pedro has trained essentially to serve as the ears of the mission. They go out into the wider community and listen to people to learn about their lives and needs, and they, of course, evangelize while doing so. In addition, the youth stage theatrical performances, organize retreats, help out with the clothing and food banks, and cook and sell food at every mission function. We have been quite struck by the depth of their devotion to Our Lady of Guadalupe, a central form of imported religious faith that shows no sign of waning across generations or borders. Equally impressive is Padre Pedro's unwavering support of the youth groups. He serves as a model spiritual leader and inspiration, and he never misses their meetings.

On a more pastoral level, the mission youth groups play a major role in preparing and overseeing the various Easter celebrations, including a staged performance of the Passion of Christ. On Good Friday youth group members venture to one of the labor camps to lead the faithful in praying the Stations of the Cross (*El Vía Cruces*). In a moving display of Catholic devotion, four young children cordon off a large square with white rope to delineate the expansive ritual performance space. Throughout this space the fourteen stations are each posed sequentially on white poster board affixed to a respective tree. Outside the square Padre Pedro slowly maneuvers and positions his SUV to cast its headlights on the ritual and broadcast the narratives and prayers as the worshippers follow those enacting the dramatic ritual, stopping at each station for prayer in the rural darkness broken only by the two headlights and hundreds of candles. Toward the end, a young boy is tied to a wooden cross that is hoisted erect and driven into a hole in the ground. Prayerful and solemn, the ritual powerfully transports the entire gathering.

Among adult laypersons at the mission, no one is more active than Minerva, a thirty-year-old woman of unwavering commitment and seemingly boundless energy. She attends every group meeting, often staying long after they are over, organizes and sometimes leads various group sessions, and generally avails herself to the many people who come to her for advice. Born in Mexico, Minerva arrived in Homestead in 1988 when she was ten years old. Once in Florida, her father struggled to hold a gainful job, and so at just age fourteen Minerva began working to help support her family, picking lemons and tomatoes after school with her siblings. The only member of her family to go to college and graduate, Minerva today holds a bachelor's degree in psychology from Miami-Dade College, where she now works in student advisement. She aspires to enter graduate school. Gaining residency in the United States was to her a godsend, a divine blessing for which she is eternally grateful and one that helps her understand keenly the trials and tribulations as well as the hopes and dreams of the many immigrant students whom she advises at the college. They come to her for guidance, and she in return gives them hope and serves as an excellent role model. She does so, too, by volunteering at the mission, a sincere expression of her gratitude to Our Lady of Guadalupe for giving her everything that she has.

The Feast of Our Lady of Guadalupe at St. Ann Mission

Though challenged in recent decades by a growing and literally iconoclastic Protestant Evangelical movement, Mexican national identity is inextricably intertwined with Catholicism and especially with the cult of Our Lady of Guadalupe. This makes Guadalupe of double importance to Mexican immigrants in the United States in the sense that this manifestation of the Virgin Mary empowers them in their struggles past and present to improve their and their families' lives through settlement in the United States. Guadalupe is also funda-mental to maintaining a sense of Mexican identity abroad. Not surprisingly, then, for St. Ann Mission's congregation the feast of Our Lady of Guadalupe is the most important religious and cultural event of the year. It is an occasion of inti-mate and joyful communion with Guadalupe that reifies their Mexican-ness and beckons them to meld joyous expressions of thanks to the Mexican Virgin with nostalgic recollections of the homeland and their loved ones there.

Preparations for the Feast of Guadalupe at St. Ann Mission begin months in advance, as Padre Pedro oversees fund-raising initiatives for the event, while the nuns focus the choir's rehearsals on the hymns to be sung during the four days and nights of Marian celebrations and fellowship. In 2002, *la Guadalupana* (as the feast is affectionately called in Mexican Spanish, as are Guadalupe her-self and her female devotees) carried additional meaning because of the recent canonization of St. Juan Diego, receiver of the apparition of Guadalupe in 1531 and the first indigenous American to join the Catholic communion of saints. For Mexicans of Native American origins, like most of the St. Ann Mission's faithful, this made the 2002 feast additionally powerful, legitimating, and wondrous.

The feast takes place outdoors over the entirety of the parking lot and the mission yard, much of which is covered by an enormous tent to shelter some of the two thousand pilgrims in attendance. Beneath the tent are hundreds of metal folding chairs in neatly arranged rows, while surrounding it are tables decorated with flowers and ribbons, where hungry pilgrims can buy *carnitas* (fried pork) and *pozole* (pork and corn soup), cheeseburgers, French fries, rosaries, saint cards, *veladoras* (votive candles), and other food and religious paraphernalia. Front and center stands an altar supporting a large icon of Our Lady of Guadalupe, surrounded by flowers, candles, and Mexican blankets. Next to her, for the first time, is an icon of St. Juan Diego.

December 12, 2002

La Guadalupana is celebrated annually on December 12, which in 2002 fell on a Thursday. Mass this evening at St. Ann Mission is celebrated by Msgr. Augustín Román, auxiliary bishop of Miami and spiritual father of the city's Cuban exile community. He is draped in a white robe embroidered with the image of Our Lady of Guadalupe, patroness of the Americas. Before the Mass four young men, Raul Cepeda, Juan Antonio Valdés, Rodolfo García, and Edwin Lopez, offer flowers to Guadalupe upon completion of their eighteen-kilometer run to the mission from the chapel in the Redlands labor camp. They are welcomed by Román to a thunderous applause from the hundreds of worshippers in attendance.

Valdés is a twenty-four-year-old Mexican immigrant with long, straight, jet-black hair and hands that are well worn from work in the fields. He has lived in Homestead for seven years. Dressed in a T-shirt bearing the images of Guadalupe and Mexican rock star Alex Lora, he explains the faith underlying his run, "I have run for four years for *la Virgencita.* I promised her because she cured my mother. This year I even convinced my friends to run with me. I cannot explain my feelings for Guadalupe, but I feel just happiness deeper inside of me, she has given me so much. . . . As long as my legs are strong I will always run for her."

Bishop Román explains to the crowd that he has a very special love for the Mexican community of Santa Anna; this is the reason that this important feast is celebrated here instead of at the archdiocesan Cathedral of St. Mary or at the recently consecrated Church of Our Lady of Guadalupe in Doral, a more northern area of the county. "You are a role model for the whole archdiocese because of your devotion to Mary, Mother of God, who came from heaven one day to Tepeyac and spoke to San Juan Diego." The bishop explains that Mary opens to the faithful the gates to heaven, a place full of spiritual riches beyond compare with the material riches after which so many misguidedly aspire in this world. His sermon concludes by recounting the miraculous story of Guadalupe's apparitions appearing to Juan Diego, by explaining Guadalupe's rich hagiography, by recollecting the papacy's declaration that Our Lady of Guadalupe is patroness to all the Americas, and by proclaiming that Latin America is the most important part of the Catholic world.

Following a beautiful Mass, hundreds of communicants line up to receive the bishop's benediction. Dozens of others kneel before Guadalupe, offering her candles and flowers in gratitude for her intervention in their lives and in the history of their nation and its people. Among them is Rutilio, a middle-aged man who brought a small statue of Guadalupe to be blessed by the bishop. He explained to us the reasons for his participation, which, incidentally, reflect the rich and syncretic nature of Mexican folk Catholicism: "I have always asked the Virgin all sorts of things, and she always listens to me. I live close by, by Naranja, and I have some animals, some cows and goats. Well, fifteen years ago, one day suddenly all my animals got sick and started to die. My mother, who knows a lot about Guadalupe, told me that I had to choose the prettiest cow and sacrifice it for the Virgin. Then I did as my mom told me, chose the cow, killed her, and offered her to the Virgin. Then all my animals got better and they haven't been sick since then. Guadalupe liked my sacrifice and protects them since then."

December 13, 2002

Every year the youth group of St. Ann Mission, directed by José Miguel Roja, stages a performance of the appearance of apparitions of Our Lady of Guadalupe to Juan Diego and his subsequent pleas to the local bishop, Monsignor Juan de Zumárraga, to affirm the authenticity of his experience. The stage is very simply decorated. Its backdrop is a movie screen on which are projected the images of Tepeyac, the mountain on which the apparitions of 1531 occurred, and of Juan Diego's humble abode juxtaposed with Bishop Zumárraga's opulent palace.

The play unfolds before an enraptured audience. No one is more animated by the spectacle than the dozens of children who are huddled front and center before the stage. At the very moment of the play's climax, when Juan Diego furls open his cape (on which Guadalupe's image had miraculously formed) to throw into the air the flowers that the Virgin had planted to confirm her apparitions to the poor Indian, the children explode into cheers, applause, and laughter. The play complete, and the actors having taken their bows, the entire mass of the faithful stands to sing "La Porra de la Mission" (the Mission Cheer):

> Estamos todos tristes?
> No No!
> Estamos muy contentos?
> Sí, sí!
> Entonces cantaremos todos nuestra porra,
> Entonces cantaremos todos nuestra porra,
> Cristo Rey
> Cristo Rey
> Cristo Rey, Rey, Rey.
> Estamos todos tristes?
> No, no.
> Estamos muy contentos?
> Sí, sí.
> Entonces cantaremos todos nuestra porra,
> Entonces cantaremos todos nuestra porra,
> María Reina
> María Reina
> María Reina, Reina, Reina.
> (Are we all sad?
> No, no!
> Are we all happy?

Yes, yes!
Then let's sing our cheer!
Then let's sing our cheer!
Christ the King!
Christ the King!
Cristo the King, the King, the King!
Are we all sad?
No, no!
Are we all very happy?
Yes, yes!
Then let's sing our cheer!
Then let's sing our cheer!
Mary, Queen!
Mary, Queen!
Mary Queen, Queen, Queen!)

Members of the youth group consider it a great honor to perform in the annual play for la Guadalupana, and their efforts are much appreciated by everyone in attendance. They are motivated by their faith, central to which is the Marian devotion passed on to them by their parents and the mission. Martín Fernández, age seventeen, and Amanda Tecina, age sixteen, played Juan Diego and Guadalupe, respectively, this year. Martín was born in Texas and moved to Homestead with his immigrant parents in 1995, while Amanda was born in Homestead to parents who immigrated from Michoacoan. They both speak Spanish with a decidedly American accent, sprinkled with English words, what some might call "Spanglish." To Martín, Guadalupe represents both the sacred and his Mexican roots: "The Virgencita always makes me think about my abuela [grandmother] lighting candles and praying to her and telling me that Guadalupe is my mother in heaven and that there's no place like Mexico because God willed for Guadalupe to appear there." Amanda shares these feelings, but also highlights the unifying power of Guadalupe, which is one of the taproots of the mission's bonding social capital for South Florida's Mexican immigrants: "I have attended Santa Ana all my life; I was baptized here and would never change it for nothing. It's a very close community and we all look after each other. We take care of the children, teach catechism, wash cars, and sell food after the Sunday Mass to collect money for the poor. The Little Virgin keeps us together and gives us strength to fight every day."

Victor, who played Bishop Zumarraga, is the only one among the three main characters, and the only member of St. Ann Mission's youth group, who was actually born in Mexico, in Guanajuato. In 2000, he left his parents' home there to accept an invitation from his cousin to come and work in Homestead. After a very difficult journey, replete with episodes of pursuit by the U.S. Border Patrol in Texas and a hungry and cold four-day refuge in a desert cave, today he lives with his cousin and earns thirteen dollars an hour as a construction worker. Victor is convinced that Our Lady of Guadalupe helped him to survive his migration ordeal; and, like so many of his co-congregants, his participation at St. Ann Mission is largely driven by his need to express his gratitude to the Virgin Mary: "When I arrived to Homestead, the first thing I did was to ask for a church with the image of Our Lady of Guadalupe, my *Virgencita*, and I went on a procession on my knees to thank her. Since then, I always come to Santa Anna. Santa Anna is a poor church with a very rich heart. We are all very happy to have God and the Virgin of Guadalupe in our hearts. This is the church of all the Mexicans and for all the Mexicans. . . . We are Mexicans and we have to respect our traditions and roots. Guadalupe goes beyond the border."

December 14, 2002

On an unusually cold (by South Florida measures), windy Saturday evening, the mature solemnity of a communal recitation of the rosary is eclipsed by the childlike and riotous joy of the breaking of a large piñata. Bishop Román had blessed a large stash of blue and white plastic rosaries during his visit to the mission two days prior (blue and white are the colors of the Virgin Mary in Catholic hagiography). Once the nuns have distributed the prayer beads to the hundreds of faithful Catholics in attendance, a group of teenaged candidates for the Sacrament of Confirmation lead the gathering in praying the rosary. The youths are divided into subgroups from their respective labor camps, and they take turns leading the prayers. Two altar boys, meanwhile, meditatively swing incensories during the recitation; the smoke slowly rises in wafting unison with the hundreds of worshipful Our Fathers and Hail Marys said on this, the third day of la Guadalupana. Then, the teens receive the Sacrament of Confirmation.

When the prayers finally end, Father García approaches the altar and invites all of the children present to come to him for a blessing. Laughing excitedly and pushing people out of their way, they scurry to get near their beloved priest. One by one, he blesses them and then somehow gets them all to form a single line to take turns trying to strike the large piñata, which was donated to the mission by a local business for the occasion. With the piñata bursts open and its contents greedily horded by the children, a party ensues, complete with festive music and a sumptuous selection of Mexican food: *pozole, buñuelos, churros* (pastries), and *champurrado* (a thick hot chocolate drink with masa, almonds, and spices). The crowd soon disperses, however, as the next day will begin early with a sunrise vigil for Our Lady of Guadalupe.

December 15, 2002

It is 5:00 a.m. and still dark at St. Ann Mission, where mariachis and dancers in native Mesoamerican costumes gather with some two thousand pilgrims to await the arrival of Padre Pedro for *las mañanitas*. Many have brought paintings and sculptures of Guadalupe, rosaries, prayer cards, and even entire home altars to be blessed. The gathering is almost baroque in appearance, as hundreds of women are dressed in colorful sequined dresses bearing Guadalupe's image, while as many men are in broad-brimmed sombreros, cowboy boots, and hats, and others wave flags for la Virgencita.

Once Padre Pedro arrives, the singing begins and lasts for some five hours. Some weep, some close their eyes, while others scream for joy, their voices united in a sweeping expression of religious fervor, longing, and joy. We are puzzled as to why everyone holds leaves of paper with the lyrics to the hymns, for no one seems to need them. The verses are known by heart, learned in Mexico or in Homestead during countless supplications before the image of Guadalupe. The range of emotions is altogether stupefying, an arresting communal expression of catharsis and nostalgia, of gratitude and longing, of fulfillment and need, of pride and joy.

> Buenos días paloma blanca.
> Hoy te vengo a saluda,
> Saludando tu belleza
> En tu reino celestial.
> Madre mía de Guadalupe,
> Dame ya tu bendición
> Recibe estas mañanitas
> De un humilde corazón.
> (Good morning, white dove.
> Today I come to say hello,
> Recognizing your beauty
> In your heavenly kingdom.
> My dear mother of Guadalupe,
> Give me your blessing.
> And receive this morning prayer
> From my humble heart.)

It all ends with eight nearly naked teenagers taking the stage and dancing to the rhythms of Aztec bells and drums for Tonatzín, the pagan goddess believed by many to have portended the cult of Guadalupe in Mexico.

Though this might seem a hard act to follow, the ensuing Eucharistic Mass is equally transfixing, in part because a priest from the homeland, Father Roberto Valverde of the Guadalupan Missionaries of the Holy Spirit, has joined St. Ann Mission's faithful today to conduct the service.[7] His sermon touches on the subjects of religious syncretism, divine revelation, devotion to Our Lady of Guadalupe, the history of Mexico, and Mexican immigration to the United States. He explains that all these factors culminate in the establishment of so many Mexican congregations in the United States, making Mexican devotion to Guadalupe, indeed, one of the cornerstones of "American" Catholicism.

Having received Communion and Valverde's blessings and encouragement, and having fulfilled their promise to "wake up the Virgin in song," the faithful are now spiritually quenched as the four-day Feast of Guadalupe draws to a close. Once more, they sing, dance, and share the foods of the homeland, where so many of their loved ones live out their hopes and struggles under the same loving guidance of Our Lady of Guadalupe. In large part, for the congregants and others attending, the four days of celebration at St. Ann Mission were about Mexican pride and spiritual renewal and were a collective expression of faithful petition to be empowered anew by the Mother of God and the Mother of all Mexicans. This included Martín, Amanda, and all of the youths of St. Ann Mission, many of whom have never been to Mexico, though Mexico is clearly their spiritual homeland, thanks to the mission and to the transtemporal and translocative power of Our Lady of Guadalupe.

Devotion to Guadalupe: Bonding the New Land and the Homeland

The social capital produced by St. Ann Mission Catholic Church is almost exclusively bonding social capital. The only bridging and the only way that St. Ann Mission produces civic social capital (CSC) is bridging between Mexicans who attend the church regularly and other Mexicans who only infrequently attend or who come for the Feast of Guadalupe and the primarily metaphorical, symbolic bonding with their homeland. In the wake of Hurricane Andrew, St. Ann Mission offered significant bridging and linking social capital with resources provided by the archdiocese and the federal government. Once those resources dried up, St. Ann Mission became a focus of primarily bonding social capital among exclusively Mexican immigrants. While St. Ann Mission does offer some social services, social relations pivot primarily on religious and spiritual activities, a focus that is consistent with other studies of immigrant Mexican religion. Pablo Vila concludes that religious faith in general is for Mexican immigrants "one of the most important subject positions people have to deal with on the border in order to construct a more or less coherent self" (2005, 7). Jeanette Rodriguez, meanwhile, states that Mexican American women "relate to Our Lady of Guadalupe as a role model to whom they pray, a mother, one who intercedes, heals, affirms, gives them strength, and gives direction for a new world based on love, compassion, help, and defense" (1994, 161).

Although the Mexican community centered at St. Ann Mission is much younger than its counterparts in the southwestern United States, Guadalupe's cult is as vital to the Mexicans of Homestead as it is to those of, say, Albuquerque or San Diego. Still, the Homestead Mexican community's relative newness and its marked minority status among Hispanic groups in South Florida, including its incumbent political marginalization, surely have much to do with the relative lack of bridging civic social capital at St. Ann Mission, even though its potential for development in this regard was amply demonstrated by the mission's response to the disaster of Hurricane Andrew.

For the Cuban pastor of St. Ann Mission, meanwhile, the awesome presence of Our Lady of Guadalupe in the lives of his Mexican flock surely reminds him of his own people's devotion to the Virgin of Charity of El Cobre, Cuba's patron saint. Here are a Hispanic people who, like his own, have been driven by destructive social forces (poverty for Mexicans, and political oppression for Cubans) to cross water into the United States often under unspeakably harsh and perilous conditions. In both cases, it is the Virgin Mary, as so many of these immigrants resolutely believe, who ensured their safe passage and their establishment of a new home and a new life in Miami. Tweed (1997) was so struck by Cuban exiles' appreciative and prayerful devotion to Caridad in Miami that he was inspired to develop one of the most impressive theories of religion to have emerged in recent decades, in which he defines religions as "confluences of organic-cultural flows that intensify joy and confront suffering by drawing on human and superhuman forces to make homes and cross boundaries" (2006, 54).

Padre Pedro's leadership is critical to producing the intense bonding manifest through the celebration of Our Lady of Guadalupe. The mission has few material resources, nor does it have either significant bridging or linking CSC. Padre Pedro has invested his energies, therefore, not in CSC but in religious and spiritual activities that resonate deeply and fulfill profound needs among the local Mexican community.

In the case of the Marian devotion of Mexicans at St. Ann Mission, Our Lady of Guadalupe is one especially impressive example of what Tweed calls a "superhuman" force who empowers her devotees to "cross boundaries" (literally and figuratively, both of which are explicitly intended by Tweed) and "to make homes" in Homestead, domestically, culturally, and spiritually.

In creating the rituals surrounding the veneration of Our Lady of Guadalupe, the mission youth are central. They organize and coordinate the celebrations that fill the middle of December before Christmas. Contrary to the findings of studies of immigrant youth for whom the process of Americanization alienates them from their parents' religion (Ebaugh and Chafetz 2000a, 2000b; Stepick 2005), these Mexican youth at St. Ann Mission are the embodiment of their parents' devotion to Our Virgin of Guadalupe.

We have offered a glimpse of some of the "suffering" confronted by these people and some of the "joy" that is intensified by the "organic-cultural flows" that comprise their religious practice, from the weekly Mass to the four-day celebration of la Guadalupana. And just as they are swept downstream by the various "confluences" that flow together in the cult of Guadalupe, so, too, do they carve out new tributaries that further enrich this extraordinary tradition, whether in sacrificing a cow for the Virgin Mary in South Florida, performing the miracle of 1531 in American-accented Spanish, or following a Cuban bishop in procession for Guadalupe near a labor camp in the bean fields of South Florida. At the same time, this powerful devotion has limitations. The Mexican immigrants at St. Ann Mission do not cross ethnic boundaries. The bonding that Our Lady of Guadalupe produces and symbolizes is limited to Mexican immigrants.

NOTES

1. At around the same time that Mexicans began settling in southern Miami-Dade County, another Mexican immigrant community was taking root to the northwest in and around the fields of Immokalee in Collier County. Immokalee's Our Lady of Guadalupe Catholic Church dates to 1957, even though until the 1970s there was no significant Mexican community there (Williams and Loret de Mola 2007, 236; Thissen 2002, 89).

2. Founded in 1958, the Diocese of Miami was upgraded to the Archdiocese of Miami ten years later, in 1968.

3. An important exception to this rule is the recently established Feast of St. Ann, July 25, which attracts hundreds of Haitians each year.

4. The camp ministry's effectiveness is revealed when the case of Homestead is contrasted with that of Immokalee in Collier County, Florida, where "most migrant farmworkers are not spiritually connected to the Catholic Church" (Williams and Loret de Mola 2007, 243).

5. Hurricane Katrina's damage to southern Louisiana and Mississippi in 2005 surpassed that of Hurricane Andrew. There were also earlier hurricanes in Florida in 1926 and 1933 that caused more deaths (Pielke and Landsea 1998).

6. Although we did not measure for this in our broader project, we do have the impression that Mexican immigrants at St. Ann Mission are highly successful in passing on their religious devotion to their children in a decidedly Mexican form.

7. We have found such occasions as these, when clergy from their homelands visit immigrants' congregations in Miami to lead religious services, to be considered highly important by religious members of all the immigrant ethnic groups covered in this book. Sometimes their presence can effect more than a tripling in church attendance.

REFERENCES

Aguirre, B. E., K. P. Schwirian, and A. J. LaGreca. 1980. The Residential Patterning of Latin American and Other Ethnic Populations in Metropolitan Miami. *Latin American Research Review* 15(2): 35–63.

Brading, D. A. 2001. *Mexican Phoenix: Our Lady of Guadalupe: Image and Tradition across Five Centuries.* New York: Cambridge University Press.

Davis, J. D. 2002. Religious Groups Joined Forces to Help Hurricane Andrew's Victims. *South Florida Sun Sentinel*, August 24.

Ebaugh, H. R., and J. Saltzman Chafetz. 2000a. Dilemmas of Language in Immigrant Congregations: The Tie That Binds or the Tower of Babel? *Review of Religious Research* 41(4): 432–452.

————, eds. 2000b. *Religion and the New Immigrants: Continuities and Adaptations in Immigrant Congregations*. Walnut Creek, CA: AltaMira Press.

Hall, L. B. 2004. *Mary, Mother and Warrior*. Austin: University of Texas Press.

Miami-Dade County. 2000. *Census 2000*. Florida Electronic Data Depository Library. www.uflib.ufl.edu/fefdl/census/miamidadecensus; accessed on May 13, 2006.

————. 2003. Demographic Profile, Miami-Dade County, 1960–2000. Miami, FL.

Pielke, R. A., and C. W. Landsea. 1998. Normalized Hurricane Damages in the United States: 1925–95. *Weather and Forecasting* 13(3): 621–631.

Portes, A., and R. G. Rumbaut. 2001. *Legacies: The Story of the Immigrant Second Generation*. Berkeley and Los Angeles: University of California Press.

Rodriguez, J. 1994. *Our Lady of Guadalupe: Faith and Empowerment among Mexican-American Women*. Austin: University of Texas Press.

Stepick, A. 2005. God Is Apparently Not Dead: The Obvious, the Emergent, and the Unknown in Immigration and Religion. In *Immigrant Faiths: Transforming Religious Life in America*, ed. K. Leonard, A. Stepick, M. A. Vasquez, and J. Holdaway, 33–44. Lanham, MD: AltaMira Press.

Thissen, C. A. 2002. *Immokalee's Fields of Hope*. Lincoln: University of Nebraska Press.

Tweed, T. A. 1997. *Our Lady of the Exile: Diasporic Devotion at a Cuban Catholic Shrine in Miami*. New York: Oxford University Press.

————. 2006. *Crossing and Dwelling: A Theory of Religion*. Cambridge, MA: Harvard University Press.

United States Census Bureau. 2000. *United States Census 2000*. http://www.census.gov/main/www/cen2000.html; accessed August 5, 2007.

United States Department of Energy. 1994. *Tomorrow's Energy Today for Cities and Counties: When Disaster Strikes, the Sun Can Still Shine Through*. DOE/CH 10093–282 DE940000–289, March 1994 reporting document.

Vila, P. 2005. *Border Identifications: Narratives of Religion, Gender, and Class on the U.S.-Mexican Border*. Austin: University of Texas Press.

Williams, P., and P. F. Loret de Mola. 2007. Religion and Social Capital among Mexican Immigrants in Southwest Florida. *Latino Studies* 5(1): 233–253.

10

The Struggle for Civic Social Capital in West Indian Churches

TERUYUKI TSUJI, CHRISTINE HO, AND ALEX STEPICK

> We can't just be in a little box here, because the Bible says we're supposed to be witness to everyone around our neighborhood.
>
> —Sandy, a Sunday school teacher, Emmanuel Apostolic Church, Perrine

The West Indian[1] churches in this study typically have not been sites for the development of civic social capital (CSC). Similar to Sandy, quoted above, West Indian congregants commonly speak of the need to reach out, but the perceived need is usually not matched by deeds. While welcoming outsiders, as they did us in our fieldwork,[2] they do not actively reach out to them. Typical of West Indian immigrants, the congregants possess relatively large amounts of human and cultural capital with above-average education for immigrants and a native fluency in English, resources frequently associated with CSC. Yet their churches are more likely to focus on advancing individuals' morality and economic well-being or social relationships with co-ethnics, rather than engaging in civic or charitable affairs beyond the congregation.

This chapter explores the forms of social capital discovered in congregations with significant West Indian membership throughout Miami-Dade County.[3] We found West Indian churches in South Florida to emphasize one or more of three different types of social relationships and associated capital: (1) The majority of churches we studied, which were Pentecostal, stress the development of human capital through church-based social activities that are limited overwhelmingly to interactions within the same congregation; (2) the Catholic and Episcopal churches promote social relationships that promote primarily bonding but also bridge to co-ethnics who do not attend those churches; and (3) we found one Baptist church that actively promotes CSC and engages the broader South Florida community. In short, West Indian immigrant churches in South Florida constitute a community; but, with the one Baptist church exception, their reach extends only to those who are most like them, primarily, other West Indians in their own congregation and, secondarily, to West Indians outside their congregation. The congregations and their members embody much more bonding than bridging social capital.

This chapter addresses the three types of social relations and associated social and civic capitals that these diverse congregations manifest. Pentecostals are both the most numerous and the least likely to engage in CSC activities. Social interactions focus instead on cultivating and promoting human capital, i.e., individual skills and knowledge that will increase one's economic well-being. The ministry of these churches is emphatically spiritually oriented. Indeed, their theology legitimizes the pursuit of individual material well-being as a constituent element of the spiritual.

Catholic and Episcopalian churches that have significant numbers of West Indian congregants were found to have both local and transnational co-ethnic ties beyond their congregations. In these congregations social relationships are actively cultivated through national and ethnic events, such as the celebration of a West Indian carnival. The social relationships embodied in these events have the potential to be social capital, i.e., to produce economic consequences, as these social ties may overlap with business or work relationships. However, this potential is not explicitly recognized. Moreover, the congregations of these churches reflect a minority of the immigrant West Indian population because Catholicism was largely limited to Trinidad and Tobago while the Episcopalian church integrated primarily the upper and middle classes in Jamaica and the other islands.

The congregation of Sierra Norwood Baptist Church actively promotes CSC through membership in an ecumenical organization that has mounted a number of successful political initiatives addressing specific social issues. While Sierra Norwood struggles to motivate its West Indian congregants to embrace its civic and political outreach, it remains unique among the West Indian churches we encountered.

West Indians in South Florida and Their Churches

South Florida has become a primary location for West Indian immigrants in the United States. Only New York has more West Indians than Florida, where Jamaicans are more numerous than any other immigrant group except Cubans and Haitians (Elliott 2001). In fact, the growth in South Florida's overall Black population is propelled primarily by immigrants from the Caribbean (Charles 2001). New York is the historical and still primary West Indian immigrant center. Its West Indian population received nearly all the scholarly attention focused on understanding the migration to the United States from the Anglophone Caribbean (see, for example, Foner 1985, 1998, 2001; Kasinitz 1992;

Waters 1994, 1999; Kasinitz and Vikerman 1998).[4] South Florida's rapidly growing West Indian population, on the other hand, remains relatively ignored by scholars (for an exception, see Kasinitz, Battle, and Myares 2001).

In South Florida, the over 150,000 West Indians concentrate primarily in two general areas, the southern part of Miami-Dade County and, increasingly, southern Broward and northern Miami-Dade Counties. Compared with other immigrant groups, West Indians have considerable human and cultural capital. According to the 1990 U.S. census, out of all the U.S. residents with origins of Jamaica and Trinidad, 68.7 percent and 74.2 percent, respectively, are the graduates of high schools or higher educational institutions. The relatively high educational level of West Indian immigrants is highlighted when compared with other immigrant groups. Only 58 percent of Haitian immigrants, for example, were high school graduates in the corresponding period. West Indians have also begun to construct some CSC with the election of a few city commissioners and one mayor of suburban cities in Broward County.

There is a popular misconception that the majority of West Indians belong to the Anglican or Episcopalian church[5] because of their recent independence from British rule. To the contrary, the religious landscape of West Indians both in their home countries and in South Florida actually spans a wide range of Christian denominations and other religions, so much so that it would be accurate to characterize it as a denominational or religious mosaic.

Historically influenced by France and Spain, in Trinidad the largest Christian denomination has remained Roman Catholicism since the colonial period. However, the proportion of Catholics has constantly decreased due to the growth of non-Christian denominations, particularly Hinduism along with Islam, and, more recently, the expansion of evangelical Christian denominations, such as Pentecostalism.[6] Historically, in Jamaica and the other former British West Indian colonies, the politically and socially dominant denomination was Anglicanism, but its influence was limited mainly to the White ruling class (Burton 1997, 115). Since emancipation in 1834, different forms of Protestantism were exported from the United States, where they flourished, especially in Jamaica. Methodists gained wide support among the colored middle-class (mulattoes), and Baptists laid a strong foundation among the Black working class (Burton 1997, 115; Rogozinski 1992, 181). At the beginning of the twentieth century, the proselytizing activities of North American Pentecostal missionaries began to engage Blacks (Burton 1997, 119); and over the past one hundred years, Pentecostalism, which is less hierarchical than mainstream Christianity, emerged as Jamaica's most popular religion, especially among the working class (Austin-Broos 1999, 219; Wedenoja 1980, 40).[7]

The denominational mosaic has been replicated in the religious landscape of West Indian immigrants to South Florida. Generally speaking, Trinidadians living in South Florida tend to be Roman Catholic, while Jamaicans tend to be

Pentecostal. Although the numbers are small, some West Indians do attend South Florida's Episcopalian churches. Episcopalianism in Miami socially parallels that of Trinidad, Jamaica, and the other islands as a symbol of middle- to upper-middle-class status. Some West Indians have joined Baptist, Methodist, and other mainstream Protestant churches, where they form a minority within those congregations.

Regardless of denomination, the majority of the congregations are made up of first-generation immigrants with a smaller proportion of second-generation children also in attendance. Congregations span a broad age range from young children to adolescents and the elderly, although middle-aged women predominate. The women organize most of the activities and do the majority of the church committee work. Some congregants, especially in the Catholic and Episcopalian churches, complained that their children attended different churches from themselves because they found the services and Mass of the parents' church too boring. In particular, they found the music was not lively enough.

"They Were Just a Part of Everyday Life": Geography versus Community

While West Indians tend to concentrate geographically in particular areas of South Florida, they have not established an institutionally complete ethnic community. In contrast to the Cuban enclave community, West Indians do not have a complete set of, for example, Jamaican-owned and operated businesses and other institutions such as schools and community organizations. Nor is there a single overwhelmingly West Indian residential area. Churches do not draw their congregants from only the immediate neighborhood, but from the broader Jamaican community throughout South Florida. They are what Helen Ebaugh, Jennifer O'Brien, and Janet Chafetz (2000) label as ethnic "niche churches," not integrated into their geographic surroundings but serving a relatively dispersed, ethnic religious community. The geographic dispersion contrasts to the organization of churches in the home countries, which immigrants remember as being integrated into more intimate communities back home in Jamaica. As Mary James of the Emmanuel Apostolic Church explained, "[Back in Jamaica] you knew everybody; which church they went to; what they did; whatever who had; who didn't have. When I was growing up, my father was a pastor, so we'd have like people who would . . . need. Their needs are always met by the church."

The memory of the church back home conforms to Ebaugh, O'Brien, and Chafetz's (2000) "parish" structure, in which the church is integrated into a particular neighborhood and fulfills multiple functions. Drawing upon Benedict Anderson's notion of "imagined community," Kenneth Bilby (1999) argues that religion in Jamaica traditionally provides the "displaced," i.e., those not lifted up by Jamaica's economic development, with symbolic means by which they imagine, retain, and expand their "communities." Religion, according to Bilby, has played a critical role in the formation of a new social place for the economically displaced to restore their integrity as social beings. In the language of this book, they create bonding social capital.

Immigration disperses a congregation's members, who then can no longer remain "a part of everyday life." West Indian churches in South Florida are generally established in neighborhoods characterized by shifting demographics. While there may be significant numbers of co-ethnics (i.e., other West Indians) and even co-nationals (e.g., Jamaicans), the neighborhoods obviously contain neither all their former neighbors nor all the people who attended the same church in the home country. The church is the one institution that regularly embodies the imagined community of the homeland. Under these conditions of fluid demographics, the bonding social capital of community must be constructed consciously and deliberately. As one congregant declared, "Jamaica is so different from America because we're so different here, so many different nationalities. Here you actually have to have a ministry to do something to *know* people in the community" (evangelist, Emmanuel Apostolic Church).

Community, for West Indian immigrants in South Florida, is thus more imagined and less connected to the geography of the church than in their homelands. Struggling to reestablish community as envisioned through the lens of shared memory has usually led West Indian immigrants to an investment of bonding social capital in co-ethnics. This is particularly the case for the largest West Indian religious group in South Florida, Pentecostals.

Pentecostals

Repeatedly, both in sermons and individual interviews, congregants of the numerous West Indian Pentecostal churches in South Florida emphasized their personal relationship to God. "The church is a body, a fellowship that will help you to reach out, but the whole identifying with God is a personal relationship with God that only you and God—you have to develop that. You know, you can come and you can shout and you can have a good time but the truth and reality is that there must be a personal relationship with God. You got to know Him for yourself" (minister, Emmanuel Apostolic Church). This fundamental concept underwrote and legitimized social activities that sanctioned and promoted individual financial success. In other words, the Pentecostal congregations are a site of the promotion and development of individual human capital. Nearly all their social activities are also intracongregational, i.e., they focus on developing bonding social capital. The few activities that extend beyond the congregation incorporate only other Pentecostals. While these may constitute bridging social capital, they are very short, familiar bridges. We examine, first, the theological basis they articulated for this approach, and then how it was implemented, particularly for women and youth.

Pentecostalism focuses on an individual's personal relationship to God. Cementing one's relationship to God is the key both to ultimate salvation and to coping with the problems of everyday life. Changing the world as you find it through social and political action is not encouraged. In a sermon, Pastor Emmanuel Gordon of the Emmanuel Apostolic Church exhorted, "Whatever your [skin] color is, . . . things sometimes go against us. . . . I have no control how I came into this world. I have no control over my gender. It was decided by appointment. We came to this world by appointment. It was a required appointment. We sometimes regret. . . . But let me tell you this, . . . all can be changed while you stay in the same system. . . . Stop complaining. Even if you are in the gutter, you have to get up and go forward. . . . We can do it."

Instead of "complaining," or instead of taking social and political action, Pentecostals often strongly encourage individual economic advancement. For example, just before Easter in 2002, Emmanuel Apostolic Church had a visiting pastor, one of the "Twelve Elders" of the home church in Jamaica. Toward the end of the service the visiting pastor asked all the attendants to come to the altar. As he walked through the attendants gathered by the altar, the pastor gave each one of them a "cleansed" coin, a quarter, and then calmly proclaimed, "That's yours. You can do whatever you want with it. This is a seed. Plant it, cultivate it, and then bring back the harvest. Bring back whatever you can get. But I don't want to see a quarter again. Bring back at least a dollar bill." This infusion of materialism into a sacred service was typical. The de facto Pentecostal dictum is that "God helps people in material ways," with the corollary that "God helps those who help themselves." Ignoring Christianity's anti-materialist themes, South Florida's Jamaican Pentecostals see no moral contradiction between being religious and being prosperous. Indeed, many of the Pentecostal churches consciously promote individual economic prosperity.

At a regular Sunday service at Monument of Faith Church, an affiliate of the Church of God, the pastor gave a signal to begin projecting a video that had been taped from a religious TV channel and featured a minister well known to the pastor and the congregation. The sermon began with the observation that money is the root of all evil. However, it continued by arguing, "It is OK to be rich as long as one loves God." The television preacher used himself as an example. He recounted his poverty-stricken childhood, remembering eating government-issued peanut butter, which was so hard it caused him to bend all his spoons. He boasted that today he is a rich man and has a Lear jet that is paid for. There is nothing wrong with his wealth because he got all his money by loving God, not by loving money. The key is to worship God and not money. If God makes you rich, money is not evil. What is evil is worshiping money, not God. Throughout the sermon, congregants applauded and shouted agreement. The sermon was followed by the collection of money. The pastor who showed the video of the TV evangelist was himself formerly a stockbroker for Merrill Lynch.

He described himself as a "prosperity specialist." He proclaimed, "I used to do seminars and conferences and speak at some of those as well as the independent outreach I do. Actually, I was scheduled to be returning from South Africa today, prior to the September 11 [2001] disaster. I was going to do some speaking on prosperity and on hate, which are two of my gifted areas."

Similarly, the pastor of First Born Christian Center has a parallel background that he related:

> I have a second degree in accounting which probably helps me as a pastor to understand how to run the church, . . . basically, because there's a business aspect to it. It's not just a theological stream; it is a business. . . . There's an important marriage between businesses and us. We brought about thirty-five business people to church here . . . and we put on a dinner when we brought the business people in. Then we exacted from them monies that they helped us to sponsor this thing. We raised over about ten thousand dollars . . . raised from local businesses . . . island business people, friends of mine, because I am bi-vocational. I teach financial seminars all over the world, corporate financial seminars, to banks, General Electric and Chase and Citibank. So I have built relationships with these guys, so we brought them in, and they came in and we showed what we were doing and we voiced our intent to them. And they helped us finance activities that reached several hundred kids. . . . Most of them were Caribbean-based, but we had others.

First Born Christian Center also promoted business opportunities in Jamaica. The church hosted a town hall meeting featuring the Victoria Mutual Building Society, the premier savings and loan association in Jamaica. At this meeting the president of the Victoria Mutual Building Society invited Jamaicans living in Miami to open savings accounts in Jamaica in U.S. dollars, not only because the interest rates on such accounts were three to four times higher than those being offered in the United States, but also because the accounts were tax free in Jamaica as long as the funds originated in the United States and the holders were U.S. residents. For those interested in investing in property in Jamaica, he also offered mortgage loans at rates higher than those in the United States but low by Jamaican standards. In addition, he offered appraisal and property management services. Finally, he offered them investment opportunities in the Jamaica Stock Exchange and in a line of high-yielding fixed-income instruments. At the end, the pastor announced that in a few weeks First Born Christian Center would also be sponsoring a workshop on how to start a small business. He closed stating, "We must work hard to be prosperous because prosperity is one way to get closer to God."

Monument of Faith Church and the First Born Christian Center are not the only South Florida West Indian churches in which the sacred and the secular are fused. Unity Light of the World, a non-denominational church, includes as a regular feature of its Sunday service the singing of the Prosperity Exercise:

All financial doors are now open.
All financial channels are now free.
God's rich substance is manifesting
for Unity Light of the World, right now!
In the name and through the power of Jesus Christ.
It is done!
God is manifesting
as our infinite supply now.
Amen.

This song is immediately followed by a recitation of the Prosperity Affirmation: "Divine love through me blesses and multiplies all that I have, all that I give, and all that I receive. Thank you Father, Mother God for providing for all our needs."

The Reverend Veda Wong-Chuck, perhaps the only female Jamaican pastor in South Florida, describes the church's principles in this way: "We are non-denominational. . . . We teach practical Christianity, something to live by day to day. . . . We do not take the Bible literally. . . . We do not teach about sin because we feel that sin is an error, a mistake which can be corrected. . . . We teach that you can do anything that you want to do because with God all things are possible. . . . We do not preach down to the congregation. . . . And we don't preach about the Devil and Satan. . . . Rather, in the beginning we got freedom of choice and we sometimes choose things that are not good for us. We make mistakes, but these mistakes can be corrected."

In Pentecostal churches, an active commitment to prosperity is not fortuitous. As Diane Austin-Broos (1999, 222) has observed, Pentecostalism's emphasis on materialism in its religious practices has invited censure from other denominations for promoting the growing "church-business" in Jamaica. The term is hyphenated because these two dimensions of life, the secular and the sacred, that are often regarded as distinct and contradictory, are consistently fused in the Pentecostal world. For Pentecostals the two are in principle inseparable; the "secular" forms a part of the "sacred," and vice versa.

Most of the Pentecostal Church leaders are males. But, the majority of Pentecostal congregants are females. Women do participate in the activities aimed at improving individual economic well-being, but they also have other activities that are specifically for them.

Pentecostal Women

A female evangelist addressed the Women in Warfare retreat, a gathering of between forty and fifty females, all West Indian, primarily Pentecostals, except the Japanese Buddhist male researcher. Referring to the Scriptures, she emphasized the necessity to pursue a "corporate victory" to solve the common "troubles" of women:

> Two types of woman are mentioned in the Bible. . . . I want you to know that there are several issues common to these two types of women in the scripture. Number one, none of the names are mentioned. It means a lack of identity. Identity crisis is one of the problems of women. When you have your name, it identifies you in person. It tells you who you are. A man calls me "Hey, ya!" I said, "You're talking to me?" Because I am not "ya." I have a name. Every human being got to have their own name. People don't know who you are. Women have an identity crisis. . . . Number two, they both got sick and died. You should say to God, "We got a lot of troubles." . . . The Black people have a trouble. Poor people have a trouble. Women have a trouble! Our troubles are all different. But the end is the same. Death. They were both sick and died.

According to the evangelist, women confront the common "troubles" that they are neither allowed "identity" nor "invited to Jesus' last supper." To overcome these troubles, women must unite in struggle, in a war. At the Women in Warfare retreat helmets and sleeping bags are strewn about the floor, making the venue look like an army camp. Before the female evangelist spoke, the Praise Team, a core group of female youth, began singing, "I'm a soldier in the army under the Lord! I'm a soldier in the army! I'm a soldier in the army! I'm a soldier in the army!" The leader of the youth group encouraged the audience: "Tell neighbors you're a soldier. Hey, march. March. March!" Everyone began marching around the "house" in a line led by the evangelist, who was waving a flag. A number of female congregants wearing army camouflage followed the flag-carrying leader. The Praise Team continued to sing, "I'm a soldier in the army! I'm a soldier in the army! I'm a soldier in the army!"

In Jamaica, Pentecostal churches have been constructed by poor women who have built a community with similar women in locally based, close-knit, small-scale units, albeit usually led by men (Burton 1997, 120). Equally, Jamaican women found strength in the Pentecostal emphasis on salvation through a personal relationship with Jesus. In this way, Pentecostalism has allowed poor Jamaican women to imagine "utopias" and communities beyond racial and gender hierarchies (Austin-Broos 1999, 217).

The Emmanuel Apostolic Church embodies Jamaican feminized Pentecostalism. The founder was a woman, Pastor White, who even after her death remains an important source of gender-oriented pride and identity. As one congregant explained, "She was a woman of God. I mean a real woman that could, you know, see through you and tell you things, you know. 'Brother, you need to stop doing those things you used to with the woman, or you need to get your life straighten up and don't go that way.' She could read you and tell you right as it is, you know, from the spirit."

At the Women in Warfare retreat, the messages were directed toward not just the "fellow soldiers," but also the "Reserves," that is, female youth who appeared to be from five to fifteen years old. Only the youth were chosen to "receive the Holy Ghost." The young women, one after another, were individually called up to the stage and prayed for. Even if the young women still do not have actual experiences of common troubles, such an occasion of intergenerational communication provides them with potential or imaginary experience. Social and cultural capital is passed on to the next generation through maternal lines. Female youth, for the evangelist and other adult congregants, are not simply members of the church, but, more importantly, "daughters," as one of their favorite phrases suggests, who inherit their legacies. This Women in Warfare retreat was also the only West Indian Pentecostal event that we witnessed that demonstrated any form of bridging CSC, albeit of a limited nature. The women present were all Pentecostals, but they were from different congregations. Every other Pentecostal event that we observed included only individuals from the same congregation. The retreat also reflected the Pentecostals' emphasis on youth, the topic of the next section.

Passing the Mantle On: The Development
of Civic Social Capital among Youth

On a Friday night, five or six youngsters squat on the ground absorbed in conversation in front of a small grocery store. One of them starts rocking his body to the hip-hop music blaring from a nearby car radio. A few minutes later, another car drives into the parking lot. Another group of youngsters jumps out. While they are not much different in appearance from the first group, they do not join them. Instead, they disappear into the building next door. They are members of the youth group of the Emmanuel Apostolic Church, a storefront Pentecostal church. Before long, their lively singing from inside the church nearly drowns out the loud, "cool" music outside. The youth meet every Friday. Sometimes there are nearly fifty youth, at other times just a few show up. But the youth service is always active and serious. And once it starts, there is seemingly no end to the vivacious singing and shouting and the sound of clapping and stamping, by which the youth commune with "Him" far into the night.

Since its official founding in 1992, young people have accounted for roughly two-thirds of the congregation of Emmanuel Apostolic Church. One of the founding members of the church explained, "I guess when we started as a church . . . there from the beginning we started with like thirty people. Of that thirty we had like probably eighteen young people. When you're like that in an environment you have no choice but to use what you have." A congregant, who is another founding member, agrees: "They were all that we had, and we had to make the best use of what we had."

One minister, who was installed as the first president of the youth department when the church was founded, indicated that church leaders have made concerted efforts to develop their "adults of tomorrow," not merely because there is "no other choice" but also because the youth are the "wisest investment." All the same, church leaders are well acquainted with the fact that "investment in youth" is by no means a smooth undertaking because, as the minister states, "Youths move." They are constantly evolving, changing their ideas and, perhaps, their congregational affiliation. Indeed, regardless of their denomination, the youth leaders all recounted how difficult it is to "keep them." Mr. Hamilton of the Church of the Ascension, an Episcopalian church, believes it is crucial for the church to become a "role model" for the youth. He lamented the "disappearance" of one particular youth: "His mother was a very devoted member of this church. And he was also a very devoted member of this church. And then suddenly he disappeared, and then I heard he was going to some other church. He is at other churches with music. They take away our younger members because they like it; they like the drama of the [other] church."

The youth preferred the high drama and "cool" music of the Pentecostal churches, which are far more successful than the staid Episcopalians in recruiting and retaining young people. Pentecostal music is "rocking," and the loud preaching and the "catching of the spirit" provide dramatic excitement. The mobility or flexibility that youth usually display, in contrast to the stability of adults, is highly valued among the church leaders in the Emmanuel Apostolic Church. They regard young people not simply as an uncertainty but also as a necessary energy for the church to survive. One pastor related, "If you don't get active youth, you'll just sit and be dormant and you'll finally die." In the Pentecostal churches, the high rate of mobility of youth is not considered instability, but unlimited potential to expand. Compared with adults, youth have talents by which they can easily transcend geographical, ethnic, and socioeconomic boundaries, penetrating into different segments of society. Church leaders are well aware of the lack of responsibility and the persuasiveness among youth, which, paradoxically, they consider as necessary for community outreach activities. A leader at Emmanuel Apostolic Church explained:

> I believe that our outreach may really concentrate with young people or stuff relating to the youth because that's what we have. . . . The important thing for each church is to identify what you have and not to say, well, this church is doing that so why shouldn't we be doing it. . . . That's using young people to do something they probably can't do outside the ministry. You can send them on the street witnessing, but they don't have as much effect; a number of people don't give much respect to them in terms of, you know, relating the Scriptures. People don't think they're grown enough or have gone through enough trials to be able to be such a good witness. But they get along easily with people. . . . That's what we have. We have such a talented group of young people who is going to give the message in a different way.

The leaders of Emmanuel Apostolic Church, as in other churches, are uncertain when, with what form, and even where they will receive the dividends from their investments in young people. Thus, "youth moves," so that "whatever seeds you sow in them," even if they are blown away and land in a remote region, "will bring fruit."

Put differently, the synthesizing of the sacred with the secular facilitates the mutual conversion of cultural capital (i.e., cultural knowledge that can be converted into something more tangible) into social capital (Bourdieu 1986, 252–255). For instance, at Talent Night, an event held within the regular youth service at Emmanuel Apostolic Church, one of the leaders related the "Word of God" to children, teens, and young adults, then continued by explaining, "About talents, some have five, some have two, and some have one. It is according to the measure of one's ability. God gave each and every one of you in the house at least one talent." Talent Night allows the youth group to display a variety of talents, including singing, dancing, playing instruments, and reading poetry, all of which are enthusiastically individually cultivated and socially appreciated. The congregation conceives of these expressions as examples of their individualistic "freedom of worship." Those who can sing can worship Him by singing. Those who can dance can worship Him by dancing. Such talents are nurtured to "pay back" God, yet they also simultaneously express cultural capital that can be used for what would otherwise be considered the secular purposes of establishing a career. For example, a group of youths in this church, in collaboration with members of other Pentecostal churches, produced and sold a musical CD to subsidize the annual international Pentecostal youth camp. The music from this CD was later broadcast on the radio, leading some of the performers to aspire to careers in the entertainment industry. Their serious efforts to come closer to and sacrifice for Him gave them a drive and orientation for the creation of theologically sanctioned strategies that also promoted individual interest-oriented actions.

The youth also do not necessarily draw a stark boundary between their religious activities and civic social activities that their parents are likely to label as "politricks," a Rastafarian phrase that has been adopted by many Jamaicans to express their cynicism toward electoral politics. For younger immigrant Pentecostals, their experience in U.S. schools has engendered a more optimistic yet still thoroughly religious perspective on politics. Ann, a young adult congregant from the Emmanuel Apostolic Church, reflected both her negative feelings and a call for change in political engagement: "To be honest with you, I really think you need a spiritual eye to run this country. If we are going to get anywhere we need some spiritual leaders up there to help the direction. If our leaders of this country rely on the source from above we'd be all right, because He's the awesome God. He's the universal. You know the only problem with politics; it's all politricks! Maybe we could get some of that garbage cut out of it and have a real life. And then we wouldn't have it so bad. I really think that spiritual leaders should take more active roles."

In summary, West Indian Pentecostals in South Florida do not engage significantly in the production of CSC. They eschew the civic, and socially they concentrate on their own congregations, producing deep bonding social capital among themselves, fellow West Indian, primarily Jamaican, Pentecostals. Generally, we have found that the Pentecostal sense of civic is theologically limited. Instead of engaging the broader civic social world, South Florida's West Indian Pentecostals focus on changing themselves spiritually. This, in turn, they believe, can effect material changes, exemplified through the lectures and social contacts dedicated to improving congregants' human capital, i.e. the skills and education specifically related to money-making opportunities. Our observations further revealed that they socially interacted overwhelmingly with other Pentecostals and primarily with Pentecostals who are co-ethnics, i.e., other West Indians, usually Jamaicans. Episcopalians and Catholics also interact primarily with co-ethnics, but their social range is broader and they do not explicitly use religion to advance human capital and associated individual economic well-being.

Episcopalian and Catholic Ethnic Solidarity and Community Construction

The Curry-Q (a Trinidadian adaptation of a barbecue) at Christ the King Catholic Church was supposed to be all set up by 11:30 a.m. Teruyuki (Terry) Tsuji, the Japanese Buddhist author, who had lived and worked in both Trinidad and Jamaica, had been attending services at the church and had volunteered to help. He arrived at 11:10 a.m. and observed that things were nowhere near being ready. Ricky, the chair of the Trinidad and Tobago Committee at Christ the King, greeted Terry and introduced him around. Terry and the committee members there to set up queried each other about their backgrounds. They asked Terry where and when he lived in Trinidad, and he inquired what part of Trinidad they were from, when they came to the United States, when the last time was that they went home, and the like. The "Trinis" were not from a single town, let alone a single congregation in Trinidad. Most came during Trinidad's economic difficulties of the 1980s, and most also did not initially settle in Miami. The volunteers then turned to discussing Trinidadian politics, with most voicing their support of the majority Peoples' National Movement, and they angrily assailed the opposition United National Congress. The discussion took precedence over preparations for Curry-Q, and set up wasn't complete until 12:30.

When they opened the doors, people rushed in, most picking up plates of curry or BBQ chicken, *roti, paratha,* rice and peas, potato salad, and corn soup, along with Trinidadian soft drinks. After the initial rush, other people continued to trickle in. Many bought their food and directly left, though as the afternoon wore on more and more lingered about. Most who attended were parishioners, and virtually all were Trinidadian. By 2:30 p.m., when someone arrived with a couple of bottles of rum, the event was effectively transformed into what Trinidadians call "liming," the social art of doing nothing (Erickson 1990). They discussed how successful the Curry-Q was (three hundred meals sold, which was more than the previous year), sports, the upcoming Mother's Day Dance ,and the Florida Memorial College Steel Orchestra, each of which was advertised by flyers passed out to attendees. One of the Curry-Q organizers asked the limers to quiet down when the 5:30 Mass began inside the church. They quieted, but continued on to 6:30, talking while cleaning up. Finally, they dispersed, promising to see each other at one of the upcoming events.

The Church of the Ascension, the Episcopalian (i.e., Anglican) church directly across the street from Christ the King, annually hosts an even larger event, the Annual International Carnival Bash, which includes entertainers from the Caribbean and a live radio broadcast on the local West Indian–oriented AM radio station. Brightly colored booths represented Jamaica, Trinidad and Tobago, Guyana, Barbados, and the Bahamas. Each booth flew a national flag from one corner. There was also an American booth, complete with U.S. flag, selling hotdogs. The only booth without a national flag was offering free medical checks for blood pressure and diabetes testing. Church of Ascension parishioners working the carnival all wore polo shirts embroidered with "Church of Ascension" and also the name of their homeland country. Those working the booths included not only Church of the Ascension parishioners, but also some from Christ the King Catholic Church from across the street. The event lasts all day, even longer than the neighboring Catholics' Curry-Q, because it is one of several occasions for the Trinidad and Tobago community, scattered across more then two geographically large counties, to come together and create community rather than imagine it.

Christ the King and Church of the Ascension each have numerous events like these throughout the year that celebrate West Indian culture. The congregations of both the Episcopalian and Catholic churches are multinational, perhaps the only West Indian congregations in Miami that are *primarily* multinational. The Episcopalian Church of the Ascension has a congregation composed of Jamaicans (the majority) plus Trinidadians, Barbadians, Guyanese, Vincentians (from St. Vincent), Bahamians, Haitians, Venezuelans, and Panamanians. Christ the King Catholic Church has a similar national mix of Caribbean ethnicities, but also includes Haitians, Vietnamese, Filipino, and Cuban and other Latinos. It is consistent with the slogan of the church, "Love is international." Yet the social activities are almost all nationally specific. The Curry Q is organized by the Trinidad and Tobago Catholic Community, which not only plans and sponsors many cultural events throughout the year, but also organizes transnational exchanges between churches in Trinidad and Christ the King Catholic Church. They also sponsor a special Mass, Annual Thanksgiving Mass, every year in September to celebrate the political independence of

Trinidad and Tobago. It has been customary to invite a parish priest and a choir group from Trinidad to officiate the Mass. The Most Reverend Anthony Pantin, the then archbishop of Port of Spain, accepted the invitation for the occasion of the fifteenth anniversary of this special Trinidadian Mass. This Mass has become so famous that it is attended not only by Catholic Trinidadians from the entire South Florida area, who travel far for this Mass, but also Trinidadians of other denominations.

The events contribute to the re-construction of the immigrants' imagined national communities, based in South Florida, but also reaching back to their homeland, i.e., they are transnational as they not only imagine themselves as part of the dispersed, for example, Trinidadian or West Indian communities, but also concretely bring religious leaders and performers from the homeland to South Florida West Indian Catholic and Episcopal church activities. In this sense, they constitute primarily bonding social capital, but also a form of bridging social capital back to the homeland. The social activities are also more inclusive and thus also more bridging than those in the Protestant Pentecostal churches. Among the Episcopalians and Catholics, for example, social activities are directed toward and appeal to those who are socially much like themselves, co-nationals (i.e., from the same nation, such as Trinidad or Jamaica) and co-ethnics (English-speaking West Indians), not just to those who are in the same religious congregation. While some people undoubtedly have more than imaginary ties to others, and perhaps even business relationships, these churches have none of the activities promoting individual economic well-being, as observed in the West Indian Pentecostal churches. Thus, whereas they do have civic social capital potential, that potential is not realized as the participants are not necessarily civically engaged themselves. Civic activities, particularly home country politics, are certainly discussed, sometimes quite passionately. Civic activities also are not theologically discouraged as in most West Indian Protestant Pentecostal churches. Nevertheless, civic concerns are not the focus or intent of these activities. We found only one West Indian church in which civic activities, particularly civic activities that concentrated on South Florida, were a focus, and it was neither Pentecostal nor Catholic nor Episcopalian.

Building Civic Social Capital:
Sierra Norwood Calvary Baptist Church and PACT

Sierra Norwood Calvary Baptist Church is located in northern Miami-Dade County, in the heart of a predominantly West Indian neighborhood. Characterizing himself as the chief shepherd leading a flock, its Jamaican-born pastor, Richard Ledgister, described his congregation of nearly four hundred as international, although in his estimation about 65 to 70 percent are Jamaican. The remainder of the congregation migrated from Trinidad, Guyana, Antigua, the Bahamas, Nicaragua (mainly the Bluefields area, which is primarily English-speaking), Panama, Haiti, and Nigeria. There are also a couple of African Americans. The history of this church mirrors the history of demographic changes in this part of the county over the past fifty years. Established in 1952 as the Sierra Norwood Baptist Church, it had an all-White congregation for about thirty years. Then West Indians began to move into the area in the early 1980s and the White congregation moved out. Meanwhile, a mission church called Calvary Baptist Church, then headed by Norwood's present Jamaican pastor, began to flourish next door in a recreation center because West Indians were not welcome in the White congregation. With his church on the brink of financial collapse, the White pastor approached the Jamaican pastor about merging congregations. It took several years, but the merger in name and congregation finally took place in 1988.[8]

Apart from its ethnic history of adapting to demographic change in its immediate neighborhood, Sierra Norwood Calvary Baptist Church stands out as the single most civically engaged West Indian church that we encountered in our study. One of its forays into territory outside of the church is through its overseas missionary work. Although a member of the Southern Baptist Convention, the Florida Baptist Convention, and the Miami Baptist Association, Sierra Norwood has been sponsoring overseas missions to Haiti and Guyana on its own as an autonomous church for the past five years. It provides financial support for these missions from its own budget and recruits members of its congregation (young and old) to volunteer to travel to Haiti and Guyana to provide the labor to help build churches and provide schooling (using the church building as a school during the week).

Locally, Sierra Norwood Calvary Baptist Church manifests its outreach through its participation in People Acting for Community Together (PACT). Founded in 1988 as a multi-denominational coalition of religious bodies, PACT "seeks to build community power and overcome systemic injustices that affect low to moderate-income communities" in Miami-Dade County (see http://www.miamipact.org/). As a nonprofit, its funding comes from a combination of membership dues from participating congregations; donations from small businesses, individuals, and corporations; and grants from various private foundations. PACT is comprised of twenty-one congregations plus one housing association. Ten of these are Catholic churches, seven are Methodist churches, one is a Presbyterian church, one is a Moravian church, one is a Baptist church (Sierra Norwood), and one is a Jewish synagogue, plus the Little Haiti Housing Association. The people served by PACT are mostly immigrants from Latin America and the Caribbean, so meetings are held in three languages: English, Spanish, and Haitian Creole. At these meetings members identify public concerns that are common to their communities and try to use the power of numbers to negotiate with public officials about important issues that affect their lives.

These goals are articulated on its Web site in PACT's explicit motto: "Building Stronger Communities with Social Capital," which is accomplished by establishing networks of relationships within and between its diverse congregations. Through a process of one-on-one visits and house meetings, members of PACT share their dreams and identify commonly held community concerns, but they do not stop at problem identification. PACT's motto is twinned with its strategy of "Finding Solutions and Holding Officials Accountable" (http://www. miamipact.org/). Congregation leaders conduct extensive research to find solutions to community problems and find out which public officials have the power to implement the solutions. PACT then holds direct-action meetings, attended by hundreds of its members, while PACT leaders make requests of the appropriate public officials. PACT has a long history of success at community empowerment and is one of Miami's largest grassroots organizations.

In 1990, PACT succeeded in convincing the City of Miami to demolish more than three hundred crack houses in low-income neighborhoods. In the domain of housing, PACT participated in establishing the Homeless Trust to provide more county resources to help the homeless, and in 1994 it also secured an agreement with two local banks to provide $38 million for low-income, affordable housing programs. In 1998, PACT participated in a policing program in the Norland/Norwood section of Miami-Dade and succeeded in increasing the number of officers who can speak Haitian Creole as well as targeting hotspots of drug dealing and prostitution. In 1999, the organization convinced the U.S. Immigration and Naturalization Service to adopt a mandatory two-day training program in cultural awareness for all staff to improve its customer service, and also to speed up the immigration process for potential permanent residents and citizens.

One of PACT's strongest initiatives is educational reform. As a result of strong pressure from PACT, Miami-Dade County Public Schools implemented a phonics-based reading program called Direct Instruction, and the organization was also awarded $7.25 million in state funding for the reading program, which has positively impacted twenty-seven elementary schools. PACT's latest project aimed to double the bus fleet of Miami-Dade's Public Transportation system. The combination of not enough buses, erratic scheduling, frequent breakdowns, overcrowding, and long waits resulted in people being habitually late and losing their jobs. Although he initially rejected the demands of more than one thousand members of PACT in early 2001, then–county mayor Alex Penelas finally succumbed to pressure in early 2002 by formulating a transportation plan to increase the sales tax to establish a "dedicated source of funds" for doubling the number of buses and other improvements to public transportation. In November 2002, Miami-Dade County voters overwhelmingly passed a transportation initiative that sought to address PACT's goals by levying a 0.5 percent county sales surtax.

Not only is Sierra Norwood Calvary Baptist's involvement in a multi-ethnic and multicultural coalition unique among West Indian churches, but also its membership in PACT demonstrates its conscious commitment to civic engagement. As its pastor declared,

> Another thing that PACT does, apart from sensitizing people in the church to know that they have a voice and can influence or change things that are affecting them in the community, it also helps the members to realize that there is what we call "the work of the church," not just "church work," where people think that you [only] come to the church and get involved in committees of the church and come to prayer meeting on Sunday. They must realize that the church must get out of the four walls and go out in the community to impact the community by trying to bring about change in the community that would improve the livelihood or conditions of people. So we do not see this at cross purposes with what the church stands for; it's a part of being a good neighbor and being your brother's keeper.

Sierra Norwood's pastor, Richard Ledgister, not only endorses PACT, but is also one of its leaders. Firmly believing in the spirituality of civic engagement, he has hosted meetings of PACT's board of directors, and his congregation is one of the organization's largest financial contributors. However, membership in PACT should only be considered a partial success at generating CSC. First, its origins were not within the congregation, but among outsiders who solicited support from the congregation. More importantly, while the pastor remains enthusiastic, the congregation is less so. Indeed, the pastor admitted in an interview that it is difficult to sustain the momentum of community outreach:

> One problem with PACT is it is difficult to sustain because people lose interest, and to try to keep the interest going is not easy, especially after the issue they feel passionate about is completed. . . . You will find that the turnout will be dominated by the Haitian people and Hispanic people. But the rest of the Caribbean people, you will find that they are more slow in putting in their efforts. . . . They see that almost as external, secular stuff, not spiritual matters. So they don't want to get involved in that. They just want to come to church. They need to understand the importance of helping other people in the community. To mobilize them, you have to keep nagging them and nagging them, but it must be done because numbers are important. You cannot make an impression if you go with ten people. When you go with one hundred or one thousand it is totally different.

Several internally driven ministries envisioned by the pastor have also been difficult to launch. For example, he would like to expand the church school to a full elementary school beyond the third grade, create a combination music and anti-drug program to "get the kids off the streets," begin a retirement home for the elderly, and reach out to people with AIDS. None of these programs has yet come to fruition.

A West Indian Reservoir of Civic Social Capital

The majority of West Indian congregations in South Florida are not fonts of CSC in the sense of creating social activities that link individuals to forces of civic power or social change. As immigrants, most of the congregants perceive a loss of community compared to memories of the homeland. Their homeland churches are remembered as having had "organic" relationships with their communities, a relationship that is not natural in South Florida. The social activities these churches have then focus on re-creating this bonding social capital they lost through immigration.

West Indian Pentecostal churches, regardless of their historical common roots, act primarily independently of each other in South Florida. They may share many elements of their theology and style of worship in addition to the congregants' common homeland, and occasionally women join together for revivalist meetings, but socially they are far more isolated from each other than they are united. As a result, their possibilities for building CSC are limited.

The Pentecostals do, nevertheless, embody social relationships that are more than simply spiritual. Their churches are sites of activities that both legitimize and provide human and social capital for advancing individual economic well-being. A theological focus on an individual's relationship to God legitimizes individual pursuit of wealth and simultaneously attenuates and subverts desires to reach out to the community beyond the congregation. An uncompromising belief that their "level of worship" is much higher than that in mainstream churches inscribes theological boundaries that block participation in any trans-denominational or inter-church activities, such as PACT. Contrary to many African American churches, which have historically been politically active, Jamaican Pentecostal churches, and especially the older congregants, hold a deep cynicism toward politics, a cynicism that is further buttressed by Pentecostalism's affirmation of the status quo. Pentecostal theology, encouraged by the leaders we observed, greatly enhances the conversion of cultural capital into social capital. Pierre Bourdieu has argued that the power of this conversion lies precisely in the concealment of the economic motivation and accordingly disguised forms of economic capital (Bourdieu 1986, 252; see also Portes and Landolt 2000, 531; Rey 2004, 333). In this way, social ties within the Pentecostal community have provided individuals, as well as the congregation as a whole, not only with the "goods of salvation" (Bourdieu 1986), but also with the potential to maximize material well-being.

Whereas the Pentecostals' activities we observed do not directly promote CSC, they do contain "seeds" that may eventually lead to greater community involvement. Pentecostalism's theological principles that fuse together the sacred and the secular potentially disencumber the members from the moral injunctions against the instrumental use of religion. Currently, their theology frees them to pursue material resources through their membership in church networks, but it could also legitimize civic involvement if leaders did not so strongly emphasize the acceptance of the social status quo.

The strong initiatives of female West Indian Pentecostals also contain the potential to expand social networks. Female solidarity that stems from their shared experience confronting common problems was the only example that we found of Pentecostals overcoming denominational differences as they joined together in cross-denominational revivals. Actually, among other events organized by the members of Emmanuel Apostolic Church, the Women in Warfare retreat was the only occasion where the researcher encountered participants who were not Pentecostals. Moreover, all the community-based outreach activities, though they had not been activated yet, were planned under the strong initiative of female congregants, such as nursery and prison-visiting programs. The younger generation of Pentecostals who are socialized in the United States also contain the potential for church-based development of CSC. Unlike many second-generation immigrant youth who are alienated from the congregations of their parents, the Pentecostal youth are thoroughly integrated. Church leaders recognize youths' flexibility and mobility, which are likely to push them to bridge impediments and boundaries and move toward establishing wider and closer relationships with community. While the elder generation view these characteristics as potentially hazardous to the church, the younger generation is more likely to view the civic domain as important to assuring their rights as individuals and, thus, their ability to do God's work.

Catholic and Episcopalian West Indian congregants do not have activities that explicitly promote human capital or social capital linked to economic well-being. Instead, they focus on reconstructing the social communities fractured by immigration. Their social activities bond co-nationals and bridge to West Indians in general. They welcome whoever might be interested in a West Indian breakfast, curry, or carnival. Many of the events sponsored by Catholic and Episcopalian churches are also explicitly transnational, bringing in representatives from the home countries. Indeed, the primary result of these events appears to be to embody the imagined national and co-ethnic communities, i.e., to epitomize bonding social capital. The role of religion may be peripheral, as with a Curry-Q, or central, as with a Mass to celebrate Trinidad's national independence. Typically, the activities and the talk surrounding most activities are less religious and more social. Politics, particularly homeland politics, may occupy a small place in the informal discourse that occurs during these events, but it is not central. The events do not encourage participants to engage in any specific civic or political activities. In short, the West Indian Catholics and Episcopalians have the potential for building both individual and social capital. Constructing their imagined homeland communities also contains the potential for transforming these social relations and associated solidarity into CSC, but at this point it is only unrealized potential. While they talk informally of homeland politics, the churches are not the sites of any forceful mobilization of CSC.

Sierra Norwood is an exception. It actively promotes building and using CSC. Moreover, with the exception of its overseas missions, it focuses its civic social activities not on the homeland, but on South Florida, and does so largely through PACT. It also actively incorporates not only West Indians in South Florida, but those from other ethnic groups, too. As a mainstream Protestant church, moreover, it also has ready institutional ties to other churches, and a leader who chooses to use those ties for the production of CSC. Sierra Norwood confirms the literature's emphasis on denomination and leadership. Sierra Norwood's pastor is clearly a critical reason that it so actively promotes CSC. His leadership, combined with the theological orientation and social links to other mainstream Protestant congregations through PACT, produced CSC. Among West Indians, CSC emerged only in this case where a mainstream Protestant denomination combined with a leader who endorsed and enacted CSC. Although Sierra Norwood's pastor struggles to maintain the commitment of his congregation, his congregation has accomplished much more civically, especially in South Florida, than any of the other West Indian congregations in our study.

NOTES

1. By West Indies we mean the Anglophone Caribbean, former colonies and the remaining overseas territories of the United Kingdom. The most important in terms of immigration to the United States are Jamaica, the Bahamas, and Trinidad and Tobago. They also include Anguilla, Antigua and Barbuda, Barbados, Belize (formerly British Honduras), the Cayman Islands, Commonwealth of Dominica, the British Virgin Islands, Grenada, Guyana, Montserrat, St. Kitts and Nevis, St. Vincent and the Grenadines, St. Lucia, and the Turks and Caicos Islands.

2. Teruyuki Tsuji is a native of Japan; Alex Stepick is a native of the United States; Christine Ho is a native of Trinidad.

3. We also include some churches in southern Broward County, which is adjacent to Miami-Dade County, because a concentration of the West Indian population in South Florida straddles the border between the two counties.

4. Outside of the United States, large West Indian immigrant settlements are concentrated especially in London and Toronto (Foner 1985).

5. The Episcopal Church was formally separated from the Church of England in 1789 so that the U.S. clergy would not be required to accept the supremacy of the British monarch. Since the West Indian colonies remained firmly under British rule until the mid-twentieth century, they retained the Anglican name and ties to the Anglican Church of England.

6. According to the Trinidadian 2000 census, religious affiliation is as follows: Anglican, 7.8 percent; Baptist, 7.2 percent; Jehovah's Witness, 1.6 percent; Methodist, 0.9 percent; Pentecostal, 6.8 percent; Presbyterian, 3.29 percent; Roman Catholic, 25.98 percent; Seventh-Day Adventist, 4.0 percent; Hindu, 22.5 percent; Muslim, 5.6 percent; Other, 10.8 percent.

7. The period when Pentecostalism started expanding its influence among the Jamaican poor, in general, and among working-class women, in particular, corresponded to the worst-ever stagnation in the Jamaican economy in the 1920s and 1930s, linked to the decline of the sugar industry as well as to the Great Depression that resulted in massive internal migration from rural to urban areas (Wedenoja 1980).

8. Today the church complex has three separate congregations. Apart from the English-speaking congregation that meets in the main sanctuary, there is a detached chapel (the original church), which houses a mission church offering services in Spanish. In addition, services in Creole with a Haitian pastor ministering to a Haitian congregation are offered on the top floor of the school in the back of the church. The church complex comprises several buildings, including a day-care center, a preschool, and a school that goes up to third grade.

REFERENCES

Austin-Broos, D. J. 1999. Pentecostal Community and Jamaican Hierarchy. In *Religion, Diaspora, and Cultural Identity*, ed. J. Pulis, 215–245. Amsterdam, The Netherlands: Gordon and Breach Publishers.

Bilby, K. 1999. Neither Here nor There: The Place of "Community" in the Jamaican Religious Imagination. In *Religion, Diaspora, and Cultural Identity*, ed. J. Pulis, 311–351. Amsterdam, The Netherlands: Gordon and Breach Publishers.

Bourdieu, P. 1986. Forms of Capital. In *Handbook of Theory and Research for the Sociology of Education*, ed. J. G. Richardson, 241–258. New York: Greenwood Press.

Burton, R. D. E. 1997. *Afro-Creole: Power, Opposition, and Play in the Caribbean*. Ithaca, NY: Cornell University Press.

Charles, J. 2001. West Indians Lead Black Growth. *Miami Herald*.

Ebaugh, H. R., J. O'Brien, and J. S. Chafetz. 2000. The Social Ecology of Residential Patterns and Membership in Immigrant Churches. *Journal for the Scientific Study of Religion* 39(1, March): 107–116.

Elliott, A. 2001. South Florida's Caribbean Population Has Almost Doubled. *Miami Herald*.

Erickson, T. H. 1990. Liming in Trinidad: The Art of Doing Nothing. *Folk* 32: 23–43.

Foner, N. 1985. Race and Color: Jamaican Migrants in London and New York City. *International Migration Review* 19(4, winter): 708–727.

———. 1998. West Indian Identity in the Diaspora: Comparative and Historical Perspectives. *Latin American Perspectives* 26, (3, issue 100): 173–188.

———, ed. 2001. *Islands in the City: West Indian Migration to New York*. Berkeley: University of California Press.

Kasinitz, P. 1992. *Caribbean New York: Black Immigrants and the Politics of Race*. Ithaca, NY: Cornell University Press.

Kasinitz, P., J. Battle, and I. Myares. 2001. Fade to Black? The Children of West Indian Immigrants in Southern Florida. In *Ethnicities: Children of Immigrants in America*, ed. R. Rumbaut and A. Portes, 267–300. Berkeley: University of California Press.

Kasinitz, P., and M. Vikerman. 1998. Ethnic Niches and Racial Traps: Jamaicans in the New York Regional Economy. In *Migration, Transnationalization, and Race in a Changing*

New York, ed. H. R. Cordero-Guzman, R. C. Smith, and R. Grosfoguel, 191–211. Philadelphia, PA: Temple University Press.

Portes, A., and P. Landolt. 2000. Social Capital: Promise and Pitfalls of Its Role in Development. *Journal of Latin American Studies* 32(2): 529–547.

Rey, T. 2004. Marketing the Goods of Salvation: Bourdieu on Religion. *Religion* 34: 331–343.

Rogozinski, J. 1992. *A Brief History of the Caribbean: From the Arawak and the Carib to the Present.* New York: Meridian.

U.S. Bureau of the Census. 1990. Census of Population and Housing, 1990: Summary Tape File 3 on CD-ROM. Prepared by the Bureau of the Census. Washington: Bureau, 1992.

Waters, M. C. 1994. Ethnic and Racial Identities of Second-Generation Black Immigrants in New York City. *International Migration Review* 28(4, winter): 795–820.

———. 1999. *West Indian Immigrant Dreams and American Realities.* Cambridge, MA: Harvard University Press.

Wedenoja, W. 1980. Modernization and the Pentecostal Movement in Jamaica. In *Perspectives on Pentecostalism: Case Studies from the Caribbean and Latin America*, ed. S. D. Glazier, 27–48. Washington, DC: University Press of America.

11

Religious Practice and Civic Social Capital among Miami Youth

YVES LABISSIERE, ANN REEDER GORACZKO, AND ALEX STEPICK

I wouldn't say that I liked the church when I was over there [Mexico]. I would just go to Mass on Sunday. I think it wasn't until I got here that I began to get involved in the church.

—Victor, a first-generation Mexican immigrant youth

The previous chapters in this book focus on particular immigrant and native minority congregations. This chapter assumes a complementary perspective through the examination of a large cross-section of Miami youth to assess the relationship between their religious practice and civic social capital (CSC). We focus on youth, and particularly immigrant youth, for two reasons. First, the impact of immigration on the United States is not solely immediate but is also expressed in the longer term by immigrant youth who mature into adults in the United States. Second, while the literature reviewed in the first chapter demonstrates the central role that religious institutions play in meeting both the spiritual and material needs of their immigrant members, most of these studies have a focus on immigrant adults. While the literature on adults leads us to hypothesize that immigrant youth will also have a high level of religious participation, few studies have empirically examined the religious lives of the children of immigrants.

The literature on immigrant youth describes a well-established dynamic: when children begin to absorb and express U.S. cultural norms and values, they often clash with their immigrant parents, who may associate their children's behaviors with immorality and U.S. secularism (Portes and Rumbaut 2001; Stepick, Dutton Stepick, et al. 2001). For many first-generation immigrants, secularism often amounts to a loss of cultural identity and a wholesale rejection of their heritage. In an effort to mitigate this loss, immigrants often rely on their places of worship to develop programs for their children that emphasize the importance of faith, encourage religious involvement, and maintain and rein-force cultural knowledge (Warner and Wittner 1998; Stepick and Dutton Stepick 2002; Stepick 2005; Portes and Rumbaut 2006).

Do these parental efforts work? Are the children of immigrants religiously engaged? Is their engagement any different from that of native-born Americans? More specifically, do parents' concerns about their children's secularization result in immigrant youths' religious participation being insular, focused chiefly on promoting and reproducing their home country beliefs and culture and not linking them to the broader society? In the theoretical terms of this book, does the religious participation of immigrant youth result in their having lower repositories of CSC? Do immigrant youth in South Florida have relatively low levels of engagement in civic activities and few links to the broader society?

This chapter addresses the connections between religious practice and CSC for a sample of college freshmen in South Florida. As college freshman, these youth are on the brink of independence and adulthood, yet they remain close to their adolescent years when they were more fully under parental control. As such, they provide an opportune population for assessing the CSC of the children of immigrants. Analytically, we proceed, first, by quantifying and exploring religious practice among this sample of youth; next, by examining the effects that religious practice has on various forms of CSC; and, finally, because we want to know how immigrant youth may differ from others, we compare immigrants' and non-immigrants' religious practices and beliefs. The literature also indi-cates that religious affiliation affects civic engagement. Accordingly, we contrast the sample's three major religious types: Protestants, Catholics, and unaffili-ated. Relevant to the preceding chapters in this volume, we compare African Americans, Cubans, Nicaraguans, Mexicans, and Jamaicans.

Who Are These Youth?

In the fall of 2001, we administered an extensive survey to the freshman English classes at Florida International University (FIU), the state university of Florida in Miami. At that time, FIU had a total student population of over thirty-two thou-sand. While FIU has students from outside of Florida (3 percent from most of the fifty U.S. states) and outside the United States (another 9 percent from more than 130 countries), the student body is primarily from South Florida (88 per-cent). Consequently, it reflects the diversity of Miami-Dade County with nearly 70 percent of student enrollment from minority groups, including a Latino stu-dent majority of 55.7 percent and another 12.9 percent Black.[1]

Our sample survey consisted of 1,334 respondents who were broadly repre-sentative of the general FIU population and the surrounding Miami-Dade County. The typical respondent is more likely to have been born in the United States than the general Miami-Dade population, which has the highest foreign-born population of any U.S. county. Nevertheless, about the same percentage of the sample are of immigrant origins, i.e., either first generation, one-and-one-half-generation, or second generation, as the general Miami-Dade County population. The one-and-one-half-generation youth are those who are foreign-born but migrated to the United States when young, in this case less than twelve years of age. The second-generation youth are those who have at least one parent who was foreign-born.

Many of FIU's students are first-generation college students. Only 22 percent of their fathers and 23 percent of their mothers have a college degree. This is still higher than in the surrounding county, the state, or the United States overall. Similarly, the median family household income for this sample is higher than that in the county, state, or United States. In short, the sample has immigrant origins, is ethnically comparable to Miami-Dade County, and is slightly better off socioeconomically than the surrounding county.[2]

The 253-item survey focused on religion-related activities and opinions, civic engagement, and demographic and other background characteristics.[3] Concerning religion, the survey asked about church attendance, activities done at or through church, importance of church in one's life, reasons for attending church, and if the respondent attended the same church as family or friends, along with the Duke University Religion Index (DUREL) (Hood and Hill 1999) and Hoge's Intrinsic Religious Motivation Scale (Hood and Hill 1999). From these questions, we created measures of church attendance, church involvement style, and church commitment. For civic engagement, we asked about participation on 26 items, first in high school and then since attending college. For each item, the respondent indicated whether they participated in these activities very often, often, sometimes, rarely, once, or never. In this chapter, we focus on variables relating to beliefs and practices of religion and those concerning civic engagement, plus various demographic variables.

Throughout this chapter, we complement the survey results with data derived from ethnographic work that we have done with adolescents. The specific quotes that exemplify the survey results below are drawn primarily from focus groups done with high school students slightly before the survey was administered.

Religious Practices

Most college freshmen, both nationwide and among our sample in South Florida, are religious. Significant majorities believe in God (90 percent), spend time in prayer (70 percent), and both attend church (74 percent) and practice their faith at home (70 percent). South Florida's college youth are slightly less attached to religious institutions than similar youth across the country, but a higher proportion have faith as expressed by a belief in God (90 percent versus 79 percent for a national sample of college freshmen (Sax et al. 2001).

Our sample youth are less likely to attend church than youth nationwide (74 percent versus 81 percent). Some are skeptical of church, such as Amber, a first-generation Nigerian student who explained, "I like the more personal relationship with God. I talk about God and everything, but some people feel that in order to be a Christian you have to go to church. But I think there's more bad people going to church than out on the street." Others, such as Georgette, a second-generation Cuban immigrant student, are less skeptical but adopt a personal religious perspective without a reliance on the institution of church: "I think you can pray anywhere. You can call upon God in the way you believe and the way you are. Like going to church is more like a support group. Everybody is together and you believe the same thing and helping each other out with the same faith." Robert, a first-generation Colombian immigrant student, ignores institutional religion even more and states, "You can pray by yourself. You don't have to go every Sunday to church."

Nevertheless, nearly three-fourths of our sample attend church at least sometimes, even if only one-third do so weekly. For that one-third, church can be central to their lives, as Clifford, a West Indian immigrant student explains, "My friend, right, he used to be bad and stuff. Then he got to know God, so now he's going to church every day. Now he's trying to bring me to church every day." Similarly, Edner, a first-generation Haitian student, credited religion with being the most important influence in his life: "I never thought I'd graduate high school, 'cause I didn't like high school. But thanks [to] God, I did. I learned how to pray. I learned a lot of stuff. I learned about helping people. I learned more about God, too."

Is immigrant youth's commitment to church any different from that of non-immigrant youth in South Florida? We constructed an overall measure of Church Commitment that includes frequency of church attendance, service activities performed for the church, and how important the respondent ranks church is in his or her life. By this measure, all of the immigrant generations demonstrate greater Church Commitment than non-immigrants. The difference between first-generation immigrants and non-immigrants is especially large (3.07 versus 2.80), while the one-and-one-half- and second-generation immigrants are intermediate in Church Commitment and relatively close to each other. Thus, the more one is socialized in the United States (as reflected in immigrant generations), the less one becomes committed to church.

In our survey, females are consistently more committed to church than males. In fact, the differences between males and females are more dramatic than those among immigrant generations or between immigrants and non-immigrants. The lowest church-committed female group, those of a non-immigrant background, still has a higher average of Church Commitment than the highest church-committed male group, first-generation immigrants (2.94 for female non-immigrants versus 2.89 for male first-generation immigrants). This finding agrees with the literature, which consistently reports higher rates of church attendance among females in general, and especially among African

American females, than among their male counterparts (Ellison 1992; Levin, Taylor, and Chatters 1994).

Not surprisingly, those who profess to be unaffiliated with any religion, almost by definition, demonstrate less religious commitment than those who profess either Protestant or Catholic affiliation. A more substantively important finding is the difference between Catholics and Protestants. Not only is our constructed variable, Church Commitment, higher for Protestants (3.55 versus 2.94 for Catholics), but also Protestants are much more likely than Catholics to assert that religion affects their day-to-day lives.

African Americans, a group wholly comprised of non-immigrants, have the highest proportion who identify as Protestants, nearly 90 percent. Accordingly, we found that statistically significant differences also exist between ethnic groups. African Americans have the highest Church Commitment of all the ethnic groups (3.92). Ethnicity, however, is not a perfect proxy for Church Commitment, though race certainly may be. Haitians, a primarily Black Catholic group, rank just below African Americans in their Church Commitment (3.41). African Americans and Haitians were also the most likely to report that religion affects their day-to-day lives. The other mostly Black group, Jamaicans, demonstrates the third-highest Church Commitment (3.27). All of the Black groups, namely, African Americans, Haitians, and Jamaicans, thus demonstrate higher Church Commitment than any of the Latino groups, i.e., Nicaraguans (3.22), Cubans (3.02), or "other Latinos" (2.90). At the other end of the scale, European Americans (2.51) fall notably below all other groups in terms of their Church Commitment.

Thus far the data establishes that religion and religious participation are important in the lives of the youth in our sample population for everyone except the minority (9 percent) who claim no religious affiliation. First-generation immigrants, females, Black ethnic groups, and Protestants are the most religiously committed.

Previous research consistently indicates that religious involvement correlates with numerous forms of civic engagement, including community service (Youniss, McLellan and Yates 1999), voting, and other forms of civic involvement (Serow and Dreyden 1990). Religious involvement also reportedly contributes to a range of healthy outcomes that include life satisfaction, academic achievement (Muller and Ellison 2001), effective coping (Balk 1991), and low drug and alcohol usage (Cochran 1993). We anticipated, therefore, that religious commitment and practice would be associated with increased CSC among the youth in the sample.

Civic Social Capital

We conceive of participation in the twenty-six political, service, and social activities listed on the questionnaire as potentially contributing to overall CSC.

Following and slightly altering another study (Keeter et al. 2002), we have grouped CSC activities into three types: political, bridging service, and social. Political activities include registering to vote,[4] discussing politics, attending a demonstration, being a club officer, and seeking information on current events through newspapers or the Internet. These activities conform to a narrow definition of civic engagement. They do not easily fit the distinctions between bonding, bridging, and linking social capital since some, such as registering to vote or seeking information, do not require significant social interaction. Bridging service activities are those designed to help other people individually or through formal service organizations and programs. Because Miami is such a heavily immigrant area, we included in this list a number of activities specifically related to immigrants, such as helping a non-English speaker. The category of social activities extends that study (Keeter et al. 2002)[5] to incorporate types of activities relevant to Robert Putnam's interest in the social aspects of community (Putnam 1993). Social activities are those that are generally excluded in discussions of civic engagement. We include them first to provide a context for the overall activities in which these youth engage, but also because some of them do fit an extended definition of civic engagement, such as participating in sports and attending church.

South Florida high schools have followed the current national trend of required community service activities as a pre-requisite to graduation. Seventy-five percent of the college freshmen reported having had some form of a community service requirement in high school. Accordingly, most FIU freshmen spent some time during their high school years engaged in a service project to benefit their school or some part of the broader community. The range of experiences and, especially, the students' reactions to and evaluations of them are remarkably diverse. Table 11.1 indicates what percentage of the sample participated in each type of activity during high school either very frequently or frequently. Since the freshmen had only been in college for a few months when we administered the survey, we do not include here their college activities. The sample appears to be highly active in all three realms. Over 90 percent discussed politics with family or friends. Over 87 percent had engaged in volunteer or community service. And a majority belonged to an ethnic club. Yet closer examination reveals a more nuanced profile.

Bridging Service Activities

Table 11.1 indicates that nearly 90 percent of the college freshmen volunteered or performed community service during high school. Much of this activity, however, may not be completely voluntary as it stems from a high school community service requirement. Some students were utterly negative, many expressed mixed reactions, and some spoke positively of their high school community service. Patrick, a second-generation Haitian immigrant student, explained,

TABLE 11.1

Bridging Service, Political, and Social Activities of College Freshmen When in High School

	% who participated frequently or very frequently
Bridging service activities	
Volunteered or did community service	87.1
Tutored someone	77.5
Helped non-English speaker write	75.2
Helped senior citizens	74.7
Participated in community fund-raiser	70.5
Helped someone who can't read	48.6
Helped a recent immigrant	44.3
Donated blood	36.6
Political activities	
Discussed politics with family/friends	90.3
Used Internet for current events/news	90.2
Read a newspaper for current events	86.8
Participated in organized demonstrations	65.3
Was officer of club/student government	46.6
Registered to vote	46.1
Social activities	
Had friends over to your home	97.9
Visited relatives	96.7
Hung out with other ethnic/racial group member	94.0
Ran errands for relatives	89.2
Attended church/other religious activity	83.9
Participated in athletic activities	81.6
Attended family reunions	77.3
Watched over younger siblings	62.8
Was active in ethnic club	53.1

"We weren't doing anything in class, so I had to do something that would take up my time. A lot of the [service] stuff was stuff that interested me anyway. I don't ever remember doing too much in high school. I don't remember having homework in high school. I don't remember any of that. I just remember going there and having fun. The reason why I had fun was because I was in all these different [service] groups. I knew all these different people, so I was always doing something different. I used to look forward to going to school because I knew I was going to have fun." Similarly, Julio, a first-generation Cuban immigrant student, indicated, "Yeah, everybody liked it, 'cause, I mean, it was fun. You show up to the meetings and then you go out. On a Sunday you would go out to Key Biscayne and pick up trash [on the beach] or we would go to the dog pound to feed the animals, walk the animals. So it was cool. It was a nice thing to do, and you would get community service out of it." Jamal, a first-generation West Indian, added, "Participating is very important. I guess I wish I did more of it. I didn't realize how important it was. You are able to, in a way, get out of class a lot, see the world a lot, experience things, and you meet other people. If you're a shy type of person this is perfect."

On the other hand, some students, referring to precisely the same activities, expressed their resentment of the community service requirement. Ramon, a second-generation Cuban, proclaimed, "I needed some community service by the end of the year, 'cause I hadn't done anything. . . . But I never did anything, 'cause it was like go to the beach and clean stuff! I'm not gonna go to the beach and clean stuff. That's stupid!" When we asked Luvy, a second-generation Haitian, to explain the acronym of one organization, DYFYIT, a school-based drug-prevention program, she responded, "I don't know! I don't know nothing about DYFYIT! We were just in there 'cause they would take us to field trips and stuff. That's all it was about."

Regardless of their motivations, the majority of the sample engaged in some form of service activity beyond fulfilling their high school community service requirement, including helping senior citizens, tutoring others, and helping a non-English speaker write something—an activity commonly needed in Miami, where more than one-half the population speaks a language other than English at home. As Gladys, a second-generation Cuban student, explained, "For half of the year we went to Coral Park Elementary. We helped the LD [learning disabled] kids learn math and English and stuff they had problems with. That was cool. I liked that. Yeah, I helped this one girl. She was hurting herself physically. She was like burning herself. She would talk to me a lot. It makes me feel better. I feel bad if I do something selfishly. If I know I could have helped somebody, and I didn't, it doesn't make me feel good." Midchi, a first-generation Haitian, even joined a predominantly Latino club, Aspira, so that she would have more opportunity to provide service: "I always had this in my mind: if I am in any club, I will be helping people. Aspira is helping people in a way and helping yourself in another way."

To analyze bridging service activities, we created a summary index that summed up each individual's participation in bridging service activities. We then calculated the mean for each subgroup of gender, immigrant generation, denomination, and ethnicity. Within these categories, we found the highest average of Bridging Service Activities was among females (15.9), non-immigrants (15.4), Catholics (15.1), and Cubans (15.8). As with Church Commitment, females had the highest average of any subgroup. Unlike in Church Commitment, however, Protestants, immigrants, and the different Black ethnic groups are not the other highest subgroups. Latinos, who are primarily Catholic, have a higher average in Bridging Service Activities than any of the Black ethnic groups or the European American group. Nicaraguans and Cubans were especially likely to help immigrants, most frequently helping a non-English speaker to write. Nicaraguans especially stood out with 80 percent helping non-English speakers, compared to over 60 percent for Cubans. Among Haitians also, 50 percent helped non-English speakers, and this contributed to them having the highest average in Bridging Service Activities of the Black groups. In short, young immigrants who are non-native speakers of English perform significant service to fellow immigrants who have yet to learn English.

Political Activities

As reflected in table 11.1, nearly two-thirds of the sample indicated that they had participated in a political demonstration of some kind. This relatively high percentage, however, was affected by the timing of the survey. During what was, for most of the respondents, their senior year of high school, Miami was the epicenter of a dramatic 2000–2001 political struggle over the custody of Elián Gonzalez, the six-year-old Cuban boy who survived a raft trip to Miami while his mother drowned and his father remained in Cuba. The Miami Cuban community insisted that Elián remain in Miami rather than return to Cuba. Fidel Castro along with Elián's father equally adamantly insisted that the boy should be reunited with his father in Cuba. For months, demonstrations enveloped Miami and seized national attention (Acosta 2001; De La Torre 2003; Stepick, Grenier, et al. 2003).

Before the arrival of Elián, most of the Latino youth whom we had been studying ethnographically had been politically disengaged. They tended to demean and dismiss their parents' and grandparents' obsessions with Castro and Cuba as irrelevant to their lives. The controversy surrounding Elián, however, captured their attention and morphed many of their opinions. Ronald, a second-generation Cuban student, noted, "Like with Elián, that's when you hear about everything. That's when things start like surfacing. . . . But, like that was completely and totally out of proportion because all it would show in the news was people, you know, setting trash cans on fire, getting in fights with the cops. When you see stuff like that and it's about you, you realize that, you know, they wanted to make us look like the angry Cubans. Right? To make everybody hate us." Like many other Latinos, Ronald suddenly felt as if he was perceived as different and that perception prompted political engagement. Ronald and other youth frequented the daily demonstrations in front of the house where Elián stayed. While a few claimed that others were there just to check out the girls (or boys), all the youth with whom we spoke were there to express their solidarity. Ramon, another second-generation Cuban student, explained, "It was like a feeling that this was wrong, and what can be done to show that this is not just going to be accepted by the [Cuban community]?"

As Table 11.1 indicates, these South Florida college freshmen generally attempt to stay informed on current events and news, with over 80 percent reading the newspaper and over 90 percent using the Internet to access information. Over 90 percent also reported that they discuss politics with family or friends. On the other hand, just over 46 percent registered to vote. Nadege, a first-generation Haitian, reflects a relatively cynical political assessment: "I mean, I think y'all's vote don't change anything. The decision is already made. It's just like a game you know." Erica, an African American, also expressed little faith in the power of the vote: "I ain't fixin' to vote for somebody and then when they get in office they be messing up, you know. I'll be mad. I'd be saying, "Dang, if I wouldn't have voted they wouldn't have won." Well, probably they would've won anyways. But still, they be lying and I don't know why should I vote for them. So I be like, forget about it. So I just don't vote."

Notwithstanding Nadege's and Erica's opinions, females were slightly more politically active than males. Females also were more likely to have been an officer of a club or to have taken part in a demonstration, although females and males were equally likely to be registered to vote. These gender differences persisted in college activities, too.

Immigrants were not any different from non-immigrants according to the Political Activities summary index we constructed. While non-immigrants had a slightly higher average on this index, it was not significantly different from any of the immigrant groups. In short, in terms of the most narrow definition of civic engagement, i.e., political activities and staying informed, immigrants and the native-born were equal.

We did find that Protestants and Catholics had a notably higher average Political Activities summary index than those who were not religiously affiliated. Protestants were more likely to be registered to vote with over 47 percent registered, compared to just over 40 percent for both Catholics and nondenominationally affiliated respondents. This population of college youth thus conforms to the literature finding that religious affiliation is related to a narrow definition of civic engagement. Nevertheless, all of the denominational groups (i.e., Protestants, Catholics, and those not affiliated) are equally likely to be politically informed, and all are more or less equally likely to have participated in a demonstration. Thus, although being religious increases political civic engagement, it does not matter, at least for this group of college freshmen, the kind of religion in which one is engaged.

Among ethnic groups, African Americans have the highest average political activities index. Over 60 percent of African Americans are registered to vote and more than 80 percent discussed politics with family and friends. Chenel, an African American student, asserted, "I just wanna make sure my future is the way I want it to be. And you're not gonna do that if you don't participate in anything. I mean, you hear all the time, the people who didn't vote are the ones complaining. You know, and I don't want that to be me. You know, that's my motivation, my future."

The relatively higher degree of political engagement of African Americans is one of the most significant substantive findings from this survey of South Florida college youth. Cubans are the most powerful group in local politics, and Cuban adults are highly politically engaged locally (Warren and Stack 1986; Moreno and Warren 1992; Stepick and Grenier 1993; Moreno 1997; Warren 1997; Moreno and Hill 1999; Moreno and Warren 1999; Warren and Moreno 2003). Among contemporary immigrant groups, Cubans have high rates of becoming citizens and voting once they are eligible. For the past forty years, Cubans in Miami have politically overshadowed African Americans and Haitians. Although not an absolute majority, Cubans are locally the single largest ethnic group. Their political dominance is thus unlikely to change with any speed even if the younger generation, like the college students that we surveyed, appears to be less engaged than their elders. The relatively high political engagement of African American youth indicates, however, that their voices are likely to be raised and heard. In contrast, this data indicates that the political power of Nicaraguans and West Indians is not likely to increase as youth come of age. While Nicaraguans informally helped each other, as reflected in their service activities, and a significant proportion of West Indians engaged in at least tutoring, neither of these two groups, at least judging by this sample, engaged in significant political activities.

Social Activities

Central to the notion of social capital are social relations, particularly social relations that can instrumentally lead to a material result such as finding a job. Putnam's conception of social capital emphasizes the group benefits of social relations, rather than the individual benefits, such as finding a job, associated with the sociological use of social capital (cf. Putnam 1993 and Portes 1998). Yet most work influenced by Putnam focuses on social relationships that are immediately linked to civic engagement, i.e., those kinds of activities we have covered in bridging service activities and political activities. For youth, such as the college freshmen we surveyed, relationships that appear to be solely self- or family-centered may potentially lead to activities that have political or service results. Translating for one's grandmother, for example, may be motivated solely by a sense of family responsibility, but it can produce an awareness of the needs of others and the ability of one to address those needs. Similarly, while Putnam (2000) may lament the decline of participation in various voluntary organizations from unions to PTAs, attending family reunions or a youth church group may have a similar ultimate effect upon one's sense of community. Accordingly, to obtain a more complete view of these youth's civically related activities, our questionnaire included social activities ignored by those who study solely political and bridging service activities.

During their high school careers, a majority of the college freshman engaged in each of the social activities on the list. As reflected in table 11.1, the largest majorities engaged in peer group activities, such as having friends over, "hanging out" with people of the same ethnic or racial group, or athletic activities. Clyford, a first-generation Haitian student, noted, "Being on the soccer team was like being around a family." Indeed, significant majorities engaged in family activities, such as running errands, attending family reunions, and watching over younger siblings, an activity commonly mentioned in the literature as required of immigrant youth, especially females (M. Suárez-Orozco 1987, 1989; Suárez-Orozco and Suárez-Orozco 1995; Stanton-Salazar 2001; C. Suárez-Orozco 2001; Fuligni and Pedersen 2002).

We constructed a summary index for social activities with averages overall and for subgroups. The social activities category is the one case where males' activities outpace females' activities. Statistically, males are more socially engaged than females, whereas males had statistically significantly lower bridging service and political activities. Specifically, males are more likely to engage in athletic activity in high school, although the majority of females did, too, but to a lesser extent. Also, college males are more likely to be in a fraternity than females are to be in a sorority.

Differences among other subgroups were very small and statistically insignificant. The religiously affiliated, for example, are not any less likely to engage in secular social activities such as athletics or joining an ethnic club. The religiously unaffiliated, however, are an exception. They engage in significantly fewer social activities, similar to their lower than average bonding service and political activities. While European Americans were most likely to be religiously unaffiliated, they do not have the lowest average level of social activities. Thus, being religiously unaffiliated and being European American are not proxies for each other. Regardless of ethnicity, the religiously unaffiliated have the lowest levels of all three types of activities, political, bonding service, and social ones. They are clearly less engaged on all dimensions.

Nicaraguans are the only ethnic subgroup that is statistically significantly different from the others. Likely for cultural reasons that are noted in Aidil

Oscariz's chapter on Our Lady of Divine Providence Catholic Church, Nicaraguans have the lowest level of social activities. Nicaraguans, however, generally do help other immigrants with English at higher levels than any other ethnic group. This could be re-interpreted as both a social activity and a service activity, in which case Nicaraguans would not be statistically significantly different from other ethnic subgroups.

So far we have demonstrated that the majority of these college freshmen are religious in terms of both their beliefs and their activities and that many of them also engage in significant bridging service, political, and social activities. Our last question is, Do religious belief and, especially, practice relate to other forms of civic social capital?

Linking Religious Practice and Civic Social Capital

Gena and Yvette offer divergent perspectives on the link between religious-based activities and CSC. Gena, a second-generation Haitian student, said, "I was a teacher's assistant. They had Saturday church. I would go and assist and help some of the kids who couldn't read. I would sit next to them and help them read. You know, the little boys that are nervous to talk in class, so I would sit in the back and help them read or help them learn the prayers. Whenever the Sister, which was the main director of the whole organization, she would need help and I would go ahead and help her." Yvette, a second-generation Haitian immigrant student, noted, "We went camping, went on Disney trips. Disney would have this thing, Night of Joy, where you would go and it's all Christian music. We went to Costa Rica. I went twice to Costa Rica for community service projects to build houses and churches and stuff and do VBS [Vocational Bible School] with little kids and stuff. Then you would go to KIC [Kids in Christ] on Thursday nights or Monday. They had different nights for each grade. I mean, you are supposed to be learning about God, but you know how these kids [are] . . . 'cause the attraction is going places, like camping!" Gena and Yvette, articulate opposing explanations of the relationship between religious practices and civic social capital. Gena reflects the conclusion of the broader literature that those who are more involved in religion are also more likely to be civically engaged, in particular, to perform service activities as a direct consequence of religious participation. Yvette, meanwhile, describes her religious participation as producing primarily social results and only secondarily service. Which of these young women most represents the college youth of South Florida?

The survey establishes that young South Florida college students are highly religious and that many engage in bridging service, political, and social activities. Is there a direct relationship between being religious and engaging in these activities? Do those who are more religiously active also have higher levels of bridging service, political, or social activities? Paul Djupe and Tobin Grant

(2001) found, for example, that while civic skills gained at church did not directly affect political participation, religious institutions did bring parishioners into the political process through recruitment and by communicating the connection between church activity and political consequences. Is this also true among South Florida's largely immigrant population of young people?

With survey data, the most common approach to assess the relationship among variables is multiple regression. We calculated multiple regression equations for each of the three types of activities, bridging service, political, and social.[6] We included as independent variables our measure of Church Commitment, which we used earlier in this chapter,[7] along with other variables that either the literature or data indicate are likely to be important in producing civic engagement. These included gender, ethnicity, denomination, and immigrant status. In the analysis, we distinguish Latinos and Blacks, Catholics and Protestants, and immigrants (i.e., first-, one-and-one-half-, and second-generation immigrants) and non-immigrants.[8]

The results of the multiple regression analysis confirm that Church Commitment is critical to civic engagement. For Bridging Service activities, Church Commitment was twice as important as gender or grade point average (GPA) and about four times as important as being an immigrant or child of an immigrant. Being female, a non-immigrant, and having a high GPA all contribute to being more involved in Bridging Service Activities, but Church Commitment is still the most important of all the variables. Parental income, ethnicity, and denomination played no significant role for those we surveyed.

For political CSC activities, Church Commitment stands out even more starkly. It was the only variable that was significant. Gender, GPA, parental income, immigration status, ethnicity, and denomination all made no difference in predicting political activities. Our analysis above on political CSC activities indicated some differences, specifically with African Americans being more politically involved. The multiple regression analysis reveals that African Americans' political CSC activities are actually related to their higher Church Commitment. For African Americans, religion and politics are inseparably intertwined.

Males were more likely to engage in social activities than were females. Church Commitment was also significant; in fact, it was the only other variable that was statistically significant, but it was not as important as gender.

Revisiting Religion and Civic Engagement

The survey of college freshmen in Miami complements the ethnographies of the relationship between religion and civic engagement among Miami youth and largely confirms the ethnographies and other studies of American youth in general. As in the ethnographic chapters for both adults and youth, the college freshmen are highly religious. Moreover, their religious involvement is the single most important factor in promoting civic engagement, a finding also similar to other research (Youniss, McLellan, and Yates 1999).

Other college-age youth in the United States are similar to those in South Florida in matters of church membership, church attendance, faith, and belief (Regnerus, Smith, and Fritsch 2003). Similar to youth in national studies (Sax et al. 2001; Youniss, McLellan, and Mazer 2001), South Florida youth are involved in more volunteer activities than political ones. As is the case nationwide, female youth are both more religious and more engaged in volunteer activities than males (Regnerus, Smith and Fritsch 2003; Dote, Cramer, Dietz and Grimm 2006; Marcelo, Lopez and Kirby 2007). Also consistent with other studies (Regnerus, Smith and Fritsch 2003), African American youth are also both more religious and more civically engaged.

The unique contribution of this chapter is the direct comparison of immigrant and non-immigrant youth. Some commentators expect immigrants to be less civically engaged (Huntington 2004). The South Florida immigrant youth, however, are as engaged as natives. Personal immigration history did not influence either religious practice or civic engagement. Immigrants are slightly, but not statistically significantly, more religious than their non-immigrant peers. Immigrants are slightly less likely to engage in bridging service activities, but they are equally as likely as non-immigrants to be involved in political or social activities. Once young immigrants arrive, they apparently become involved in their churches and in broader civic and social activities statistically as much as their peers who are not of immigrant origin.

Immigration, however, did affect the type of volunteer activities. Immigrant youth took advantage of their particular cultural skills, i.e., knowledge of English and the U.S. system, to help other immigrants. They translated for other immigrants and they tutored extensively. In this sense they were both bonding and bridging. They bonded to other immigrants at the same time they were bridging, often between generations or between themselves and more recently arrived immigrants. They also embody a bridge between the homeland cultures of the immigrants and U.S. culture.

The influence of denomination is mixed. When looked at separately, Protestants were more religiously committed while Catholics engaged in more bridging service activities. The students who claimed that religion turned their or a friend's life around were all Protestants. On the other hand, those who claimed a belief in God but did not think it necessary to attend church were more likely to be Catholic. Yet these denominational differences did not have an impact on bridging service, political, or social activities. Protestants and Catholics were equally likely to be engaged in any of the bridging service activities listed on the survey.

Ethnicity has similarly mixed effects. Our analysis revealed that, similar to national studies (Regnerus, Smith, and Fritsch 2003), all the Black groups demonstrate high levels of both religious and civic engagement. Cubans, however, engaged in slightly more bridging service activities, while African Americans were more involved in political activities, and Nicaraguans were the only group significantly lower in social activities. But all of these differences were insignificant in the multiple regression equations. Their importance was washed out by other variables, most notably Church Commitment. In short, South Florida college freshmen are as religious as the adults and youth depicted in the ethnographic chapters. Immigrants are different from the native-born only in being slightly more religious and using their cultural skills to help other immigrants bridge cultures.

NOTES

1. A more detailed version of this chapter, including all the tables, can be found at http://www.fiu.edu/~iei/index/religion_imm.html.

2. Throughout this chapter, we complement the survey results with data derived from ethnographic work that we have done with adolescents. The previous chapters were based on ethnography specifically focused on religion. Since the mid-1990s we have conducted numerous projects on immigrant and native minority adolescents in South Florida on various topics, including civic engagement, education, ethnic identity, and inter-ethnic interactions (Stepick 1998; Teed 2000; Konczal 2001; Morgan 2001; Stepick and Dutton Stepick 2001a, 2001b, 2002; Stepick, Dutton Stepick, Eugene, et al. 2001; Fernández 2003; Stepick, Grenier, et al. 2003).

3. The questionnaire also incorporated questions from previously validated scales, including the Rosenberg Self-Esteem Scale (1965); various scales created by Jennifer Crocker, et al. (2004), including a Collective Self-Esteem (CSE) Scale, which consists of a Private CSE Scale, a Public CSE Scale, an Importance to Identity CSE Scale, and a Membership CSE Scale; the Personal Threat Scale; the Positive Feelings Toward the US Government Scale; the Support War Scale; and the Attachment to American Values Measure. For greater detail on the survey, see Goraczko (2003).

4. Few actually had an opportunity to vote as the median age of the sample was eighteen and the survey was administered in an off-election year, 2001.

5. Keeter et al. (2002) divide engagement into just two kinds: the political and the civic. For the political they focus on activities that relate to electoral politics. We broaden the definition of political engagement to include activities pertaining to seeking information on current affairs. Keeter et al.'s civic category is roughly equivalent to our service activities. They do not have a category similar to our social engagement.

6. Before correlating these variables, we made one change. Our original scale of social CSC included church-related social activities. To leave this in for our correlation with religious practice would be at least partially circular. We therefore recalculated our measure of social CSC without the church-related activities.

7. We also correlated the measures of activities with other measures of religion. Specifically, we used Church Attendance (which measures frequency of church attendance), Church Involvement Style (a constructed scale that incorporates doing some kind of service for the church), the Duke Religion Index (which assesses church attendance along with prayer or religious study and intrinsic dimensions of religion (Hood and Hill 1999), and the Hoge Intrinsic Religious Motivation Scale (which assesses an individual's psychological impetus for religious participation). All of the measures replicated the results of the correlations with Church Commitment.

8. In the analysis, we also included measures of citizenship and whether someone was foreign-born or not, along with whether an individual had been required in high school to perform community service. None of these were significant. We also examined other forms of immigrant background, such as separating first-, one-and-one-half-, and second-generation immigrants from non-immigrants, but combining first-, one-and-one-half-, and second-generation immigrants produced the most robust results. The full multiple regression analysis can be found at http://www.fiu.edu/~iei/index/religion_imm.html.

REFERENCES

Acosta, I. 2001. Boy Exile Turned Saint: Elián Gonzalez as a Contested Religio-Ideological Symbol among Cuban-American Catholics. Master's thesis, Florida International University.

Balk, D. E. 1991. Sibling Death, Adolescent Bereavement, and Religion. *Death Studies* 15: 1–20.

Cochran, J. K. 1993. The Variable Effects of Religiosity and Denomination on Adolescent Self-Reported Alcohol Use by Beverage Type. *Journal of Drug Issues* 23(3): 479–499.

Crocker, J., R. K. Luhtanen, and S. R. Sommers. 2004. Contingencies of Self-Worth: Progress and Prospects. *European Review of Social Psychology* 15: 133–181.

De La Torre, M. A. 2003. *La Lucha for Cuba: Religion and Politics on the Streets of Miami*. Berkeley: University of California Press.

Djupe, P. A., and J. T. Grant. 2001. Religious Institutions and Political Participation in America. *Journal for the Scientific Study of Religion* 40(2): 303–314.

Dote, L., K. Cramer, N. Dietz, and J. R. Grimm. 2006. *College Students Helping America*. Washington, DC: Office of Research and Policy Development, Corporation for National Community Service.

Ellison, C. G. 1992. Are Religious People Nice People? Evidence from the National Survey of Black Americans. *Social Forces* 71(2): 411–430.

Fernández, P. 2003. Academic Orientations of African American Adolescents in Miami-Dade County. PhD diss., Florida International University.

Fuligni, A. J., and S. Pedersen. 2002. Family Obligation and the Transition to Young Adulthood. *Developmental Psychology* 38(5): 856–868.

Goraczko, A. R. 2003. The Effects of Religious Participation on the Civic Engagement of Children of Immigrants and Immigrant Youth in South Florida. Master's thesis, Florida International University.

Hood, R. W., and P. C. Hill, eds. 1999. *Measures of Religiosity*. Birmingham, AL: Religious Education Press.

Huntington, S. P. 2004. The Hispanic Challenge. *Foreign Policy* 141(March/April): 30–45.

Keeter, S., C. Zukin, M. Andolina, and K. Jenkins. 2002. *The Civic and Political Health of the Nation: A Generational Portrait*. College Park, MD: CIRCLE, Center for Information and Research on Civic Learning and Engagement, University of Maryland.

Konczal, L. 2001. The Academic Orientation of First and Second Generation Nicaraguan Immigrant Adolescents. PhD diss., Florida International University.

Levin, J. S., R. J. Taylor, and L. M. Chatters 1994. Race and Gender Differences in Religiosity among Older Adults: Findings from Four National Surveys. *Journals of Gerontology* 49(3): 137–145.

Marcelo, K. B., M. H. Lopez, and E. H. Kirby. 2007. Civic Engagement among Young Men and Women, Center for Information and Research on Civic Learning and Engagement (CIRCLE), University of Maryland. On-line series, no. 24.

Moreno, D. 1997. Cuban-American Political Empowerment. In *Pursuing Power: Latinos and the Political System*, ed. F. C. Garcia, 208–226. Notre Dame, IN: University of Notre Dame Press.

Moreno, D., and K. Hill. 1999. *The Political Attitude of Young Cubans: Second Generation Cubans.* Miami: Florida International University.

Moreno, D., and C. L. Warren. 1992. The Conservative Enclave: Cubans in Florida. In *Latinos in the 1988* Elections, ed. R. de la Garza, 169–184. Boulder, CO: Westview Press.

———. 1999. Pragmatism and Strategic Realignment in the 1996 Election: Florida's Cuban Americans. In *Awash in the Mainstream: Latino Politics in the 1996* Elections, ed. R. O. de la Garza and L. DeSipio, 211–237. Boulder, CO: Westview.

Morgan, J. 2001. Un-Equal Opportunity: Sex and School among First and Second Generation Mexican Immigrant Adolescent Girls. PhD diss., Florida International University.

Muller, C., and C. G. Ellison. 2001. Religious Involvement, Social Capital, and Adolescents' Academic Progress: Evidence from the National Education Longitudinal Study of 1988. *Sociological Focus* 34(2): 155–183.

Portes, A. 1998. Social Capital: Its Origins and Applications in Modern Sociology. *Annual Reviews in Sociology* 24: 1–24.

Portes, A., and R. Rumbaut. 2001. *Legacies: The Story of the Immigrant Second Generation.* Berkeley and New York: University of California Press and Russell Sage Foundation.

———. 2006. *Immigrant America: A Portrait.* Berkeley: University of California Press.

Putnam, R. D. 1993. The Prosperous Community: Social Capital and Public Life. *American Prospect* 13: 35–42.

———. 2000. *Bowling Alone: The Collapse and Revival of American Community.* New York: Simon & Schuster.

Regnerus, M., C. Smith, and M. Fritsch. 2003. *Religion in the Lives of American Adolescents: A Review of the Literature.* A research report of the National Study of Youth and Religion. Chapel Hill, NC: National Study of Youth and Religion, University of North Carolina and Chapel Hill.

Rosenberg, M. 1965. *Society and the Adolescent Self-Image.* Princeton, NJ: Princeton University Press.

Sax, L. J., J. A. Lindholm, A. W. Astin, W. S. Korn, and K. M. Mahoney. 2001. *The American Freshman: National Norms for Fall 2001.* Los Angeles, CA: Higher Education Research Institute, UCLA Graduate School of Education & Information Studies.

Serow, R. C., and J. I. Dreyden. 1990. Community Service among College and University Students: Individual and Institutional Relationships. *Adolescence* 25(99): 553–566.

Stanton-Salazar, R. D. 2001. *Manufacturing Hope and Despair: The School and Kin Support Networks of U.S.-Mexican Youth.* New York and London: Teachers College Press.

Stepick, A. 1998. *Pride against Prejudice: Haitians in the United States.* Boston: Allyn & Bacon.

———. 2005. God Is Apparently Not Dead. The Obvious, the Emergent, and the Unknown in Immigration and Religion. In *Immigrant Faiths: Transforming Religious Life in America*, ed. K. Leonard, A. Stepick, M. A. Vasquez. and J. Holdaway, 11–37. Lanham, MD: Alta Mira Press.

Stepick, A., and C. Dutton Stepick. 2001a. *Generation X Speaks Out on Censuses, Surveys and Civic Engagement: An Ethnographic Approach, the Case of Miami.* Miami: Immigration & Ethnicity Institute, Florida International University.

———. 2001b. Power and Identity: Miami Cubans. In *Latinos: The Research Agenda*, ed. M. Suarez-Orozco and C. Suarez-Orozco, 75–92. Berkeley: University of California Press.

———. 2002. Becoming American, Constructing Ethnicity: Immigrant Youth and Civic Engagement. *Applied Developmental Science* 6(4): 246–257.

Stepick, A., C. Dutton Stepick, E. Eugene, D. Teed, and Y. Labissiere. 2001. Shifting Identities and Inter-Generational Conflict: Growing Up Haitian in Miami. In *Ethnicities: Children of Immigrants in America*, ed. R. Rumbaut and A. Portes, 229–266. Berkeley and New York: University of California Press and Russell Sage Foundation.

Stepick, A., and G. Grenier. 1993. Cubans in Miami. In *In the Barrios: Latinos and the Underclass Debate*, ed. J. Moore and R. Rivera, 79–100. New York: Russell Sage Foundation.

Stepick, A., G. Grenier, M. Castro, and M. Dunn. 2003. *This Land Is Our Land: Interethnic Relations in Miami*. Berkeley: University of California Press.

Suárez-Orozco, C. 2001. Immigrant Families and Their Children: Adaptation and Identity Formation. In *The Blackwell Companion to Sociology*, ed. J. R. Blau, 128–139. Malden, MA: Blackwell.

Suárez-Orozco, C., and M. M. Suárez-Orozco. 1995. *Transformations: Migration, Family Life, and Achievement Motivation among Latino and White Adolescents*. Stanford, CA: Stanford University Press.

Suárez-Orozco, M. M. 1987. Hispanic Americans: Comparative Considerations and the Educational Problems of Children. *International Migration* 25(2): 141–164.

———. 1989. *Central American Refugees and U.S. High Schools: A Psychosocial Study of Motivation and Achievement*. Stanford, CA: Stanford University Press.

Teed, D. 2000. Voices at the Shore: Ethnolinguistic Identity among Adolescent Haitian Students. PhD diss., Florida International University.

Warner, R. S., and J. G. Wittner, eds. 1998. *Gatherings in Diaspora: Religious Communities and the New Immigration*. Philadelphia: Temple University Press.

Warren, C. L. 1997. Hispanic Incorporation and Structural Reform in Miami. In *Racial Politics in American Cities*, ed. R. P. Browning, D. R. Marshall, and D. H. Tabb, 223–246. New York: Longman Publishers.

Warren, C., and D. Moreno. 2003. Power without a Program: Hispanic Incorporation in Miami. In *Racial Politics in American Cities*, ed. R. P. Browning, D. R. Marshall, and D. H. Tabb, 281–308. New York: Longman Publishers.

Warren, C. L., and J. F. Stack Jr. 1986. Immigration and the Politics of Ethnicity and Class in Metropolitan Miami. In *The Primordial Challenge: Ethnicity in the Modern World*, ed. J. F. Stack Jr., 61–79. Westport, CT: Greenwood Press.

Youniss, J., J. A. McLellan, and B. Mazer. 2001. Voluntary Service, Peer Group Orientation, and Civic Engagement. *Journal of Adolescent Research* 16(5): 456–468.

Youniss, J., J. A. McLellan, and M. Yates. 1999. Religion, Community Service, and Identity in American Youth. *Journal of Adolescence* 22(2): 243–253.

12

Conclusions

Religious Leadership and Civic Social Capital

ALEX STEPICK, SARAH J. MAHLER, AND TERRY REY

Through case studies of Christian congregations and a survey of college fresh-men, this volume has examined the relationships between civic engagement and religion for immigrants and African Americans. Through the concept of civic social capital (CSC), it most fundamentally addresses these relationships within the context of the social and cultural transformation of U.S. society in the wake of the largest influx of immigrants in its history.

CSC focuses on social capital that specifically ties individuals to the larger civic society in which they are embedded. We created this concept to overcome what we view as deficiencies in the ways others have extended but also muddled the notion of social capital. For sociologists, the concept is an extension of econ-omists' notions of financial and human capital. The original and still primary use of social and the other forms of capital has been to explain individual eco-nomic achievement. The political scientist Robert Putnam, however, employed the same phrase but theorized it fundamentally differently. His formulation emphasized the social capital of communities, not individuals; and he was more concerned with the general civic life of a community than with economic achievement. We share Putnam's interest in civic relations, but we seek to develop a concept that avoids the communalistic pitfalls of his application of the term "social capital." In this vein we employ the term "civic social capital" (CSC) largely to shift focus away from social capital's emphasis on economic benefits to individuals toward activities that are civic.

Since this is a volume of primarily ethnographic studies and the first attempt to analyze civic social capital, we employed a broad, inclusive definition of "civic" activities, one not limited only to participation in electoral politics. We have sought to reveal empirically a range of civic relationships and, in par-ticular, to understand why some congregations turn inward and others reach out. That is, while congregations are known to generate bonding social capital to help members deal with their problems, we were particularly interested in understanding what causes congregations to engage in activities that bridge and link them to people and institutions beyond themselves. In this chapter, we integrate the findings of the empirical chapters to construct theoretical generalizations concerning the relationships between civic engagement and religion for immigrants and African Americans.

A Typology of CSC

The volume's congregational case studies and chapter on the survey of college freshmen reveal an array of CSC activities that can be located on a continuum that measures social distance. The continuum begins with activities that bond those who are socially and religiously similar and then moves to activities that bridge and link people who are different in the greater Miami community and, further afield, beyond Miami and the United States. Each congregational case study examines the different types of social capital—bonding, bridging, and linking. Every congregation demonstrates some form or forms of bonding social capital. While bonding can be considered to have a civic element in that one may bond or come together with people one did not know before and who may be different in some ways, bridging and linking social capital, by definition, are more civic; they join people who are socially and possibly religiously different. Many congregations examined in this volume exhibited bridging CSC. Importantly but not surprisingly, fewer congregations are involved in civic social activities that create linking social capital to organizations that provide access to material power and resources.

Clearly, some congregations and some individuals display far more CSC than others. Each chapter includes explanations for the author's findings, but they add up to more than a sum of particularistic conclusions. In table 12.1, we offer a typology that organizes our empirical findings on two dimensions: (1) geographic focus and (2) categories of civic social activities that also reflect different types of social capital. As in all typologies, exceptions and nuances in the data are underplayed in order to show predominant patterns.

Bonding Social Capital: Social and Congregational Activities

An important concept in religion is the axis mundi, the locus of a group, around which the group orders the rest of the world. For immigrants who have gone through complex processes of geographic, social, and cultural uprooting and transplanting, there is a powerful need for a rudder that stays firm despite passage through turbulent seas. We have observed in all the congregations studied and in the youth survey as well that religion and faith provide much of this needed continuity and comfort. It is not surprising, then, that bonding social capital activities are most prevalent in the immigrant congregations, for they

TABLE 12.1

Typology of Civic Social Capital Activities Exhibited by Congregations and College Youth

Geographic focus of activity and type of social capital	Type of activity			
	Civic social capital		Bonding social capital	
	Linking social capital	Bridging social capital		
	Formal politics	Service, volunteering	Social and cultural	Religious and spiritual
Local	African American mainstream Protestants, Sierra Norwood Baptist, Disciples' Nazarene	Refugees 7th-Day Adventist, college youth	Christ the King, Church of the Ascencion, San Juan Bosco, St. Agatha, Divine Providence, Notre Dame d'Haiti	Pentecostal West Indians, St. Ann Mission, Divine Providence, Refugees 7th-Day Adventist
U.S. national	African American mainstream Protestants, Notre Dame d'Haiti, Miami Catholic Archdiocese	College youth		
Transnational	Notre Dame d'Haiti, St. Agatha	St. Agatha, Divine Providence	Refugees 7th-Day Adventist, San Juan Bosco, St. Agatha	Pentecostal West Indians, St. Ann Mission, Notre Dame d'Haiti

are the church home to people whose social ties have been strained, if not severed altogether.

Our research also concurs with a most common theme in other literature on immigrants and religion, that is, religion helps reproduce the culture of the immigrant's homeland. Religious activities do this in manifold ways, through use of native language, sermons that refer to one's roots, rituals and worship styles that are peculiar to or have a homeland twist, symbolic representations of the homeland in flags, paintings and murals, guest pastors and priests from the homeland, and celebration of homeland national holidays and religious festivals. All of these were abundantly evident in the congregations we studied. Notre Dame D'Haiti has both a mural and stained glass representations of Haiti and of Haitian refugees coming to the United States. It also devotes an entire week to celebrating the feast of Haiti's patron saint, Our Lady of Perpetual Help (Rey 2004). St. Agatha has a festival remembering Guantánamo-Baracoa. West Indian Catholics celebrate Trinidad's independence, while across the street West Indian Episcopalians put on a carnival fête. St. Ann Mission celebrates Mexico's patron saint, Guadalupe, and Our Lady of Divine Providence celebrates the Feast of La Purísima, the patron saint of Nicaragua, and the feast days of the patron saints of other Latin American nations which have congregants at this church.

In each of these cases, the members of a congregation or a subgroup within a congregation have moved its axis mundi to the new land. In most cases the repositioning is symbolic but nonetheless emotionally and spiritually supportive. In the case of the primarily Cuban Refugees' Seventh-Day Adventist church in Hialeah, the repositioning was material as well as spiritual; the congregation built a new sanctuary as a near-perfect simulacra of their previous building in Havana. These connections provided by houses of worship, though commonsensical and patently functionalist, must be acknowledged and appreciated for they embody the immigrants' axis mundi. In a fundamental but not always appreciated way, they lay the foundation for congregations to do civic work. The key, then, is to examine these processes of strengthening and note what moves congregations to the civic building blocks of bridging and linking social capital that reach into the broader community.

Congregations frequently take this next step to the bridging and linking social capital that constitutes CSC through evangelization and other outreach programs that are geared toward building membership. In our typology, we characterize these activities as exhibiting bonding social capital but focus on religious and spiritual concerns. A religious retreat such as the West Indian Pentecostals' Women in Warfare program is a good example. Women in Warfare brought together women from different congregations for a weekend of intensive social bonding as well as religious renewal. The Disciples' church in Hialeah innovated many ways to bring people to its congregation through prayer groups and services at all hours of the day and by bringing homeless and the poor to their doors for meals. Offering social assistance as a means to engage potential new members is certainly not new. We highlight it, rather, as a point along a continuum we are documenting of immigrant churches' activities that span civic engagement from that closest to home to that furthest away. Activities that must be characterized as overwhelmingly bonding are typically the supports upon which the latticework of bridging and linking civic social capital typically is laid.

Bridging Social Capital: Service and Volunteerism

Much of the debate in the current literature on civic engagement focuses on service activities and volunteering. Indeed, participation in these types of activities is typically the threshold for measuring civic engagement. Still, if service and volunteering are valid measures, then our volume provides a counterpoint to other research suggesting that civic participation is on the wane. For example, in our survey of college freshmen the majority reported having engaged in service activities including tutoring, helping immigrants and senior citizens, and participating in community fund-raisers. Our congregational studies also illustrate a wealth of service provision and volunteering, including English-language and after-school programs, medical clinics, day-care centers, emergency help for housing, food and clothing, disaster relief, and so on. We found individuals in each congregation who supported volunteering and are confident that if we conducted a survey of everyone, respondents in each congregation would have endorsed their church's involvement in unpaid service activities that benefit the needy.

Translating stated willingness and desire to help others outside of one's own congregation into actual service behavior, however, is more difficult. In chapter 10, the pastor of Sierra Norwood, the West Indian Baptist Church that was a part of PACT, also encouraged volunteering for such activities as Habitat for Humanity, but he had a very difficult time motivating his parishioners to participate. Similarly, when asked about volunteering activities, the West Indian Pentecostals talked about how they were going to organize hospital visits. In over two years of research with this congregation, however, they never got around to actually visiting hospitals and, in fact, were never observed discussing it except when a researcher brought up the subject. And the "Brother 100" sermon offered by a Cuban Adventist pastor in chapter 2 largely fell on deaf ears. In fact, in most of the congregations we observed, volunteer activities were episodic at best, engaged in when people responded to specific events such as disasters or particularistic initiatives, but not as part of the congregation's general set of activities.

Some congregations and individuals within congregations, however, emphasize and take part in extensive volunteer activities. The Disciples' Nazarene Church in Hialeah, described in chapter 2, engaged in service volunteering more than any other congregation we studied. Why? Sarah Mahler argues that leadership is key, and we shall return to this point below. The Disciples' church uses charity as a form of advertising their congregation and of building membership.

We also observed this in other churches. For the Disciples' Nazarene and other churches, these service activities, however self-serving, also do bridge their congregations to the larger society. Whatever the motivation, the effect is that typical sociological dividing lines of class, race, neighborhood, immigration status, ethnicity, and religious convictions are crossed. The lines that divide become ties that bind. In metropolitan areas all around the world there is great need for such healing work. Indeed, the fact that immigrant congregations are involved in so many programs that serve the greater good is particularly inspiring given these churches' disproportionate need to help their own congregants find comfort and care in new, unfamiliar settings. What limits their ability to do more service beyond their walls, however, is the obligation to attend not merely to their own congregants' needs but also to their deficit of knowledge about and ties to resources in the greater society, that is, linking social capital. Nonetheless, some congregations we researched have achieved this level of connectedness.

Linking Social Capital: Political Activities

A major preoccupation of recent scholarship addressing immigration and religion, particularly but not solely in Europe, is the rise of religious extremists dedicated to political projects. While our research did not yield instances of this, despite the fact that our research window opened in the years immediately following the September 11, 2001, attacks, we have found in our work that most civic activities that can be labeled as involving linking social capital are political in nature. They are distributed across different geographic spheres of influence from the local to the transnational, and they reflect access to different types of resources.

Local Linking

Formal politics are those that fit the most narrow, restricted definition of civic engagement or citizenship, i.e., individual voting and individuals or groups directly attempting to influence elected or appointed political figures and structures. At the local level, the most obvious examples in our empirical research were the African Americans, describing both those people who linked to locally elected officials and those who organized their neighborhood, as in the case of the Perrine churches, noted in chapter 4, and the Overtown African American churches involved in the preservation of Virginia Key, described in chapter 7. Sierra Norwood, the West Indian Baptist Church described in chapter 10, is an active member of a local ecumenical organization, PACT, whose primary strategy is action directed toward local politicians.

National Linking

The primary case we have of religious organizations involved in formal politics and linked to national figures is the African American community in Perrine.

They utilized local ties to gain access to then U.S. attorney general Janet Reno, who was from Miami. As described in chapter 3, the Haitian Catholic Church, Notre Dame d'Haiti, focused primarily on politics in Haiti, but because the U.S. government was so involved in Haitian politics, some of Notre Dame's political efforts could also be conceived as directed toward the U.S. government. And, historically, when Cubans began arriving in Miami, the Miami Catholic Archdiocese directly worked with the U.S. government on Cuban resettlement. This kind of involvement is less important now and was not visible in the ethnographies of the two Cuban Catholic churches, but it continues to influence the work at St. Agatha parish, as described in chapter 5, and at San Juan Bosco parish, described in chapter 6.

African American churches' access to elected leaders at the local and national levels comes as no surprise. It is the legacy of decades and generations of activists whose foundational work, overwhelmingly cultivated within Black churches, produced the civil rights movement. The attention paid by Haitians and Cubans in Miami and by other immigrant groups in other locations to lobbying elected officials on behalf of their interests has been learned by modeling themselves after other successful immigrants. Cuban American leaders, for example, studied the Jewish lobby on behalf of Israel. Immigrant churches in Miami and elsewhere nurture this linking social capital by both cultivating leadership and providing ready-made audiences that elected leaders seek to access with their messages.

Notable by its absence in the chapters of this volume is the religiously based political set of issues that receives most media attention, i.e., school prayer, abortion, and homosexuality, associated with such organizations as Focus on the Family and, formerly, the Moral Majority. Individuals in and leaders of the congregations we studied certainly had opinions on these issues, opinions that were almost always consonant with the broader public religion debate. If we had done a survey of congregants on these issues, we feel confident that the majority would be opposed to abortion and homosexuality and would support prayer in schools. The leaders of the congregations would occasionally address these issues. Pastors would mention them in their sermons, and at least the Catholic Church consistently made anti-abortion pamphlets available. There are also a few congregations in the Miami area that do actively organize around these types of issues. In particular, there is one Hispanic Protestant congregation that has led the anti–gay rights movement in Miami-Dade County. Yet these morally conservative political efforts are *not* typical of congregations in Miami. Among African Americans, fighting against discrimination and its legacy of inequality is the primary focus of civic social engagement in formal local and national politics. Increasingly, this is true for Haitians, too, while Nicaraguans, Mexicans, and other Latin American immigrants are concerned with the politics of U.S. immigration policy.

Transnational Linking

Among immigrants we studied, the majority of their political activities were oriented toward their homelands. The Haitian Catholic congregation's involvement in Haitian presidential politics was undoubtedly boosted because a former Catholic priest, Jean Bertrand Aristide, was running for and obtained the presidency of Haiti. Cubans' religiously based involvement in formal politics is more complicated. On the one hand, San Juan Bosco, the primary church in Little Havana, which subsequently came to serve Nicaraguans more than Cubans, denies nearly fifty years of recent Cuban history by ignoring the country's formal political changes, such as the creation of a new division of provinces, and treats Cuba as if it were still the same country émigrés left in 1959. On the other hand, St. Agatha implicitly acknowledges Castro's socialist regime but works around it by engaging in a parish-to-parish relationship with the Cuban diocese of Guantánamo-Baracoa. In order for St. Agatha to accomplish its transnational humanitarian and political goals, the congregation also has to bridge and link to a wide variety of local secular businesses and organizations which underwrite these activities.

Regardless of the motivation or source of resources, all of these examples of transnational linking illustrate CSC, i.e., civic engagement that links congregations to the wider social fabric. However tempting it is to end our discussion on this positive note, the data obligate us to go a level deeper into this analysis.

Civic Social Capital: Beneath the Veneer

The social capital literature tends to emphasize the positive benefits of social capital. The bridging and linking varieties are characterized, for instance, as promoting civic responsibility, helping to overcome divisiveness and insularity, and as encouraging not only tolerance but also the cooperation necessary to resolve large-scale social problems (Portes and Landolt 1996; Skocpol and Fiorina 1999; Wuthnow 2002).

Other case studies, however, reveal that bonding and linking relationships can also have negative consequences that are neither democratic nor empowering (Portes and Landolt 1996). This revelation seems particularly apt when analysis distinguishes between the two ends of the hierarchy implicated in linking social capital, those who give and those who receive. The Cuban service providers in San Juan Bosco evinced condescending attitudes toward the Nicaraguans to whom they provided services. Similarly, the congregants at St. Agatha who raised funds for the Guantánamo-Baracoa diocese referred to those in Cuba as *los pobrecitos* (the poor ones) in a way that clearly communicated the donors' self-identity as superior. While bridging and linking relationships do expand CSC, they may produce greater alienation than solidarity. Bonding social capital generally implies that those who are not bonded are excluded or marginalized through, for example, condescension and disparagement. While this is not a necessary consequence of linking or bridging CSC, a patronizing attitude can attenuate the positive benefits of bridging and linking. Simon Szreter argues that linking social capital assumes "a democratic and empowering character where those involved are endeavoring to achieve a mutually agreed beneficial goal (or set of goals) *on a basis of mutual respect, trust and equality of status*, despite the manifest inequalities in their respective positions" (2002, 579, emphasis added). The cases of San Juan Bosco and St. Agatha certainly imply that mutual respect, trust, and equality of status are not necessarily the end result of linking social capital.

The St. Agatha and San Juan Bosco examples of condescension tied to linking social capital also demonstrate that the empirical reality of social capital in its various forms is more complicated than conveyed by the broad and seemingly bordered distinctions among bonding, bridging, and linking. While it is generally true that religious and secular activities, along with social and cultural ones, embody bonding social capital, they also contain elements of bridging and linking.[1] St. Agatha's La Noche Cubana, for example, bonds Cuban Catholics, but it also bridges to Cubans from Guantánamo who otherwise do not attend St. Agatha's, and it relies upon links to local merchants who make donations to underwrite the event. St. Ann Mission's celebration of Guadalupe similarly bonds Mexican congregants, but the festival also bridges to and incorporates other Mexicans who do not regularly frequent church. Also at St. Ann Mission, while the primary work is done by the congregation's Mexican youth, it is overseen by the resident Cuban priest. And while the Disciples' Nazarene resident program for substance abusers is based upon common rituals that bond the recovering addicts, the program reached out to them while they were on the streets to bring them in and to convert them to sobriety and Christianity.

That which appears at first glance to promote bonding may also introduce such tension that it divides as much or more than it unites. The Seventh-Day Adventist Church in Hialeah, described in chapter 2, bonds all congregants in some ways, but it also strains them in others. In this case, the stresses are along generational lines in particular. The discussion of the Trinidadian Catholic Curry-Q and the Episcopalian carnival in chapter 10 also calls for a more critical approach to the strength of ties that bind. These public events bridge to the relatively broad West Indian community, but some in this community, in particular the small group that organizes these events, are clearly more bonded to each other than those who simply come to pick up their curry take-out order.

Regardless of its particular form—bonding, bridging or linking—social capital (or CSC) is fundamentally relational (Narayan 1999; Portes 1996). It is not inherent in a particular individual or activity. Rather, it emerges from individuals' and organizations' negotiations of their positions with others in a complex social structure, a social structure permeated by inequalities (Szreter 2002;

Bourdieu 1987). Moreover, CSC is contextually relational; an individual's CSC and that which organizations engender in groups vary over levels of analysis, over time, and with respect to different activities. The African American congregations, for example, link hierarchically to formal political power at the same time they bridge horizontally to White environmental organizations and to the broader African American community. Similarly, the Cubans who administer San Juan Bosco's service programs link hierarchically to their sponsors in the diocese along with non-governmental and governmental organizations at the same time they condescend toward those congregants and clients whom they view as socially inferior.[2]

Following Pierre Bourdieu, what matters is not so much the label identifying specific forms of capital, but whether or not and to what degree any form of capital solidifies or improves one's access to power (Rey 2007). In Bourdieu's inimitable and, for our purposes, apt language, can the relationship be "transubstantiated"? Lindon Robison, Allan Schmid, and Marcelo Siles (2002) argue that capital is not worthy of the name unless it can be transformed into something else. This question and point inexorably lead to an inquiry into what causes these transformations? In our case, what triggers a congregation that has been principally focused on bonding social capital activities to build bridges and links to the wider society? We turn to this fundamental question now.

What Produces CSC?

In the previous section we have argued that the commonplace categories used to characterize social capital, and by extension our concept of civic social capital, are useful analytic lenses, but they must be understood more as ideal types than as categorical isolates. Rather, people and their institutions often exhibit multiple varieties at any one time and, also, there is great fluidity over time. As social scientists we are not content to merely describe a phenomenon but prefer to engage in a deeper level of analysis aimed at explanation. We turn, then, to asking what factors are most implicated in determining whether congregations participate in linking, bridging, and bonding CSC.

Denominational Determinants

As discussed in the first chapter, Catholic and mainstream Protestants are generally more likely to bridge and link, while other Protestants, such as the Pentecostals we observed, are more likely to be self-referential, to emphasize relationships with others who have been "saved."[3] Many of our cases fit these denominational predictions. The West Indian Pentecostals embody primarily bonding social capital within their congregation and with those who share their same religious beliefs. The mainstream African American churches epitomize bridging and linking CSC. At first glance they may appear to embody primarily bonding with other African Americans, but a deeper gaze exposes that their activities clearly are designed to both bridge them to the broader African American community and link them to formal, mixed-ethnic political structures. All of the Perrine African American churches place a strong emphasis on training leaders, not just of the church but of the broader African American community. At the same time, the Pentecostal churches in Perrine had an ambivalent relationship to the mainstream Protestant denominations. When drugs and violence most disrupted the community, mainstream and Pentecostal congregations united, but at other times the Pentecostals distanced themselves from the others, disparaging them as morally hypocritical and therefore not worthy of leadership.

The West Indian Baptist congregation that was a member of the ecumenical coalition PACT also conforms to the literature's generalizations about bridging and linking social capital, as do the Miami Catholic Archdiocese and the various Catholic churches we studied, which provide an array of social services, including welcoming Mariel Boatlift Cubans and then Nicaraguan refugees, sending money and medicines to the Cuban Catholic community, providing a health clinic and after-school program that serves Nicaraguans and other Central Americans, advocating on behalf of Haitian refugees, and being the de facto center of the Miami Haitian community. Yet not all of the congregations readily fit the generalizations of the literature. The West Perrine Christian Association contained both mainstream Protestant and Pentecostal members. The Catholic Notre Dame d'Haiti evinced much higher CSC, for example, than two other Catholic churches, Divine Providence and Santa Ana. At the same time, while the Disciples' Nazarene Church had its origins as a mainstream Protestant church, its current leadership, worship style, and theology are more closely evocative of charismatic or even Pentecostal services; yet it exhibits the highest CSC of any immigrant congregation in our study. What explains the anomalies, i.e., congregations where denomination does not predict the kind and level of CSC engendered? We believe that the best explanation lies in the role of leaders and their charisma.

Leadership

Although our research design did not expressly seek congregations with charismatic leaders, we found them in several congregations and, subsequently, have been convinced by our data that leadership is a critical determinant of congregations' engagement with the broader society. The volume's case studies reveal a number of charismatic leaders. Father Thomas Wenski, the founder of Notre Dame d'Haiti, who later was elevated to bishop, made his church into the most important institution in Miami's Haitian community. His embodiment of liberation theology's "base communities" forged a congregation filled with CSC as it participated strongly in efforts to support Jean Bertrand Aristide as president of Haiti and to seek justice for Haitian refugees in the United States. Reverend Al González of the Disciples' Nazarene Church resurrected a congregation that had nearly completely dissolved. Following the inspiration of one of his female congregants, Flor, he constructed a compassion ministry that not only aided people to leave the streets but also helped them recover from their substance abuse. Subsequently, the church established a live-in rehabilitation center for substance abusers. Pastor Walter Richardson of the Baptist congregation in Perrine confronted a similar problem with gangs and drug abusers. However, rather than focusing on rescuing those involved with drugs, he brought together the broader community to combat the violence and devastation produced by the local drug trade. He and other African American ministers and congregants used linking social capital to marshal resources. These clerical religious leaders forcefully inspired effective social ministries.

All of these leaders exemplify Max Weber's description of natural leaders, which we discussed in the introduction. They all have what Weber labeled as "charisma," an inherent quality that renders them natural, effective, and inspirational leaders. Weber also referred to natural religious leaders as "prophets," a slightly different use of the word than in common English, where it usually refers to someone who foretells the future. "Prophet," in English and for Weber, also means someone who has divine inspiration. Leaders such as Father Wenski, Reverend González, and Pastor Richardson lead through reference to the will of God, but they also lead by example. Father Wenski conducted a human rights mission to Haiti. Reverend González tromped the streets offering services to substance abusers, and Pastor Richardson led the marches against drug dealers in Perrine. By combining their own charisma with moral teachings from their faith backgrounds, they engendered enthusiastic and wide ranging CSC. They transformed the moral authority of their religious position into active, effective CSC for their congregants.

The Divine Providence Catholic Church also became a primary producer of CSC soon after its founding. Within a year of its 1979 opening, it became a refuge for Mariel Boatlift Cuban refugees. The church's priest, Father Ernesto Garcia-Rubio, was a Cuban who had a personal history as a refugee, and this informed his cultivation of service projects at the parish. With help from the Theatine Sisters of the Immaculate Conception and congregation volunteers, the church offered an extraordinary array of services. To the Mariel Cubans and, subsequently, Nicaraguan refugees who began arriving in the 1980s, the church provided legal aid, job placement, housing assistance, food distribution, economic aid, and psychological counseling. In the early 1980s, the Cuban priest led his primarily Cuban congregants to bridge to the newly arrived Nicaraguans. They both shared an anti-communist worldview, as the Nicaraguans were fleeing the left-wing Sandinista government. Even when a few years later this initial solidarity eroded as factionalism emerged both among Nicaraguans and between Nicaraguans and Cubans, Father Garcia-Rubio's charismatic leadership was strong enough to bridge these yawning divides. Yet, much as social capital has both positive and negative manifestations, leaders have their flaws as well. For Father Garcia-Rubio his sexual improprieties became not only his own downfall, but that of his parish as well. The priests who replaced him have not shared his charismatic leadership qualities, and the church's social mission projects and youth program have withered in the aftermath.

Padre Pedro, the Cuban pastor to St. Ann Mission's Mexican congregation, is also charismatic, an admired, esteemed, and effective leader of his Mexican congregants. Yet he and, consequently, his congregation differ significantly from the civically engaged charismatic leaders such as Father Wenski, Pastor González, and Pastor Richardson. The limited resources of his poor parish and his own hectic schedule clogged with responsibilities for meeting his congregants' immediate spiritual needs take up all of his time and energy. His charisma results in more insular spiritual and cultural activities, that is, in more attention to bonding than bridging or linking social capital. The most important celebration in the church's calendar is the feast of the Virgin of Guadalupe, which contains elements of redemption from repression that have been used by clerical leaders in the Southwest to civically engage Mexicans with respect to issues of immigration and employment (Hondagneu-Sotelo et al. 2004; Hondagneu-Sotelo, Gaudinez, and Lara 2007). Padre Pedro's focus, however, remains spiritual. We did not observe him making an effort to emphasize the social theology of the Virgin of Guadalupe, nor has he mobilized his congregants to advocate for immigration reform. He is extraordinarily successful at generating a bridge between himself, a Cuban refugee, and his devout Mexican congregants who attend church regularly and to the broader local Mexican community. He also has fostered and promoted the leadership of the youth in his congregation, who have assumed most of the organizational responsibilities of the Guadalupe celebration. These accomplishments are estimable. They do not, however, constitute significant CSC as they reach only into the local Mexican community.

In most of the cases that we have studied, the impetus for civic engagement flows downward from clerical leadership to the laity, and Weber is apt for understanding these cases where leaders seem to be naturally endowed and have an inherent social vision. However, we also observed congregations in which leadership is not, so to speak, top-down, but derived from a dialectical relationship between the congregation and the broader society. In the Disciples' Nazarene Church, the interaction between church leaders, the congregants, and the immediate broader society of the neighborhood is crucial. Reverend González's transformation of his church into our most outstanding example of CSC was begun by one of his congregants. Reverend González struggled mightily to engage the interests and needs of those he rescued from the streets with those who had already been attending his church. And he built a lay leadership cultivation program that constantly cycles in new potential leaders under the mentorship of the active and more senior models.

Monsignor Estévez achieved more limited results in his efforts at St. Agatha to promote ties between his older Cuban congregants and Catholics in Cuba, addressed in chapter 5. Known for his open-mindedness and strong, ongoing relationship with and support of the Catholic Church in Cuba, Monsignor Estévez embraced Archbishop John Favalora's plan for creating formal ties of support between Miami's Catholics and those in Cuba. Well aware that his own congregation was vehemently anti-Castro and unlikely to support anything that involved the island, Father Estévez's homilies framed the prospect of ties with Cuban Catholics in such broad terms of Christian values of love and fraternity that they could span the geographic and political distances involved, analogous to Christ's Disciples spreading the Word millennia ago. In addition, he had the foresight to create a ministry that would specifically dedicate itself to the planned church-diocese partnership. For this, he intentionally selected lay leaders whom he knew were open-minded enough to look beyond the dominant, anti-Castro exile politics. It is a tribute to Monsignor Estévez's charisma that the transnational ministry continues successfully even after he left St. Agatha's. Yet, because his charisma does not mesh well with the overriding anti-Castro worldview of his parishioners, Monsignor Estévez was not able to transform his congregation as comprehensively as Reverend González at the Disciples' Nazarene or Father Wenski at Notre Dame d'Haiti; nor has he transformed the local community as much as Pastor Richardson and others have accomplished in Perrine.

All of these examples demonstrate the critical role of religious leadership, particularly as it responds to the needs and concerns of its congregants *and* as it motivates them to move beyond their individual needs and congregation-centered concerns. Leadership and denomination are not fully independent variables for, as we have discussed, some denominations and, above all, some groups' histories within denominations, African Americans in particular, are known for their cultivation of leaders. To date, leadership has not received the same attention that denomination has received when researchers attempt to explain civic engagement among the faithful. We argue that denomination provides an initial approximation of how CSC is produced, but this needs to be complemented by drawing upon Weber's analysis of charisma. But Weber is also insufficient. He does not address the relationship between the charismatic leaders and the needs and concerns of followers, what Bourdieu called the religious *habitus* (the matrix of perception) of the laity. Bourdieu argues that "prophecy can play such a role only because it has as its own generative and unifying principle, a habitus objectively attuned to that of its addressees," i.e., congregants (1987, 131). Our cases of leadership overwhelmingly confirm Bourdieu's insight. The successful leaders matched their charisma to the matrix of perception, the perceived needs and interests of the congregants.

Eileen Smith-Cavros's analysis in chapter 7 of the Virginia Key Trust and the Richmond Heights tree-planting initiative demonstrates that local African

American churches have developed a habitus that promotes social activism as a way of doing "God's work." While each project had some volunteers who were also church pastors, they also were propelled by many volunteers who were simply congregants committed to the cause. Several of the Black churchgoers involved in the Virginia Key Trust were active in Miami's civil rights movement and fought for the integration of beaches, schools, and politics. Their roots in the African American church had engendered such a strong habitus of civic social capital that individual charismatic pastors were not necessary to induce them to become civically engaged.

Pastor Richard Ledgister of Sierra Norwood, the Jamaican Baptist Church described in chapter 10, presents a converse case. Pastor Ledgister had charisma but confronted a gap between himself and his congregants' habitus. Pastor Ledgister and Sierra Norwood as a congregation were members of PACT, a local ecumenical social action ministry. Pastor Ledgister even assumed a leadership role in PACT. He was personally committed to achieving social justice through bridging and linking social capital, similar to Father Wenski, Reverend González, and Pastor Richardson. And Pastor Ledgister achieved some success. The congregants strongly support the church's independent, autonomous missionary work in Haiti and Guyana. Pastor Ledgister was also able to motivate some and occasionally many of his congregants to attend PACT events. But his congregants were reticent. Many still often evinced the island-based notion that politics is "politricks" and not worth their time. As he says, they see PACT activities as "external, secular stuff, not spiritual matters." In spite of being a mainline Protestant church that the literature argues should be inclined to produce CSC through service activities, Pastor Ledgister's congregants often react more like Pentecostals, more concerned with spiritual and individual issues than social issues. They have not transformed their habitus to that of Pastor Ledgister's broader commitment to bridging and linking social capital that embodies CSC. Habitus may also be different across generations.

Generation

Immigrant parents and their children often differ over religion. The children of immigrants frequently prefer English to their parents' language. They may also prefer churches that place less emphasis on the homeland. They may prefer a different style of worship than their parents. In Miami, we saw some congregations confronting precisely these issues. The Adventist Church in Hialeah with a congregation of mixed Hispanics, described in chapter 2, had particular difficulty integrating their youth, who questioned the authority of the adult leaders and insisted on knowing why things were done in a particular way. A West Indian Episcopalian church, discussed in chapter 10, noted that the Episcopalian youth preferred the more stimulating sermons and exciting music that Pentecostals offered. The youth at Divine Providence Catholic Church, discussed in chapter 8, remained in the church of their parents, but the adult leader assigned to guide them resigned and the youth felt directionless. The Cuban leaders of the after-school program at San Juan Bosco, portrayed in chapter 6, certainly were concerned with the Nicaraguan youth who were their students. However, they had a narrow, ethnocentric, and patronizing vision of how to help youth as they emphasized the upper- and middle-class values of the early-arriving Cuban exiles in Miami.

We also encountered numerous congregations that successfully integrated their youth. Padre Pedro of St. Ann Mission, depicted in chapter 9, nurtures his young Mexican congregants, who have assumed literally center stage in the celebrations of the Virgin of Guadalupe. The adult West Indian Pentecostals in chapter 10 self-consciously invest in their youth, whom they believe have a necessary energy to keep their church "alive." Similarly, African American pastors described in chapter 4 self-consciously prepare their youth for leadership roles.

The difference between those congregations that encounter difficulty and those that successfully integrate their youth, again, seems to be in style of leadership. Adult leaders who devote time and, particularly, are open to listening and giving responsibility to youth are able to integrate them into the broader congregation. This appears to mesh well with the habitus of young adults, in particular, the high value most older adolescents place on being listened to, respected, and able to assume responsibility. How individuals are accepted and treated, whether by church leadership, established congregants, or the broader society, contributes to the production of social capital.

Context of Reception

In the early 1980s when imprisoned Cuban refugees from the Mariel Boatlift were rioting in an Atlanta prison, then Monsignor and now Bishop Augustín Román was appointed by the U.S. government to negotiate a peaceful resolution. That there were Cuban refugees in an Atlanta prison reflects that not all Cubans have been positively received. Those who came in 1980 through Mariel particularly confronted negative stereotypes after Fidel Castro labeled them as "worms" and "scum" and included former prison inmates among the refugees (Portes and Stepick 1993). Compared to Cubans who came in the 1960s and 1970s, a higher proportion of these 1980 Mariel Cuban refugees were also Black. and they encountered racism both from established resident Americans and from fellow Cubans. As Sarah Mahler indicates in chapter 2, the Adventists felt discriminated against in Cuba for their religious beliefs and then encountered further difficulties in Miami because of the color of their skin.

In contrast, the extraordinarily positive context of reception for Cubans who arrived in the 1960s made the Miami Catholic Church the progenitor of tremendous CSC and established a worldview that continues to reverberate nearly fifty years after the Cuban exile began. It also provides a framework for understanding San Juan Bosco and its peculiar relationship to the Nicaraguan community. The head priest at San Juan Bosco, Father Emilio Vallina, was one of the early Cuban Catholic exiles. He participated fully in the construction of Miami's Cuban Catholic community. He saw how Cuban refugees arrived with nothing, attended Catholic schools and churches, and went on to become successful. What he and the Cuban Catholic lay workers he employs do not see, however, is how the elite status of the early exiles, combined with the unparalleled support provided to them by the Catholic diocese and U.S. government, propelled many Cubans into Miami's elite. In contrast, the Nicaraguans who attend San Juan Bosco and participate in its extensive service programs come from far more modest backgrounds and have experienced far less assistance and even rejection from the U.S. government. Through the 1980s and 1990s, Nicaraguans had to politically struggle for legal immigration status. They had no federally funded benefits, let alone the unparalleled ones provided to earlier Cubans. Overlooking these differences, the Cubans who work at San Juan Bosco can sincerely, unself-consciously, and misleadingly attribute the Nicaraguan's modest success in the United States to their lack of appropriate values.

Haitians have confronted a context of reception that is even more negative than that of Nicaraguans. From the beginnings of the massive inflow of Haitian refugees into Miami, local authorities and federal officials have branded them as unwanted and have made every effort to deter their arrival and impede their settlement. If it were not for the heroic efforts of leaders such as Father Wenski and others in the civil rights and human rights communities, Haitians would have had even greater difficulties establishing a community in Miami (see Stepick 1998). This discrimination and the struggle against it have been key motivators for the development of CSC among Haitians in Miami. As such and arguably not surprisingly, given their African heritage, Haitians' experience in the United States has much in common with that of the long-standing African American communities, such as those in Perrine, whose CSC pivots on responses to discrimination and the devastation it has caused. As Su Oltman Fink (citing Chidester 1988) indicates in chapter 4 on African Americans in Perrine, conflict can produce CSC.

For most of the immigrants in Miami, context of reception is not perceived as something that affects their religion. They notice that Cubans are generally treated better by the federal government than other groups, but they see this as affecting the need to fight for immigration status and, perhaps, employment prospects, not as something that affects religious practice. The Cubans at San Juan Bosco certainly never mentioned that the resources heaped on Cubans by the U.S. federal government greatly boosted the Miami Archdiocese and thus helped individual Cubans. Neither does context of reception have the obvious effects that denomination, leadership, or generation have. It is a background variable that requires contrast to emerge.

African American churches are certainly aware of how their "reception" by the broader society affects them, both their history as segregated churches and the associated development of civic social capital within churches. If we had focused more on non-Christian congregations, particularly those who practice Santería or Vodou, context of reception would have also been more evident to those "congregants." As mentioned in chapter 1, a leading Lukumi congregation in Hialeah won a victory in 1993 in the U.S. Supreme Court that ruled in favor of animal sacrifice for religious purposes (Supreme Court of the United States 1993). The victory, however, did not eliminate the tension between the estimated one hundred thousand practitioners of Santería (or related traditions in Miami) and the broader community. Context of reception obviously affects religious practices in this case, but it also has a more subtle, yet still important influence in the Christian congregations in Miami.

Are Immigrants Really Different?

Are immigrants different in terms of their civic social capital from the broader U.S. public and from particular racial or ethnic groups within that broader public? The two chapters with case studies of African American congregations and communities do make their CSC appear to be different from immigrants. First, in the African American congregations we observed, CSC is thoroughly infused with and fundamentally inseparable from religion. Many of the most important community leaders we encountered are based in churches. Churches self-consciously prepare youth for community leadership. Moreover, their CSC projects, marshaling resources to protect the community from violence, preserving historical heritage, and making environmental improvements, are all firmly rooted locally in South Florida. They focus fundamentally on the challenges they see as stemming from race, and racial bonding provides the initial basis for their CSC, although that bonded solidarity does have a fracture that divides Pentecostals from mainstream Protestants. Moreover, racial bonding is insufficient. All of the successful African American CSC projects required bridging and linking capital. In the early years of Perrine, when segregation was still legal, Black community institutions bridged to sympathetic White landowners. In the post–civil rights era, these linkages have been fortified and extended beyond the neighborhood to include powerful locally and nationally based Whites.

In some ways the African American experience does parallel that of immigrants. For example, immigrants' CSC projects tend to be directed toward their own group (as defined by nationality, but often as also defined by race, ethnicity, and class). The difference appears in the distance involved and the borders to contain or to bridge. African Americans' and other established residents' CSC activities rarely extend beyond national borders, although international missions are a prime exception, while immigrants' CSC activities are frequently transnational. Examples from our case studies include St. Agatha's assistance to

Guantánamo-Baracoa Catholics, Divine Providence's aid to victims of Hurricane Mitch in Nicaragua, Notre Dame d'Haiti's involvement in Haitian presidential politics, and West Indian Pentecostals' hosting of a seminar soliciting investment in Jamaica. Some transnational ties are more spiritual than civic, such as the West Indian Pentecostals presenting guest preachers from Jamaica; West Indian Catholics hosting visiting Trinidadian pastors and church musical groups, St. Ann Mission's celebration of the feast of Mexico's patron saint, the Virgin of Guadalupe; and Divine Providence's Feast of La Purísima, the patron saint of Nicaragua. Such ties can cultivate an imagined transnational or Diasporic community, such as those at San Juan Bosco who imagine Cuba to still have the same political geographic boundaries that it had before the revolution nearly fifty years ago and the shrine to Cuba's patron saint, which is on Miami's seashore, not Cuba's.

At the same time, the survey of local college freshmen indicates that at least among youth, immigrants' CSC is not significantly different from natives' CSC. According to this self-reported data, immigrants and native college youth are equally civically engaged, and they are engaged in similar activities. Moreover, they are involved in formal politics similarly; they volunteer at similar rates; and they engage in social and cultural activities much the same. The only difference is that Miami's immigrant youth tend to be slightly more religious than natives, with the exception of African Americans, who are the most religious of those we surveyed.

We believe, however, that the survey of college freshmen reveals a generational change, that the second generation of immigrants, those born and/or raised in the United States, focuses its CSC more locally and less transnationally than their immigrant parents. In this sense, they are more "Americanized."[4] We hesitate, however, to argue that the second generation has more CSC or is more civically engaged than their immigrant elders. The case studies in this volume amply demonstrate that many of the adult immigrant first generation have considerable CSC, although they may exercise it differently than the second generation. The differences between immigrants and those born in the United States, thus, is less about the amount of CSC they generate and more about its focus. Those who were born abroad are more likely, but not exclusively, to focus on transnational activities. Those born in the United States, regardless if they have immigrant or native-born parents, are more likely to focus on local projects.

These data forcefully argue that American civic engagement will not decline because of immigrants. It is certainly misleading to conclude, for example, as Samuel Huntington does, that Hispanics, in general, remain more loyal to their home countries than to the United States and are unwilling or unable to assimilate (Huntington 2004a, 2004b). While our case studies do provide some examples of Hispanics who seemingly remain more attached to their homeland than to Miami or the United States, many of Miami's Hispanics and other immigrants also are deeply civically engaged in the United States. The first generation may focus more abroad, but the second generation adopts a worldview and projects in line with those of natives. Huntington and the populists who worry about the future of American democracy because of immigration are too short-sighted.

Critique of Social Capital

What about the utility of social capital and our construction of civic social capital for understanding civic engagement and religion? The concept of social capital has matured considerably since its rather indiscriminate use through the 1990s, when it reduced the complexity of social relations to a single concept. The distinctions between bonding, bridging, and linking social capital convey a more nuanced understanding that indicates the different ways in which social capital can operate. It also has become evident that no kind of social capital is inherently "good" or necessarily productive of social civic bonds beyond one's family and immediate friends. Bonding brings solidarity among those it envelops, but it logically excludes others. Moreover, bonding social capital can mask tension within a community, such as that between Cuban and other Hispanic Seventh-Day Adventists or between Pentecostal and mainstream Protestant African Americans.

Similarly, not all bridging social capital is the same. For formal politics, not all bridges go to the same place. Bridges that link people to different power structures and their associated resources are critical. All of the CSC related to formal politics that we studied involved not just bridging but linking social capital, specifically. Without access to social relationships with those who have more power, Cubans would not have fundamentally transformed Miami's Catholic Church or achieved such political and economic power. Similarly, African Americans would not have been as able to withstand the violence of legal segregation and then the local drug dealers. Relationships of power, i.e., linking social capital, are critical to the political fortunes of established residents and immigrants alike.

Leadership plays a central, necessary role in linking social capital. Without effective leadership, without prophets to lead the way, the power of bonding social capital likely will not be transformed into the very bridging and linking social capital that accesses resources. Leadership transubstantiates bonding capital into bridging and linking social capital. Religious leadership that focuses on social ministry is essential to transubstantiating that capital into effective linking social capital that constitutes and further propagates civic social capital.

The argument that diversity ipso facto diminishes bridging social capital and consensus (Putnam 2007) is questionable. There may, indeed, be a valid statistical relationship, for Miami has been the subject of considerable tension and struggle related to diversity and, particularly, to the influx of immigrants. But correlation is not causation, and our analysis indicates that the relationship between diversity and consensus is spurious. The context of reception for and subsequent success of Cubans indicates that when diversity is welcomed by those with power, positive outcomes follow. Diversity, or, more particularly, immigration that leads to changing demographics, is not the critical element. The relationships among diverse groups, rather than the groups' internal characteristics, determine the outcome. Critical to determining these relationships is the welcome offered by natives and those with power, those who can extend benefits to ease settlement and change the structure of their own institutions, including churches, to accommodate the newcomers.

While we believe that our empirical data and analysis construct a strong case for the concept of CSC and for the previously neglected importance of linking social capital and leadership, we acknowledge that our work has limitations. Our analysis is based upon the case of Miami. Miami today is not representative of many other U.S. cities, but we suggest that with its high degree of ethnic diversity it is more in line with what U.S. cities' future will be like than other metropolitan areas where similar research could have been done. Consequently, we feel that our findings should be viewed as harbingers of America's third century; and the prognosis we offer, an antidote to dire warnings of decline, is one of a healthy civic life in the offing.

NOTES

1. We remind the reader that Wuthnow (2002) refers to this as status-bridging social capital.

2. An incidental peculiarity to Miami's power relations is that the overwhelming majority of all the relationships we describe, whether bonding, bridging, or linking, are among people and organizations of native minority and immigrant backgrounds. Native Whites, or, more precisely, non-Hispanic Whites, who are dominant and quite visible in the rest of the United States, have faded into the background and even history of Miami. The Disciples' Nazarene Church, for example, emerged when the White pastor of a mainstream Protestant church turned over the church to the current Hispanic pastor after nearly all the White Anglo congregants had departed. The Roman Catholic Archdiocese of Miami has been led by Whites, but it was created out of the larger South Florida diocese because of the influx of immigrants, and the majority of Catholic churches have priests who are of Latin American or Caribbean origins. The West Indian Pentecostals had their origins in American missionaries to the West Indies, primarily Jamaica. But the White American leadership returned to the States long ago and the immigrant West Indian congregations in Miami are all led by immigrant West Indians.

3. Kniss and Numrich (2007) broaden the framework to include non-Western, non-Christian religious traditions. Rather than referring to differences among denominations, therefore, they discuss sectarianism (how religiously "pure" and distinct from others a particular religious group considers itself) and whether moral authority is conceived as individually or collectively based.

4. A considerable literature on second-generation immigrants has emerged since the late 1990s. Opinions are quite divided on whether they are Americanizing (or assimilating) versus either retaining their ethnic heritage or emulating a part of a native U.S. minority group, such as African Americans or Chicanos. Portes and colleagues have argued extensively that many second-generation immigrants are assimilating to native minority groups, particularly those who grow up amongst native minorities and whose parents do not have the financial or social capital to place their children in other social environments (see, for example, Portes and Zhou 1993; Portes 1996; Portes and Rumbaut 2001; Portes, Fernandez-Kelly, and Haller 2005). Waldinger and Feliciano (2004), on the other hand, claim that it is too early to tell. Specifically concerning the transnational orientation of second-generation immigrants, Levitt and Waters (2002) have argued that the second generation is not predictably transnational.

REFERENCES

Bourdieu, P. 1987. Legitimation and Structured Interest in Weber's Sociology of Religion. In *Max Weber, Rationality, and Modernity*, ed. S. Whimster and S. Lash, 119–136. London: Allen and Unwin.

Chidester, D. 1988. *Patterns of Power: Religion and Politics in American Culture*. New York: Prentice Hall.

Hondagneu-Sotelo, P., G. Gaudinez, and H. Lara. 2007. Religious Reenactment on the Line: A Genealogy of Political Religious Hybridity. In *Religion and Social Justice for Immigrants*, ed. P. Hondagneu-Sotelo, 122–138. New Brunswick, NJ: Rutgers University Press.

Hondagneu-Sotelo, P., G. Gaudinez, H. Lara, and B. C. Ortiz. 2004. "There's a Spirit That Transcends the Border": Faith, Ritual, and Postnational Protest at the U.S.-Mexico Border. *Sociological Perspectives* 47(2): 133–159.

Huntington, S. P. 2004a. The Hispanic Challenge. *Foreign Policy* 141(March/April): 30–45.

———. 2004b. *Who Are We? The Challenges to America's National Identity*. New York: Simon & Schuster.

Kniss, F., and P. D. Numrich. 2007. *Sacred Assemblies and Civic Engagement*. New Brunswick, NJ: Rutgers University Press.

Levitt, P., and M. C. Waters, eds. 2002. *The Changing Face of Home: The Transnational Lives of the Second Generation*. New York: Russell Sage Foundation.

Narayan, D. 1999. *Bonds and Bridges: Social Capital and Poverty*. Washington, DC: World Bank.

Portes, A. 1996. *The New Second Generation*. New York: Russell Sage Foundation.

Portes, A., P. Fernandez-Kelly, and W. Haller. 2005. Segmented Assimilation on the Ground: The New Second Generation in Early Adulthood. *Ethnic and Racial Studies* 28(6): 1000–1040.

Portes, A., and P. Landolt. 1996. The Downside of Social Capital. *American Prospect* 26: 18–21, 94.

Portes, A., and R. Rumbaut. 2001. *Legacies: The Story of the Immigrant Second Generation*. Berkeley and New York: University of California Press and Russell Sage Foundation.

Portes, A., and A. Stepick. 1993. *City on the Edge: The Transformation of Miami*. Berkeley: University of California Press.

Portes, A., and M. Zhou. 1993. The New Second Generation: Segmented Assimilation and Its Variants. *Annals of the American Academy of Political and Social Sciences* 530: 74–95.

Putnam, R. D. 2007. *E Pluribus Unum*: Diversity and Community in the Twenty-First Century. The 2006 Johan Skytte Prize Lecture. *Scandinavian Political Studies* 30(2): 137–174.

Rey, T. 2004. Marian Devotion at a Haitian Catholic Parish in Miami: The Feast Day of Our Lady of Perpetual Help. *Journal of Contemporary Religion* 19(3): 353–374.

———. 2007. *Bourdieu on Religion: Imposing Faith and Legitimacy.* London: Equinox.

Robison, L. J., A. A. Schmid, and M. E. Siles. 2002. Is Social Capital Really Capital? *Review of Social Economy* 60(1): 1–21.

Skocpol, T., and M. P. Fiorina, eds. 1999. *Civic Engagement in American Democracy.* Washington, DC, and New York: Brookings Institution Press and Russell Sage Foundation.

Stepick, A. 1998. *Pride against Prejudice: Haitians in the United States.* Boston: Allyn & Bacon.

Supreme Court of the United States. 1993. *Church of Lukumi Babalu Aye v. Hialeah.* No. 91–948.

Szreter, S. 2002. The State of Social Capital: Bringing Back in Power, Politics, and History. *Theory and Society* 31(5): 573–621.

Waldinger, R., and C. Feliciano. 2004. Will the New Second Generation Experience "Downward Assimilation"? Segmented Assimilation Re-Assessed. *Ethnic and Racial Studies* 27(3): 376–402.

Wuthnow, R. 2002. Religious Involvement and Status-Bridging Social Capital. *Journal for the Scientific Study of Religion* 41(4): 669–684.

CONTRIBUTORS

NOEMÍ BÁEZ currently works for the New York City Civilian Complaint Review Board and plans to continue working with immigrant and political issues. Her 2003 masters thesis, "Religion and Ethnic Identity among Mexican Youths in Homestead, Florida," was in Latin American and Caribbean studies at Florida International University.

ISABEL DEL PINO-ALLEN was baptized Catholic in her native Cuba against her atheist father's wishes but participated in Presbyterian services with her Protestant mother when she came to the United States as a child. She teaches at Miami-Dade College and is working on her dissertation at Florida International University.

SU OLTMAN FINK received a masters in religious studies at Florida International University. Her thesis is entitled "Politics and Prayer in West Perrine, Florida: Civic Social Capital and the Black Church" and charts a hundred-year history of Perrine.

ANN REEDER GORACZKO is the associate director of the Institute for Public Opinion Research (IPOR) at Florida International University (FIU). Her 2003 masters thesis, "The Effects of Religious Participation on the Civic Engagement of the Children of Immigrants and Immigrant Youth in South Florida," was in comparative sociology at FIU. She has supervised IPOR's FIU/Florida Poll, Cuba Poll, and other surveys for over ten years. She also teaches research methods in FIU's School of Journalism and Mass Communication. Her research interests include spirituality and civic engagement in higher education.

KATRIN HANSING is the associate director of the Cuban Research Institute at Florida International University and an anthropologist. She is the author of *Rasta, Race, and Revolution: The Emergence and Development of the Rastafari Movement in Socialist Cuba.*

CHRISTINE HO is currently on the faculty of the Fielding Graduate University. She received her PhD in anthropology from the University of California at Los

Angeles. Her most recent book is *Globalization, Diaspora, and Caribbean Popular Culture*, which she edited with Keith Nurse. She is a native of Trinidad and Tobago.

YVES LABISSIERE, a social psychologist by training, is an associate professor at Portland State University. A former Ford Foundation fellow, he is a core faculty member of Portland State's general education program, University Studies. His research interests focus broadly on intra- and inter-group relations and, more specifically, on the negotiations of racial and ethnic identities among groups categorized as Black in the United States.

SARAH J. MAHLER is an associate professor of anthropology and former director of the Center for Transnational and Comparative Studies at Florida International University in Miami. Her research and publications focus primarily on transnational ties linking Latin American and Caribbean migrants in the United States with their communities of origin. She has particularly emphasized the importance of bringing gender into the transnational migration perspective.

AIDIL OSCARIZ was born in Cuba and left when she was three years old. She grew up in Miami and currently lives in West New York, where she is the New Jersey chapter director for the Cuban-American Commission for Family Rights. Currently attending Fordham University, she is scheduled to receive her law degree in 2008. She was a Florida Bar Foundation 2007 Legal Services summer fellow. Previously, she worked for the Southwest Voter Registration Project.

MARÍA DE LOS ANGELES REY, a native of Mexico City and graduate of Universidad Intercontinental, is a journalist and immigrant health care advocate who currently lives and writes in Philadelphia.

TERRY REY was formerly professeur de sociologie des religions at l'Université d'Etat d'Haïti and is currently associate professor and chair of religion at Temple University. He is the author of *Our Lady of Class Struggle: The Cult of the Virgin Mary in Haiti* and *Bourdieu on Religion: Imposing Faith and Legitimacy* and co-editor, with Jacob K. Olupona, of *Òrìsà Devotion as World Religion: Global Yòrubá Religious Culture*.

EILEEN M. SMITH-CAVROS is an environmental sociologist at Nova Southeastern University in Fort Lauderdale, where she enjoys the outdoors with her husband, George Cavros, an environmental lawyer. She is the author of the Association of Partners for Public Lands award-winning book *Pioneer Voices of Zion Canyon* as well as various journal articles on the relationships between people and nature. Her 2003 PhD dissertation in comparative sociology at Florida International University was "Black Churchgoers, Environmental Activism, and the Preservation of Nature in Miami, Florida."

ALEX STEPICK is the director of the Immigration and Ethnicity Institute and a professor of anthropology and sociology at Florida International University. He is co-author, with Alejandro Portes, of *City on the Edge*. His most recent books are *Immigrant Faiths*, edited with Karen Leonard, Jennifer Holdaway, and Manuel Vasquez, and *This Land Is Our Land: Immigrants and Power in Miami*, written with Guillermo Grenier, Max Castro, and Marvin Dunn.

TERUYUKI TSUJI received his PhD in comparative sociology at Florida International University and currently is a visiting professor at Nova Southeastern University. After the completion of his MA in Latin American and Caribbean studies at the University of Tsukuba in Japan, he worked for the Japanese government as a foreign service officer, holding positions in Trinidad and Tobago and Jamaica. His research has focused on transnational identity construction and its relations with religious practices in both contexts of the Caribbean and of West Indian migrant communities in South Florida. His 2006 dissertation was "Hyphenated Cultures: Ethnicity and Nation in Trinidad."

INDEX